MW01115505

Information Technology and Global Governance

Series Editor
Derrick Cogburn
American University
Bethesda, MD, USA

Information Technology and Global Governance focuses on the complex interrelationships between the social, political, and economic processes of global governance that occur at national, regional, and international levels. These processes are influenced by the rapid and ongoing developments in information and communication technologies. At the same time, they affect numerous areas, create new opportunities and mechanisms for participation in global governance processes, and influence how governance is studied. Books in this series examine these relationships and influences.

More information about this series at
http://www.palgrave.com/gp/series/14855

Charley Lewis

Regulating Telecommunications in South Africa

Universal Access and Service

Charley Lewis
Fish Hoek, South Africa

Information Technology and Global Governance
ISBN 978-3-030-43526-4 ISBN 978-3-030-43527-1 (eBook)
https://doi.org/10.1007/978-3-030-43527-1

This Palgrave Macmillan imprint is published by the registered company Springer Nature Switzerland AG
The registered company address is: Gewerbestrasse 11, 6330 Cham, Switzerland

Acknowledgments

To Shafiah.
Mi kariemho.
For believing in me.
For sharing this journey.
For being both patient and persistent.
For always listening and endlessly cajoling me along the way.

This has been a project of long incubation, but it is a story that had to be told.

My thanks go to all those who commented on drafts and chapters and sections, giving wise feedback and making helpful suggestions - in particular to Stephen Louw from the University of the Witwatersrand, and to my friend and colleague, Ewan Sutherland, whose detailed comments on drafts of several chapters were both insightful and valuable. To Robert Horwitz, whose seminal work on South Africa's ICT transition was a beacon and an inspiration. And to my son, Stuart Lewis, whose surgery helped prune an unwieldy bush into a trimmer shrub.

I also owe a lasting debt to the many friends, colleagues and acquaintances who were so willing to put up with this party bore on universal access and service, and to respond to my interview questions and emailed queries, who were so unstinting of their time, so willing to share their views and memories of the last twenty years, so ready to share documents and make comments. I hope you find this a useful contribution to our shared history, to our joint endeavour, to history and scholarship.

Not least to the many nameless South Africans, in poor households and remote communities, those still without service, those struggling to find affordable, good quality telephony, those still cut off from the cornucopia of the Internet, bypassed by broadband, and the victims of fibre to other people's homes. May these lessons be used to help your livelihoods and enrich your lives.

Praise for *Regulating Telecommunications in South Africa*

"An original contribution to the fields of both politics, policymaking and telecommunication studies generally, and more specifically in the niche area of internet penetration and universal service and access…A well-researched and consistently interesting study."

—Victoria Graham, *Associate Professor of Politics, Philosophy and International Studies, Monash University, South Africa*

"The empirical analysis of these [policy] failures is arresting and important and is a substantial contribution to the scholarly field. I salute Dr. Lewis' powers of observation and analysis."

—Robert B. Horwitz, *Professor of Education, the University of California, San Diego, USA*

"*Regulating Telecommunications in South Africa* is a shrewd, critical and engagingly written overview of the deep digital donga that separated 'white' and 'black' South Africa in the immediate aftermath of apartheid. Charley Lewis showcases his in-depth knowledge of universal access service initiatives around the world, their successes and failures and their impact on the South African regulatory environment. In this book, he manages to provide historical context for a topic that remains highly contentious in contemporary (South) Africa, and also succeeds in balancing local responses to global best practice in a manner that uplifts the voice of the resource poor without condescension. This is a master feat."

—Viola C. Milton, *Professor, University of South Africa, South Africa*

"The detailed narrative and the development of universal access and service policy in relation to best practice norms is unprecedented…an extraordinarily detailed and rich discussion."

—Ahmed Veriava, *Lecturer in the Department of Political Studies, the University of the Witwatersrand, South Africa*

Contents

List of Figures

List of Tables

CHAPTER 1

The Digital Donga

In 1990, when Nelson Mandela walked out of Pollsmoor Prison and stood before the people of South Africa, he faced a country starkly divided by years of racial oppression and economic exploitation. White minority *apartheid* rule had ensured that 'white' South Africans prospered, with access to the best housing, the most well-resourced schools and hospitals, the best-paying jobs, whilst the country's 'black' majority were systematically excluded and deprived in every facet of life and society. It was a society deeply divided along the sharp lines of racial categorisation in respect of almost every socio-economic indicator: income, education, employment, health, housing and telecommunications.

1.1 1990: Two-Tier Telephony

Access to telephony[1] was one amongst many socio-economic divisions afflicting South Africa under *apartheid*. Both academic literature and common parlance use the term 'digital divide' to refer to the division—between those who have access to telephony and those who do not. Commonly, the 'digital divide' reflects differential access to telecommunications and other information and communications technology (ICT) services. Its fault lines run along key demographic categories, such as income

[1] Voice telecommunications services. See the Glossary for more formal definitions of 'telephony' and other technical terms used in the analysis.

C. Lewis, *Regulating Telecommunications in South Africa*,
Information Technology and Global Governance,
https://doi.org/10.1007/978-3-030-43527-1_1

level and geographic location, but also extend into gender, linguistic, educational, literacy and disability. In South Africa, however, it was the racial categorisations imposed and fostered by *apartheid* that were the prime predictors and indicators of lack of access to telecommunications and other ICTs.

In 1990, access to telephony meant access to fixed-line telephones, provided over copper cables to black bakelite handsets, by a single state-owned entity, South African Posts and Telecommunications (SAPT). Mobile telephony was still in its infancy globally and had yet to arrive in South Africa. Email was still the playground of academics and geeks, and the concept of the Internet had only just been born.

In 1990, the overwhelming majority of 'white' South Africans had such a telephone in their homes; less than one in a hundred of their 'black' fellow countrymen enjoyed this privilege (ANC, 1994, Section 2.8.1). The first proper national census, conducted a few years later (when there were already two mobile operators in the market), underscores the point. It reports that 88.5% of 'white' South Africans had a "telephone in dwelling/cellular phone"[2] compared to a mere 11.3% of 'black' South Africans (Stats SA, 1996, p. 80). Only 0.8% of 'white' South Africans had "no access to a telephone" compared to 24.4% of their 'black' counterparts. Further, access was heavily skewed in favour of the more urbanised economic centres of the country, with many homes in the Western Cape (55.2%) and Gauteng (45.3%) reporting a "telephone in dwelling/cellular phone", while high proportions of homes in provinces containing former bantustans had no access to telephony (45.3% in the Eastern Cape and 30.5% in the then Northern Province).

It was this stark divide—this yawning chasm between affluent, mostly suburban, 'whites' with easy access to telephone services, and the 'black' majority, economically disadvantaged and largely consigned to urban ghettoes and rural slums—that confronted the African National Congress as it contemplated what policies and practices to adopt in the lead-up to South Africa's first democratic general election in 1994.

Mandela would have been familiar with the dongas that scarred the brown hills where he grew up in Qunu, deep red scars slashed across the landscape, angry signs of deprivation and drought. The deep and lasting scar of a donga is therefore an appropriate metaphor for the particular

[2] Still in its infancy in South Africa at the time, cellular nonetheless already had almost 20% of the total voice telephony market, mostly more affluent users.

South African flavour of the profound digital divide inflicted by *apartheid* on the country, a chasm that cut the majority of the country's population off from access to telecommunications services, primarily on the basis of racial categorisation.

1.2 ICT Access Today

Dramatic shifts have shaped the telecommunications market since then. Today South Africa has many more mobile phones than inhabitants, and the fixed-line customer network is now in terminal decline. With over 88 million 'active' mobile SIM cards in a population of some 56 million, and Telkom's main line subscriber base having shrunk to under 3 million (below what it was in 1993), it is a radically altered landscape. With burgeoning access to the Internet via laptops and smartphones, the rollout of broadband networks and FTTH connectivity has assumed centre stage. It is no longer a simple telephony landscape. Increasingly, the environment is perceived as an integrated ecosystem (Fransman, 2010) driven by a complex and dynamic interaction involving the previously disparate domains of telecommunications, broadcasting, the Internet and computing.

Further, the disparities in access to telephony today are dramatically less starkly racialised, as can be seen from the graph below, which compares telephony access enjoyed by South Africa's racial groupings between 1996 and 2013 (Fig. 1.1[3]).

The stark and yawning divide between 'black' and 'white' South Africa of 1996 has now narrowed dramatically. While the percentage of 'white' South African households with either a fixed-line or a mobile telephone in their homes has increased to 99.4% (an increase of 12%), access to fixed-line or mobile telephony in 'black' households has soared by some 730% to reach 94.1%. The digital divide today is far more closely linked to issues such as income and geographic location, and it is these axes of the digital divide that Statistics South Africa now focuses on in its reporting.

[3] The categories in this book reflect those inherited from *apartheid*, and still in use to track progress in respect of many metrics. 'Black / African' refers to the country's mainly Bantu-speaking majority, comprising around 80% of the total population. 'Coloured' refers to those of Khoisan/mixed-race descent, comprising some 9% of the population. 'Indian/Asian' refers to those descended from immigrants out of the Indian subcontinent, comprising 2% of the population. 'Whites' comprise the remaining 8%, down from 11% in 1996.

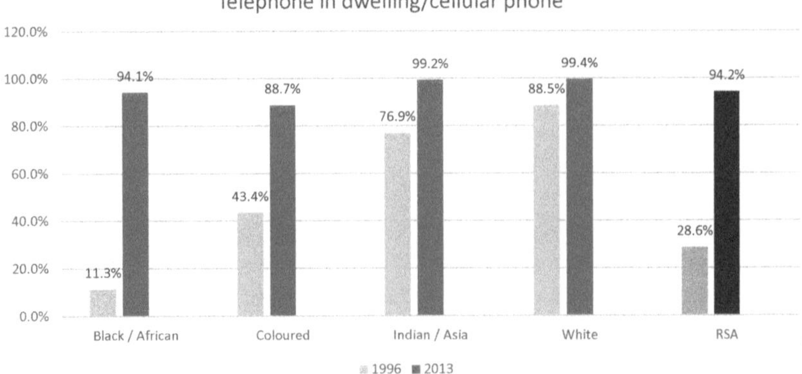

Fig. 1.1 Households with telephony by race: 1996 vs 2013 (*Source* Author, data from Stats SA [1996, p. 80, 2015, p. 25])

1.3 'The People Shall Call'

Confronted with the deep digital donga of 1990 that separated 'white' South Africa from 'black' South Africa, that cut the majority of the country's population off from the economic, social and cultural benefits of access to telephony, it is hardly surprising that the new ANC government made "providing access to these essential services for all South Africans" the centre plank of its telecommunications policy as it prepared to contest the country's first democratic elections (ANC, 1992, p. 53). The stated national telecommunications policy intention of the new government sought to ensure the "provision of basic universal service in telecommunications to disadvantaged rural and urban communities" (RSA, 1996a, p. 1). It is a policy commitment attested to, as this book shows, by a series of specifically-targeted policy and regulatory interventions over the ensuing 20 years, aimed in various ways at ensuring that those disadvantaged and deprived by *apartheid* secured access to telecommunications services.

The levels of access to telecommunications services have both skyrocketed and become substantially more equitable in the intervening 20 years. It would appear, therefore, on the face of it, that policy-makers can claim an easy victory, a clear policy success. But yet commentators—both academic (Gillwald, 2005; Hodge, 2004; Lewis, 2010; Msimang, 2006) and in the press (Business Day, 2006; Guest, 2006; Vecchiatto, 2006, 2007;

Perry, 2010)—have almost universally been sceptical of the effectiveness and impact of those very interventions.

Such widespread negative assessment implies at least some level of fracture between policy intention and policy impact. Possibly the overall policy thrust towards universal access and service was ill-conceived and inappropriate for a developing country such as South Africa. Perhaps it was the concrete implementation of universal access and service policy that was badly flawed, either due to failures at institutional and human capacity level, or because of policy slippages, or the modalities of policy transfer. It may also be that the dynamics of access were simply overtaken by other developments, such as technological evolution, or the changing nature of the sector, or the incoming tide of the market. More likely, some complex interaction of multiple factors, some internal, others external, underpins what unfolded.

1.4 The Evolution of Universal Service

What, then, was the international policy backdrop for the new ANC government's avowed intention to ensure that the country's 'black' majority secure access to telecommunications?

The call for universal access to telecommunications services was to become a commonplace policy and regulatory component within the globally-widespread series of changes to market structure, institutional frameworks and ownership arrangements that swept through the broader information and communications technologies (ICT) sector from the mid-1980s onwards.

Together these changes form part of the phenomenon widely referred to as "telecom reform" (Melody, 1997), whose central features comprise:

- Privatisation of the state-owned incumbent providers of telecommunications services;
- The introduction of competition into the telecommunications market;
- The establishment of an independent regulator to oversee the market (Wallsten, 2001, p. 3).

'Telecom reform' included a number of policy and regulatory interventions aimed at ensuring widespread access to telecommunications services within the changed market environment. These measures fall under the umbrella of what is variously referred to as 'universal service', 'universal access', 'universality' and 'universal access and service' (the term in common parlance today).

Universal access and service (UAS) is a complex pair of closely-related concepts, both conceptually and programmatically. UAS is a concept widely applicable and widely applied—from the developed countries of the North America and Europe, across the board to the underdeveloped countries of sub-Saharan Africa—albeit with shifting content, depending on concrete national circumstances and differing levels of development. Furthermore, it is a concept that has been applied over the years to an evolving spectrum of information and communications technologies (ICTs), from fixed-line telephony, through the Internet, to broadcasting and, latterly, broadband. And under the umbrella of UAS, a wide spectrum of policies and programmes in a range of country jurisdictions has been proposed and implemented. Further, there has been considerable debate in both academic and expert circles (not only in South Africa, by any means) as to the appropriateness, success and impact of such UAS interventions.

Universal access and service thus has a lengthy pedigree. The concept stretches back at least to the 1907 use of the term "universal service" by AT&T President Theodore Vail (Mueller, 1993, p. 353) and the company's subsequent advertising campaign was based on a ringing clarion call for "One Policy, One System, Universal Service" (Thierer, 1994).

But the "universal service" flag flown by Vail had little to do with any altruistic commitment to widespread public service provision. Rather it was aimed at bolstering AT&T's position as a monopoly provider of telecommunications services. Nevertheless, the slogan has since been adopted under the modern welfare-state paradigm of "universal telephone service…[focused on] reaching every member of society, no matter how remote or poor….[and hence implying] a legal obligation to serve" (Mueller, 1993, p. 353). It is this conceptualisation that has since become central within telecommunications policy discourse, as market structure and policy paradigms have evolved.

The modern emphasis on UAS arises from and is linked to much of the early literature on the digital divide. For example, the 1985 Maitland Report of the International Telecommunication Union (ITU) pointed to a "gross and growing imbalance in the distribution of telecommunications throughout the world" (ITU, 1985, p. 3).

It was, however, some years later that the concept of 'universal service' was introduced into law in the United States of America (Mueller, 1997a; USA, 1996), by which time it had already been in current usage for some years by the European Commission (EC, 1987, 1996) and had for some time been part of academic debate (Hudson, 1994). It would not be long before it was formalised as part of international good practice by the ITU (1998). Against this background, it is unsurprising that telecommunications reform in South Africa was accompanied by a strong policy commitment to achieving UAS.

Although 'universal service' was the term in common parlance initially, it would not be long before a conceptual distinction between 'universal service' and 'universal access' began to be made, as the discussion moved to address the situation in developing countries. In 1998, the ITU formally tabled the distinction, defining 'universal service' as "focused upon connection of individual households to the public telephone network"—in contrast to 'universal access' which it described as the "notion … that everyone, at home or at work, should be within a reasonable distance of a telephone" (1998, p. 61). Current usage still retains the distinction between widespread private access at the individual or household level (universal service) versus widespread shared access via public facilities such as payphones (universal access), but adopts the portmanteau term 'universal access and service (UAS)' to cover the broad policy and regulatory field (Blackman & Srivastava, 2011, pp. 153–154). UAS policy and regulatory interventions, therefore, aim to redress the gap between those who are able to make use of ICT services and those who, mainly by reason of poverty or geographical remoteness, are not. They thus implicitly form part of a wider range of social upliftment policy interventions, but with a specific focus in the arena of telecommunications.

1.5 Telecomms in Transition, South African Style

This body of international best practice, together with its evolution and its influence upon policy, law and regulation, will be discussed much more fully in subsequent chapters. It was, however, one the factors influencing South Africa's ANC as it moved to define the telecommunications component of its post-*apartheid* social and economic policy.

South Africa's engagement with ICT sector reform was also definitively shaped by being swept up in the flurry of policy reform and legislative activity that took place in the immediate aftermath of South Africa's transition to democracy in 1994. The country had emerged from a racially discriminatory history of systemic and systematic denial of access for the majority of the country's population to telecommunications services, *inter alia*. This had led to the enormous disparities in telecommunications access between 'black' and 'white' South Africans alluded to above. The new government accordingly sought to ensure that redressing those inequalities was at the core of its policy and legislation. In the words of Horwitz, "the principle of universal service, enshrined in [South Africa's] telecommunications reform process, embodied a commitment to equalizing social access to information and communication as a democratic norm" (2001, p. 19). South Africa's engagement with universal access and service was therefore an important component of its multi-pronged endeavour to 'build a better life for all'.[4] This is not to say that the ICT policy thrust was an entirely altruistic and disinterested one: opportunities for rent-seeking and personal enrichment were to abound in the margins of the new sectoral regime, coexisting with more noble objectives.[5]

1.6 Universal Service: A Better Life for All

The ANC's early commitment to social upliftment and service delivery as being integral to the democratic transformation was thus aligned to emerging international good practice. The vision of "universal affordable access for all" (ANC, 1994, Section 2.8.4) animated the country's engagement with the ICT sector policy reform process. It was a commitment that served to ensure that universal access and service was placed at the forefront of communications policy and legislation, a vision that has continued to animate subsequent policy and regulatory interventions (Hodge, 2004; Msimang, 2006).

South Africa's adherence to the principle of UAS can be traced through the major policy documents that punctuated the process of reforming the ICT sector (ANC, 1994; RSA, 1993, 1995, 1996a). It culminated in the keystone legislation that was the centrepiece and outcome of that

[4] ANC election slogan.

[5] As the ongoing exposure of endemic corruption and 'state capture' during the Zuma years attests.

reform process, the 1996 Telecommunications Act.[6] Here, the objective to "promote the universal and affordable provision of telecommunication services" (RSA, 1996b, Section 2[a]) is listed as foremost amongst its 17 objectives. It was only with the passage of the 2005 Electronic Communications Act (RSA, 2005)—by which time substantial strides had been made towards securing universal access to telecommunications services for all South Africans—that this overarching goal of universal affordable access shaded into a less strongly-formulated commitment to "promote the universal provision of electronic communications networks and electronic communications services and connectivity for all" (RSA, 2005, Section 2(c)). The notion of universal access and service appears in documents as diverse as the broadcasting Triple Enquiry Report (IBA, 1995), the National Information Society and Development Plan (PNC on ISAD, 2007), and the Presidential Infrastructure Coordinating Commission (RSA, 2014) and continues to be alluded to in almost every annual Presidential State of the Nation Address (USAASA, 2014, pp. 1v1–17ff).

1.7 Intervening for UAS in South Africa

This policy and legislative backdrop formed the *mise en scéne* for a series of concrete interventions undertaken to increase access to ICT goods and services. On the one hand, South Africa followed global best practice (Intven, 2000; ITU, 1998, pp. 91, 92) by imposing universal service obligations[7] on licensees (Hodge, 2004; Lewis, 2010, pp. 4–5; Msimang, 2006, pp. 232–236) and by establishing a Universal Service Fund[8] (Lewis, 2010, p. 6; Msimang, 2006, pp. 224–230). On the other hand, establishing of a dedicated entity[9] to deal with UAS issues, and the subsequent experiment in the awarding of geographically restricted licences

[6] Since replaced by an updated 2005 Electronic Communications Act (RSA, 2005).

[7] Mandatory stipulation imposed on operators, requiring, for example, network rollout or service provision to under-serviced areas and communities.

[8] A fund into which contributions imposed upon operators are paid, and which is used to provide ICT infrastructure and services to under-serviced areas and communities, or to individuals who cannot afford such services on their own.

[9] Initially the Universal Service Agency (USA), later the Universal Service and Access Agency of South Africa (USAASA).

in under-serviced areas[10] (Gillwald, 2002, 2005), were both, in different ways, groundbreaking.

1.8 Less Than Universal Acclaim

As indicated earlier, many of these interventions are widely regarded in the press as having failed, or at least as having been subject to serious implementation problems. The academic and expert literature, although rather more nuanced, is not a great deal more sanguine.

At best, the analyses that have attempted a macro-level view (Barendse, 2004; Msimang, 2006; Oyedemi, 2009) or that have touched tangentially on UAS policy (Schofield & Sithole, 2006) suggest equivocal outcomes for South Africa's engagement with UAS. Msimang's guarded overall assessment of the various interventions as having produced "mixed results" (2006, p. 244) is representative.

Where analysis and commentary has focused on specific aspects of UAS policy and regulatory intervention, it has tended to be negative. For example, Lewis (2013) gives an assessment that is negative in respect of each of the major interventions examined. More specifically, Hodge (2004) paints a gloomy picture of the failure of the universal service obligations imposed via licence conditions on Telkom in respect of fixed-line telephony, which he describes as a "roll-out disaster" (2004, p. 221). Hodge has also pointed to institutional problems with the then Universal Service Agency, categorising its track record as one of "agency failure" (2004, p. 221). Calandro and Moyo have suggested that the Universal Service Fund has "not [been] utilised in an effective way" (2010, p. 14). Others (Gillwald, 2005; Thornton, 2006; van Leijden & Monasso, 2005) have expressed profound scepticism about the likely outcomes of the under-serviced area licensing intervention.

1.9 Universal What?

Both technology and markets have undergone dramatic shifts as the telecommunications landscape has evolved towards a complex, integrated,

[10] The so-called Under-serviced Area Licences (USALs), introduced from 2001, requiring successful bidders to provide telecommunications infrastructure and services to areas with low fixed-line teledensity.

dynamic ICT ecosystem. As the landscape has shifted, the nature of the digital divide too has evolved (Hilbert, 2016). And, in consequence, so too have the challenges facing policy-makers seeking to advance the goals of UAS (ITU, 2003, pp. 32–35).

While the racial dimension of the telephony divide in South Africa has largely disappeared, other dimensions remain. For instance, while Statistics South Africa reports that 96.5% of all households have functional access to telephony, this falls to 90.3% in the largely rural Northern Cape compared to 98.5% in the country's urban heartland of Gauteng (Stats SA, 2017, p. 49). The discrepancy is far from stark, but it does suggest that an urban versus rural divide continues to persist.

Further, the technological basis of the digital divide in South Africa has shifted away from telephony to the Internet and towards broadband. The same report shows that access to the Internet is very far from universal. Only 9.5% of South Africans have access to the Internet at home, but, worse, the Internet divide between metropolitan Western Cape (where 27.3% of households have access at home) and rural North West (only 0.6% of households) is stark (Stats SA, 2017, p. 51).

A recent edition of Arthur Goldstuck's influential report on the Internet in South Africa underlines the point (World Wide Worx, 2017, pp. 1–22). It describes the Internet divide as a vast and multidimensional one "that stretches across almost every imaginable sector of society, from geography and location to income and education" (World Wide Worx, 2017, p. 7). While income disparities are starkest (the report finds 82.4% of rich South Africans have access[11] to the Internet, compared to only 30% of the poorest), geography reflects similar levels of polarisation (Internet penetration is 67.6% in "major metropolitan areas" compared to a mere 32.6% in "smaller cities and towns"). Importantly, given South Africa's history of starkly-racialised divisions in levels of telephony access, the racial digital donga remains disturbingly prominent when it comes to Internet access, with 69.1% of 'white' South Africans enjoying Internet access, compared to levels of under 50% for the other three standard racial categorisations (Fig. 1.2).

A similar trend is evidenced from an earlier Stats SA analysis, examining household access to the Internet in 2013. The graphs are not directly comparable, of course, given that they reflect data taken several years

[11] The report adopts a fairly relaxed definition of 'access', which it defines as "as having personally accessed the Internet in the last 12 months" (World Wide Worx, 2017, p. 10).

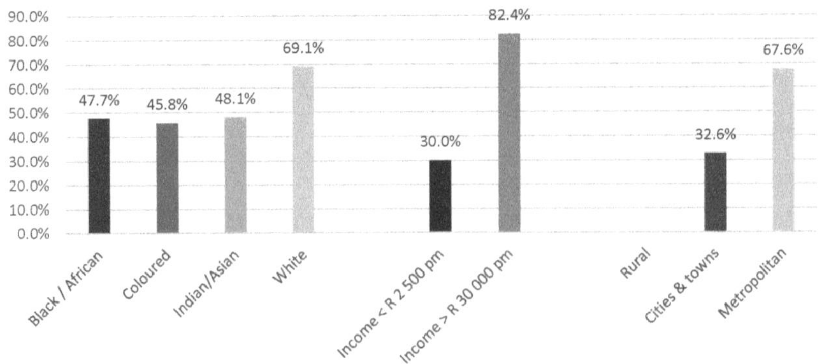

Fig. 1.2 Axes of the Internet divide (Urban South Africa, 2017) (*Source* Author, data from World Wide Worx [2017, pp. 1–22])

apart, and use slightly differing definitions of access. In addition, Goldstuck's smaller sample excludes rural respondents. However, both show that the income-based Internet divide is far more pronounced than the racially-based one. Regression analysis on the earlier Stats SA data suggests that rich households are 10 times more likely to have Internet access in the home than poorer ones, whereas 'white' households are 5 times more likely to have Internet access at home than their 'black' counterparts (Stats SA, 2015, p. 41) (Fig. 1.3).

Such a multidimensional Internet divide (urban vs rural, rich vs poor, 'white' vs 'black') is likely to be further exacerbated by the recent, dramatic proliferation of super-fast fibre-to-the-home Internet access (Sidler, 2016), with FTTH rollout targeting wealthy, formerly-white suburbs in the country's major cities. As a result, concerns about securing universal access to the Internet have been voiced by sources as divergent as Facebook founder Mark Zuckerberg (Vermeulen, 2016) and international NGO, the Alliance for Affordable Internet (Mzekandaba, 2016).

The technology may have changed, and the axes of deprivation may have shifted to some extent, but the policy challenge of securing universal access and service to ICTs remains.

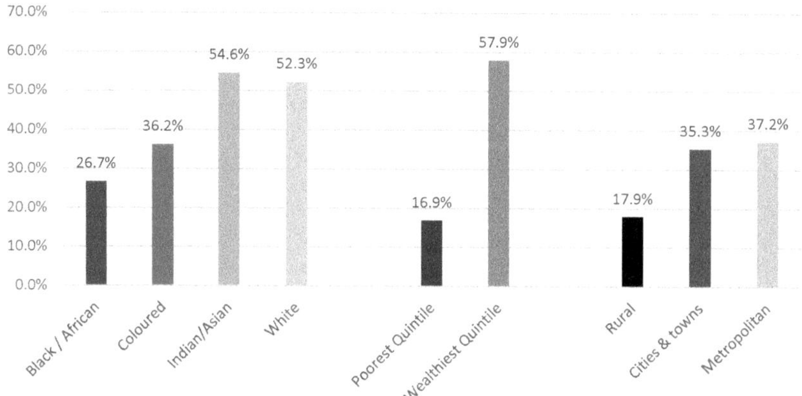

Fig. 1.3 Access to the Internet via mobile (South Africa, 2013) (*Source* Author, data from Stats SA [2015])

1.10 UAS: Policy Disjunctures

Taken together, the picture that emerges is one of a substantial disjuncture between policy intention and implementation outcomes.

At the same time, it appears as if the 'digital donga' of 1990 has largely dissipated when it comes to access to telephony. The extent to which this has occurred in consequence of the various targeted interventions, rather than as a result of market forces and trends, however, appears to be highly debatable.

Meanwhile, new fissures of the 'digital donga' continue to emerge, as broadband assumes centre stage in policy, and the fibre-to-the-home market explodes. With South Africa poised to undertake major policy shifts (DTPS, 2016) and embark on key ICT programmes (DoC, 2013; DTPS, 2017a), understanding the chain between policy intention and implementation outcomes is both essential and urgent.

Questions clearly arise as to the extent of the historical policy disjunctures, the factors accounting for them, and the implications of this for ongoing universal access and service policy and regulation.

1.11 Through a Conceptual Lens

This book sets out a case study, examining the history of universal access and service in South Africa. As such, it draws on several strands of theory, each appropriate to a specific arc of the analysis. For example, regime theory illuminates the rise to hegemony of the cluster of concepts and interventions that have come to constitute 'international best practice' for telecomms reform, under the ITU, the WTO, the OECD and the EU. The theories of policy diffusion and policy transfer form the lens through which to analyse the adoption and adaptation of these good practices and specific interventions in South Africa. Policy success and policy failure theory is the heuristic framework adopted to describe, analyse and critique the individual interventions and their outcomes.

Figure 1.4 illustrates the conceptual framework underpinning the analysis.

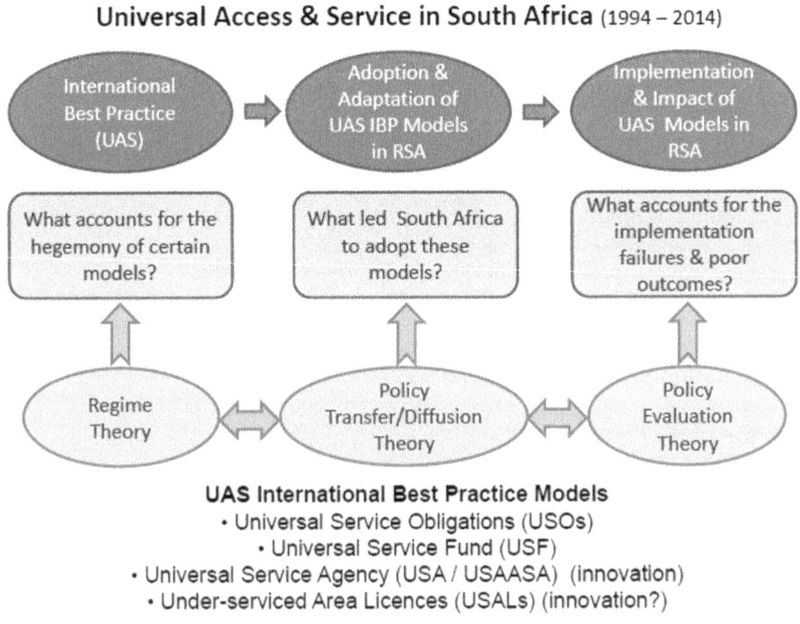

Fig. 1.4 Forces driving reform of the telecommunications sector (*Source* Author)

1.12 A South African Trajectory

The chapters that follow seek to illuminate the road travelled by South Africa in its efforts to ensure universal access, initially to telephony and, latterly, to a broader range of ICTs, over a 20-year period. International good practice was adopted and adapted, then implemented, with varying degrees of policy success and failure.

The analysis seeks to chart that trajectory, and to draw conclusions from that story. It is largely a history of UAS in relation to South Africa, but a history illumined through the lens of an appropriate conceptual and analytical framework. It is the first complete study of South Africa's interventions in pursuit of the policy goal of universal access and service.

The rise of UAS within the broader context of ICT sector reform will be documented and accounted for. In addition, the book charts how the various components of what has come to be considered international good practice in respect of UAS, coalesced and achieved good practice hegemony.

Then, the book further examines the factors that led to the adoption of UAS as the key component of South Africa's ICT sector reform programme, analysing how these factors influenced the adoption and implementation of UAS interventions, and assessing how the process impacted on policy outcomes. Factors will include those internal to the South African sociopolitical context—some of a structural nature, others driven by the various actors—as well as those impacting from external sources.

Further, the book seeks to account for and explain how the policy objectives were translated from their initial conception into specific programmatic interventions. This will entail an examination of appropriate theoretical frameworks accounting for policy adoption, implementation and impact in the broader context of regulatory theory. Inter alia, regime theory, along with the bodies of theory relating to policy transfer and diffusion and to policy success or failure will be drawn on to conceptualise South Africa's experience of universal access and service policy and regulation.

The book adopts a specific time frame, focusing on the 20 years between 1994 and 2014. This is not an arbitrary choice, but one that covers a defined era for South Africa's ICT sector. 1994 marks the election of the first ANC government, which preceded and kick-started the formal process of ICT sector reform.

2014 marks the widely commemorated anniversary of 20 years of democracy in South Africa. It also marks the fourth re-election of the ANC to power, albeit with a reduced majority, under the leadership of the then already deeply-discredited and scandal-ridden President Jacob Zuma. It also marks an attempt to unscramble the convergence egg, when, in a widely condemned move, the Ministry of Communications was dismembered and broken into two, with Faith Muthambi as Minister of Communications, and Siyabonga Cwele as Minister of Telecommunications and Postal Services.

The book thus provides, on the one hand, the first comprehensive history of South Africa's engagement with universal access and service over a 20-year period. On the other hand, however, its insights seek to contribute to a theoretical understanding of how policy is adopted and implemented, of what constitutes policy success and failure, and of the complex conjunction of forces that can cause the policy process to go awry. These lessons aim to contribute to a broader understanding of policy adoption and implementation within a changing political context. Such lessons may then suggest a more comprehensive, better balanced, more nuanced matrix of best practice UAS interventions, one perhaps more widely applicable to developing countries.

Although the ICT landscape, both in South Africa and globally, has changed substantially since the mid-1990s, universal access and service continues to remain a central preoccupation of both academics (Batura, 2016; Eliassen & From, 2009; Hudson, 2017; Xavier, 2008) and policy-makers (DTPS, 2017b; EU, 2010; Lewis & Maddens, 2011; Maddens, 2009) in many parts of the world.

It is also true that scepticism around the effectiveness of universal access and service interventions is neither recent, nor limited to South Africa. The work of Mueller, for example, which seeks to expose the concept of 'universal service' in the USA as an "ideology" (1993, p. 352; 1997b), with all the pejorative overtones of the term, has at its roots a profound scepticism as to the value of such interventions. Others have critiqued specific interventions, such as the establishment and operation of a Universal Service Fund (Berg, Jiang, & Lin, 2011; Hazlett, 2006).

Much of the current global ICT policy-making centre of gravity has now moved firmly to focus on issues pertaining to broadband and its deployment, both globally (ITU/UNESCO, 2011; Kim, Kelly, & Raja, 2010) and in South Africa (DoC, 2013). Thus, a clear understanding of the contingent factors affecting the adoption of international good practice, derived from earlier generations of telecommunications, and of the challenges of ensuring effective implementation, may offer a greater degree of policy success when it comes to intervening in order to ensure UAS in respect of broadband.

In addition, I hope the book makes a small contribution to a significant area of academic discourse, the theory of policy and regulation for UAS in the developing country context. As such, it may hold important practical implications for developing countries like South Africa as they grapple with the twenty-first-century goal of universal, affordable access within a converged and evolving ICT ecosystem.

References

ANC. (1992). *Ready to govern: ANC policy guidelines for a democratic South Africa.* Johannesburg: African National Congress. Retrieved from http://www.anc.org.za/show.php?id=227.

ANC. (1994). *The Reconstruction and development programme: A policy framework.* Johannesburg: African National Congress.

Barendse, A. (2004). Innovative regulatory and policy initiatives at increasing ICT connectivity in South Africa. *Telematics and Informatics, 21,* 49–66.

Batura, O. (2016). Can a revision of the universal service scope result in substantive change? An analysis of the EU's universal service review mechanism. *Telecommunications Policy, 40*(1), 14–21. doi:http://dx.doi.org/10.1016/j.telpol.2015.11.007.

Berg, S., Jiang, L., & Lin, C. (2011). Universal service subsidies and cost overstatement: Evidence from the US telecommunications sector. *Telecommunications Policy, 35,* 583–591.

Blackman, C., & Srivastava, L. (2011). From availability to use: Universal access and service. In C. Blackman, & L. Srivastava (Eds.), *Telecommunications regulation handbook* (pp. 151–177). Washington, DC, Washington, DC, and Geneva: World Bank, infoDev, and International Telecommunication Union. Retrieved from http://www.infoDev.org/en/Document.1069.pdf.

Business Day. (2006, September 21). Mobile phone operators await ICASA nod on roll-out for poor in South Africa. *Business Day.*

Calandro, E., & Moyo, M. (2010). Is the universal access fund in Africa creating an enabling environment for ICT infrastructure investment in rural and perceived uneconomic areas? *5th Communication Policy Research Conference.* Xi'an. Retrieved from http://ssrn.com/abstract=1724465.

DoC. (2013, December 6). South Africa connect: Creating opportunities, ensuring inclusion—South Africa's broadband policy. *Government Gazette* (37119).

DTPS. (2016, October 3). National Integrated ICT Policy White Paper. *Government Gazette, 616* (40325).

DTPS. (2017a, April 7). National e-Strategy. *Government Gazette* (40772).

DTPS. (2017b). *Internet for all concept document.* Pretoria: Department of Telecommunications and Postal Services. Retrieved from http://www.ellipsis.co.za/wp-content/uploads/2017/07/Internet_For_All_Concept_Document.pdf.

EC. (1987). *Towards a dynamic European economy: Green Paper on the development of the common market for telecommunications services and equipment.* Brussels: Commission of the European Communities. Retrieved from http://ec.europa.eu/green-papers/pdf/green_paper_telecom_services__common_market_com_87_290.pdf.

EC. (1996). *Universal service for telecommunications in the perspective of a fully liberalised environment: An essential element of the information society.* Brussels: European Commission. Retrieved from http://aei.pitt.edu/3989/1/3989.pdf.

Eliassen, K., & From, J. (2009). Deregulation, privatisation and public service delivery: Universal service in telecommunications in Europe. *Policy and Society, 27*(3), 239–248.

EU. (2010). *Telecoms: Consultation on future universal service in digital era.* Brussels: European Union. Retrieved from http://europa.eu/rapid/pressReleasesAction.do?reference=IP/10/218&format=PDF&aged=0&language=EN&guiLanguage=en.

Fransman, M. (2010). *The new ICT ecosystem: Implications for policy and regulation.* New York: Cambridge University Press.

Gillwald, A. (2002). *Under-serviced area licences in South Africa: Steps to achieving viable operators.* Johannesburg: LINK Centre, University of the Witwatersrand. Retrieved from http://link.wits.ac.za/papers/usal.pdf.

Gillwald, A. (2005, Summer). A closing window of opportunity: Under-serviced area licensing in South Africa. *Information Technologies and International Development, 2*(4), 1–19.

Guest, K. (2006, October 2). A licence to fail. *Brainstorm.* Retrieved from http://www.brainstormmag.co.za/technology/10308-a-licence-to-fail.

Hazlett, T. (2006). *"Universal service" telephone subsidies: What does $7 Billion buy?* Chicago: The Heartland Institute. Retrieved from http://www.heartland.org/custom/semod_policybot/pdf/19520.pdf.

Hilbert, M. (2016). The bad news is that the digital access divide is here to stay: Domestically installed bandwidths among 172 countries for 1986–2014. *Telecommunications Policy, 40*(6). doi:http://dx.doi.org/10.1016/j.telpol.2016.01.006.

Hodge, J. (2004, March). Universal service through roll-out targets and licence conditions: lessons from telecommunications in South Africa. *Development Southern Africa, 21*(1), 205–225.

Horwitz, R. (2001). *Communication and democratic reform in South Africa.* Cambridge: Cambridge University Press.

Hudson, H. (1994). Universal service in the information age. *Telecommunications Policy, 18*(8), 658–667.

Hudson, H. (2017). *When regulation fills a policy gap: Toward universal broadband in the remote north.* Social Science Research Network. Retrieved from https://ssrn.com/abstract=2944295.

IBA. (1995). *Independent broadcasting authority report on the protection and viability of public broadcasting services, cross media control of broadcasting services, local television content and South African music.* Johannesburg: Independent Broadcasting Authority.

Intven, H. (2000). Universal service. In H. Intven (Ed.), *Telecommunications regulation handbook.* Washington, DC: infoDev. Retrieved from http://www.infoDev.org/projects/314regulationhandbook/module6.pdf.

ITU. (1985). *The missing link: Report of the independent commission for World Wide telecommunications development.* Geneva: International Telecommunication Union. Retrieved from http://www.itu.int/osg/spu/sfo/missinglink/The_Missing_Ling_A4-E.pdf.

ITU. (1998). *World telecommunication development report 1998: Universal access.* Geneva: International Telecommunication Union. Retrieved from http://www.itu.int/ITU-D/ict/publications/wtdr_98/.

ITU. (2003). *Trends in telecommunications reform 2003: Promoting universal access to ICTs—Practical tools For regulators.* Geneva: International Telecommunication Union.

ITU/UNESCO. (2011). *Broadband: a platform for progress: A report by the broadband commission for digital development.* Geneva and Paris: International Telecommunication Union and United Nations Educational, Scientific and Cultural Organisation. Retrieved from http://www.broadbandcommission.org/Reports/Report_2.pdf.

Kim, Y., Kelly, T., & Raja, S. (2010). *Building broadband: Strategies and policies for the developing world.* Global Information and Communication Technologies (GICT) Department. Washington, DC: World Bank. Retrieved from http://siteresources.worldbank.org/EXTINFORMATIONANDCOMMUNICATIONANDTECHNOLOGIES/Resources/282822-1208273252769/Building_broadband.pdf.

Lewis, C. (2010, August 26–28). Achieving universal service in South Africa: What next for regulation? *International Telecommunications Society Conference on Telecommunications: Ubiquity and equity in a broadband environment.*

Wellington. Retrieved from http://link.wits.ac.za/papers/Lewis-2010-USA-RSA-regulation-ITS-paper.pdf.

Lewis, C. (2013). Universal access and service interventions in South Africa: Best practice, poor Impact. *African Journal of Information and Communication* (13). LINK Centre, University of the Witwatersrand.

Lewis, C., & Maddens, S. (2011). *Update of SADC guidelines on universal access and service and assessment report*. Geneva: International Telecommunication Union. Retrieved from http://www.itu.int/ITU-D/projects/ITU_EC_ACP/hipssa/events/2011/Docs/universal_access-e.docx.

Maddens, S. (2009). *Trends in universal access and service policies: Changing policies to accommodate competition and convergence*. Geneva: International Telecommunication Union. Retrieved from http://www.itu.int/ITU-D/treg/Events/Seminars/GSR/GSR09/doc/USPolicy_ITUEC.pdf.

Melody, W. (Ed.). (1997). Telecom reform: Principles, policies and regulatory practices. Lyngby: Den Private Ingeniørfond, Technical University of Denmark. Retrieved from http://lirne.net/resources/tr/telecomreform.pdf.

Msimang, M. (2006). Universal service and universal access. In L. Thornton, Y. Carrim, P. Mtshaulana, & P. Reyburn (Eds.), Telecommunications law in South Africa. Johannesburg: STE Publishers. Retrieved from http://www.wits.ac.za/files/buads_542496001393429228.pdf.

Mueller, M. (1993). Universal service in telephone history: A reconstruction. *Telecommunications Policy, 17*(5), 353–369.

Mueller, M. (1997a, March). Universal service and the telecommunications Act: Myth made law. Communications of the ACM, 40(3), 39–47.

Mueller, M. (1997b). Universal service: Competition, interconnection, and monopoly in the making of the American telephone system. Cambridge, MA and Washington, DC: MIT Press and AEI Press.

Mzekandaba, S. (2016, February 22). High internet costs threaten universal access. ITWeb. Retrieved from http://www.itweb.co.za/index.php?option=com_content&view=article&id=150024:High-Internet-costs-threaten-universal-access&catid=260.

Oyedemi, T. (2009). Social inequalities and the South African ICT access policy agendas. International Journal of Communication, 3, 151–168.

Perry, S. (2010, May). The operators' missing millions. Brainstorm. Retrieved from http://www.brainstormmag.co.za/index.php?option=com_content&view=article&id=3855&catid=70:cover&Itemid=108.

PNC on ISAD. (2007). *Towards an inclusive information society for South Africa: A national information society and development plan*. Pretoria: Presidential National Commission on the Information Society and Development.

RSA. (1993, October 29). Multiparty implementation agreement. Government Gazette (15232). Retrieved from https://secure1.telkom.co.za/apps_static/ir/pdf/financial/pdf/exhibit10_5.pdf.

RSA. (1995). Telecommunications Green Paper. Pretoria: Ministry of Posts, Telecommunications and Broadcasting. Retrieved from http://www.polity.org.za/html/govdocs/green_papers/telecomms.html.

RSA. (1996a). White paper on telecommunications policy. Pretoria: Ministry for Posts, Telecommunications and Broadcasting.

RSA. (1996b). Telecommunications Act, 1996. No 103 of 1996. Pretoria: Republic of South Africa.

RSA. (2005). Electronic Communications Act, No 36 of 2005. Pretoria: Republic of South Africa.

RSA. (2014, June 2). Infrastructure Development Act. Government Gazette, 588 (37712).

Schofield, A., & Sithole, H. (2006). Achievement of the telecommunications Act objectives: Analysis of the extent to which the objectives of the telecommunications act (103 of 1996), as amended were achieved (in the period 1997 to 2004). Johannesburg: Universal Service Agency. Retrieved from http://www.usa.org.za/docs/gen/Achievements%20of%20the%20Objectives%20of%20the%20Telecom%20Act%20of%201996%2020.pdf.

Sidler, V. (2016, March 29). Fibre to everywhere is in South Africa's near-term future. Business Tech. Retrieved from http://businesstech.co.za/news/industry-news/118194/fibre-to-everywhere-is-in-south-africas-near-term-future/.

Stats SA. (1996). The people of South Africa: Population census, 1996. Pretoria: Statistics South Africa. Retrieved from https://apps.statssa.gov.za/census01/Census96/HTML/CIB/CIB1996.pdf.

Stats SA. (2015). Information and communication technologies (ICT): In-depth analysis of the general household survey data 2002–2013. Pretoria: Statistics South Africa. Retrieved from http://www.statssa.gov.za/publications/Report-03-18-05/Report-03-18-052013.pdf.

Stats SA. (2017). General household survey 2016. Pretoria: Statistics South Africa. Retrieved from http://www.statssa.gov.za/publications/P0318/P03182016.pdf.

Thierer, A. (1994, Fall). Unnatural monopoly: Critical moments in the development of the bell system monopoly. Cato Journal, 14(2). Retrieved from http://www.cato.org/pubs/journal/cjv14n2-6.html.

Thornton, L. (2006). *Recommendations on how the USA and other stakeholders might assist USALs to ensure sustainability*. Johannesburg: Universal Service and Access Agency of South Africa.

USA. (1996). Telecommunications Act of 1996. Washington, DC: United States of America. Retrieved from http://www.fcc.gov/Reports/tcom1996.pdf.

USAASA. (2014). *The national strategy on universal service & access report*. Johannesburg: Universal Service and Access Agency of South Africa.

van Leijden, F., & Monasso, T. (2005). Beware Dongas! An assessment of the road ahead for under-serviced area telecommunications operators in South Africa. Southern African Journal of Information and Communication (6).

Vecchiatto, P. (2006, March 8). USALs in deep trouble. ITWeb. Retrieved from http://www.itweb.co.za/index.php?option=com_content&view=article&id=113363:usals-in-deep-trouble&catid=260.

Vecchiatto, P. (2007, March 6). USF cash not flowing back into industry. ITWeb. Retrieved from http://www.itweb.co.za/sections/quickprint/print.asp?StoryID=171374.

Vermeulen, J. (2016, February 22). We shouldn't just build faster Internet for rich people: Mark Zuckerberg. MyBroadband. Retrieved from http://mybroadband.co.za/news/internet/156093-we-shouldnt-just-build-faster-internet-for-rich-people-mark-zuckerberg.html.

Wallsten, S. (2001). An econometric analysis of telecom competition, privatization, and regulation in Africa and Latin America. *The Journal of Industrial Economics, 49*(1), 1–19.

World Wide Worx. (2017). *Internet access in South Africa 2017: A comprehensive study of the internet access market in South Africa, and its key drivers.* Johannesburg: World Wide Worx.

Xavier, P. (2008). From universal service to universal network access? info, 10(5/6), 20–32.

CHAPTER 2

Universal Access and Service: The Rise of International Good Practice

The global telecommunications market was swept by a number of profound changes in the last quarter of the twentieth century, changes that were to have a lasting impact on the face and complexion of ICT policy and regulation, changes which still shape its features today.

The opening moves in what is now known as 'telecom reform' (Melody, 1997) came from the UK's Thatcher government (OECD, 2002, p. 7ff). In 1981, new legislation introduced competition into what was then a state-owned monopoly market. British Telecom (BT) was split off from the Post Office, with a new entrant, Mercury Communications, being licensed the following year. The new legal framework also established Oftel (Office for Telecommunications, now Ofcom, Office for Communications) as the sector regulator, and imposing universal service obligations on BT. The Thatcher government then moved to privatise BT, by floating 51% of the company on the London Stock Exchange.[1]

These developments effectively put in place in the UK what are still today considered to be the three core features of ICT sector reform: privatisation of the incumbent operator, the introduction of competition into the market, and the creation of an independent sector regulator (cf. ITU, 2014).

At much the same time, on the opposite side of the Atlantic, the US telecommunications market was also undergoing equally fundamental

[1] Further listings in 1991 and 1993 have now left BT fully in private hands.

C. Lewis, *Regulating Telecommunications in South Africa*,
Information Technology and Global Governance,
https://doi.org/10.1007/978-3-030-43527-1_2

changes. In early 1982, faced with a long-running antitrust lawsuit, AT&T agreed to break up its local fixed-line operations into 7 regional operators.[2]

Although the US market had long been subject to regulation under the national Federal Communications Commission (FCC) and individual state-level regulatory commissions, the 1982 break-up of A&T ushered into the market profound competitive changes that continue to be felt today.

These fundamental changes were driven partly by economic forces and partly by technology pressures. The forces at play were both multifaceted and dynamic (Beardsley, von Morgenstern, Enriquez, & Kipping, 2002) and have been the subject of much international scholarship, perhaps pre-eminently through the seminal work of Manuel Castells (Castells, 1999). Further, they have been extensively analysed through the lens of regime theory.

These changes were accompanied by the rise, influence and hegemony of an epistemic community of 'international good practice', which prescribed ICT sector reform more broadly, and universal access and service more specifically. The development of 'international good practice' (Overman, 1994, p. 69) is linked in turn to regime formation through the political contestation for hegemony amongst individuals, organisational entities and state actors. It involves the development of a set of "implicit or explicit principles, norms, rules, and decision-making procedures around which actors' expectations converge" (Krasner, 1982, p. 186).

2.1 Contestation and Hegemony: The ITU and the WTO

The role of the International Telecommunication Union (ITU), and the ITU's relationship to the General Agreement on Tariffs and Trade (GATT) and its successor, the World Trade Organisation (WTO), have been examined from the perspective of regime theory by a number of analysts (Aronson & Cowhey, 1988; Cowhey, 1990; Drake, 1994; Levi-Faur, 1998; Woodrow, 1991; Zacher, 1996, 2002). However, from the point of view of universal access and service policy and practice, it is

[2] Known as the 'Baby Bells'. AT&T was thereby able to keep its *de facto* long-distance monopoly.

less important to deliberate on the dynamics of the political forces at play than to analyse their product.

Writing before the advent of the WTO and its Agreement on Basic Telecommunications, as well as before the 1992 restructuring of the ITU, Cowhey (1990) offers an early examination of the upheavals that were beginning to reshape the structure of the telecommunications market. The features he sketched out were picked up by subsequent commentators and included: the role of politics in shaping and driving international policy dispensations and the importance of 'epistemic communities' in conceptualising and formulating changes in regime dynamics.

2.1.1 *The ITU's Cosy Cartel*

The *ancien* telecommunications regime centred on the ITU (Drake, 1994) was essentially based on an economic market model widely characterised as a "cartel" (Cowhey, 1990; Zacher, 1996)—an association of commercial enterprises, co-operating in order to restrict competition in the market or to maintain artificially-inflated prices. Based on the normative presumption of the telecommunications network as a "'natural monopoly'… [with] a single entity in charge of production and distribution" (1990, p. 183), the ITU was established in 1865 to bring together telegraph companies, mostly state-owned national monopolies. The "central normative guideline" (Zacher, 2002, p. 194) for this late nineteenth-century collaboration was the need to ensure functioning international interconnection of networks in order to provide cross-border telegraph services, increasingly important for business and trade in the late nineteenth century. With the advent of telecommunications, similar norms and rules were adopted. Much of the work of the ITU, therefore, came to be focused on the interconnection of networks and on the agreement of the necessary technical standards upon which this relies, along with the high-level co-ordination and management of spectrum, and, later, the allocation of satellite orbits (Zacher, 2002, pp. 191–197).

The ITU provided a platform for the disparate national telecommunications operators to negotiate mutually-beneficial agreements on economic arrangements, market shares and pricing. In the words of Zacher, they adopted the "traditional cartel norm [which] prescribed that all state telecommunications administrations should co-operate in determining market shares, setting rates, and dividing revenues" (Zacher, 1996, p. 161). It was an accommodation with considerable mutual benefit.

Largely, this was achieved through setting international prices well above cost in order to cross-subsidise domestic service prices, either to support universal service or, in the case of many developing countries, to provide income to the fiscus via the state-owned monopoly operator. Accordingly, the cartel adopted rules preventing unwanted competition and protecting state monopolies (Zacher, 1996, pp. 164–166).

2.1.2 *Pressures for Change*

It was only towards the middle of the twentieth century that a number of complex, multifaceted and shifting pressures began to undermine the comfortable status quo. The main drivers, however, included: technological advances, commercial imperatives and global power dynamics.

Key amongst these technological changes were developments in the information technology and electronics environment, starting in the 1970s and clustered predominantly in the US (cf. Castells, 1999, pp. 28–76), which had substantial impacts on both industrial development and business models. But for business to deploy and benefit from this information technology revolution, improved telecommunications networks and the new services they enabled were of key importance. The impact of this increasing integration of information technologies and telecommunications has variously been articulated as the "death of distance" (Cairncross, 1997) and the "compression of time and space" (Harvey, 1990), or as the "space of flows" (Castells, 1999).

This central nexus between computing and telecommunications is closely linked to the notion of globalisation, for which the new information and communications technologies are both a driver and a product. The changes wrought by the new ICTs were in turn to drive changes in the international telecommunications regulatory environment.

The pressures were fundamentally economic, based on the imperative of business firms seeking market reforms either to reduce input costs or to exploit the business opportunities a restructured market would open up. The commercial entities pressing for reform were powerful, large users of telecommunications services in information-intensive sectors such as banking and financial services, for whom "price, efficiency, and quality of service were becoming increasingly more important" (Zacher, 2002, p. 200), along with the emerging computer companies and a range of "service and equipment producers" (Cowhey, 1990, pp. 187,188).

Several business and commercial user associations, such as the International Telecommunications Users' Group (INTUG) and the International Chamber of Commerce (ICC), also played a significant role in pushing for liberalisation of leased lines and value-added services (Drahos & Joseph, 1995, p. 624; Drake, 2000; Levi-Faur, 1998, p. 21).

Political pressures and geopolitics also shaped the pressures for change. The analysis of Hills, while allowing for the changes wrought by technological innovations and the role of business in attempting to exploit the opportunities thus created, posits a model that is a fundamentally political, which has neo-imperialist, hegemonic designs driven by the US at its core. In her view, the changes to the international telecommunications regime are about the exercise of power. Her central thesis is one in which "the United States as the world's dominant economic and military power attempted to restructure the international market of telecommunications to expand its direct and indirect control over the domestic markets of other governments [whilst] at the same time, it protected its domestic market from foreign penetration" (Hills, 2007, p. 2). While there were clearly strong political pressures at play, her model is a touch too one-dimensional, with insufficient space for the complex and unpredictable dynamics of the interplay between technology, the economy and political hegemony, and for the mediating role of epistemic communities.

What was important was the coalition between business interests and governmental agendas, with political support for the business lobby in favour of greater ICT sector liberalisation a key factor behind shifts in the regime (Hills, 1994; Zacher, 2002, pp. 191–206).

There were clearly also counterpressures. The US in particular sought liberalisation abroad while engaging in protectionism of its domestic telecommunications industry (Hills, 2007, p. 2; Zacher, 1996, p. 160). And the countervailing need to protect national incumbent monopolies and retain sovereignty in domestic telecommunications policy is what underlay the bitter opposition to the US agenda from the EU and from most developing countries (Zacher, 1996, p. 171). At bottom, therefore, the contestation centred on the opening up of telecommunications markets, both domestic and international, to competition and international investment.

The transformation of a tightly controlled telecommunications market presided over by a state-owned monopoly into a more competitive environment contained within itself a tripartite logic.

Firstly, introducing competition implies a key role for private sector investment and opens up opportunities for national operators to seek profitable investments abroad.

Secondly, attracting private sector investment implies the need to privatise the state-owned incumbent, which also provides opportunities for national operators to secure lucrative investments in foreign countries.

Finally, competition and privatisation in turn imply the need for regulatory structures to optimise market functioning, enforce interconnection and ensure that public interest objectives are met—something Hills suggests had also been promoted strongly by the World Bank and the IMF (2007, pp. 149–174).

The ensuing struggle unfolded on several fronts.

2.1.3 *Sites of Struggle: The ITU*

Domestic reform provided both an exemplar and a source of international pressure. As Cowhey notes, the three pioneering ICT sector reform countries (the US, the UK and Japan) possessed "formidable" power to "drive the world market", partly because they alone accounted for "almost 60 percent of the world telecommunications market", but also because of their role as centres of global finance and manufacturing (1990, pp. 191,192).

This, in turn, put pressure on the Europe to change its rules. A 1987 telecommunications Green Paper was an explicit response to the pressures of technological developments and the demands of business, along with the "measures taken in the United States and Japan" (EC, 1987, pp. 1–2). The Green Paper set the stage for the liberalisation of 'value-added' but not 'basic' (i.e. telephony) telecommunications services (EC, 1987). It also made the case for a "separation of the regulatory and operational functions" (EC, 1987, p. 94). Two key directives ensued, effectively liberalising the VANS component of the (EC, 1990a, 1990b).

Across at the ITU, pressure for telecomms reform had begun to make itself as early as its 1982 Nairobi Plenipotentiary Conference, at which a consensus was reached on the need to establish a "broad international regulatory framework for all existing and foreseen new telecommunication services" (ITU, 1982). But it was at the 1988 key World Administrative Telegraph and Telephone Conference, where the early impetus towards changing the shape and face of the ITU, and altering the rules of the regime, made itself felt. Here, the separate sets of regulations for telegraph and telephone services were replaced by an integrated set of International Telecommunication Regulations (ITRs), which still today remain in force (albeit with a highly contested 2012 set of revisions [Hill, 2013]) as the fundamental treaty of the ITU.

The 1988 ITRs are widely regarded as both influenced by and paving the way towards the "privatization, liberalization and the growth of the Internet and mobile networks" (Hill, 2013, p. 313). They were also the subject of bitter contestation between those developed countries seeking to institutionalise telecommunications liberalisation, spearheaded by the US, and the countries of the Third World seeking to forestall competition, led by India and Brazil (Langdale, 1989), with the outcome representing a compromise between the two groupings (Hill, 2014, p. 9).

Subsequently, ITU Secretary-General Richard Butler (1983–1989)[3] set up an Advisory Group of experts to write a report on the implications of the changes in the sector and to make recommendations on the way forward. The group comprised: Denmark's Poul Hansen (as chair), former telecomms academic Rita Cruise O'Brien, US-based consultant Lynne Gallagher, academics Dale Hatfield and Bill Melody (principal drafter), ITU staffer Terrefe Ras-Work, MD of India's fixed-line incumbent Mahendra Shukla, Panaftel Co-ordinator Gabriel Tedros and the World Bank's Bjorn Wellenius.

The report was highly influential: it lent legitimacy to the arguments in favour of liberalisation, privatisation and independent regulation within the developing world (Hills, 2007, pp. 122–123). More broadly, as Hills suggests, the report marked a shift in the role of the ITU from merely a technocratic one towards a far greater degree of policy and developmental involvement (Hills, 2007, pp. 122–123), and presaged the creation of its developmental wing, ITU-D.

Indeed, the report's starting point is the incipient reform of the sector, the "current state of debates on the structure, management and ownership of telecommunication entities" (ITU, 1989, p. v). The language used to describe these changes—as "policy adjustments based on market-led approaches, placing limitations on the scope of the traditional telecommunication monopoly and permitting a certain amount of competition" (ITU, 1989, p. 4)—is surprisingly oblique by today's standards, suggesting the degree of contestation.

[3] Butler's key catalytic role in telecomms reform was recognised by both Andile Ngcaba (interview, 28 January 2015) and Bill Melody (personal communication, 20 April 2015).

The report emphasises the issues and challenges facing developing countries. Although it recognises that "appropriate policies and institutional structures for progress in telecommunication development are not likely to be the same as those for industrialized countries", it notes "human resource development" as a key constraint, and emphasises the "unique and positive role that ITU could play in respect of the special problems of telecommunication expansion in developing countries" (ITU, 1989, p. 28). The report thus sought to place the ITU as a key bearer and interpreter of the gospel of ICT sector reform in the developing world.

The report's emphasis on the key functions of the ITU as being

a. Standardization matters: related to equipment and system operation and interconnectibility,
b. Regulatory matters: frequency allocation, satellite orbital positions, telecommunication operations, etc.,
c. Development and extension of networks and services (ITU, 1989, p. 30),

also paved the way for its reorganisation a few years later into the current divisions dealing with radio communication (ITU-R), standardisation (ITU-T) and development (ITU-D), the latter being the major 1992 innovation.

Hills points to a number of strong-arm tactics on the part of the US, aimed at imposing its agenda on the ITU. Apart from direct political pressure on other delegations, partly through its ability to field large well-resourced delegations, she points to the exercise of financial muscle as a principal funder of the ITU, along with some rather more nefarious tactics such as "late submission of papers", *ex parte* meetings and "agenda manipulation" (2007, p. 115).

In the following year, influenced by the Hansen Advisory Group report, the ITU's 1989 Nice Plenipotentiary Conference moved to make further changes, adopting a permanent Constitution, and establishing a Telecommunication Development Bureau (BDT) to provide support to developing countries.

The Nice conference also laid the groundwork for an

> in-depth review of the structure and functioning of the Union, in order to study and recommend, as necessary, measures to ensure greater cost-effectiveness... with a view to ensuring that the Union responds effectively to the demands placed on it by the changing nature of the telecommunications environment. (ITU, 1990, p. Resolution 55)

The restructuring was later formalised at a special Plenipotentiary Conference held in Geneva (ITU, 1992). As a result, the ITU was restructured into three sectoral arms, viz. Radio communication (ITU-R), responsible primarily for the management of international radio frequency spectrum and the allocation of satellite orbits; Standardisation (ITU-T), responsible for global telecommunications standards, excluding radio; Development (ITU-D), responsible for spreading equitable, sustainable and affordable access to ICTs. The process was welcomed by the US as enabling the ITU to be "more effective in responding to the changes taking place in telecommunications" and "more responsive to the needs of the Unites States Government and private sector" (Clinton, 1996).

Nonetheless, the US was less than successful at imposing its full agenda on the ITU than it had hoped. The outcome was more of a compromise, reflecting the balance of forces within the ITU, none of whom were willing to sacrifice the entire telecommunications regime as the price of enforcing their specific positions. Developing countries were thus able to retain the principle of "state sovereignty" over domestic telecommunications markets, although the liberalisation of the telecommunications market was now firmly on the agenda (Hills, 2007, p. 115).

Over the next few years, the ITU held a series of important regulatory policy colloquiums under the umbrella of 'The Changing Role of Government in an Era of Telecom Deregulation'[4]:

- 1993, February—focusing on "the exchange of insights and experiences about alternative approaches to telecom regulation" (ITU, 1993, p. 5);
- 1994, November—dealing with Global Mobile Personal Communications Systems (ITU, 1994a);
- 1994, December—which "considered how regulators can promote universal service and facilitate the application of innovations in telecommunications" (ITU, 1994b, p. 2);

[4] Interestingly, the ANC's Andile Ngcaba, who features prominently in Chapter 3, attended at least four of these colloquiums.

- 1995, April—focusing on the regulatory issues pertaining to interconnection;
- 1995, December—dealing with the regulatory implications of GATS and the WTO (ITU, 1995);
- 1996, December—looking at the regulatory implications of convergence (ITU, 1996b);
- 1997, December—which sought to address "the present crisis in the international… accounting rate system" (ITU, 1997);
- 1998, December—dealing with electronic commerce.

The set of colloquiums, interestingly, addresses many of the issues identified in the preceding discussion on telecomms reform: interconnection, the accounting rate regime, trade in services. This attests to the normative influence of the work of the ITU on national regulators (Cowhey, 1990, p. 181; Zhao, 2002).

The ITU was both responding to the various pressures for telecomms reform and influencing its member states to do likewise—a strictly normative role. It was a different arena, the negotiations over trade in services, including telecommunications, that offered agreements with considerably more binding effect.

2.1.4 Sites of Struggle: The WTO

Those pressing for ICT sector reform saw a parallel opportunity to achieve telecomms liberalisation through the platform offered by the Uruguay Round of multilateral trade negotiations, which had commenced in 1986 within the framework of the General Agreement on Tariffs and Trade (GATT). The shift in focus was driven partly by the need to engage in all available forums as part of a multifaceted approach. But it also formed part of a deliberate and more cynical strategy of "forum-shopping" (Hills, 2007, p. 21), where the choice of negotiating platform shifts according to the likelihood of achieving the desired outcome.

The Uruguay round of talks sought to include new service-based areas within the GATT framework, including trade in telecommunications services. An agreement was finally signed in Marrakesh, Morocco, on 15 April 1994, by ministers from most of the 123 participating governments. It was this agreement which established, with effect from 1 January 1995, the World Trade Organisation (WTO) and the General Agreement on Trade in Services (GATS).

The GATS agreement included an Annex on Telecommunications (WTO, 1995), but this covered only "value-added or specialized telecommunications" (Singh, 2002, p. 253) because of the failure of the negotiating countries to reach agreement on the contentious issue of basic, voice telecommunications (Hills, 2007, pp. 194–195).

Under the WTO now, a Negotiating Group on Basic Telecommunications was constituted to carry forward the unfinished attempt to reach agreement. It was a difficult balancing act to agree a "progressively higher level of liberalization in services on a mutually advantageous basis with appropriate flexibility for individual developing country members" (WTO, 1997).

Progress was slow and disputatious. But by April 1996 the group was able to reach agreement on a Regulatory Reference Paper (WTO, 1996b) and to table an agreement (WTO, 1996a) giving member states until late 1997 to make commitments concerning basic telecommunications. By early, some 55 schedules of commitments had been submitted, including from the US, the EC (a common offer from all 15 member states), Australia, Brazil, India, Japan—South Africa was one of 6 African countries to do so (WTO, 1997). The strongest offers, though, had come from OECD members (Aronson & Cowhey, 1988, p. 163).

The "incorporation of regulatory principles into a trade policy framework" was seen in some quarters as a "remarkable achievement" (Drake & Noam, 1997, p. 806). Likewise, Cowhey and Klimenko categorise the WTO Agreement on Basic Telecommunications Services as a "major achievement" that goes to the "heart of sound regulation in the market" (2000, p. 274).

The Regulatory Reference Paper was a key milestone. It codified the core principles of ICT sector reform,[5] thus playing an important normative role in setting forth the rules of the new regime (Cowhey & Aronson, 2009, p. 164; Cowhey & Klimenko, 2000; Drake & Noam, 1997; Fredebeul-Krein & Freytag, 1997),[6] and remains influential today. It was a broad-based document, originally instigated by the FCC, but drawing on both the EC's Open Network Directive and the 1996 US

[5] The six core issues covered are: competitive safeguards; interconnection; universal service; public availability of licensing criteria; independent regulators; allocation and use of scarce resources.

[6] It has currently been acceded to by 82 of the WTO's 157 members.

Telecommunications Act, with the final wording primarily from the hand of Japan (Hills, 2007, pp. 198–204).

The negotiations had brought powerful vested interests to the fore, with access to foreign markets and the protection of the domestic telecommunications sector at stake. For the reformers, the application of GATT principles would serve to institutionalise the norm of market access for telecommunications companies, opening up domestic markets to foreign investment, providing for international oversight in respect of network standards, pricing, consumer protection and regulation (Cowhey, 1990, pp. 174, 194).

On the other hand, the very nature of the negotiations precluded straightforward outcomes that favoured only a limited number of participants. The multiplicity of negotiating stakeholder parties (which included a number of developing countries), together with the wide range of issues on the table—"multi-actor plurality and multi-issue plurality" (Singh, 2002, p. 242)—mitigated against one-sided outcomes.

Further, the very nature of the settlement being negotiated allowed countries both to accede to the agreement in principle, and to control in practice—through their commitments—the extent and pace of their own country's telecomms reform.[7] Accession was probably further facilitated by the fact that developing countries too faced similar sets of sectoral pressures—principally technological change and business imperatives driving the need for global integration and liberalisation of their telecommunications sectors.

The principles of the new WTO telecommunications regime included reciprocity and non-discrimination in respect of trade in telecommunications services through the Most-Favoured Nation (MFN) principle, the opening up of domestic markets to external firms and foreign investment through the principles of equal market access and equal national treatment, all supported by the principle of transparency (cf. Drahos & Joseph, 1995, p. 622; Singh, 2002, p. 253). This ensured a predictable and structured process of liberalisation, governed by the commitments offers of the

[7] South Africa, for example, made a complex set of commitments, including, amongst others: the preservation of Telkom's monopoly until 2003, and of the Vodacom/MTN duopoly until 1998, followed by the introduction of an additional licensee in each subsector; the gradual liberalisation of resale from 2000; a foreign investment cap of 30% (WTO, 2003). All of these have since fallen away.

signatory states. Together, buttressed by the normative role of the Regulatory Reference Paper, this constituted what Drahos and Joseph characterise as the "emerging supranational regulatory regime" (Drahos & Joseph, 1995).

What arose, therefore, is an internationally negotiated regime framework with strong normative characteristics, one that is diffuse in nature, centred primarily around two institutions. Indeed, in many respects the ITU, the WTO, the World Bank, the IMF have functioned as a quartet of institutions, the component pillars of a loosely integrated ICT sector regime, with a converging and relatively consistent set of principles, norms, values, rules and procedures aligned with 'Washington consensus' thinking.

Indeed, there has been fairly extensive collaboration between the ITU and the World Bank, including hosting (with the Commonwealth Telecommunications Organisation) a joint 1991 seminar involving over 40 countries to "examine the experience of implementing reforms in the telecommunications sector" (Wellenius & Stern, 1994, p. ix). Until recently, the two bodies also worked together via *info*Dev and have published a number of ICT policy and regulatory handbooks (Blackman & Srivastava, 2011a; Intven, 2000), along with an online ICT Regulatory Toolkit.[8]

2.2 Building an Epistemic Community for Telecomms Reform

These shifts in the global telecommunications regime—driven by technological change and the needs of business, mediated through the structural changes and substantive policy shifts negotiated at the ITU and through the WTO telecommunications process—have established an overall epistemic framework embracing and advocating privatisation, liberalisation and regulation. It was also through these changes that the notions of universal access and service first rose to prominence within international good practice. It is a regime that has had a powerful influence upon developing countries like South Africa as they grappled with the pressures and challenges of ICT sector reform.

[8] Housed online at http://www.ictregulationtoolkit.org/en/home.

The ITU/WTO policy regime was to develop a close relationship with the professional epistemic communities aligned to the principles and norms it sought to institutionalise. Both shared the phraseology of a common discourse, framing the issues and debates in overlapping terms. This implies a complex interplay of mutual influence and legitimation, where the political forces striving for hegemony within the regime turned to existing epistemic communities engaged in analytical enquiry and academic discourse for the cognitive frameworks and normative agendas and specialist knowledge needed to legitimate the framing of problems and the definition of solutions (Cowhey, 1990, pp. 172,3; Drahos & Joseph, 1995, p. 628).

For example, General Secretary Butler deployed what was in effect an epistemic community in the formulation of the key report (ITU, 1991) that launched the ITU reform movement.

On the other hand, such epistemic communities benefit from the political support they receive, becoming influential in their own right. The adoption of their cognitive frameworks by the political actors influences in turn how such actors frame problems and define solutions. Further, the political agendas of the actors in turn influence the content and direction of the self-same epistemic communities.

The development of the telecomms reform regime was thus in part a struggle for supremacy of ideas. And what the analysis here is concerned with, in particular, is the values, norms and good practices associated with the question of universal access and service.

Within the broader sweep of the evolving global ICT regime, the relevant questions are: why universal access and service came to be one of its key issues; how the problems of UAS came to be framed; and what solutions, strategies and interventions were developed to address the challenges of UAS.

2.3 Codifying International Good Practice

The question of universal service entered the epistemic discourse in response to objections raised by operators and countries that introducing competition and opening their markets to foreign or private investment would prevent them from meeting the socially desirable objective of providing telecommunications services to all—universal service.

Faced with the pressures for telecomms reform, operators and policymakers sought justifications for retaining state-owned monopoly provision. Acceding to sector liberalisation, they argued, would undermine the ability to sustain the implicit public policy objective of delivering universal service through cross subsidies and support from the state (Bauer, 1999; Gasmi, Laffont, & Sharkey, 2000; Melody, 1999, pp. 23–24; OECD, 1991, pp. 28–29). Indeed, Tim Kelly, who had been working at the OECD at the time, describes universal service as "the fig-leaf of the monopolist" (interview 27 October 2014).

Faced with these objections, and drawing on the expertise of loose epistemic community of academics (e.g., Martin Cave, Dale Hatfield, Bill Melody, Patrick Xavier) and ICT policy experts (e.g., Tim Kelly, Björn Wellenius), a number of reports were commissioned to make the counter-argument. What emerged gradually began to cohere as a canon of international good practice in relation to universal access and service.

2.3.1 Maitland's Missing Link

Commissioned by the 1982 Nairobi Plenipotentiary meeting of the ITU "to recommend ways in which the expansion of telecommunications across the world could be stimulated" (ITU, 1985, p. 1), highly regarded and widely influential, the 'Missing Link' report of the Maitland Commission provides an important UAS baseline.

Although the Maitland Report makes no mention of the specific term 'universal service', it is imbued with many of the concerns later to surface within the UAS body of knowledge. And it offered an early focus on the phenomenon that was later to become characterised as the 'digital divide', the developmental *raison d'être* for universal access and service interventions.

The Maitland Report starts by recognising the important role of telecommunications as an enabler of economic growth and social development, and a source of cultural enrichment, recognising:

> the vital role telecommunications play not only in such obvious fields as emergency, health and other social services, administration and commerce, but also in stimulating economic growth and enhancing the quality of life. (ITU, 1985, p. 65)

The report's central concern is the global disparity in access to telecommunications, the need to address this access gap and to ensure the widespread provision of telecommunications services. While "advanced industrialised societies have virtually comprehensive services" (ITU, 1985, p. 65), it notes that:

> In most developing countries the telephone service is still far from universal and the more sophisticated forms of telecommunications are almost unknown, except, in some of the larger towns and business centres. In many countries there are great tracts of territory with no telecommunications at all. (ITU, 1985, p. 14)

While treading a cautious path in relation to telecomms reform, the Maitland Report calls for joint efforts to address the imbalance, through increased investment in the sector, the adoption of improved technologies, and increased funding and financial support for telecommunications rollout (ITU, 1985, pp. 65–69). However, the report fails to provide recommendations on how to increase penetration for the under-serviced.

2.3.2 *Europe's Green Paper*

Aside from its role in paving the way for the liberalisation of value-added telecommunications services, Europe's 1987 telecommunications Green Paper is important for its defence—in the name of 'universal service'—of the monopoly provision of basic, voice telephony. It also provided the first definition of services "offered on a universal basis", as those provided:

i. with general geographical coverage...
ii. on demand to all users on reasonably the same terms regardless of the users' location... and the cost of connection to the network (EC, 1987, p. 66).

In terms of current UAS good practice thinking, the Green Paper's proposals are rudimentary, including:

- [cross-subsidies for] certain public service goals, such as universal service;
- a complex [pricing] trade-off between commercial considerations and universal service goals;
- specification of a number of end-to-end services to be provided with universal availability (EC, 1987, pp. 77, 79, 118).

Importantly, though, the Green Paper explicitly squares off against the public service argument for universal service as a central defence against the introduction of competition—this despite the fact that the very concrete measures referred to above are not readily sustainable in a fully competitive environment.

2.3.3 *Universal Service in the OECD*

It was from the OECD that universal service in the context of ICT sector policy and regulation received its first serious international attention—in a report (1991) examining two of the main issues flagged as obstacles to telecomms liberalisation by the European Commission. These were the questions of universal service and of the application of cost-based pricing and rate rebalancing to telecommunications tariffs.

Then comprising 25 (mainly European) members, as well as the US and Japan, the OECD was a useful platform for carrying the debate of telecommunications liberalisation forward.

Tim Kelly, then an OECD staffer, points to an explicit agenda to tackle the objections to liberalisation of the sector:

> what we tried to do in our work at the OECD was to point out that it was perfectly possible to have universal service and a competitive market structure, and that in many ways competition was the best way to achieve that. (interview, 27 October 2014)

Likewise, other commentators have pointed to the influential role of the OECD within the emerging 'supranational telecommunications regulatory regime' of the time, noting its "considerable power to set agendas and create influential models. (Drahos & Joseph, 1995, p. 626).

The OECD report also reflects a concrete move to draw on the expertise of the academic epistemic community already researching and writing in this area. The two main sections of the report were written by prominent English academics, Prof Nicholas Garnham[9] and Dr Robin Mansell,[10] respectively.

[9] Then at the Centre for Communication and Information Studies, Polytechnic of Central London, UK.

[10] Then at the Centre for Information and Communication Technologies, Science Policy Research Unit, University of Sussex, UK.

The report typifies much international good practice literature: country benchmarking, examining situations and practices in a number of jurisdictions[11]—accompanied by an analysis distilling generally applicable lessons and guidelines.

The UAS section describes itself as the "first comprehensive study of universal service in the countries of Western Europe" (OECD, 1991, p. 3) and, in line with its normative intention, sets out to tackle the

> arguments used to justify the retention of public, or publicly-controlled, telecommunications monopoly structures [which] are based on the claim that only through such structures will there be an assurance of maintaining universal telecommunication service. (OECD, 1991, p. 23)

The report addresses a number of issues and areas that would later come to characterise the policy debate. Flagging the importance of definitional questions, it points out that the "concept of universal service is ... too imprecisely defined to serve as a useful guide to policy" and identifies the consequent need to set "distinct, realizable and measurable goals" (OECD, 1991, p. 83).

It also contains the first outlines of what would become the UAS mantra of 'availability, accessibility and affordability' that permeates international good practice to this day, by breaking down of the notion of universal service into the "distinct subsidiary concepts" of:

- universal geographical availability;
- non-discriminatory access, that is, the equal treatment of all users [in respect of tariffs and quality of service]...
- reasonable costs or affordability (OECD, 1991, p. 26).

This framework was to inform subsequent ITU thinking. It was picked up at a 1994 ITU workshop, which suggested that the universal service "regulatory obligation" should cover "universal geographical availability ... non-discriminatory access ... [and] reasonable costs or affordability" (Blackman, 1995, p. 172). The framework subsequently became the ITU best practice catchphrase: "availability... accessibility... affordability"

[11] The report covers: Belgium, France, Germany, Ireland, Italy, the Netherlands, Portugal, Spain, Sweden and the UK.

(ITU, 1998, p. 63), remaining so ever since (cf. Blackman & Srivastava, 2011a, pp. 155–156; infoDev, 2009, pp. 2–3).

Recognising the tension between the objectives of universal service and those of market competition and cost-based pricing, the report concludes that

> there is no institutional reason why universal service should not be required of and delivered by either public monopolies or regulated private competitive operators. (OECD, 1991, p. 85)

It is a conclusion somewhat equivocally appeasing to monopolists, but one that does show that universal service and competition can be policy bedfellows.

Although it lists a "number of tools in the regulators [sic] armoury, such as access charges, life-line service and universal service contracts", as well as "universal service obligations" (OECD, 1991, pp. 86,87), the report gives little detail on what precisely is meant by these interventions or on how they might be applied.

Strangely too, the report makes little reference to the clear linkages between the two questions under consideration. Rate rebalancing clearly impacts consumer tariffs and thus the affordability of telecommunications services. And the question of affordability as a universal service *sine qua non* is an issue that threads its way through much of the subsequent discourse.

2.3.4 *Costing Universal Service Obligations*

A few years later, a duo of reports (EC, 1994; OECD, 1995) served to take forward the formulation of international good practice, for the first time explicitly foregrounding and framing the issue of universal service obligations (USOs), an intervention that was to become part of the UAS canon (Intven, 2000, pp. 6–1, 6–56).

Both reports place themselves squarely within the debate over the impact of a liberalising telecommunications landscape on the policy objective of universal service. Both conclude that competition is not antithetical to universal service objectives. The OECD report explicitly tackles the universal service argument, noting that it is exploited by monopoly providers as a justification for opposing market liberalisation and argues conversely that "prohibiting competition could serve, in fact, to impede progress towards universal service" (1995, p. 5).

Similarly, the European Commission sees "no reason in principle why universal service obligations cannot be satisfied in the framework of competition" (EC, 1994, p. 4).

The academic epistemic community is again central to both reports.[12] Both sets of authors also draw explicitly on the academic literature in the framing and justification of their arguments. Both reports also engage in the cross-country benchmarking approach characteristic of international good practice literature.[13]

Both reports debate the nature of universal service, its characteristics and criteria. The European Commission report is rather briefer, identifying four key components to UAS:

1. Achieving universal geographic coverage;
2. Offering residential services at geographically averaged prices;
3. Pursuing universal access through widely subsidised residential access;
4. Offering Targetted [sic] Telephone Subsidies (EC, 1994, pp. 6–13).

Similarly, the OECD report provides an extensive discussion of a similar cluster of core dimensions underpinning the UAS service objective, viz.:

a. Universal geographic access: subscribership and penetration levels;
b. Universal affordable access;
c. Universal service quality;
d. Universal access by the disabled;
e. Tariffs for universal service (OECD, 1995, pp. 36–49).

[12] The EC report was authored by Prof Martin Cave (Brunel University), Claire Milne (Antelope Consulting) and Mark Scanlan (Brunel University), while the OECD report was written by Patrick Xavier (Swinburne University of Technology, with a chapter by Professor Martin Cave (Brunel University).

[13] The European Commission report covers: Australia, Finland, New Zealand, Sweden, UK and the US (EC, 1994); while the OECD examines: Australia, Japan, New Zealand, the UK and the US (OECD, 1995, p. 17).

Both reports thus echo the concepts of geographic availability, non-discriminatory access and affordability from the earlier OECD report (1991), albeit without much greater clarity. But ensuring both universal geographic coverage and consumer affordability are common policy objectives and performance criteria throughout. And, the EC report, in particular, focuses on a number of specific pricing interventions as proxies for ensuring affordability.

Both reports adopt similar public interest, social equity approaches to the imposition of USOs. According to the European Commission, USOs are imposed in respect of those:

> services which an operator is required to supply and supplies efficiently, yet which impose losses upon the operator... [and] typically require a "basic service" to be provided at a specified quality of service. (EC, 1994, p. 5)

The OECD report adopts a similar position, stating that USOs:

> constitute a requirement to provide basic telephone service to all who request it at a uniform and affordable price even though there may be significant differences in the costs of supply. (OECD, 1995, p. 13)

Both definitions emphasise the provision of 'basic' voice telephony to (usually residential) consumers. Both recognise that providing such services is likely to be unprofitable for operators in terms of both location and revenue, the two dimensions of the 'access gap' that will be discussed below. The cost of supply to remote, usually rural, locations is high because of the distances involved. Conversely, revenue from less affluent customers, with consequent low levels of usage, is low.

The requirement imposed on an operator to provide telecommunications services to remote and often relatively impoverished communities and customers to meet public interest objectives remains the essence of USOs as understood within UAS good practice today (Blackman & Srivastava, 2011b, p. 160; Intven, 2000, pp. 6–19).

Because of the uneconomic nature of USOs, both reports devote considerable attention to analysing and quantifying the costs of meeting such requirements, a full chapter in each case. But, of more interest from the good practice perspective, is the range of interventions they recommend supporting the sustainability of USOs under competition.

The rather tentative recommendations from the EC report include:

- financing USOs from general taxation (which it rather discounts as a viable option);
- cross-subsidising USOs through a levy on operator profits or on existing customers in order to fund loss-making customers, a proposal similar to the now common USF levy;
- competitive tendering for the provision of USOs—akin to the least-subsidy auction approach, of which Chile is perhaps the best-known example (Wellenius, 2002);
- proposals for middle-income countries, including: restricting competition to certain market segments (e.g. international calls); a rather complex, averaged access deficit calculation; or the award of "non-overlapping franchises", possibly subsidised, to provide services to unserved areas (EC, 1994, pp. 61–62)—the latter proposal with some seeds of the under-serviced area licensing approach adopted much later in South Africa (see Chapter 6).

Although the later OECD does consider a number of country cases, its focus instead is on "providing a framework and set of principles for (re)considering the identification, costing, funding, reporting and monitoring of universal service" (OECD, 1995, p. 16). The principles proposed aim to delineate good practice guidelines to develop USO programmes rather than offer a set of implementation models:

a. Universal service objectives and coverage need to be clearly and specifically articulated;
b. Identify barriers to universal service;
c. Identify schemes which could cost-effectively address the identified barriers to universal service;
d. Estimate the cost of universal service programmes;
e. Consider the relative merits of alternative mechanisms for funding universal service;
f. Progress in universal service should be regularly and publicly reported;
g. Performance in universal service delivery should be regularly monitored and evaluated (OECD, 1995, pp. 135–139).

In both reports, many of the proposals are derived from the assessment of practices adopted in the countries considered. A number of the conclusions, however, are on the vague side, and thus fall short of achieving a catalogue of international good practice.

However, as a result of the various reports, UAS as an issue was now firmly on the agenda, in the context of telecomms reform, and the focus was shifting to concrete policy proposals and regulatory interventions.

2.3.5 *Universal Service in Africa*

As the ITU sought further to hegemonise sector reform, it issued what it was later to describe as a series of "flagship reports... [offering] guidelines for governments embarking on reform of the telecommunication sector and as a tool to practically assist regulators facing the many challenges encountered in promoting the sector" (ITU, 2011a).

Amongst these was the 'African Green Paper' (ITU, 1996a).[14] Self-consciously modelled on the EC's own 'Green Paper', it set out to "elaborate and formulate suitable recommendations" for an "'African Information and Telecommunication Policy and Strategy" (ITU, 1996a, pp. 80–81), for the OAU and PATU.

Given its developing country context, the Africa Green Paper was relatively circumspect in its approach to telecomms reform, defining the key challenge facing Africa as the need to "adapt the sector in a coherent and systematic manner to market forces", qualified by a relatively timid and "prudent approach to liberalization". At various points, it refers to:

- The operational "separation of postal and telecommunication services";
- Measures to "improve the operational efficiency and productivity of Public Telecommunication Organizations (PTOs)";
- The "initial opening to regulated competition of market segments for which demand remains to be satisfied";
- The "creation of a separate national body for the regulation of telecommunications" (ITU, 1996a, p. 4).

[14] Others included 'Telecommunication policies for the Arab Region—The Arab Book', and 'Telecommunication Policies for the Americas: The Blue Book'.

The main pillars of telecomms reform are all there, albeit circumspectly stated, and with the contentious (in the context of Africa) notion of privatisation receiving the barest of mentions as something that "may be a useful tool among others" (ITU, 1996a, pp. 3–10).

Surprisingly, given the low levels of teledensity across Africa, the consideration of 'universal service' is scant and weak. The document only considers the concept in relation to "basic telecommunication services… covering the whole geographical area… provided on demand to all users" (ITU, 1996a, p. 38). Universal access, already then on the horizon as an issue, receives nary a mention. USOs are viewed solely in relation to the incumbent telco.

The African Green Paper does not appear to have had a great deal of direct influence, subsumed in the welter of contemporaneous developments, including as the launch of the African Information Society Initiative (AISI) and the Information Society and Development (ISAD) Conference, both in the same year.

UAS began slowly to surface more strongly in Africa's ICT sector reform discourse, although the concept was not without its detractors. For example, Mustafa, Laidlaw, and Brand were dismissive of the notion, largely on the basis of its prohibitive costs, stating baldly that, for "low-income countries, providing universal service, as commonly understood, is impossible" (1997, p. 32). Others were considerably more sanguine: "from its inception [the African Information Society Initiative] was concerned with creating universal access to ICT in Africa, emphasizing public over individual access" (Hafkin, 2002, p. 118).

2.4 Globalising Good Practice

Globally then, UAS first came to prominence within the context of the processes of telecomms reform that were changing the nature and face of the global ICT sector regime. The consequent sets of changes placed liberalisation firmly on the table, and that positioned the ITU to fulfil a normative role with respect to sector reform in the face of developing country concerns. This was further reinforced through the 1996 WTO General Agreement on Trade in Services (GATS) and its associated Agreement on Basic Telecommunications Services and the Regulatory Reference Paper.

The various reports discussed above clearly show the mounting pressures for a shift of policy in the direction of liberalisation. They also reflect the tensions between the social objective of universal service imperatives and the market drive towards the introduction of competition.

Faced with a defensive response on the part of countries and monopoly providers, who argued that telecomms reform would undermine universal service, those arguing for telecommunications reform needed to demolish this argument by showing that competition and universal service were in practice not incompatible.

Further, it then became necessary to identify a range of options for intervention which would ensure that universal service could still be achieved under market competition. Many of these were still embryonic in articulation and would require further engagement and development on the part of UAS policy-makers.

Within this context, the normative role of the institutions associated with the emergent ICT sector regime, along with the involvement of largely academic epistemic communities in the drafting of many of the reports, is significant. Academic sources feature in the various report bibliographies, and many reports later resurface, repurposed as academic journal articles.

While this did serve to ensure that UAS entered mainstream regulatory practice, it remained weakly formulated and, in the views of some, the "main shortcoming of the regulatory framework" (Fredebeul-Krein & Freytag, 1997, p. 491).

Despite its normative intention and standing as an instrument of policy transfer, even the WTO's Regulatory Reference Paper remains relatively circumspect and unspecific in respect of UAS, merely stating that:

> Any Member has the right to define the kind of universal service obligation it wishes to maintain. Such obligations will not be regarded as anti-competitive per se, provided they are administered in a transparent, non-discriminatory and competitively neutral manner and are not more burdensome than necessary.... (WTO, 1996b, p. Clause 3)

2.4.1 From Universal Service to Universal Access

However, the ITU was soon to engage far more substantively. Its report to the 1998 World Telecommunication Development Conference (ITU, 1998, p. 1) marked a qualitative shift towards establishing a more comprehensive canon of international UAS good practice.

The report can be viewed as a landmark in relation to UAS. It provided the first explicit formulation of the concept of 'universal access' as a differentiated policy objective for developing countries, explicitly distinguishing it for the first time from the more established concept of 'universal service'.

'Universal service', as defined by the ITU in this report, is "focused upon connection of individual households to the public telephone network" and is viewed as a policy objective more appropriate to developed countries (1998, p. 61).

The objective of 'universal access' policy, by contrast, is to ensure that "everyone, at home or at work, should be within a reasonable distance of a telephone" (ITU, 1998, p. 61) and is viewed as a policy objective more appropriate to developing countries.

The categorisation of these two concepts and their differentiation remains a fundamental tenet within the field to this day (SADC, 2011, p. 5), with 'universal access' focused on widespread community-level, shared access, and 'universal service' focused on individual or household-level, private access.

Sadly and strangely, the report proffers little substantive information as to the derivation of the concept of universal access that it was so instrumental in placing on the table. This is an oblique reference to a United Nations "decision to embrace the objective of establishing universal access to basic communication and information services for all" (UN, 1997, p. Para 7), but without noting the UN's further elaboration on the concept: "universal access in basic communication and information services to the developing world would thus make it advisable to focus on the community level … rather than the household or individual level" (UN, 1997, p. Para 14).

There are some suggestions pointing to an access/service distinction in some of the earlier academic and expert literature. For example, Wellenius and Stern note that the concept of 'universal service':

> varies among countries, from having a telephone in every home and business in the wealthier countries, to most inhabitants' being within a certain distance or time away from a public telephone in developing countries. (1994, p. 744)

There are also hints of the distinction in earlier work by Milne on developmental stages in the progress towards universal service that was later published academically (1998).

Where 'universal access' appears in the academic literature, it is often used loosely as a synonym for 'universal service' or in the context of access to the Internet and the information society (Clement & Shade, 1996; Compaine & Weinraub, 1997). Drawing on Compaine, Xavier[15] elaborates the notion of "public access... to the networks and services of the information society" and proposes "public access points" as means of achieving this (Xavier, 1997, p. 837). Former Director General of Communications, Andile Ngcaba, who was active in the ITU at the time, is unclear as to the origins of the concept, ascribing it to a "collective effort", although he does count himself a "firm advocate of the idea" (interview, 28 January, 2015).

This distinction between universal access and universal service forms the basis for a series of recommended differential policy interventions in the ITU report (1998, p. 65ff), which also articulates clearly and precisely for the first time the formulation of 'availability, accessibility and affordability' that has remained the mantra of UAS policy since then:

- **Availability.** There should be nationwide coverage of telephone service, wherever and whenever required;
- **Accessibility.** Users should be treated alike; there should be non-discrimination in terms of price, service and quality, irrespective of geographical location or race, sex, religion;
- **Affordability.** Telephone service should be priced so that most users can afford it (ITU, 1998, p. 63).

While geographic 'availability' and pricing 'affordability' had regularly featured in preceding UAS studies, the dimension of 'accessibility' appears to bring together concerns over uniform quality of service, provision of services for disabled users and geographically-averaged tariffing. It is only very recently that changes have been proposed to this formulation, with a rather tentative argument for the addition of two further dimensions for UAS to broadband services, namely 'awareness' and 'ability':

[15] Principal author of the 1995 OECD report on universal service obligations (OECD, 1995).

> "awareness" and "ability" are fast becoming central tenets of universality as the Internet and broadband services are included in the scope of universal service, and access enabling the use of ICTs is a factor. (Msimang, 2012, p. 83)

These are clearly more information society concepts, and it remains to be seen whether they will be adopted more widely.

For developing countries, the 1998 report recommends that 'universal access' should occupy centre stage in policy and regulation, with 'universal service' a more appropriate objective for developed countries. The specific best practice interventions recommended in the report are still relatively underdeveloped and include the imposition of operator obligations, cross-subsidies, access charges,[16] the establishment of universal service funds and financial assistance to needy users (ITU, 1998, pp. 86–90).

This time the report draws on an epistemic community largely internal to the ITU: the authors—Michael Minges, Dr Peter Lovelock and Dr Tim Kelly—were all senior staffers within the ITU at the time, although Minges and Lovelock also had several academic journal articles to their credit. The report was edited by Dr Colin Blackman, then editor of the leading journal in the field, the prestigious *Telecommunications Policy.*

Universal access has continued to be mentioned in every edition of the ITU's (approximately) annual report, 'Trends in Telecommunication Reform', from 1999 onwards, either in specific sections or chapters, or in relation to other substantive policy and regulatory issues or challenges.

2.4.2 Practical UAS Tools for Regulators

Universal access and service policy and regulation was again specifically revisited in far greater depth by the ITU a few years later, when 'Trends in Telecommunication Reform' devoted itself to providing policy-makers and regulators with a "well-developed toolkit… to address the true access gap that remains unbridged even after sector reforms occurred" (ITU, 2003, p. 124).

[16] More commonly referred to nowadays as 'access deficit charges', and applied for a time in India.

This report was the product of a more diverse team, most of them either ITU staffers[17] or ICT consultants,[18] with Dr Michael Best, then at MIT, the lone academic. Many of them continue to be active in the field of ICT policy and UAS to this day.

Detailed good practice recommendations from the report include: strengthening ICT sector reform; establishing universal service funds; using minimum subsidy auctions; and promoting telecentres (ITU, 2003).

International good practice for UAS has continued to remain a focus of policy research and regulatory recommendation. More recently, the ITU undertook an evaluation of existing UAS "mechanisms, including market reform, the imposition of universal service obligations on certain or all market players, the designation of universal service providers, the financing of universal service obligations, the creation of universal service funds, as well as... innovative measures such as public-private partnerships, business-NGO partnerships" (Maddens, 2009, pp. 2–3). The outcome was a framework of policy and regulatory best practice in UAS, including: ensuring a proper institutional framework; defining universal access and service; imposing universal service obligations; strengthening regulatory reform; ensuring a multi-pronged approach in pursuit of universal access and service; and establishing mechanisms to finance universal access and service, including a Universal Service Fund (Maddens, 2009).

Based on this approach, the ITU undertook an international good practice assessment of UAS policy and practice for countries affiliated to the Communication Regulators' Association of Southern Africa (CRASA) (Lewis & Maddens, 2011). The project resulted in two further good practice documents—a set of policy and regulatory guidelines in respect UAS for the Southern African Development Community (SADC, 2011) and a toolkit for the establishment and operationalisation of USFs (ITU, 2011b).

It is clear that there was an ongoing, substantial effort to derive a relatively coherent set of guidelines in respect of policy and regulation pertaining to UAS in the ICT sector. Driven by the need to sustain and achieve the objectives of UAS under conditions of ICT sector liberalisation, principally with the introduction of competition, most of the

[17] Including Doreen Bogdan-Martin, Michael Minges, Susan Schorr and Nancy Sundberg.

[18] John Alden, Andrew Dymond, Sonja Oestmann, Mandla Msimang, Edgardo Sepulveda and David Townsend, many of whom had previously done work for the ITU.

guidelines derive from the growing body of international good practice emanating from multilateral institutions and their associated epistemic communities.

Although not a tightly prescriptive body of practice, certain common threads run through it. Two features stand out across many of the recommendations from 1998 onwards[19]:

1. The imposition of universal service obligations upon operators, usually through licence conditions;
2. The creation of a Universal Service Fund to finance access interventions in under-serviced areas.

2.4.3 *Mapping the Access Gap*

The conceptual dimensions of availability, accessibility and affordability underpin the good practice precepts identified above.

Similarly, designing UAS interventions derives from an analysis the digital divide between those users who already enjoy the benefits of ICT services and those to whom such benefits are denied. The notion of an access gap attempts, therefore, to conceptualise, quantify and map the digital divide in respect of UAS.

A number of analysts have attempted to map the gaps in UAS over the years. Perhaps the earliest attempt can be found in a briefing report examining regulation and universal service, prepared for an ITU regulatory colloquium on UAS in December 1994 (ITU, 1994b). Drawing on 12 country case examples (including South Africa), the report seeks to identify and plot the "logical distinctions between different categories of current telecommunications users and potential future users" (1995, p. 5) (Fig. 2.1).

Lead author Mike Tyler suggests the model derives from considering three questions:

1. How do we judge the degree to which universal service has or has not been achieved?
2. How can that be linked to the extent to which customers who can be served commercially (i.e. profitably) are in fact being served?

[19] Both continue to feature as key components of international good practice today (Blackman & Srivastava, 2011b).

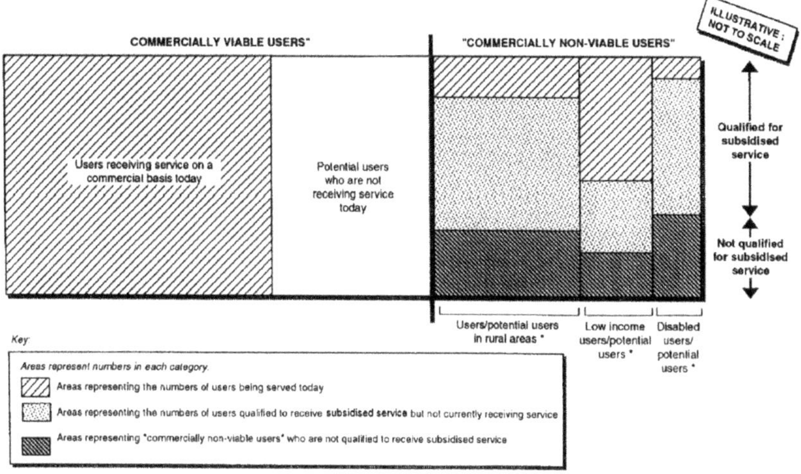

Fig. 2.1 Commercially viable vs non-viable users (*Source* Tyler, Letwin, and Roe [1995, p. 5])

3. For customers who cannot be served commercially (i.e. profitably), how that be linked to the extent to which the customer is eligible for subsidy, on grounds of their rural location, low income, or disability? (personal communication, 27 May, 2019).

The primary axis of the diagram is that of affordability, although there is some disaggregation to cater for those in rural areas (availability) or affected by disability (accessibility).

The distinction between those users who are "commercially viable" and those who are "commercially non-viable" implies that, properly managed and regulated, the market can serve numbers of those currently unconnected. As Tyler, Letwin and Roe point out, the model aims to examine "how cost-effectively resources are or could be applied [sic] to achieving those targets, and thus address the problem of choosing the right economic means for bringing telecommunications to each different segment of potential users" (1995, p. 6). In other words, modelling the 'access gap' offers both a diagnostic tool and an intervention map.

The value of the report lies less in the recommendations—it remains averse to the normative prescription of 'international good practice' because of the need to ensure that objectives and interventions are grounded in and derived from the circumstances specific to each country. In its own words: "the 'pros and cons' of these alternatives are so specific to the regulators' operational and institutional circumstances that it is not useful to attempt to offer any general summary" (Tyler, Letwin, & Roe, 1995, p. 20). Rather its value lies in the conceptual map it offers to policy-makers and regulators.

An updated version of the 'access gap' model (Fig. 2.2 below), was subsequently developed by Navas-Sabater, Dymond, and Juntunen for a World Bank discussion paper (2002), and takes an important step forward in aligning the 'access gap' model more closely with some of the standard axes of the digital divide.

Likewise intended as a diagnostic tool, aimed at providing targeted normative guidance for policy-makers and regulators, it is analytically more complex than its predecessor. Using slightly different terminology, it instead maps two key "dimensions — poverty and geographic isolation"—related, respectively, to affordability and availability—that account for and align with lack of access (Navas-Sabater et al., 2002, p. 8). This allows the telecommunications market to be segmented into "commercially feasible" users, and those afflicted by the "access gap". The latter

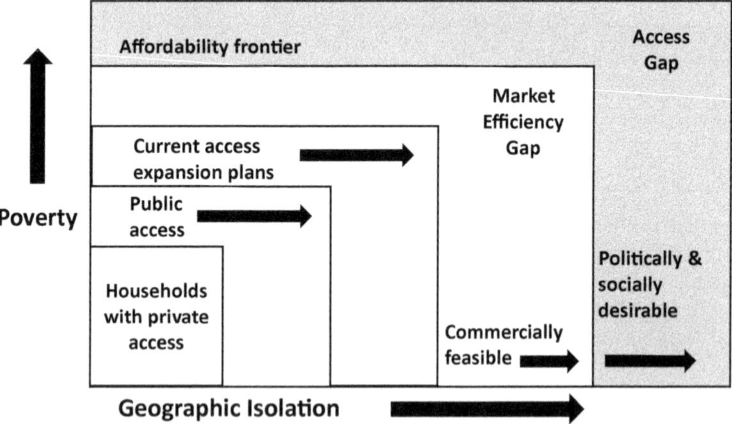

Fig. 2.2 The Access Gap (2002) (*Source* Author, adapted from Navas-Sabater, Dymond, and Juntunen [2002, p. 8])

are those who are too remote or too poor to be commercially feasible, but where access remains desirable for political and social equity reasons.

Apart from market-oriented regulatory interventions to address the 'market efficiency gap', the report points to the imposition of "US/UA Obligations" and the establishment of a Universal Service Fund, from which "smart subsidies" can be deployed to support service rollout and to subsidise poor users (Navas-Sabater et al., 2002, p. 34ff).

The origins of the revised diagram remain somewhat elusive. ICT consultant David Townsend suggests it was rooted in the broader epistemic community of academics and consultants working on UAS and in the "evolving set of ideas around these concepts for several years... [where] a variety of versions of the diagram were utilized in various documents by different experts" (personal communication, 12 February 2015). Andrew Dymond suggests the access gap diagram was developed for the first time for the World Bank paper, written in July 2000. He attributes its origin to Navas-Sabater who, he says, "initially put the concept down onto paper in an informal meeting we had when we planned the publication" (personal communication, 19 November 2014) (Fig. 2.2).

Further development of the 'access gap' model took place at the hands of Andrew Dymond's company, Intelecon Research (infoDev, 2009). The primary improvement involves breaking down the 'access gap', by making a distinction between those potential users who can secure access through some form of one-off intervention (the "smart subsidy zone") and those who require ongoing support and intervention (the "true access gap") (infoDev, 2009, pp. 10–12). It is this conceptual model that is widely in use today.

A somewhat different version of the access gap model was to appear a few years later in a study evaluating the experience of UAS programmes in Latin America and making recommendations for future interventions (Stern, Townsend, & Monedero, 2006, pp. 8–14). But it is the version of the 'access gap' diagram below that continues to appear in and inform international good practice literature to this day (Blackman & Srivastava, 2011b, p. 157; Msimang, 2012, p. 84) (Fig. 2.3).

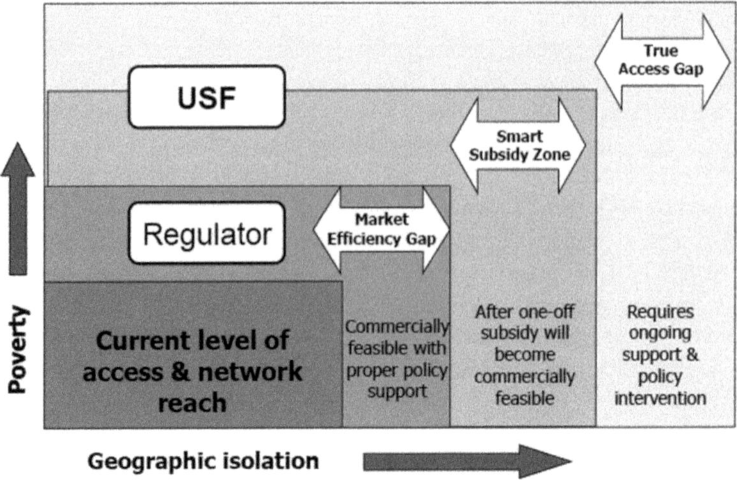

Fig. 2.3 The Access Gap (2009) (*Source* Author, adapted from infoDev [2009])

2.5 Conclusion

As we have seen, ICT sector reform was a complex process, driven principally by technological changes that undermined the monopoly rationale in the telecommunications sector, and by the demands of business interests seeking to exploit the benefits enabled by the combination of computing and information technologies, coupled with advances in telecommunications services.

The ensuing changes in the existing telecommunications regime were primarily driven through the existing multilateral institutions such as the OECD and the EU, and then globally through the International Telecommunication Union (ITU), and through the formation of the World Trade Organisation (WTO), as well as being influenced by the World Bank.

If the WTO regime drove the broad ICT sector reform agenda and raised the question of how signatories should comply with the new market imperatives through privatisation of monopoly incumbents, and through introducing competition and establishing independent regulation, it was the ITU that supplied the normative international good practice solutions.

This set of sector reforms in turn raised the question of how to meet the non-market imperative of universal access and service, with many jurisdictions using the universal service imperative as a justification for retaining the status quo, so much so that universal service came to be seen as the 'fig leaf of the monopolist'.

This in turn led to the sustained international development of a set of good practice UAS interventions, designed to demonstrate the compatibility of UAS with a competitive marketplace. Drawing on concepts like availability, accessibility and affordability, on the distinction between universal access and universal service, and on the notion of the access gap, this recommended, principally, the:

- imposition of universal service obligations upon licensees;
- creation of universal service funds to finance access and service projects;
- adoption of a range of implementation models, including telecentres, least-subsidy auctions and the licensing of rural operators.

There was clearly involvement from a broader epistemic community in the development of that set of international good practices, with figures like Garnham, Xavier and Milne party to much of the formulation. Many of these people knew each other, and interacted and worked with each other.

Despite the caveats from Milne (1998) and Tyler et al. (1995) that policy-makers should base their interventions upon in-country realities, this remains essentially a policy transfer (Dolowitz & Marsh, 2000) regime. The analysis will now move on to how that policy was transferred and diffused to South Africa, how it was adopted and adapted in the specific country context.

References

Aronson, J., & Cowhey, P. (1988). *When countries talk: International trade in telecommunications services*. Lexington, MA: Ballinger.

Bauer, J. (1999). Universal service in the European Union. *Government Information Quarterly, 16*(4), 329–343.

Beardsley, S., von Morgenstern, I., Enriquez, L., & Kipping, C. (2002). Telecommunications sector reform: A prerequisite for networked readiness. In

G. Kirkman, P. Cornelius, J. Sachs, & K. Schwab (Eds.), *The global information technology report 2001–2002: Readiness for the networked world*. Oxford University Press. Retrieved from http://cyber.law.harvard.edu/itg/libpubs/gitrr2002_ch11.pdf.

Blackman, C. (1995). Universal service: Obligation or opportunity? *Telecommunications Policy, 19*(3), 171–176.

Blackman, C., & Srivastava, L. (Eds.). (2011a). *Telecommunications regulation handbook*. Washington, DC, Washington, DC, and Geneva: World Bank, infoDev, and International Telecommunication Union. Retrieved from http://www.infodev.org/en/Document.1057.pdf.

Blackman, C., & Srivastava, L. (2011b). From availability to use: Universal access and service. In C. Blackman, & L. Srivastava (Eds.), *Telecommunications regulation handbook* (pp. 151–177). Washington, DC, Washington, DC, and Geneva: World Bank, infoDev, and International Telecommunication Union. Retrieved from http://www.infoDev.org/en/Document.1069.pdf.

Cairncross, F. (1997). *The death of distance: How the communications revolution will change our lives*. Boston: Harvard Business School Press.

Castells, M. (1999). *The information age: Economy, society and culture* (Vols. 1–3). Hoboken, NJ: Wiley-Blackwell.

Clement, A., & Shade, L. (1996). What do we mean by "Universal access?": Social perspectives in a Canadian context. *Proceedings Inet 96*. Internet Society. Retrieved from https://www.isoc.org/inet96/proceedings/f2/f2_1.htm.

Clinton, W. (1996, September 13). Message to the senate transmitting the constitution and convention of the international telecommunication union. Washington, DC: US Government Publishing Office. Retrieved from http://www.gpo.gov/fdsys/pkg/CDOC-104tdoc34/html/CDOC-104tdoc34.htm.

Compaine, B., & Weinraub, M. (1997). Universal access to online services: An examination of the issue. *Telecommunications Policy, 21*(1), 15–33.

Cowhey, P. (1990). The international telecommunications regime: The political roots of regimes for high technology. *International Organization, 44*(2), 169–199.

Cowhey, P., & Aronson, J. (2009). Trade and the global network revolution. In P. Cowhey & J. Aronson (Eds.), *Transforming the global information and communications market: The political economy of innovation* (pp. 149–174). Cambridge, MA: MIT Press.

Cowhey, P., & Klimenko, P. (2000). Telecommunications reform in developing countries after the WTO agreement on basic telecommunications services. *Journal of International Development, 12*(2), 265 ± 281.

Dolowitz, D., & Marsh, D. (2000). Learning from Abroad: The role of policy transfer in contemporary policy-making. *Governance: An International Journal of Policy and Administration, 13*(1), 5–24.

Drahos, P., & Joseph, R. (1995). Telecommunications and investment in the great supranational regulatory game. *Telecommunications Policy, 19*(8), 619–635.

Drake, W. (1994). Asymmetric deregulation and the transformation of the international telecommunications regime. In E. Noam & G. Poggorel (Eds.), *Asymmetric deregulation: The dynamics of telecommunications policies in Europe and the United States.* Norwood, NJ: Ablex Publishing Corp.

Drake, W. (2000). The rise and decline of the international telecommunications regime. In C. Marsden (Ed.), *Regulating the global information society* (pp. 124–177). London: Routledge.

Drake, W., & Noam, E. (1997). The WTO deal on basic telecommunications: Big bang or little whimper? *Telecommunications Policy, 21*(9/10), 799–818.

EC. (1987). *Towards a dynamic European economy: Green Paper on the development of the common market for telecommunications services and equipment.* Brussels: Commission Of The European Communities. Retrieved from http://ec.europa.eu/green-papers/pdf/green_paper_telecom_services__common_market_com_87_290.pdf.

EC. (1990a, June 28). Commission Directive 90/388/EEC of 28 June 1990 on competition in the markets for telecommunications services. *Official Journal of the European Communities*(L 192 / 24).

EC. (1990b, July 24). Council Directive of 28 June 1990 on the establishment of the internal market for telecommunications services through the implementation of open network provision (90 / 387 / EEC). *Official Journal of the European Communities*(L 192 / 1).

EC. (1994). *Meeting universal service obligations in a competitive telecommunications sector.* Brussels: European Commission. Retrieved from http://bookshop.europa.eu/en/meeting-universal-service-obligations-in-a-competitive-telecommunications-sector-pbCV8394757/.

Fredebeul-Krein, M., & Freytag, A. (1997). Telecommunications and WTO discipline: An assessment of the WTO agreement on telecommunication services. *Telecommunications Policy, 21*(6), 477–491.

Gasmi, F., Laffont, J., & Sharkey, W. (2000). Competition, universal service and telecommunications policy in developing countries. *Information Economics and Policy, 12*(3), 221–248.

Hafkin, N. (2002). The African information society initiative: A seven-year Assessment (1996–2002). *Perspectives on Global Development and Technology, 1*(2), 101–142.

Harvey, D. (1990). *The condition of postmodernity: An enquiry into the origins of cultural change.* Cambridge, MA: Blackwell.

Hill, R. (2013). WCIT: Failure or success, impasse or way forward? *International Journal of Law and Information Technology, 21*(3), 313–328.

Hill, R. (2014). *The new international telecommunication regulations and the internet: A commentary and legislative history*. Berlin: Springer.

Hills, J. (1994). A global industrial policy. US hegemony and GATT. The liberalization of telecommunications. *Review of International Political Economy, 1*(2 [Summer]), 257–279. Retrieved from http://www.jstor.org/stable/4177102.

Hills, J. (2007). *Telecommunications and empire*. Champaign, IL: University of Illinois Press.

infoDev. (2009). *Universal access and service: Executive summary*. Washington, DC and Geneva: infoDev and International Telecommunication Union. Retrieved from http://www.ictregulationtoolkit.org//Mod4ExecSummary.

Intven, H. (Ed.). (2000). *Telecommunications regulation handbook*. Washington, DC: infoDev.

ITU. (1982). *Resolution No 10: World administrative telegraph and telephone conference*. Geneva: International Telecommunication Union. Retrieved from http://www.itu.int/dms_pub/itu-s/oth/02/09/S020900000B5201PDFE.PDF.

ITU. (1985). *The missing link: Report of the independent commission for World Wide Telecommunications development*. Geneva: International Telecommunication Union. Retrieved from http://www.itu.int/osg/spu/sfo/missinglink/The_Missing_Ling_A4-E.pdf.

ITU. (1989). *The changing telecommunication environment: Policy considerations for the members of the ITU*. Geneva: International Telecommunication Union.

ITU. (1990). Final Acts of the Plenipotentiary Conference, Nice 1989. Geneva: International Telecommunication Union. Retrieved from http://www.itu.int/dms_pub/itu-s/oth/02/01/S02010000224002PDFE.PDF.

ITU. (1991). *Tomorrow's ITU: The challenges of change—Report of the high level committee to review the structure and functioning of the international telecommunication union (ITU)*. Geneva: International Telecommunication Union.

ITU. (1992). *Final acts of the additional plenipotentiary conference (Geneva, 1992)—Constitution and convention of the international telecommunication union, optional protocol, resolutions, recommendation*. Geneva: International Telecommunication Union. Retrieved from http://www.itu.int/dms_pub/itu-s/oth/02/09/S020900000C5201PDFE.PDF.

ITU. (1993). *The changing ROLE of Government in an era of telecom deregulation: Report of the colloquium held at ITU headquarters 17–19 February 1993*. Geneva: International Telecommunication Union.

ITU. (1994a). *The changing role of government in an era of telecom deregulation: Global mobile personal communications systems (GMPCS)*. Geneva: International Telecommunication Union. Retrieved from https://www.itu.int/newsarchive/wtpf96/gmpcs.html.

ITU. (1994b). *The changing role of government in an era of telecom deregulation: Report of the second regulatory colloquium held at the ITU headquarters 1–3 December 1993.* Geneva: International Telecommunication Union.

ITU. (1995). *The changing role of government in an era of telecom deregulation—Trade agreements on telecommunications: Regulatory implications.* Geneva: International Telecommunication Union. Retrieved from https://www.itu.int/newsarchive/wtpf96/trade.html.

ITU. (1996a). *The African Green Paper: Telecommunication policies for Africa.* Geneva: International. Telecommunication Union.

ITU. (1996b). *The changing role of government in an era of telecom deregulation: The regulatory implications of telecommunications convergence.* Geneva: International Telecommunication Union. Retrieved from https://www.itu.int/itudoc/osg/colloq/chai_rep/sixthcol/37003.htm.

ITU. (1997). *The changing role of government in an era of telecom deregulation: Transforming economic relationships in international telecommunications.* Geneva: International Telecommunication Union. Retrieved from http://www.itu.int/osg/csd/wtpf/wtpf98/trade/reg_coll/7th/chair_report.html.

ITU. (1998). *World telecommunication Development report 1998: Universal access.* Geneva: International Telecommunication Union. Retrieved from http://www.itu.int/ITU-D/ict/publications/wtdr_98/.

ITU. (2003). *Trends in telecommunications reform 2003: Promoting universal access to ICTs—Practical tools for regulators.* Geneva: International Telecommunication Union.

ITU. (2011a, November 2). New regional telecommunication / ICT reform studies. *BDT/IEE/RME/DM/120.* Geneva: International Telecommunication Union. Retrieved from http://www.itu.int/net4/ITU-D/CDS/circulars-dm/DM/DM_2011/pdf/DM-120_RME_PartnersRegulatoryReformStudy_PUBLISH_Web_en.pdf.

ITU. (2011b). *SADC toolkit on universal access funding and universal service fund implementation.* Geneva: International Telecommunication Union. Retrieved from http://www.itu.int/ITU-D/projects/ITU_EC_ACP/hipssa/Activities/SA/CRASA/Toolkit%20Final%20Report.pdf.

ITU. (2014). *Trends in telecommunication reform—Fourth-generation regulation: Driving digital communications ahead.* Geneva: International Telecommunication Union. Retrieved from https://www.itu.int/dms_pub/itu-d/opb/reg/D-REG-TTR.15-2014-PDF-E.pdf.

Krasner, S. (1982). Structural causes and regime consequences: Regimes as intervening variables. *International Organization, 36*(2), 185–205.

Langdale, J. (1989, September). International telecommunications and trade in services: Policy perspectives. *Telecommunications Policy, 13*(3), 203–221.

Levi-Faur, D. (1998). *The governance of international telecommunications competition: Cross-international study of international policy regimes.* Haifa: Department of Political Science, University of Haifa. Retrieved from http://www.isr.umich.edu/cps/pewpa/archive/archive_98/19980014.pdf.

Lewis, C., & Maddens, S. (2011). *Update of SADC guidelines on universal access and service and assessment report.* Geneva: International Telecommunication Union. Retrieved from http://www.itu.int/ITU-D/projects/ITU_EC_ACP/hipssa/events/2011/Docs/universal_access-e.docx.

Maddens, S. (2009). *Trends in universal access and service policies: Changing policies to accommodate competition and convergence.* Geneva: International Telecommunication Union. Retrieved from http://www.itu.int/ITU-D/treg/Events/Seminars/GSR/GSR09/doc/USPolicy_ITUEC.pdf.

Melody, W. (Ed.). (1997). *Telecom reform: Principles, policies and regulatory practices.* Lyngby: Den Private Ingeniørfond, Technical University of Denmark. Retrieved from http://lirne.net/resources/tr/telecomreform.pdf.

Melody, W. (1999). Telecom reform: Progress and prospects. *Telecommunications Policy, 23*(1), 7–34.

Milne, C. (1998). Stages of universal service policy. *Telecommunications Policy, 22*(9), 775–780.

Msimang, M. (2012). The more things change, the more they stay the same: Strategies for financing universal broadband access. *ITU, trends in telecommunication reform 2012: Smart regulation for a broadband world* (pp. 79–110). Geneva: International Telecommunication Union.

Mustafa, M., Laidlaw, B., & Brand, M. (1997). *Telecommunications policies for Sub-Saharan Africa.* Washington, DC: The World Bank. Retrieved from http://documents.worldbank.org/curated/en/231651468765295985/pdf/multi-page.pdf.

Navas-Sabater, J., Dymond, A., & Juntunen, N. (2002). *Telecommunications & information services for the Poor: Towards a strategy for universal access.* Washington, DC: World Bank. Retrieved from http://rru.worldbank.org/Documents/PapersLinks/1210.pdf.

OECD. (1991). Universal Service and Rate Restructuring in Telecommunications, No 23. *OECD Digital Economy, 4.* doi:http://dx.doi.org/10.1787/237454868255.

OECD. (1995). *Universal service obligations in a competitive telecommunications environment.* Paris: Organisation For Economic Co-operation And Development. Retrieved from http://www.oecd.org/sti/broadband/2349175.pdf.

OECD. (2002). *OECD Reviews of regulatory reform: Regulatory reform in UK.* Paris: Organisation for Economic Co-Operation and Development. Retrieved from http://www.oecd.org/internet/2766201.pdf.

Overman, E. (1994). Best practice research and postbureaucratic reform. *Journal of Public Administration Research and Theory, 4*(1), 67–84.

SADC. (2011, June 16). SADC guidelines on universal access and service. *Adopted by Meeting of SADC Ministers Responsible for Telecommunications, Postal and ICT, International Convention Centre, Gaborone, Botswana*. Gaborone: Southern African Development Community. Retrieved from http://www.crasa.org/tempex/doc_pub_eng80.pdf.

Singh, J. (2002). Negotiating regime change: The weak, the strong and the WTO telecom accord. In J. Rosenau & J. Singh (Eds.), *Information technologies and global politics: The changing scope of power and governance* (pp. 189–210). New York: SUNY Press.

Stern, P., Townsend, D., & Monedero, J. (2006). *New models for universal access in Latin America*. Montreal, Boston, and Madrid: Regulatel, World Bank, and ECLAC. Retrieved from http://www.ictregulationtoolkit.org/Documents/Document/Document/3511.

Tyler, M., Letwin, W., & Roe, C. (1995). Universal service and innovation in telecommunication services: Fostering linked goals through regulatory policy. *Telecommunications Policy, 19*(1), 3–20.

UN. (1997). *Statement on universal access to basic communication and information*. Geneva: Administrative Committee on Coordination, United Nations. Retrieved from http://www.unites.org/acc1997.htm.

Wellenius, B. (2002). Closing the gap in access to RURAL Communication: Chile 1995–2002. *info, 4*(3), 29–41.

Wellenius, B., & Stern, P. (Eds.). (1994). *Implementing reforms in the telecommunications sector: Lessons from experience*. Washington, DC: World Bank. Retrieved from http://documents.worldbank.org/curated/en/1994/05/441706/implementing-reforms-telecommunications-sector-lessons-experience.

Woodrow, R. (1991, August). Tilting towards a trade regime: The ITU and the Uruguay round services negotiations. *Telecommunications Policy, 15*(4), 323–342.

WTO. (1995). *Annex on telecommunications*. Geneva: World Trade Organisation. Retrieved from http://www.wto.org/english/tratop_e/serv_e/12-tel_e.htm.

WTO. (1996a, April 30). Fourth Protocol to the General Agreement on trade in Services. Geneva: World Trade Organisation.

WTO. (1996b). *Telecommunications services: Reference Paper*. Geneva: World Trade Organisation. Retrieved from http://www.wto.org/english/tratop_e/serv_e/telecom_e/tel23_e.htm.

WTO. (1997). *Report of the group on basic telecommunications*. Geneva: World Trade Organisation. Retrieved from https://www.wto.org/english/news_e/pres97_e/finalrep.htm.

WTO. (2003). *Draft converted schedule of specific commitments: S/DCS/W/ZAF*. Geneva: World Trade Organisation. Retrieved from http://www.sadc.int/files/3713/2634/9546/South_Africa_GATS_Schedule.pdf.

Xavier, P. (1997). Universal service and public access in the networked society. *Telecommunications Policy, 21*(9/10), 829–843.

Zacher, M. (1996). The international telecommunications regime. In M. Zacher (Ed.), *Governing global networks: International regimes for transportation and communications*. Cambridge: Cambridge University Press.

Zacher, M. (2002). Capitalism, technology, and liberalization: The international telecommunications regime, 1865–1998. In J. Rosenau, *Information technologies and global politics: The changing scope of power and governance* (pp. 189–210). New York: SUNY Press.

Zhao, Y. (2002). The ITU and national regulatory authorities in the era of liberalization. *Space Policy, 18*(4), 293–300.

CHAPTER 3

Universal Access and Service in South Africa

Although South Africa had been excluded from the ITU in 1965 because of its racially exclusive and oppressive *apartheid* policies, the country was not immune from the phenomenon of telecomms reform or the normative pressures of the incipient ICT sector regime, despite its status as a global pariah.

Many of the commercial and technological forces driving global change were also present in the South African market. And, once South Africa began post-1990 to move down the hesitant, conflictual path to democracy, ICT sector reform was firmly on the cards. It was, however, only after the country's first democratic election, in 1994, that reform of the sector became a concrete reality. It was, though, to be a transition to ICT sector reform unlike any other—driven by a new ANC government with limited sector experience, facing a deeply suspicious business sector and a hostile bureaucracy.

The unfolding shape of that reform is a story encompassing profound regime change—at the political level, to a degree within the economy, as well as in the ICT sector, its institutional framework, and the principles, norms and procedures that govern it. It is also a story of policy transfer, with international good practice driving of much that was put in place, alongside a degree of policy innovation. And, at a normative level, it is a story of universal access and service.

C. Lewis, *Regulating Telecommunications in South Africa*,
Information Technology and Global Governance,
https://doi.org/10.1007/978-3-030-43527-1_3

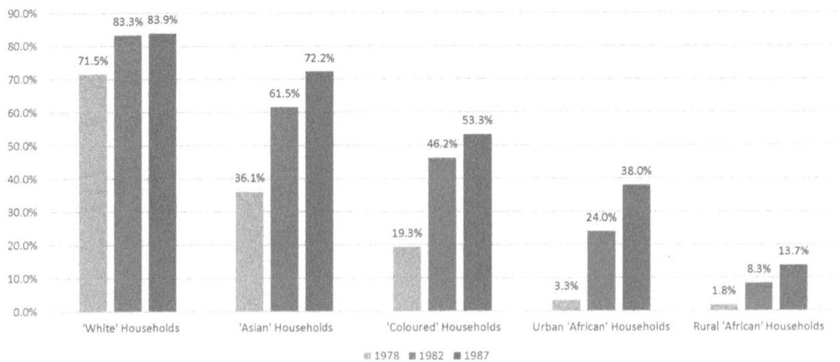

Fig. 3.1 Telephony: Household penetration by racial classification (1978–1987) (Adapted from de Villiers [1989]; Horwitz, [2001, p. 76])

3.1 Telecommunications Under *Apartheid*

The structure of the telecommunications sector in South Africa in the early 1980s was little different from what prevailed in most other countries in the world at the time. It was a substantial market too, then 15th largest in the world (Kaplan, 1990). And, in line with established global practice at the time, services were provided by an integrated state-owned monopoly, South African Posts and Telecommunications (SAPT), which was responsible for both postal and telecommunications services.

More importantly, the twisted logic of *apartheid* meant that a digital divide and access gap with a unique South African flavour had been created. As the diagram below shows, *apartheid* racial imbalances meant that while nearly 84% of 'white' households had a telephone at home in 1987, less than 14% of their rural 'black' counterparts did—this despite significant increases in access for some groups over the preceding decade (Fig. 3.1).

The figures reflect an almost saturated 'white' market, and consequent, if limited, moves to penetrate other demographic segments. They are, however, almost certainly misleading; indeed, they appear substantially to overstate telephony penetration for 'black' households.[1]

[1] The figures appear to exclude those parts of 'black' South Africa likely to have had the lowest levels of access: the so-called TBVC 'states' (Transkei, Bophuthatswana, Venda and Ciskei), as well as the six nominally self-governing 'bantustans'.

Access in the 'bantustan' parts of South Africa was even worse. Teledensity figures from some years later suggest alarmingly low levels of access to telephony across the TBVC states, ranging from 0.2% (Transkei), through 0.5% (Venda), up to 2.5% (Ciskei), this compared to 25% in "white communities" (UNDP/ITU, 1995, p. 29).[2] Similar teledensity figures from 1994 give the national average as 9.8% (as opposed to the 8.4% of the ITU) with penetration as high as 25% in "white urban areas" and as low as 0.1% in "rural TBVC areas" (RSA, 1995).

Taken together, the figures reveal a stark and dramatic digital divide, closely aligned to the hierarchical divisions imposed by *apartheid*, and dubbed a 'digital donga' by academic Peter Benjamin.[3] The causes, nature and explication of this bluntly racialised access gap are complex, multidimensional and systemic.

Many 'black' South Africans of that generation recount anecdotes of racially abusive denial of service. One interviewee recounts the never-explained rejection of her parents' first application for telephone service in the mid-1970s and the derisive laughter that met a second application (Noluthando Tungande, personal communication, 16 May 2015).

However, the SAPT may have had some semblance of a public service ethos, at least at management level. One commentator puts the substantial increases in access for 'black' South Africans, all be they off a very low base, down "in part to marketing, in part to the vision of [the Deputy Postmaster General, who] believed in state monopolies, public service, and universal telephone service to all" (Horwitz, 2001, p. 180). And there does appear to have been some shift towards rolling out telephony services to 'black' South Africans under the so-called 'reform *apartheid*' of the 1980s, the figure above suggests.

But the racialised 'digital *donga*' in access to telecommunications cannot be ascribed to the SAPT alone. *Apartheid* geographies and the euphemistically named system of 'influx control' ensured that few 'black' South Africans' enjoyed permanent residence status in the country's urban areas. Many others were sequestered in dormitory-style 'hostels' under

[2] Note that this report presents the figures for 'teledensity', or per capita access, rather than household penetration.

[3] It is an appropriate and striking metaphor in the South African context, since a donga is a narrow, steep-sided gulley formed by soil erosion, usually dry except in the rainy season.

the migrant labour system. And the 'bantustan' system kept large numbers in isolated and impoverished rural homelands. The very modalities of life and living conditions created by *apartheid*, therefore, mitigated against individual access by 'black' South Africans to telecommunications services. Thus, the standard urban–rural divide of telecommunications access was, in South Africa, stamped with and exacerbated by the characteristics of the *apartheid* state.

Although the causalities were complex and interlinked, *apartheid*'s 'digital donga'—albeit aligned with many other axes of deprivation (income, geography, education, skills, gender)—has emerged as a powerful motivation behind making universal access and service central to post-*apartheid* telecommunications policy. In the words of ITU expert, Mandla Msimang:

> The South African experience is not born out of decades of telecommunications regulation in the public interest, as is the case in many other jurisdictions. Rather, current regulation emerges from an attempt to reverse the damage caused by decades of policies that promoted racial discrimination and denied certain individuals access to telecommunication services. (Msimang, 2006, p. 218)

3.2 Tentative Telecommunications Reform

Despite the political and economic isolations of *apartheid*, the relatively advanced nature and substantial size of South Africa's telecommunications network, along with high levels of digitisation, exposed the country to many of the technological pressures felt elsewhere. Some were already calling for reforms in the upstream equipment supply chain, particularly in respect of the cosy, long-term manufacturing contracts entered into by the SAPT (Kaplan, 1990). Business users were subject to similar demands to be able to reduce input costs and to leverage the information technology revolution in order to exploit business opportunities and re-engineer business processes. For example, one grouping, claiming to speak for "major data line users in government, industry and commerce", sought to "secure more freedom for its members in the way data lines and switching techniques are used" (*Financial Mail*, 1983,

p. 30). Another, the National Telematics User Group (NTUG),[4] called for restrictions on the use of leased lines and value-added network services to be removed. Meanwhile, the National Association of Business Voice Users (NABVU) took up "voice issues... PABX competition and the like" (Mike van den Bergh, personal communication, 18 May 2015). A number later came together under the umbrella of Communications Users of South Africa (CUASA). The issues thus raised included calls for the liberalisation of customer premises equipment (CPE), such as private networks and PABXs, and protests against poor customer service from the SAPT (Snyman, 1998, pp. 90–93).

These pressures from within the sector, coincided with a more immediate and practical trigger—the increasing financial difficulties faced by the *apartheid* regime, partly due to high levels of state economic intervention, leading to the 1985 debt freeze and the need to restore "creditworthiness in terms of the ability to raise loans" (Fine, 1995, pp. 7–9).

Coupled with political admiration of the right-wing policies of British Prime Minister Margaret Thatcher, and the consequent successful privatisation of British Telecom (Horwitz, 2001, p. 107), the tipping point of the debt crisis may have created conditions under which policy emulation of deregulation and privatisation became an attractive option for the ruling National Party.

Work was already afoot to reassess the ownership, role and functioning of several key state-owned entities, with the appointment in 1983 of Wim de Villiers to investigate and report on the main state-owned entities operating in electricity supply, transport services and telecommunications.

In 1987, shortly after de Villiers completed his investigation of SAPT, the National Party Government issued a 'White Paper on Privatisation and Deregulation' (RSA, 1987). It was, however, not a particularly detailed or prescriptive document, outlining in broad brush-strokes an essentially Thatcherite strategy to curb the "public sector's involvement in the economy" and to give the private sector the "opportunity to develop and grow optimally with minimum State intervention and regulation" (RSA, 1987, p. 8). On the question of deregulation, it was again less than specific, calling only for "minimum interference by the State... [the need to] promote the optimal functioning of market mechanisms and self-regulation"

[4] Created to engage with SAPT on behalf of large data users, its members were mostly large companies with multiple offices and overseas links, such as banks, insurers and freight forwarders.

(RSA, 1987, p. 13). Albeit short on specifics, the White Paper nevertheless set the scene for a future within which the SAPT could be privatised, competition introduced and an independent sector regulator established.

3.2.1 The de Villiers Report

This, then, was the context within which the de Villiers report into SAPT (1989) saw the light of day. Preoccupied as it was with SAPT as a business, and less focused on the broader perspective of the sector as a whole, much of its attention is taken up with an analysis of the telephony market, on the demand for telephone services, the cost of service provision and an examination of revenue streams. Nevertheless, it floated the possible privatisation of the SAPT and recommended the introduction of regulatory structures to oversee the sector.

The report, however, displays limited awareness of the potential of telecommunications as a business enabler, giving almost no attention to the demands of groups like NTUG for the liberalisation of leased lines, PABX and PTNs, and making what Horwitz characterises as its "essential error in condemning SAPT's digitalization program" (Horwitz, 2001, p. 180).

Moreover, the report criticises SAPT for over-investing in capacity for rolling out services to 'black' South Africans, whose usage and revenue profiles were low. Although it does recognise the demand for telephony services amongst the 'black' majority, the notion of 'universal service' is entirely absent from its vocabulary, with suppressed demand merely ascribed to "unrest conditions in the black townships" (de Villiers, 1989, p. 3).

The ultimate point of the de Villiers report is reached in its concluding pages, with its "transformation and privatisation" recommendations. Despite an annoyingly equivocal, shifting mode of formulation, three key steps are envisaged:

- the separation of posts and telecommunications into distinct entities;
- the requirement that the various entities operate according to sound "business principles" with appropriate management and governance structures;
- eventual partial privatisation of SAPT through the sale of shares to the public (de Villiers, 1989, pp. 85–97).

Competition as an issue is dealt with ambiguously. On the one hand, the report views telecommunications as a "natural monopoly" (de Villiers, 1989, pp. 85 and 92). Indeed, it contemplates incorporating into SAPT other state-owned national networks, those of the electricity and transport parastatals, even that of the military (de Villiers, 1989, p. 95)! But it also contemplates competition in the downstream market, where "other undertakings may be established to operate value-added services by making use of the network" (de Villiers, 1989, p. 85).

The report views regulation of its partially-privatised SAPT monopoly as necessary in order to "obtain benefits for the consumer" (de Villiers, 1989, p. 86). To this end, it suggests creating two separate regulatory authorities: one to deal with "technical" issues (including spectrum, quality of service enforcement and type approvals of equipment) and the other to function as a "price controller" (de Villiers, 1989, pp. 93–94).

The report was met with less than universal acclaim, business users claiming that de Villiers had spurned their offers to contribute and voicing their criticism of a number of its findings. Business was "particularly critical of [the] recommendation that government should retain its interest in P&T's operations" (*Financial Mail*, 1989).

Overall, however, the vision of de Villiers nonetheless adheres broadly to the standard prescriptions of telecomms reform: privatisation and regulation, albeit with equivocation when it came to competition.

3.3 Political Reform

State President de Klerk's landmark February 1990 speech, unbanning the African National Congress,[5] came as a bombshell to the public of South Africa. It was still something of a surprise to the ANC, even though 'talks about talks' had been under way since the mid-1980s (Sparks, 1994). Andile Ngcaba (later Director General of Communications, but at the time in charge of the ANC's military communications in Angola) was part of the ANC's first delegation, sent to prepare for the release, a few short days later, of Nelson Mandela, imprisoned leader of the ANC, as well as for the forthcoming negotiations with the *apartheid* government (interview, 28 January 2015).

[5] Along with a number of other previously restricted organisations.

When it came to telecommunications, however, the National Party seemed to assume it was business as usual, initially steaming ahead to implement the de Villiers recommendations, introducing draft legislation to separate posts from telecommunications and to transform the latter into a commercialised public corporation overseen by a board of directors (Lambert, 1990).

However, the dynamics of the changed political situation soon forced the Bill to be postponed in the face of "intense opposition from the ANC and the unions" (*Financial Mail*, 1990). The COSATU-aligned majority union at the SAPT, the Posts and Telecommunications Workers' Association (POTWA), saw the Bill as the thin end of the privatisation wedge, arguing that the government had "no mandate to enact a major restructuring of the public sector" ahead of majority rule. The ANC too remained, in the words its telecommunications policy head, Andile Ngcaba, "entirely opposed to the principle of privatisation" (*Business Day*, 1991).

But POTWA also charged that commercialisation would undermine affordability, and hence directly impact the poor, and "inevitably lead to increased tariffs that will hit blacks hardest" (*Financial Mail*, 1991).[6]

Nevertheless, after some concessions on privatisation and labour relations (Horwitz, 2001, p. 192), the Bill was finally passed in mid-1991, creating Telkom as a commercial entity with a monopoly in telephony services (RSA, 1991). The Act fell short of creating any of the regulatory structures recommended by the de Villiers report, leaving regulatory authority over the sector firmly within the purview of the Minister (RSA, 1991, Section 119A).

South Africa's first two VANS licences were issued in short order, both to companies associated with the banks, who had been amongst those pressing for telecomms reform (Mike van den Bergh, personal communication, 18 May 2015).

South Africa's first steps in telecommunications reform were thus largely in line with international good practice. Posts had been separated from telecommunications and placed on a commercial footing. Privatisation, although contested, was nonetheless on the table. Some, very limited, competition had been introduced. And an embryonic regulatory function had been established within the Ministry.

[6]Such social equity concerns, and support for UAS-inspired interventions, were to remain a key theme in the responses of organised labour to ICT sector reform.

3.3.1 The Coopers & Lybrand Report

Meanwhile, the National Party government sought to continue its own reform agenda under the newly appointed Minister, Piet Welgemoed. Almost immediately it embarked on a new study into the sector, with international consultants engaged to undertake a further "analysis of the policy options for restructuring the country's telecommunications services sector" (Coopers & Lybrand, 1992, p. 1).

The move may not have been entirely unilateral, as prospective data communications providers continued to lobby for greater liberalisation, and aspirant mobile operator, M-Net, began to press for a licence (senior MTN executive, Karel Pienaar interview, 6 February 2015). But it was anything but transparent and consultative. Despite the consultants' claim to have "consulted widely" (Coopers & Lybrand, 1992, p. 2), the report's release late the following year provoked howls of outrage from both the ANC and several industry bodies, saying their input had not been "canvassed" (Sergeant, 1992).

More broadly concerned with the sector overall than its predecessor, the substance of the Coopers and Lybrand report is rather closer to what was developing as international good practice, and is contextualised against the "background of revolutionary changes in the telecommunications industry worldwide" and the evidence of "international experience" (Coopers & Lybrand, 1992, p. 1).

Aligning itself with the three main "policy levers" of telecomms reform, namely "competition, regulation and privatisation" (1992, p. 22), the report recognises three, somewhat contradictory, policy objectives, namely: the "social policy" aims of increasing "telephone penetration" particularly in the townships and 'black' rural areas; and the need to ensure "affordability"; as against the "market-orientated" goal of providing advanced "service levels" for business users (Coopers & Lybrand, 1992, pp. 4–5).

From this starting point, the Coopers & Lybrand report goes on to make recommendations in four main areas:

- Protection of Telkom's monopoly—in respect of long-distance and international telephony, for 5 years to prevent cream-skimming, and to provide a revenue base to finance a ramped-up rollout of services to the country's majority;

- Competition—despite the above, the report recommends licensing supplementary local network operators, opening up the markets for VANs, PTNs, VSATs and CPE; more particularly it recommends the licensing of two mobile operators, with Telkom being party to one of the licences;
- Regulation—the report emphasises the need for a separate, independent, regulator, governed by a collegial commission and subject to the law and to Ministerial policy, enjoying a wide range of what are now standard regulatory competencies, including enforcing universal service obligations;
- Privatisation—the report holds out the privatisation of Telkom in the medium term as a means of incentivising efficiency and injecting capital into the enterprise.

The report starts with a recognition of the racialised gap in access, drawing attention to the gap in access between 'white' and 'black' South Africans. Linking teledensity and income, it shows that 'white' South Africans were orders or magnitude ahead of their 'black' counterparts in terms of both wealth and access to telephony (Coopers & Lybrand, 1992, p. 9).

Coopers and Lybrand also point to "considerable suppressed demand... constrained by both [low] income levels and the non-availability of services and infrastructure" (1992, p. 9). Contemporaneous work by Morris and Stavrou concurs, finding that "over two-thirds of all rural and urban respondents and just under half of shantytown respondents interviewed wished to possess a private telephone" (1993, p. 4).

But although the report recognises the key constraint of affordability, it offers little concrete guidance in this regard. By contrast, Morris and Stavrou warn that "less than one-tenth of rural respondents, could afford to install and maintain a telephone at the present tariffs" (1993, p. 5).

One notable feature of the report is the painting of three possible future scenarios, including: "Network Expansion" (based on aggressive monopoly-provided rollout of the "availability" of basic telephony, particularly to urban and rural 'black' households); and "Competition" (based on rate rebalancing, preparing the ground for competition and the rollout of public payphones) (Coopers & Lybrand, 1992, pp. 28–32).

Coopers and Lybrand go on to advocate the imposition of "community service obligations" (today's USOs) on Telkom, in that it be "required to meet specific, quantified targets for service growth" (Coopers & Lybrand, 1992, p. 24), by extending its network to under-served areas and communities, and by increasing teledensity through providing telephony to households and through rolling out payphones. The report envisages that these obligations will be set and monitored by the newly-created regulator, specified in Telkom's licence and funded from its international and *long*-distance monopoly.

Interestingly, the report draws a distinction between household service provision (universal service) and the rollout of payphones (universal access) when it summarises how to extend the "availability of basic telephone service, particularly to the black communities in the townships and rural areas", namely:

- by improving access to public telephones, including agency phones and community phones; and/or
- by increasing the penetration of private residential access lines (Coopers & Lybrand, 1992, p. 24).

Elsewhere the report recommends the imposition of geographic coverage obligations upon the mobile licensees, drawing on the model of the UK (Coopers & Lybrand, 1992, p. 77). This was later to be carried through into the licences awarded to Vodacom and MTN, making South Africa one of the few countries in the world to do so at the time.

Together with its predecessor, the report was instrumental in aligning South Africa *de facto* with global trends in the reform of the sector. It was also an important milestone towards putting UAS at the forefront of ICT sector policy. Both were to remain key issues for the negotiations leading to democracy and in developing ANC policy positions for the sector.

Ironically, the Nationalist Party-inspired Coopers & Lybrand report closely foreshadowed the subsequent evolution of the sector, even under the incoming ANC administration post-democracy: Telkom's five-year monopoly; its universal service obligations; the liberalisation of value-added services; the licensing of two mobile operators (with Telkom having a 50% stake in one); the establishment of a sector regulator; and the partial privatisation of Telkom.

The public reception that greeted the publication of the report was divided. The ANC's Andile Ngcaba was "outraged" over the "Department's determination to restructure telecommunication systems without broad consultation" and by the report's "acceptance of privatisation", which the ANC continued to oppose. Not unexpectedly, diametrically opposed views were voiced by the business lobby, which called for speedier liberalisation and the immediate establishment of an independent regulator (*Business Day*, 1992).

3.3.2 *Preparing to Govern: The CDITP*

It was during this period that, recognising the complex, technical nature of the ICT sector and aware that the relevant expertise, research and experience were sorely lacking within its own ranks, the ANC set up its ICT policy think tank, the Centre for the Development of Information and Telecommunications Policy (CDITP).

On his formal return from exile, ANC ICT head Andile Ngcaba moved in 1991 to set up the CDITP in response to "developments in the political negotiations at CODESA in the area of broadcasting and telecommunications" (interview, 28 January 2015). The CDITP positioned itself as an "independent, non-profit-making policy research and training organisation" aiming to support the "analysis of policy options" in preparation for the "transition to a full democracy" (CDITP, 1995, pp. 2–3).

Ngcaba lists three central achievements of the CDITP:

1. securing "academic and other training" to build 'black' expertise;
2. researching and writing policy positions;
3. establishing the National Telecommunications Forum (interview, 28 January 2015).

The cadreship programme of the CDITP reached out widely to young 'black' professionals and intellectuals, sympathetic to the ANC and its positions, and usually with some exposure to the sector. Its alumni include many who subsequently went on to leadership positions at the regulator, in industry, and in government structures.

The CDITP ran training courses in South Africa, bringing in international experts such as the ITU's Tim Kelly and Australian trade unionist Kevin Morgan. A number of CDITP recruits were also sent abroad for telecommunications technical and policy training, or on study tours to Sweden, Canada and the UK (CDITP, 1995, p. 11 and 19).

The CDITP went on to produce a number of research reports and policy recommendations, including:

- 'Licensing of cellular mobile telephone services', looking at the impact of liberalising the mobile market on affordability and universal service (September 1993);
- An 'ANC policy for equity and efficiency in the telecommunications sector' (March 1994);
- 'Reform of the South African telecommunication industry', draft legislative proposals for the SA market (September 1994);
- A 'Master plan for the South African telecommunications sector' (no date given) (CDITP, 1995).

The CDITP's approach to policy combined an awareness of international good practice and ICT sector reform, tempered with a desire to ground policy formulation in the realities of South Africa and the needs of the majority of its citizens. Accordingly, the CDITP argued for the development of a "clear telecommunications policy that reflects the needs of the community, rather than directly importing models that have been developed in other parts of the world" (CDITP, 1995, p. 16).

That this was not a rejection per se of the diffusion of policy lessons from elsewhere, is evidenced by the way in which the CDITP embraced international training and study tours and engaged with international experts. However, the CDITP sought to plug into an epistemic community broadly sympathetic to the positions of the ANC in opposition to those of the National Party government.

Further, the question of universal access and service—the "challenge of getting basic services to all people", by means of a "master plan for development of the sector" involving "marked increases in telephone penetration in black communities"(CDITP, 1995, p. 15)—looms large in the work of the CDITP.

3.3.3 *Negotiating Telecommunications: From CODESA to the NTF*

While the Coopers and Lybrand team was conducting its investigations, public political attention was instead focused on political negotiations at the Convention for a Democratic South Africa (CODESA), which commenced in late 1991.

The nature of CODESA meant that telecommunications was a relatively peripheral issue. It fell within the "political neutrality of, and fair access to, state-controlled / statutorily instituted media" scope of Working Group 2, where agreement was reached to establish an "Independent Body to Regulate Telecommunications Sector", which would have spectrum management and licensing as its principal functions (CODESA, 1992, p. 1 and 8). That aside, little of substance was tabled, beyond a general commitment to universal service by ensuring that a "wide range of telecommunication services, including regional and community broadcasting program [sic] services, is available throughout South Africa" (CODESA, 1992, p. 8). CODESA, however, eventually collapsed in mistrust, acrimony and political squabbling.

The limited focus on telecommunications was largely due to the same, highly fraught nature of the political negotiations. Willie Currie, at the centre of telecomms reform at the time, wrote to the IDRC of Canada, noting that, "unlike the control and regulation of broadcasting, telecommunications was not pivotal to the fairness of the election coverage and that further policy work was [felt to be] necessary" (1994). Attention, then, shifted to creating a fully independent entity to regulate broadcasting in the broad public interest (Gillwald, 2002, p. 6).

Meanwhile, negotiations continued across a number of areas. For example, the considerable number of stakeholder forums (such as the groundbreaking National Economic Forum,[7] the National Electrification Forum and the National Housing Forum) continued to play an important role, bringing together government, organised labour and civil society actors to parley over substantive policy issues in preparation for the new post-1994 democratic government (Habib, 1997; Lodge, 1999).

These stakeholder forums functioned as sites of struggle, born out of a recognition by the various parties of the need to reach an accommodation on policy issues that none could unilaterally impose on the others. In effect they acted as incipient mini-regimes, with their own rules and decision-making procedures, and with some congruence of principles and norms, leading to a negotiated set of policy outcomes. To an extent

[7] Predecessor to the current National Economic Development and Labour Advisory Council (NEDLAC).

they also acted as epistemic communities by "getting parties previously virtually unknown to each other to comprehend the necessities and complexities of policy under the new political dispensation" (Horwitz, 2001, p. 204). They were particularly important from the point of view of the ANC-led alliance, needing to win 'progressive' positions in the face of a hostile government and state bureaucracy.

It was in this context that the National Telecommunications Forum (NTF) was conceived. Incubated, according to its first secretary-general, Fikile Khumalo, at a key telecommunications policy conference organised by the CDITP (1995), it was formally launched in November 1993 (2001) as a vehicle to "formulate recommendations on telecommunications policy and issues for the new government" (Khumalo, 2001).

The three-day CDITP conference, headlined 'Telecommunications in a Post-*apartheid* South Africa', had been a substantial event. It boasted over 100 delegates (including visibly reluctant Postmaster General, Ters Oosthuizen) and was addressed by local speakers (including representatives of industry, labour, civic organisations and academia) and international experts. Delegates were greeted by a welcome letter from then ANC General Secretary Cyril Ramaphosa, stating that "communications constitutes the nervous system of the democratisation process" (CDITP, 1995, p. 25). Somewhat hyperbolically labelled by ANC head of telecommunications Andile Ngcaba as "the most important telecommunications event in SA's history", it was clearly intended as a reminder that the National Party government had "no legitimate authority on [telecommunications] policy decisions" and that it would be "foolhardy" for them to proceed as if it were "business as usual" (*Financial Mail*, 1993a).

It was COSATU's Bernie Fanaroff who then called for the establishment of a sector forum to carry through a "coherent, integrated strategy to provide an affordable telephone service of a high quality", describing government's moves in the sector as a "disaster [with] no openness, no transparency, grossly inadequate consultation and no strategy for a universal service" (cited in Ofir, 2003, p. 20).

The conference had, crucially, also raised the banner of UAS, stating that the "objective of providing access for all to universal services [sic] is of prime importance" (CDITP, 1995, p. 24). This commitment was carried through into the NTF's subsequent formal mission statement, in which it pledged to:

> offer policy option proposals that would ensure the socioeconomic development of all the people of South Africa through universal service, as well as the economic development of the country through a well-developed, technologically-sound and appropriate telecommunications infrastructure. (cited in Horwitz, 2001, p. 209)

Ngcaba was later to describe the establishment of the NTF as "huge step as far as policy developments and the consultation process were concerned… [one marked by] intensive debate in an inclusive forum" (2001).

Despite considerable hostility from government, the NTF brought together representatives from: business (including Telkom, NTUG, the Electronic Industries Federation, the Computer Society); labour (including COSATU and the main union at Telkom, POTWA); and academia (including from the influential University of the Witwatersrand) (Andile Ngcaba, interview, 28 January 2015).

It would be in the period after the 1994 elections, as the ANC moved to change the legislation in the sector, that the NTF would really come into its own.

3.3.4 Community Service Obligations and the Arrival of Mobile

But it was the public furore surrounding the government's moves to license two mobile cellular operators[8] that occupied political centre stage during much of 1993, amidst strident opposition to the deal from the ANC and COSATU.

One strand of the ANC's hostility stemmed from an ideological anti-privatisation stance. Andile Ngcaba insisted that telecommunications should remain a monopoly, saying that "We don't want to kill Telkom by introducing competition which will steal valuable income from it. We want a national cellular network, owned by the state" (Sergeant, 1993c).

Another was anti-elitist. Mobile telephony was popularly viewed as a high-priced, low-uptake toy. As a result, the ANC had "branded cellular phones as elitist, promising to benefit only the rich with pockets deep enough to afford to buy the hand-sets and use the system" (Chester, 1993).

[8] Vodacom and MTN.

Others alleged the licensing process was skewed in favour of white capital, with aspirant bidder Naepe Maepa[9] describing the process as "tilted in favour of white businesses, with stumbling blocks to deter black participation - especially returning exiles who had honed new high-tech skills abroad" (Chester, 1993).

The resultant furore was also deeply coloured by the antagonism and contestation that had characterised the ongoing negotiations between the *apartheid* regime and the ANC. The latter's response to the licensing of cellular was thus part of its continued push back against any unilateral changes to the sector imposed by the National Party government. Makanya, for example, characterises the ANC as "adamant [that] this 'unilateral restructuring' of telecommunications must be suspended" (1993).

The public furore may have occupied centre stage in 1993, but the roots of the mobile licensing saga stretch back well before then.

The origins of the pitch for GSM services in South Africa are unclear. Both of the initial two licensees claim credit.

Alan Knott-Craig, Vodacom's long-standing CEO, points to a Telkom study tour, and credits himself with voicing the resultant unanimous recommendation to opt for the GSM mobile standard, and to propose a duopoly:

> South Africa must go the cellular route, and that it should adopt the GSM standard, digital as opposed to analogue. And what's more, we must insist on a competitive environment, with at least two cellular players – we don't want to create another Telkom. (Knott-Craig & Afonso, 2009, p. 37)[10]

MTN senior manager Karel Pienaar has a different view, and instead traces the origins of mobile in South Africa to a small new business development team sitting at pay-television company M-Net (interview, 6 February 2015), which led to serious lobbying of senior government officials. Pienaar further claims that M-Net conducted market research and set up a pilot network with 4 base stations in Khayelitsha[11] using a test licence (interview, 6 February 2015).

More likely, the truth reflects a more complex interaction of these various initial initiatives, coupled with pressure from manufacturers touting

[9] Later to serve as ICASA Chair, before resigning in the aftermath of the debacle around the licensing of the third mobile operator, controversially awarded to Cell C.

[10] His somewhat hagiographic (auto)biography is richly imbued with hindsight.

[11] Sprawling, mostly Xhosa-speaking, dormitory township outside Cape Town.

for business. It is also probable that both initiatives fed into the substance of the Coopers and Lybrand report, and influenced its recommendation for two GSM licensees along the lines of the UK model.

Knott-Craig points to an agreement between Finance Minister Derek Keys and senior Telkom executives that essentially mirrored the recommendations of the Coopers and Lybrand report:

> licences would be issued to two cellular operators... Telkom could form part of one consortium that would bid for the cellular licences, but that it could not have more than a 50% stake in the group. (2009, p. 41)

The driving idea of providing access to South Africa's unserved, largely 'black' population is pervasive in both accounts. Likely with a substantial dose of hindsight, both Vodacom's Knott-Craig and MTN's Pienaar cite altruistic service delivery motives for the move into mobile. The recognition of the profit-making possibilities offered by the pent-up demand identified in both the de Villiers and Coopers and Lybrand reports is likely a more accurate, if less charitable, interpretation.

But securing a mobile licence was also about forging business partnerships. Both local aspirants sought out potential international partners with the necessary expertise and experience. Knott-Craig reports an early approach to the UK's newly-formed Vodafone (Knott-Craig & Afonso, 2009, p. 42). M-Net, in turn, settled on Cable and Wireless as their preferred international partner (Karel Pienaar, interview, 6 February 2015). Potential local partners were also sought, such as tobacco giant Rembrandt (Knott-Craig & Afonso, 2009, p. 42). M-Net was rather more canny, recognising that in the incipient new South Africa a 'white' Afrikaner company would need a 'black' partner, and approached Nthato Motlana[12] and FABCOS.[13]

The National Party government moved to proceed along the lines of the Coopers and Lybrand report, and in accordance with its agreement with Telkom (*Business Report*, 1993). In early 1993, a tender for two cellular mobile licences was issued. With Telkom guaranteed a 50% stake

[12] Prominent Soweto doctor and anti-*apartheid* activist, founder of New African Investments Limited (NAIL) in the early 1990s as a vehicle for 'black economic empowerment'.

[13] The Federation for African Business and Consumer Services (FABCOS) was founded in 1988, with the explicit aim of bringing informal 'black' business into the mainstream of the economy.

in one consortium, the tender was effectively for a single licence (Bidoli, 1993a) with the selection of Telkom's eventual partner, Vodacom, taking place *ex parte* (Sergeant, 1993d).

The tender did give considerable emphasis to widespread provision of services to the country's underserved 'black' majority, partly as a necessary attempt to forestall ANC criticism:

> The ANC argues that government's decision on cellular phones does not address the shortage of phones, among SA's black inhabitants... A senior government source said the tender was sensitive to issues like providing telecommunications to less-advantaged communities... [and] took into account all the ANC's 'criticisms to ensure widespread penetration'. (Sergeant, 1993a)

Bidoli's summary concurs: "applicants will have to specify the extent to which their choice of technology will lead to high volumes and low costs, how they will provide a service to poor communities and how they will support SA industry" (Bidoli, 1993a).

Several commentators complained that the hefty upfront fee (R 100 million), together with a sliding-scale annual licence fee, pegged at 5% of revenue, would hamper rollout to poor communities (Sergeant, 1993b), leaving too little surplus to finance the construction of the network, with its expensive base-station towers, backhaul circuits and switching systems. They feared the impact would potentially turn cellular telephony into "just a yuppie toy" (Bidoli, 1993b), earmarked for an urban elite.[14]

Not unexpectedly, the ANC's response was one of outrage. Although the tender's UAS service provisions served, to some extent, to blunt their call for "proper planning and [a] consultative process, aimed at providing an affordable telephone service to all", the ANC demanded that government "suspend with immediate effect the unilateral call for tenders and the award of licences for the proposed cellular telephone system" (Sergeant, 1993d) Many of the ANC's concerns were voiced by Andile Ngcaba, who labelled the process as "corrupt" and without legal foundation (Sergeant, 1993e).

Engagement behind the scenes with the ANC's investment arm, Thebe Investment Corporation, in an attempt secure some support for the deal,

[14] Coopers and Lybrand had badly mis-estimated the total market size to be a maximum of 220,000 (1992, p. 76).

was rebuffed under vocal opposition from the politicians (IOL, 2000). Instead, to give additional weight to their opposition the ANC brought together a grouping calling itself the Cellular Telephone Consultative Forum, "representing black businesses, labour unions in the telecommunications and electronics sectors, civic organisations and other interest groups" (Sergeant, 1993f). Further ratcheting up the pressure, the ANC threatened to revoke the licences once it came to power "if the bidding process was not halted until the transitional executive council had been established" (Sowetan, 1993). COSATU too joined in the fray, attacking the lack of consultation, describing the process as "unilateral reconstruction in contravention of undertakings given by government to the National Economic Forum", calling for local, job-creating manufacturing requirements to be included, and restating the demand for "universal, affordable service" (Naidoo, 1993).

The waters were muddied by late attempts from some US-based telecommunications companies to have the process delayed, pending the lifting of sanctions (Sergeant, 1993g), and by 11th hour demands for a share of the spoils from a new 'black' economic empowerment grouping, the African Telecommunications Forum (ATF), which included the ANC's own Thebe Investment Corporation (Bulger, 1993).

The ruckus was further deepened when the government tried to slip through further amendments to the Post Office Act, prompting a blistering response from Ngcaba, who described them as fresh attempts to "deregulate Telkom... the most significant unilateral restructuring yet seen from a desperate government that is intent in selling off public assets in the dying days of illegitimate rule" (1993).

But the National Party government was not to be swayed. In the end, bids were received from five consortia, which included international participation from Deutsche Telekom, Telkom Finland, Cable and Wireless (MTN) and Vodafone (Vodacom). Black economic empowerment set-asides ranged around 30% (except in the case of the Telkom/Vodacom bid).[15]

The announcement in September 1993 of the winning bidders—Vodacom and MTN—took place amidst a flurry of public sabre-rattling by

[15] One bid, submitted on a single handwritten sheet of paper (Knott-Craig & Afonso, 2009, p. 53), came from SunTel CEO, Nape Maepa who infamously remarked that his company was "not managed by any ordinary kaffirs" (The Star, 1993).

the ANC and COSATU (Sergeant, 1993h) and a series of behind-the-scenes meetings involving, amongst others, Nelson Mandela and then ANC Secretary-General Cyril Ramaphosa (*Cape Times*, 1993a).

Ramaphosa[16] appears to have been central to brokering the deal (Willie Currie, interview, 18 September 2014), in one account over-riding the opposition of Ngcaba (Denis Smit, interview, 20 November 2014). But the deal which was finally struck, and which allowed the licensing to go ahead, seems remarkably thin on any real concessions secured by Ramaphosa. There was some minor reshuffling of black economic empowerment set-asides: COSATU's pension fund secured a stake in MTN at the expense of reducing Naftel's shareholding, and Hoskens Consolidated Investments secured a 5% stake in Vodacom (*Financial Mail*, 1993c).

Other reports point to counter-trade, an agreement to give at least 50% of retail outlet franchises to 'black' business, and the provision of mobile services to under-serviced areas, as key to the deal (*Cape Times*, 1993b; Chalmers, 1993; *Financial Mail*, 1993b). But the latter had already been a bid requirement, and it is unclear if any significantly greater UAS commitments were secured from Vodacom and MTN.

'Counter-trade' likely points to the mysterious 'Joint Economic Development Plan Agreement', a "plan… to assist in the development of the South African economy and in particular the telecommunications industry" (ICASA, 2004). It appears to have included a "commitment for MTN and Vodacom to each invest 1-Billion Rands million at the time in South Africa by the year 2000" (Song & Akhtar, 1995, p. 58) in schemes to provide for social and economic upliftment to disadvantaged communities through training, job creation, foreign investment and the like. But it has never been made public.

The two licences were formally gazetted a week later (DPT, 1993) but contain no details of shareholding, counter-trade or subcontracting agreements, and few specifics by way of UAS obligations. They were accompanied by a 'Multiparty Implementation Agreement', which sets out a number of technical issues, including access to spectrum, the provision of

[16]Currently President of South Africa. After stepping down from politics in 1997, he was appointed Chair of black economic empowerment group NAIL (which held a shareholding in MTN at the time), later joining the Board of MTN itself in 2001—a curious footnote to the mobile licensing agreement.

'community service telephones', the provision of backhaul by Telkom and interconnection arrangements.

The cellular licensing furore marks an early emergence of rent-seeking behaviour on the part of the ANC and its allies. These were particularly 'black' economic empowerment groupings, many of whom had hitherto played little if any role in the struggle against *apartheid*, but who saw opportunities for the accumulation of wealth in its demise. This is not to deny the role of existing (mostly 'white' or state-owned) commercial interests—the likes of Telkom, M-Net, Rembrandt, who, with the quieter assurance of vested power, were equally desirous of making money out of the mobile licences.

There were several cross-currents flowing through these events. There was clearly a real commitment, on the part of the ANC, and of individuals within it (like Ngcaba), to address the injustices that *apartheid* had inflicted on the overwhelming majority of South Africans, and which had deprived so many of access to telephony services. There were also political dynamics and ideological postures at play, underpinning the ANC's resistance to 'unilateral restructuring' of the sector and informing their opposition to privatisation. Complicating all was self-interest, commercial greed and rent-seeking conduct, which manifested itself in the unseemly jostling for a share of the cellular spoils, and, possibly, through the manipulation of the political drama for personal gain.

Importantly, however, the mobile licences represented a policy victory for universal access and service. They included significant provisions designed to ensure universal, affordable access to telecommunications services for the country's disadvantaged majority—the first universal service obligations to be imposed on any licensees in South Africa. These USOs will be assessed in detail in the next chapter.

3.4 ANC Policy on Universal Access and Service

The nature of the ANC as a liberation movement engaged in struggle—the armed struggle, mass protest struggle and diplomatic struggle—meant that it entered negotiations for the democratic transition without clear or agreed policy positions on telecommunications or UAS more specifically.

Opposition to the privatisation of Telkom, and the demand for universal, affordable access to services could serve only as broad, guiding principles. However, they needed to be backed by specific, detailed policy alternatives. The establishment of the CDITP, along with the recruitment and training of a cadre of individuals with some exposure to the sector, and the development of research and position papers, was clearly designed to fill the lacuna.

ANC policy in relation to telecommunications was slow to crystallise. For example, the ANC's key 'Ready to Govern' policy manifesto—which emerged from its 1992 National Policy Conference, following the breakdown of political negotiations, and which was intended to showcase the ANC's vision for the future, and to establish a "set of basic guidelines to policies [the ANC intends] to pursue"—makes scant mention of telecommunications, which is simply bundled together with other aspects of infrastructure such as electricity and water, subject to the following guidelines:

- The need to "promote infrastructural development in the rural areas";
- The need to provide "access to these essential services for all South Africans";
- "The equitable allocation of these resources between industry, agriculture and domestic consumers";
- "The democratisation of the control of utilities which provide these services" (ANC, 1992).

The subsequent 'Reconstruction and Development Programme' (RDP), adopted in early 1994, shortly in advance of the country's first democratic election, and developed under pressure from COSATU rather than the ANC (Lodge, 1999; Naidoo, 2010; von Holdt, 2004), sets out far firmer policy positions on telecommunications.

Arising from a growing feeling within organised labour that a "reconstruction pact [which] would commit a new government to a joint agenda" (Naidoo, 2010, p. 240),[17] the development of the RDP initially followed participatory, consultative processes. The first four drafts were developed internally within COSATU before its 1993 Special Congress, with the remaining two drafts involving Tripartite Alliance structures. The author recalls attending one such session held at the Shaft 17 Conference Centre near Soweto, at which a variety of structures and individuals from with the broader anti-*apartheid* movement were present, and at which

[17] Then head of COSATU, Naidoo, was later to serve as the second Minister of Communications.

there was intense and detailed debate on the range of issues and options, suffused with a sense of creating a shared vision of real policy alternatives.

Early drafts of the RDP contain only peremptory reference to telecommunications, calling only for "access to an affordable telephone" in a paragraph dealing with access to basic infrastructure, including water and electricity (ANC, 1993). But the RDP as a document continued to evolve and gather detail and complexity as it "drew upon a progressively broader range of tributaries" (Lodge, 1999, p. 9).

The final version of the RDP contains fairly substantial and specific policy provisions with regard to telecommunications and UAS, under a section dealing with 'Meeting Basic Needs'. Proceeding from a characterisation of South Africa's "racially distorted" telecommunications divide, the document identifies "universal affordable access for all" as a key policy priority. both in its own right and as an enabler of socio-economic development. Further, the RDP recognises the enabling role of the sector as "indispensable backbone for the development of all other socio-economic sectors", while taking a sideswipe at government's "indiscriminate privatisation" (ANC, 1994b, Section 2.8).

Later sections in the document deal with the need to retain the basic network infrastructure under public ownership, to create an independent regulator and to stimulate local telecommunications manufacturing capacity (ANC, 1994b, pp. 4.6.6–4.6.10).

The key features of the ANC's positions over the previous three years are all there: the antipathy to unilateral privatisation and restructuring, the importance of Telkom and its network for a planned approach to social development and economic growth, but, above all, the *apartheid* telephony divide and the imperative of universal access and service.

During this period, behind the scenes, the CDITP was working on a "detailed policy development which underpinned the framing" of the RDP, and its telecommunications sections in particular (1995, p. 10 and 34). Ngcaba was central to the authorship of the document, to which Pallo Jordan[18] ascribes many of the subsequent ideas that filtered through into policy (interview, 1 December 2014). However, the work had substantial input from the team at the CDITP: Aki Stavrou recalls spending months "drafting a new regulatory framework for telecommunications" as input into impending post-1994 legislation (interview, 17 October 2014).

[18] First ANC Minister in charge of telecommunications.

Indeed, 'The ANC Policy for Equity and Efficiency in the Telecommunications Sector' contains a far more detailed and comprehensive policy articulation than that of the RDP. It explicitly sets out to balance its twin eponymous goals—of addressing the *apartheid* telecommunications divide, and of promoting ICTs as an enabler of economic and social development—reflecting the 'mixed economy' approach publicly argued by ANC Secretary-General Cyril Ramaphosa (1993). But it is UAS—the "delivery of affordable universal access to the telecommunications network, irrespective of race or location"—that is placed as the pre-eminent "overriding goal" of ANC ICT sector policy (1994a, p. 4).

The document's policy proposals are comprehensive—and clearly cognisant of the international good practice precepts of privatisation, competition and regulation, with which Andile Ngcaba and the CDITP staff were familiar. It called for:

- "Separation of functions", with policy vested in the hands of government, and regulation (including in respect of UAS) undertaken by an "independent regulator", answerable only to Parliament;
- "Public ownership" and development of the "national telecommunications infrastructure" (notably Telkom, but also Transtel) to meet the goal of "universal service", with competition limited to "where it is demonstrable that the prime goal of universal telephone service will not be harmed";
- "Meeting the community's needs" by ensuring that "telecommunications services should be both physically and financially accessible to all South Africans" through dramatically increasing connectivity and payphone provision;
- Reworking the structure of "tariffs and charges" to eliminate excessive cross-subsidies and to achieve rate re-balancing;
- Support for "local industry" and "local manufacture" by means of a targeted "procurement policy", particularly on the part of Telkom;
- The promotion of human resource development and "affirmative action";
- A "review" of the mobile licences, which it still sees as "unilateral" and "unacceptable", to ensure Telkom is protected and services rolled out to the poor;
- Securing readmission to the ITU and promoting regional co-operation (ANC, 1994a).

The Policy's 'natural monopoly' defence of public ownership of basic network services, certainly influenced by the ANC's historical allegiance to nationalisation, also echoes the standard incumbent response to business demands for greater liberalisation. It also reveals a fixation on the central role of fixed-line in UAS provision that was to undermine several policy interventions going forward. And the Policy remains huffy towards the mobile licensing process, albeit stopping short of threats to revoke licences or nationalise operators.

On the other hand, the emphasis on the separation of powers and establishing an independent regulator, insulated from political interference, structured along the lines of the IBA and answerable only to Parliament, is strongly reminiscent of the prescriptions of the ITU.

The UAS emphasis of the Policy echoes the repeated public emphasis on universal service by key alliance figures (Naidoo, 1993; Ngcaba, 1993; Ramaphosa, 1993), but, curiously, lacks specificity. USOs and the creation of a USF fund were already being touted as international good practice: yet neither receives a mention.

Together, these then were the policy positions of the ANC in respect of telecommunications reform and universal access and service in the context of the South Africa's ICT sector, as the party entered the country's first democratic election in April 1994, an election from which it was to emerge at the helm of the new government.

3.5 Green Paper: Canvassing Telecomms Reform

Following the victory of the ANC, the newly appointed Minister of Posts and Telecommunications, Pallo Jordan, embarked on a thorough review and overhaul of the sector. This was effected through a Green Paper (RSA, 1995) and White Paper (RSA, 1996a) process, leading to the 1996 Telecommunications Act (RSA, 1996b).

The twists and turns of that process, its shenanigans and confrontations, have been charted in great detail elsewhere (Horwitz, 2001, pp. 178–281). It was a seminal moment, codifying and laying down the policy framework that was to shape the ICT sector in South Africa for the next 20 years. What is of interest here, however, is the role and prominence of UAS policy within that codified framework, along with the policy influences that shaped its central features.

3.5.1 Constructing ICT Sector Reform in an Unreconstructed Context

One of the key challenges facing the new ANC government as it began to reform the ICT sector was the fact that the process of review and restructuring was to be undertaken within a hostile institutional environment. The ANC's space to manoeuvre was limited by the so-called 'sunset clauses' in the 1993 Interim Constitution, which had facilitated a political settlement by guaranteeing the National Party a share in the Government of National Unity, and by protecting the jobs of those in the civil service (RSA, 1993, Sections 88 and 236).

The bureaucracy inherited from, and historically aligned to, the *apartheid* state acted as a further encumbrance on the incoming ANC-dominated administration (Maphunye, 2002). The events of the preceding years—the lack of consultation and ongoing attempts at unilateral restructuring of the sector, along with hostility to the CDITP and the NTF—had shown Ngcaba and the ANC that they faced an "unreconstructed" bureaucracy antagonistic to their agenda (Willie Currie, interview, 18 September 2014).[19] Running the telecommunications reform process through the Department was, therefore, not an option.

Animated by the RDP-inspired approach to 'democratising the state' and society—which sought to broaden policy-making from the preserve of elites into a process where "historically oppressed communities" were able to "participate meaningfully in planning processes and decision-making" (ANC, 1994b, Section 6.3)—the ANC, instead, opted for a consultative, stakeholder process.

But the ANC was at the same time distrustful of the agendas of the (almost entirely 'white') business sector, whose positions on reform issues were often self-serving and sectarian, and which was characterised by deep "dislocations" in viewpoint, in particular around "universal service" and the "introduction of competition" (Currie, 1996a, p. 1). Indeed, the stakeholder forum of the NTF had been "close to breaking up" over tensions around "universal access" versus the demands of business (*Financial Mail*, 1995a). Albeit that its nature as a stakeholder forum meant it brought most of the contending interests around one table, there were concerns that it was "driven too much by business interests" (Khumalo, 2001, p. 184). Horwitz also alludes to the "feeling that malevolent policy

[19] Co-ordinator for the ANC of the telecomms reform process.

provisions would be put in place by white bureaucrats and businessmen under the noses of the black majority" (Horwitz, 2001, p. 213), especially given the complexity and technical nature of many of the issues on the table—this despite the capacity-building work of the CDITP.

As a result, it was decided to run the process outside both government and the NTF, in order to create a "point of focus other than the NTF, where a full public debate [could] take place" (Currie, 1994). Nonetheless, the NTF was to remain an important point of consultation: a draft of the Green Paper was circulated there "for comment"; and the penultimate draft of the White Paper was "tabled for discussion" (Currie, 1996a, pp. 4–5).

Speaking some years later, Ngcaba was to describe the development of national policy and legislation through structures outside of government as a unique achievement:

> The history of policy development initiatives in this country is quite unique in the sense that it was not government-led but rather driven by non-governmental organisations championed by the African National Congress (ANC). The 90s could be said to have represented the era of mobilisation of the marginalised to be part of the policy decision-making efforts. This was evidenced by the proliferation of forums and organisations that reared up and participated in telecommunications policy debates. (Ngcaba, 2001)

The process was superintended by Willie Currie, formerly Secretary-General of the Film and Allied Workers Organisation (FAWO), who had worked with Pallo Jordan in the Campaign for Independent Broadcasting and in setting up the Independent Broadcasting Authority (IBA), but who had not been part of the CDITP. Funding for the process came from Canada's semi-independent development research fund, the IDRC, whom Currie had approached for assistance in late 1994, setting out the envisaged process and planned timescales, and identifying areas, including "universal service" (1994).

In fact, the involvement of the IDRC predates the 1994 election, and was initially conceived much more broadly as embracing national information management policy. It was from this initiative that telecomms reform then evolved, after a number of in-country meetings, as a key sub-project (Harfoush & Wild, 1994). In late 1994, with the involvement of renowned telecommunications academic Bill Melody, the focus of attention finally began to turn to the "need for a clear regulatory framework for the telecommunication sector - a framework that is perhaps managed by an independent authority" (Akhtar, Melody, & Naidoo, 1994, p. 8). Procedurally, the IDRC recommended "as widely a consultative process as possible be activated soon to engage the various players and interest groups, including the private sector, NGO-movement, key parastatals and the labour unions". Substantively, the suggested approach was based on policy diffusion, involving a "review of the policy research literature, on international experience to date, on developments in relevant international agencies, and the current situation in South Africa" (Akhtar et al. 1994, p. 9).

The response of the IDRC to the formal request for support was therefore prompt and favourable, supported by a "checklist for developing the terms of reference for the telecommunications sector Green and White Papers", covering, inter alia, "universal service / universal access" (Akhtar, Fax to Willie Currie, 1995). Thus was created the 'National Telecommunications Policy Project' (NTPP), to run a Green and White Paper process, leading to a Telecommunications Act.

The project was to be supported by a small "technical task team" (which included the ANC's Andile Ngcaba) (Currie, 1995), supplemented by an "Advisory Panel" with wider representation from the CDITP, local and international academia, COSATU and industry (*Cape Times*, 1995; DPTB, 1995). Further, the IDRC's Kate Wild played a leading role, not only as co-ordinator, but also providing substantive input (Tina James, interview, 27 November 2014).

The process was formally announced by Minister Jordan at the 'Telkom 1995' conference (*Financial Mail*, 1995a). It was thus a very diverse and highly expert team that set about identifying issues and formulating questions, and carrying through the earlier work that Stavrou and others had been engaged on at the CDITP.

Horwitz makes much of the consultative and participatory nature of the reforms hammered out in a series of stakeholder compromises that led to the 1996 Telecommunications Act (2001). Similarly, Currie's public descriptions of the process emphasise this aspect, characterising it as "participatory democracy" rather than "policy-making by Ministerial dictat" (1996a).

Certainly, such an approach would have been in keeping with the popular, consultative *zeitgeist* of the times. However, it must be recognised that the process was not a fully democratic one. The scope for participation by ordinary, individual citizens, was limited. Rather the process was participatory in an elite sense: open all organised stakeholder groupings and a wide range of vested interests.

But other voices are rather more cynical. According to Stavrou, the outcome was "largely pre-determined", even though the process was designed to accommodate and address "very strong alternative views on particular issues" (interview, 17 October 2014). It was certainly highly fractious at times: witness, for example, an angry fax emanating from unnamed "key industry stakeholders", berating the "Willie Currie Team" for acting without "broader consultation" (Anonymous, 1995).

Running the process as a project, rather than through the NTF, no doubt allowed a good deal of behind the scenes manoeuvring and *ex parte* engagement with the wide range of stakeholder interests, from organised labour to business, to address their fears and to accommodate their issues—the "set of politically delicate visits" referred to by Horwitz (2001, p. 212).

What the ANC thus sought to achieve was a delicate balance between keeping control of the process and opening it up for stakeholder input.

3.5.2 The Green Paper: 'Let All Call'

The promised Green Paper was duly released into the public domain in July 1995 to a flurry of public response. Its twin RDP-inspired themes sought to:

- redress the historic imbalances [in access] caused by [*apartheid*] policies; [and]
- make our businesses operate more efficiently and help [socio-economic] development to unfold more effectively (RSA, 1995).

Public attention centred on the latter theme, reading into Jordan's remarks at the Green Paper launch a refusal on the part of the ANC to privatise Telkom and introduce competition (*Financial Mail*, 1995b; Herbert, 1995; Lunsche, 1995), with limited attention (Rohan, 1995) accorded to UAS.

Given its background, it is not surprising that the Green Paper accords the policy "goal of universal service" primary priority. The document is structured around a string of 149 policy questions, organised into 10 chapters, each contextualised with a short background discussion. It follows the Canadian model of an "official document" containing "propositions put before the whole nation for discussion" (Franks, 2006) and is consistent with the consultative light in which the process had sought to cast itself. In an effort to ensure wide public accessibility, versions were published in four of the country's 11 official languages, and, in an innovative move for the time, made electronically available via the incipient Internet, with submissions accepted by post, fax or email.

The Green Paper contextualises itself against "drivers of change", both internal—the need to redress the "historical imbalances" in access, on the one hand, and to meet the increasingly "sophisticated" needs of business, on the other—and external.

Its list of external drivers includes many that had underpinned telecomms reform globally: "technological developments" which undermine monopoly provision; "convergence and globalisation"; the "internationalisation of network provision"; the "development of international strategic partnerships"; and the "global liberalisation of trade in telecommunications products and services, and pressures by trading partners on international bodies (such as the World Trade Organization [WTO]) to follow suit". In other words, the document recognises the context of the global telecommunications regime and the pressures for policy transfer.

UAS issues are mainly dealt with in the first two of the document's sections, explicitly featuring in 5 of its 149 questions (RSA, 1995).

'Universal service' and 'universal access' were each canvassed as distinct issues. 'Universal service' was defined as "putting a telecommunications line in every household wanting the service, at affordable prices"; 'universal access' as "placing a telephone within people's reach but not in every household, for example, by installing public or community telephones within walking distance of people's houses" and an "appropriate intermediate stage" en route to achieving universal service. Recommended interventions to achieve UAS and to provide "rural telecommunications" were also canvassed (RSA, 1995, Questions 1.1, 1.2, 2.1, 2.2 and 2.3).

This marks the first formal definition of 'universal access', along with its clear conceptual and sequential distinction from 'universal service'. Given the influence of this conceptual distinction upon subsequent epistemic discourse and international good practice for developing countries (ITU, 1998), it is curious how the model emerged so explicitly articulated in the Green Paper. Its roots likely lie in the epistemic community associated with the global telecommunications regime. Andile Ngcaba suggests that the concept was something that had been "debated in many fora", pointing out that 'universal access' reflects the "reality" in Africa where universal service "will take many, many years to achieve" (interview, 28 January 2015). He goes on to say: "I was a firm advocate of the idea, and many people would have heard me speak about it, but it wasn't my idea". It was, however, a concept that chimed with South Africa's reality, one that suggested practicable paths across the deep chasm of the country's digital donga.

The Green Paper went on to canvass several concrete UAS interventions, specifically focusing on the international good practice precepts of imposing USOs and establishing a USF:

- Should [licensees] have clear-cut universal service obligations (directly, in terms of service provision, or indirectly, in terms of some form of financial contribution) as a condition for obtaining a license?
- Should indirect (financial) contributions be paid into a 'universal service fund' which would be used to finance universal service provision directly? (RSA, 1995, Question 2.7).

The Green Paper also addresses the good practice issues of accessibility and affordability, raising the former in relation to the option for a differential "grade of services" for UAS provision (RSA, 1995, Question 2.1). Affordability receives rather more substantive treatment, raising the possibility of "special tariffs" for UAS, and noting that "closely associated with the formulation of any tariff regime are the notions of universal service and universal access". Specifically, it asks: "How can barriers to entry be lowered by making services more affordable to disadvantaged communities?" (RSA, 1995, Question 6.10).

The central issues for telecomms reform—liberalisation, privatisation and regulation—take up much of the Green Paper. A wide range of options for the market structure of the sector are flighted, ranging from various flavours of monopoly provision (including a state-owned monopoly, a "commercialised" monopoly[20] and a private monopoly), through a hybrid structure, up to full competition. The privatisation of Telkom is also floated, in order to secure the necessary investment to

[20]Telkom's fixed-line *status quo* at the time.

achieve the massive rollout of its network. Breaking Telkom up into separate operating companies, as was done with AT&T in the US, is also mooted. Fairly extensive attention is also given to managing the relationship between Telkom and potential competitors (RSA, 1995, Sections 2 and 3).

Regulation of the sector enjoys a specific section, along with the question of spectrum management. Issues canvassed include whether to create a single, converged regulator, as well as the extent of regulatory independence and funding models. Given the importance of UAS within the Green Paper, monitoring "progress towards achieving universal service" is mooted as a competence within the scope of the regulator (RSA, 1995, Section 5). At this stage, there was no consideration given to the creation of a separate institution to oversee UAS. This was to come later.

Other issues canvassed included options to promote the "economic empowerment of members of historically disadvantaged communities in the telecommunications industry" (RSA, 1995, Section 4). The Green Paper also covered the "equipment supply industry", "human resources for the sector", "regional and international co-operation" and "legislative reforms".

Predictably, it was the issues of market structure, competition and privatisation that elicited the most public debate (Dison & Markovitz, 1995; *Financial Mail*, 1995c; Johannes & du Plessis, 1995). Most responses firmly supported the privatisation of Telkom and the gradual introduction of competition. The ANC remained steadfast in its adherence to UAS as the driving imperative for the sector, with Minister Jordan apparently prepared to concede competition as a possible *quid pro quo*, when he was quoted as saying: "If competition is what we need to get universal service, then we'll have competition" (Perlman, 1995a).

Stakeholder feedback was extensive. Over a hundred written submissions were received, most, predictably, from corporates and other parties with vested, predictable interests, with a concomitant "lack of responses by the general public" (UNDP/ITU, 1995, p. 38). The notice and comment phase was followed by a groundbreaking, online public engagement (via Internet relay chat[21]) with the Minister (*Financial Mail*, 1995d) and a three-day colloquium for selected stakeholders.

[21] Itself a relatively elite forum, given the level of connectivity of the day.

3.5.3 Seeking Sufficient Consensus: 'All Shall Call'

The Mount Grace Colloquium brought together some 80 delegates from a wide range of stakeholder groupings, including: operators, manufacturers and suppliers, civil society bodies, organised labour, business (including 'black' business), broadcasters, government departments and the technical task team itself.

Minister Jordan's welcoming address set the tone, citing as "polar opposites" the affluent suburb of Sandton and the impoverished urban township of Alexandra, and foregrounding the question of universal access as a "stepping stone to universal service" (DPTB, 1995, pp. 17–18). Moving on to the more contentious key telecomms reform issues, he suggested that the Green Paper process had shown that monopoly provision and market competition were not necessarily "Manichean opposites". Accordingly, he held out the possibility of "sufficient consensus[22]" based on "limited deregulation" and the "need to protect Telkom" (DPTB, 1995, p. 18).

The colloquium broke into working groups to debate the five core sets of issues—with UAS at the forefront—posed by Willie Currie on the basis of public responses to the Green Paper, viz.:

1. Universal service, economic empowerment and development;
2. Market structure and competition;
3. Ownership and finance;
4. Regulation;
5. The equipment supply industry (DPTB, 1995, p. 19).

Presenting the first of these questions, Currie placed formally on the table for the first time the notion of establishing a dedicated UAS entity:

Question 1.1: Should there be a universal service agency to promote and advance telecommunications universal service in South Africa? If so, what should be its structure and functions? (DPTB, 1995, p. 68).

[22] An allusion to the CODESA negotiations that had led to democracy.

It was indeed a revolutionary institutional concept. South Africa was the first country either to moot or establish a structure specifically dedicated to the funding, oversight and implementation of UAS. But its genesis is unfortunately unclear.

Stavrou (interview, 17 October 2014) suggests that the notion came from the early work of the CDITP, which, according to him, had mooted a "watchdog" body to protect and ensure UAS for the unconnected majority. If so, it is strange that the possibility of a establishing such a Universal Service Agency had not been floated in the Green Paper (RSA, 2005) or in earlier CDITP or ANC documents.

Rather, it is clear that the idea had been "suggested by Minister Z Pallo Jordan at the sectoral briefing" held two weeks before the Colloquium (DPTB, 1995, p. 21), where the significance of the suggestion was initially missed, and only received perfunctory press coverage (Payne, 1995). Horwitz goes back slightly further, suggesting that the concept of a universal service agency had been pitched to the Minister by Andile Ngcaba in a private meeting (Horwitz, 2001, p. 241). Ngcaba confirms this, although he says, disarmingly, that he does not "want to claim exclusive credit" because there were a number of people involved in a collaborative effort (interview, 28 January 2015).

At the time, there were no precedents. One comment labels the proposed structure as a "unique body", noting that "at the time there was no similar organisation elsewhere" (Stavrou, Whitehead, Wilson, Seloane, & Benjamin, 2001, p. 1). The proposal was likely underpinned by an unspoken concern at the prospect of regulatory capture, a "fear that the future regulator would be captured by white business interests" (Horwitz, 2001, p. 241). Saddled with a hostile, unreformed Department and faced with powerful and vocal business interests, this must have seemed a very real threat to the achieving UAS for the marginalised majority. Irish consultant and ICT4D activist, Seán Ó Siochrú, brought in later to work on issues of UAS (1996), agrees with the creation of a separate UAS entity as an important counterweight to the possibility of regulatory capture and a watering down of the UAS imperative (personal communications, 18 August & 1 September 2014).

The remaining UAS issues seem to have mustered fairly general consensus: the distinct definitions of 'universal access' and 'universal service', the need to impose USOs and to establish a USF (DPTB, 1995, p. 20).

The debate over the universal service agency proposal, however, divided delegates. Opponents of a separate agency labelled it an unnecessary "duplication of functions", which would undermine the work of the regulator and "lead to policy battles between the agency and the regulator". Proponents argued that it would provide "more focused" attention on UAS from a less regulatory perspective and offer a watch-dog and co-ordination rule, including by managing the USF (DPTB, 1995, pp. 21–22). The debate was fierce: "Industry was adamant that it should be part of the regulator… Andile was adamant that the USA should be a separate entity" (Denis Smit, interview, 20 November 2014). The trade union delegates were particularly vocal supporters, arguing the need for a "structural mechanism" to achieve UAS (Willie Currie, interview 18 September 2014). A more careful analysis of the actual Colloquium report (DPTB, 1995, pp. 40–67) suggests, in fact, an emerging consensus favouring a dedicated structure to monitor UAS, but one either housed within or reporting to the regulator.

Consensus on the question of the universal service agency was only reached in the final plenary session, one that accommodated the objections of those who feared duplication and conflict with the regulator:

> Established by the Minister, this universal service agency's objectives would be to keep universal service at the centre of public policy concerns and on the public policy agenda. It would also facilitate community involvement in promotion and delivery of universal service-related matters…
>
> Consensus was also reached on the following structural aspects of the universal service agency:
>
> - the universal service agency should be a free-standing statutory body;
> - the Minister should appoint the director of the universal service agency;
> - the director of the universal service agency should manage a budget funded by Parliament;
> - the director should appoint a small staff to deal with substantive matters of the universal service agency;
> - the universal service agency should share the supporting structure and services of the Regulator, including administration, financial services and information resources;
> - the director and staff of the universal service agency should interact with the Regulator to ensure effective actions with respect to the achievement of universal service. (DPTB, 1995, pp. 87–88)

Surprisingly, the summary of the role, functions and institutional positioning of the proposed agency omits any mention of the role vis-a-vis the USF agreed by the Colloquium. Nonetheless, a number of key issues run through the summary. Firstly, the proposed agency is intended to ensure the primacy of UAS as a policy goal and to monitor government steps towards achieving that goal—a rationale still cited today. Secondly, a close relationship, both politically and organisationally, between the agency and the regulator, is envisaged. This includes the sharing of institutional infrastructure, but also close liaison in respect of licensing and its associated USOs, along with other regulatory interventions, and in respect of information sharing.

Further, there was an underlying assumption, both in the structure of the Colloquium and in the responses of the delegates, that UAS would be provided by Telkom. A specific question focused on this issue, with only one working group suggesting that Telkom's role was "primary but not exclusive" (DPTB, 1995, p. 26). The focus on fixed-line services as the route to universal access and service was not unique to South Africa,[23] but was to remain a policy assumption for a number of years.

The degree of consensus varied in relation to the other three key areas of international telecommunications policy good practice: regulation, competition and privatisation. Regulation produced the greatest degree of consensus that an "independent regulatory authority along the lines of the IBA should be established to regulate all telecommunications-related activities within the sector", to be merged with the IBA in the "medium term" (DPTB, 1995, p. 90). Sufficient consensus also emerged on the inevitability of competition, albeit with a stridently dissenting voice from organised labour, who remained adamantly opposed to any abrogation of Telkom's monopoly. Again with the firm exception of the unions, there was agreement that Telkom be partially privatised, and afforded the protection of a medium-term period of "exclusivity" in order to address UAS issues. The need for black economic empowerment was also discussed and agreed (DPTB, 1995, pp. 88–90).

At the conclusion of the Colloquium, a five-person task team (the so-called Eminent Persons Group, comprising representation from Telkom, labour, various shades of business) was appointed to "advise and oversee" the drafting of both the White Paper and the ensuing legislation in order to ensure that the "policy framework" agreed to by the Colloquium was carried through (DPTB, 1995, p. 92). The central issues on which there was "lack of unanimity"—the question of Telkom's exclusivity, the

[23]The potential role of mobile in respect of UAS only began to dawn on the ITU a few years later (Tim Kelly, interview, 27 October 2014).

introduction of competition, Telkom's role in the provision of UAS, the role of other parastatals—were referred to the Eminent Persons Group for resolution (DPTB, 1995, p. 88). The question of Telkom's privatisation was instead referred to the Minister because of an ongoing, parallel and highly disputatious process around the euphemistically-phrased issue of 'restructuring of state assets'.

The official press release at the end of the Colloquium highlighted, under the slogan "All Shall Call", the commitment to UAS and the creation of a universal service agency and an independent regulator. Areas of disagreement—"Telkom's exclusivity and the introduction of a strategic equity partner" and its privatisation—were downplayed (DPTB, 1995, pp. 96–97). This was met with a surprisingly muted response from a media anxious to see the anticipated legislation and still concerned about Minister Jordan's reported antipathy to competition (Perlman, 1995b).

The policy framework that emerged from the Colloquium is clearly informed and influenced by the precepts of international good practice. But it is equally clearly tailored to deal with the realities of the South African situation. Questions of market structure, sector regulation, the introduction of competition and the possible privatisation of the incumbent—all reflect the issues and questions under consideration at international level, in fora such as the EC, the OECD, the ITU and the WTO. Many of those involved in drafting the Green Paper and in conducting the Colloquium were either directly aware of how the same questions were being conceptualised and addressed internationally, or, like Andile Ngcaba, were themselves directly embedded in that environment.

However, South Africa was not engaged in mere copy and paste policy transfer of the kind that has been criticised in other jurisdictions (Muriu, 2002). President Mandela himself had defended South Africa's reluctance to liberalise—to the ITU itself. Speaking in Geneva in late 1995, he had backed South Africa's reluctance unquestioningly to adopt the telecomms reform agenda, arguing that "telecommunications cannot simply be treated as one commercial sector of the economy, to be left to the forces of the free market" and calling for "global universal service in telephony and global universal access to the information superhighway" (Mandela, 1995).

In part, this was driven a desire to ensure a path to telecommunications reform that was explicitly South African. As Minister Jordan had noted at the Colloquium, the "policy framework we come up with must be distinctly South African, rooted here" (DPTB, 1995, p. 19). Grounding

South Africa's policy framework in *apartheid*'s digital donga, and profiling primarily the need to provide universal access and service, and, to a lesser extent, the need to promote 'black' economic empowerment, gave the policy an inescapable South African flavour. The prioritisation of UAS, and the desire to balance this against the demands from business for advanced telecommunications services and for the rapid introduction of competition and privatisation, show policy learning at play.

The ANC's adoption of UAS as a defence against privatisation and competition has a very different nuance from the response of other countries when faced by pressures from the ITU and the WTO to liberalise their telecommunications sectors. In part, it shows an ANC bounded by its own historical allegiance to the concept of nationalisation of the economy, as well as the ongoing antipathy of its Alliance partners, the SACP and COSATU, to privatisation and competition. But it also appears to reflect a genuine concern that opening up the market to the private sector would undermine the objectives of UAS. Hence, the adoption of the policy trajectory that would later become known as 'managed liberalisation' became the logical compromise outcome.

3.6 Towards a Telecommunications Act

Drafting the White Paper remained a fraught process. Rather than acting as the wise arbiter envisaged, the Eminent Persons Group became yet another negotiating forum, functioning, in the words of Horwitz, "as one more instance wherein the key stakeholder representatives could negotiate on behalf of their constituencies" (2001, p. 250). At the same time, there was considerable external pressure from organised labour in the form of strikes and sit-ins to protest plans for the privatisation and restructuring of Telkom (*Financial Mail*, 1996a; Grawitzky & Soggott, 1995; Sowetan, 1995), while Telkom itself steamed ahead with plans to secure a strategic equity partner (Cavill, 1996).

A second draft of the White Paper was tabled for discussion at the start of a two-day NTF conference in early 1996. No copy of this draft survives, but it appears from press reports (*Financial Mail*, 1996b; Golding-Duffy, 1996) that it was largely the same as the final public version. The canvassing of the NTF plenary is interesting, however, for several reasons. Firstly, it indicates that the ANC remained committed to a consultative approach to policy-making. Secondly, it threw up once more the sharp divisions between organised labour, who again vociferously protested privatisation and the introduction of competition, and the business representatives on the NTF (Sergeant, 1996).

However, creating a space for these tensions to flare up again may in fact have served the Minister well, helping to position the White Paper's phased approach to liberalisation as a middle path. Perhaps most interesting, however, was Minister Jordan's finessing defence of the privatisation of Telkom, which was indicative of the ongoing shifts on the issue of privatisation within the ANC. Opening the conference, he had suggested delegates should "seriously explore if and how competition can enhance the delivery of service" (Leshilo, 1996).

He went on to defend acquiring a strategic equity partner in Telkom, claiming that "equity restructuring is not a euphemism for privatisation" and pointing out that government was simply "contemplating placing only a minority of Telkom on the market". It was a disingenuous piece of linguistic camouflage, essentially arguing that, if privatisation is only partial, it is not really privatisation at all.

The final version of the White Paper launched in early 1996. Its structure follows that of the Green Paper, meaning that universal access and service again enjoys pride of place. Like its predecessor, it contextualises itself against an international telecommunications environment marked by "changes in technology, trade liberalisation and globalisation" and seeks to balance the "provision of basic universal service to disadvantaged rural and urban communities with the delivery of high-level services capable of meeting the needs of a growing South African economy" (RSA, 1996a, Foreword and Section 1.2).

When it came to UAS policy, the White Paper formally adopted the three central policy planks that had emerged from the Mount Grace Colloquium: the establishment of a universal service agency, the creation of a USF and the imposition of USOs upon licensees.

Underpinning the establishment of a universal service agency is the rationale that "classic approaches to managing the implementation of telecommunications policy would not be sufficient to keep the focus on the goal of universal service long enough to redress the existing imbalances" (RSA, 1996a, Section 1.13). Interestingly, the agency is conceived potentially as a temporary institutional arrangement, subject to review, in consultation with stakeholders after five years, with possible absorption into the regulator on the cards (RSA, 1996a, Section 1.24).

Managing concurrent jurisdiction over UAS between the regulator and the agency is flagged as an issue, as the White Paper sets out to define and distinguish the overlapping and complementary roles of the two institutions. Noting the need to "ensure minimum overlap and maximum synergy" between "different but closely linked activities", it recommends housing the two bodies together, sharing "common administrative and financial systems and information infrastructure" (RSA, 1996a, Sections 1.15–1.18). From a legal perspective, the White Paper accords the regulator "sole power of enforcement", while the agency will "operate within the legal and regulatory framework administered by the Regulator and will be accountable to the Regulator in that sense" (RSA, 1996a, Sections 1.16 and 1.18). The role envisaged for the agency is thus more developmental, working with "community-based... [and] development organisations", fulfilling a "promotional and catalytic" role by keeping "universal service at the heart of telecommunications policy" (RSA, 1996a, Sections 1.20 and 1.19). This entails, amongst other things, "building national consensus on the meaning of affordable and accessible universal service", "establishing goals, objectives, timetables, indicators and monitoring mechanisms" and "regular reporting to the Minister" (RSA, 1996a, Section 1.22).

The structural difficulties, however, of having two entities with mandates both overlapping and complementary are not properly solved. The labyrinthine logic of this section of the White Paper suggests some of the difficulties faced by the drafting team in delineating the respective mandates of the two bodies and underpins the "bizarre regulatory space" (Limpitlaw, 2014, p. 5265) that the agency came to occupy.

The USF is also provided for in the White Paper, to be managed by the universal service agency, subject to monitoring by the regulator, and with contributions "defined by legislation and implemented by the regulator" (RSA, 1996a, Section 1.21). The White Paper proposes that these contributions be calculated as a "fixed percentage of [licensees'] revenues" and "levied on all market segments in which there is competition", but only "applicable" once "resale is permitted"—i.e. after 4 years (RSA, 1996a, Section 2.12). Existing market segments with competition—mobile, in particular (with Vodacom and MTN) and VANS—are unaccountably overlooked. The focus of the USF and its associated levy was thus viewed as restricted to fixed-line voice telephony services, rather than encompassing the full range of ICT infrastructure and services as is the norm today.

Support from the USF is envisaged as covering two areas: poor users, paid "directly to existing targeted end-users, subsidising them to promote affordability of telephone take-up and use"; and infrastructure rollout, paid "directly to fund network expansion in areas where there is no infrastructure" (RSA, 1996a, Section 2.12). Subsidies for poor users were only envisaged as kicking in once Telkom began to rebalance its tariffs (in year 4), presumably to offset the resultant increase in the price of local calls—although affordability had clearly already been identified as an obstacle under existing conditions (Morris & Stavrou, 1993).

On USOs, the White Paper accords Telkom the "primary role", notwithstanding the existing community service obligations set out in the licences of Vodacom and MTN. Aiming for a target of 20% teledensity by the year 2000, the White Paper empowers the regulator to "set reasonable targets for annual percentage growth of network penetration", as well as to "set [assisted by the agency this time] specific targets for public telephones depending on geographical area, type of settlement, and so on" (RSA, 1996a, Sections 2.9 & 2.10). The regulator thus plays an important enforcement role in relation to universal access and service goals, targets and obligations (RSA, 1996a, Section 5.9), subject to the co-jurisdictional qualifications outlined above.

On the bigger questions of telecomms reform—regulation, competition and privatisation—the White Paper largely carries through the positions emerging from the Colloquium. On the issue of regulation, however, it comes out unequivocally in favour of an "independent statutory telecommunications regulatory authority", structurally separate from both operators and suppliers, and from government itself, accountable to Parliament via the Minister, subject to the law and to the "general framework of telecommunications policy" as set by the Minister (RSA, 1996a, Sections 5.4 and 5.7). The regulator is envisaged to consist of a full-time five-member collegial council appointed by the Minister on the advice of a "panel" (after public hearings) and funded via a "telecommunications fund" (RSA, 1996a, Section 5.10). It is therefore a structure very much in line with international good practice.

On market structure and the introduction of competition, the White Paper maintains the phased approach to liberalisation that had emanated from the Colloquium. In order to protect Telkom while it addresses the backlogs in fixed voice telephony, the White Paper sets a "period of exclusivity... after which various telecommunications market segments are to be liberalised in a phased process put into motion and overseen by an independent regulator" (RSA, 1996a, Section 2.1). The transport and electricity parastatals, Transtel and Eskom, are to be allowed retain their private networks and to provide "complementarity" by leasing spare capacity to Telkom, but not to provide services to end-users (RSA, 1996a,

Sections 2.16 and 2.17). Despite its tight exclusivity provisions, the White Paper nonetheless looks to the possible licensing of a third mobile operator within two years, subject to a market feasibility study (RSA, 1996a, Section 2.10.4). In essence, therefore, the White Paper reproduces the very gradual introduction of competition that emerged from the Colloquium, over a fixed six-year timetable.

But the White Paper dodges the issue of privatisation, noting the divergent views emerging from the Colloquium, and referring the question to the ongoing process around the 'restructuring of state assets' (RSA, 1996a, Sections 3.1 and 3.2). It does, however, make its envisaged new market structure "largely contingent on the assumption that Telkom will be able to access sufficient capital" (RSA, 1996a, Section 2.2), presumably via some form of strategic equity partnership as previously alluded to by Minister Jordan.

Other issues that feature prominently in the White Paper include black economic empowerment and the regulation of tariffs, again in order to ensure the affordability so necessary to achieve universal access and service.

The White Paper is explicit about the pressures being brought to bear by the international telecommunications regime to accede to policy transfer. It explicitly refers to the "forces at work in the international arena pushing for liberalisation", citing the ITU's rate rebalancing, South Africa's WTO commitments, and technological change, including convergence. It goes on to state that "these global forces cannot be ignored, and this policy must be realistic in accommodating them" (RSA, 1996a, p. 2.4).

Behind the scenes, however, lies rather more direct influence from the international telecommunications regime on the substance of the White Paper. This involved an unreported mission to South Africa in late 1995 by a team of experts from the ITU (UNDP/ITU, 1995), which resulted in a set of recommendations which were fed into the Green and White Paper process.

Interestingly, although the team was able to meet with a number of senior officials and executives, both Telkom and Vodacom refused to co-operate or share any information with the team. Its recommendations were—understandably, considering whence they came—firmly pro-liberalisation and heavily influenced by US models—and make no substantive mention of UAS at all. For instance, the "immediate introduction of competition into the market for national long-distance and international services" and the "break-up of Telkom" into a series of monopoly "local service operators" and one "national and international carrier"—a model very much along the lines of the court-ordered AT&T divestiture in the US—is recommended (UNDP/ITU, 1995, p. 2). The team's report further recommends a US-style federal regulatory structure with "regulatory agencies on both local and national levels" (UNDP/ITU, 1995, p. 2). While the recommendations of the report had no observable influence on either White or Green papers, the work of the mission indicates the desire of the UNDP and the ITU to influence the policy process in South Africa, and a preparedness on the part of the Minister to receive policy advice from the international telecommunications regime.

3.7 From Policy to Legislation

Translating the UAS policies adopted and promulgated as part of the White Paper's overall ICT sector policy framework into the legislation that finally emerged as the 1996 Telecommunications Act proved far more of a rollercoaster ride than any had anticipated. Others have charted the events in great detail (Horwitz, 2001, pp. 258–281). The concern here, however, focuses on issues of specific importance for UAS, and, to a lesser extent, the telecomms reform international good practice within which UAS is contextualised.

3.7.1 The Changing Political Context

The process of drafting the legislation was to be beset by a number of unexpected events affecting both the sector and the South African polity.

The first of these was a cabinet reshuffle by President Mandela in early 1996, shortly after the successful launch of the White Paper, officially occasioned by the resignation of Finance Minister Chris Liebenberg. Minister Pallo Jordan found himself unceremoniously dumped and replaced by former COSATU General Secretary Jay Naidoo, whose own troubled RDP ministry was to be closed down. There has been considerable speculation as to why Jordan was axed. The reshuffle came while Parliament was debating the White Paper, and shortly after a ruckus between Jordan and one of Parliamentary portfolio committees (*Financial Mail*, 1996c)—but these are unlikely on their own to have been the reasons. One usually well-informed newspaper attributed the sacking to a series of political clashes between Jordan, long seen as an independent thinker, and ANC leadership, including spats over language and programming at the public broadcaster, together with a perceived softness towards the unions and a reluctance to accede to shifts in the ANC's position towards privatisation (Davis, 1996). Elsewhere Horwitz and Currie suggest that Jordan's failure to "get the unions on board" with privatisation was likely instrumental (2007, p. 458). Whatever the reason, the sacking of Minister Jordan deprived the White Paper and its carefully crafted consensus of its key champion at a critical juncture.

Shortly afterwards, in an unrelated development, the National Party withdrew from the Government of National Unity (NP, 1996). The withdrawal signalled the end to the spirit of co-operation and compromise with the forces of the old regime, and may have led the ANC to wish to stamp more strongly its own imprint on governance and policy, and thus paved the way for the formulation and implementation of a new, more neoliberal macro-economic strategy (ANC, 1996).

At the same time, South Africa found itself under renewed pressure from the international telecommunications regime to adopt a set of G7 information society principles at the global Information Society and Development (ISAD) conference which it was hosting. Prominent amongst the G7 principles were "promoting dynamic competition", "encouraging private investment" and "providing open access to networks" (Blake, 1996). The conference was marked by tension between developed countries (some of whom threatened a walk-out) and the developing world, which proposed a counter set of principles. In the event neither set was adopted, but the ISAD conference demonstrates the ongoing policy transfer pressure exerted on South Africa (and other developing countries), through a range of fora and structures, to accede to the pillars of global international good practice, along with ongoing resistance from developing countries.

Another contemporaneous event of a very different nature was to have an important effect on trade union opposition to privatisation. This was the launch of the COSATU-affiliated, Telkom-based Communications' Workers Union (CWU). CWU represented a carefully choreographed merger of COSATU's POTWA—a long-standing vocal voice from the left in the policy process—with two smaller racially-based unions, the ('Coloured') Post Office Employees Association (PEASA) and the ('Indian') South African Post Telecommunication Employees Association (SAPTEA) (Shopsteward, 1996). A surprise development at the merger congress was the unexpected unseating of the incumbent POTWA leadership by an internal slate, in a development described by one analyst as a “federal coup” (Lamont, 1996)—all the more surprising, given that positions in merger congresses are usually the result of prior pre-allocated agreement (Shopsteward, 1996), Horwitz suggests that the unseating of the recalcitrant incumbent leadership was a political manoeuvre intended to undercut opposition to the privatisation of Telkom (2001, p. 262). Indeed, the new CWU President was soon soft-pedalling on the question of a strategic equity partner, reportedly saying: “If we agree that bringing in a strategic equity partner is going to be enhancing, then we would have to relook into the whole thing” (Lamont, 1996). Currie and Horwitz were later to allege a corrupt *quid pro quo*, including an SBC-arranged visit to the US and a series of directorships and lucrative contracts in subsequent years (Horwitz & Currie, 2007, p. 458). The upshot left the majority union at Telkom in the hands of a leadership more malleable, more inexperienced and less effectual.

At the same time, the ANC too was moving strongly to the right, marked by the abrupt mid-1996 launch, without any consultation within the ANC or its Alliance partners, let alone any public debate, of a ‘non-negotiable’ economic policy blueprint, ‘Growth, Employment and Redistribution’ (GEAR) (ANC, 1996). Marking a major shift away from both the substance and style of the RDP, the document had been covertly prepared by a hand-picked team led by UCT academic Iraj Abedian and Development Bank economist André Roux, supported by World Bank macroeconomic modeller Richard Ketley (Gumede, 2005, p. 105). In substance, GEAR was remarkably close to a Washington Consensus programme, described by former ANC economist Joel Netshitenzhe as a “structural adjustment policy, self-imposed, to stabilise the macroeconomic situation” and was the outcome of substantial external policy transfer pressure (2005, p. 106). Predictably, GEAR evoked bitter opposition from the ANC’s Alliance partners, COSATU and the SACP, who were privately incensed at both the lack of consultation and its neoliberal content (kaNkosi, 1997). Public condemnation was rather more restrained, as, taken aback by the sudden policy shift, the SACP and COSATU sought to negotiate the moderation of the policy (COSATU, 1996; Marais, 1996).

The adoption of GEAR was significant for the telecommunications policy process in two respects. Firstly, the adoption of a macroeconomic policy framework closely aligned to the Washington consensus created a climate in which both privatisation and competition were not only acceptable but desirable. Secondly, GEAR epitomised top-down, elite policy-making and marked a sharp shift towards an authoritarian approach within the ANC, one often associated with the ascendancy of Thabo Mbeki.

The period was marked by increasingly vocal pro-privatisation pronouncements from ANC leaders. Minister Naidoo had begun to speak more directly of the need to secure strategic equity investment in Telkom (Boyle, 1996; Leney, 1996), stressing again the shortage of the necessary capital to fund UAS rollout (Lunsche, 1996a). But the most forthright statement came from President Mandela, around a mid-year visit to Germany, when he declared that "privatisation is the fundamental policy of the ANC and it will be implemented" (Reuters, 1996).

3.7.2 Enacting the Policy

Drafting a Bill based on the White Paper at first proceeded relatively straightforwardly, despite the firing of Jordan, with incoming Minister Jay Naidoo praising the degree of "consultation" thus far and committing that he would "not divert from the White Paper". He went on to restate the key trade-off that had underpinned both the RDP and the White Paper: "The goal is still to strike a balance between providing services for all and providing a service modern enough to serve the needs of our growing economy" (Volschenk, 1996).

Naidoo released a draft of the Bill just before the ISAD conference, one which closely "reflected the White Paper regarding universal service, phased liberalisation and regulation... [and] provided for the establishment of the SA Telecommunications Regulatory Authority and the Universal Service Agency" (Chalmers, 1996a).

The most prominent feature of the Draft Bill is its very detailed year-by-year liberalisation timetable, protecting Telkom's exclusivity and phasing in competition over the medium term. It contains extensive provisions relating to UAS, listing the need to "promote the universal and affordable provision of telecommunication services" foremost amongst its objectives (DPTB, 1996a, Section 2 (a)). Specific chapters deal with the establishment of a Universal Service Agency (USA) and the establishment and operations of a USF. The USA is conceived as a short-lived entity, to be absorbed into the regulator in the medium term (DPTB, 1996a, Section 65), largely fulfilling an advisory, advocacy role: words and phrases like “promote”, “encourage, facilitate and guide”, “stimulate public awareness”, “conduct research”, “survey and evaluate”, “advise” feature prominently under its functions (DPTB, 1996a, Section 60). Aside from managing the USF, its only substantive function involves undertaking a public consultation leading up to a Ministerial gazette defining ‘universal access’ and ‘universal service’ (DPTB, 1996a, Section 60 (2)).

The Agency itself is to be financed from licence and other fees, paid via the “Telecommunications Fund” previously mentioned, which is also used to finance the regulator (DPTB, 1996a, Section 62 and Chapter XIII).

The Draft Bill establishes a USF—again, strangely only from year four, as per the White Paper—administered by the USA, subject to an annual budget and expended “in accordance with the instructions” of the regulator, which in turn prescribes the contributions to the fund. Disbursements from the fund are exclusively earmarked for “subsidies”, divided in accordance with a “prescribed formula”, between “needy persons” (as determined by the regulator) and Telkom for network rollout in the first six years (DPTB, 1996a, Chapter VIII).

USOs are only specifically provided for in relation to PSTN services, at least until year six, requiring Telkom (or the envisaged second PSTN licensee) to “comply with conditions specified in the licence concerned relating to the extension of its public switched telecommunication network service to areas and communities which are not served or not adequately served by telecommunication services, with a view to the achievement of universal service” (DPTB, 1996a, Section 37 (3)). This requirement is not extended to mobile licensees, although, as noted above, both Vodacom and MTN already had commitments in this regard in their existing licences.

The Draft Bill also provides for the establishment of the South African Telecommunications Regulatory Authority (SATRA), with some entrenched degree of independence, as “independent and separate from the State and the government and its administration” (DPTB, 1996a, Section 5 (3)). The Minister remains, however, the appointing and accounting officer for the regulator, retains the ability to issue “policy directions" and is involved in a number of regulatory processes, notably licensing and the setting of the liberalisation timetable.

Behind the scenes, the Department of State Expenditure had reviewed the Draft Bill and found it wanting on a number of grounds, not all of them strictly financial.[24] A terse memo to Postmaster General Andile Ngcaba objected to the proposed Telecommunications Fund and argued that the Department and its budget be brought under the Public Service Act, with licence fees and USF levies paid through Treasury's National Revenue Fund (DSE, 1996). The memo must have come as a considerable shock to Ngcaba and Naidoo: it struck at some of the fundamental underpinnings of the Draft Bill.

A hastily convened meeting between the Eminent Persons Group and the legislative team agreed a number of far-reaching changes to the Draft Bill. These included rearranging the structural and financial arrangements governing the Department, the regulator, the USA and the IBA, for all of which the Department would now act as an "umbrella structure". The concept of a 'Telecommunications Fund' was to be "dropped", with licence fees and other income to be paid into the National Revenue Fund. Funding for the various entities was to be via normal budgetary allocation, with the USF and the human resource development fund to be "funded by allocations from levies on licensees and donations" (DPTB, 1996b).

It was the next public 14th draft of the Bill that was to provoke a public furore. It contained a further slew of changes instructed by Naidoo and Ngcaba, affecting over 50 clauses—an extraordinary number at such a late stage—ordered and effected within the space of a few days. As rumours began to circulate of these last-minute "secret changes" (Chalmers, 1996b), a number of "furious" industry players (Brummer, 1996) charged the Minster with "destroying the consensus developed by his predecessor" (Lunsche, 1996b), prompting the NTF to call for a meeting with the Minister to "ask for an explanation" (Brummer, 1996).

The extent of the changes was such that Willie Currie, whom Jay Naidoo had retained as special adviser in order to see the legislative process through, felt compelled to resign. In a fax to Minister Naidoo, he stated that "the changes that you have made to the Telecommunications

[24]The memo also queried why a new regulator, separate from the existing IBA, was being created.

Bill have made my position as co-ordinator of the national telecommunications policy process untenable… Accordingly, I have no option but to tender my resignation as your adviser" (Currie, 1996b).

Initially, the Department attempted to downplay the furore, insisting there were "no radical changes", harping on the "inclusive process" and claiming all amendments to the Draft Bill had been "done in full consultation" (Chalmers, 1996b). However, the changes were substantial, and the Eminent Persons Group initially refused to certify them as being in line with the White Paper, although they were later persuaded to toe the line (Brummer, 1996; Horwitz, 2001, p. 265).

Central amongst the changes were those relating to Telkom's exclusivity and the liberalisation schedule (Brummer, 1996; Lunsche, 1996b). The detailed, sliding timetable was now placed at the sole discretion of the Minister, as with a number of clauses protecting Telkom's exclusivity "until after a date to be fixed by the Minister" (DPTB, 1996c). In hindsight, it is difficult to understand why these changes provoked such an uproar, other than mistrust and lack of consultation. The provisions are similar to those contained in the 12th draft other than in providing more flexibility in respect of differing licence categories and in avoiding the previous rather clumsy formulations.

The introduction of greater flexibility and Ministerial discretion were intended to facilitate negotiations with strategic equity investors, and were defended as such by Ngcaba and Naidoo, who did not want their 'hands tied' in negotiations (Brummer, 1996; Horwitz, 2001, p. 265; Lunsche, 1996b).

The other major area of changes substantially reduced the independence of the regulator. Its explicit independence as an entity separate from government was substantially watered down, so that it was only required to be "impartial" and "autonomous" (DPTB, 1996c, Section 5 (3)). The Minister was to become far more involved in the substance of regulation (*Financial Mail*, 1996d) and empowered to issue regulations "on the recommendation of or after consultation with the Authority" (DPTB, 1996c, Section 96 (1)), and to be directly involved in public notice and comment procedures.

Ngcaba defended the changes, saying "We merely said Satra's regulations should be published by the minister" (Lunsche, 1996b). Some of these changes would have been occasioned by the memo from the Department of State Expenditure referred to above, but Horwitz suggests they were also prompted by the Minister's disquiet at his own lack of control over the substance of regulation, and a change of heart from Postmaster General Ngcaba now that he was at the helm of the Department and potentially able to control the direction of regulatory intervention (Horwitz, 2001, p. 266).

UAS was less substantially affected by the changes in the 14th draft of the Bill, albeit impacted by the same Ministerial arrogation of what had been regulatory functions. The USF was to become fully self-standing. Contributions to the fund, including the "basis and manner of determination of such contributions", as well as their effective date, were to become the prerogative of the Minister rather than that of the regulator (DPTB, 1996c, Section 67), as was the prerogative to prescribe the payment of subsidies to 'needy persons' (DPTB, 1996c, Section 66 (4)).

The Draft Bill finally went to Parliament in late 1996, amidst a welter of stakeholder submissions and a flurry of public hearings, and under pressure from the ANC to have it enacted before Parliament went into recess in November. The process was accompanied by acrimony and distrust, the scars of which were to be felt in the sector for years to come (West, 1996), and the Bill was adopted with only a few amendments.

There was, for example, some softening on the appointments process for the Council of SATRA, who were now to be "appointed by the President on the advice of the Parliamentary committees on communications" (RSA, 1996b, Section 9 (1))—providing for a greater degree of independence, and essentially a mirror image of the appointments process for the IBA Council.

In respect of UAS, the changes were minimal. For example, USOs remained applicable only to PSTS licensees (RSA, 1996b, Section 36 (2)). The provisions governing the establishment of the USA, along with its role, functions and envisaged life-span, remained unchanged (RSA, 1996b, Chapter VII). The provisions in respect of the USF too were largely unchanged, although the flow of USF funding received greater clarity, with licensee contributions paid into the National Revenue Fund and appropriated into the USF by Parliament (RSA, 1996b, Section 65 (2) & (3)). The attempt in the 14th draft of the Bill to ring-fence the contributions (DPTB, 1996c, Section 67 (3)) was dropped, having been contrary to Department of State Expenditure rules.[25] The determination of the universal service levy, which remained applicable to all licensees,

[25] Provisions that were effectively later to hamstring the USA in accessing the funds theoretically at its disposal.

now reverted to the regulator, with only the inception date (no longer fixed in year 4) remaining in the hands of the Minister (RSA, 1996b, Section 67). The USF was to remain a source of subsidies for network extension and for 'needy persons', with the responsibility for defining the latter now also reverting to the regulator (RSA, 1996b, Section 66 (4)).

The UAS provisions of the final Bill thus remained largely those of international good practice, with South Africa's major innovation being the creation of the Universal Service Agency, a world first. Other countries were to follow suit to some degree. Guatemala (1996), France (1997) and the USA (1997) were amongst the first to put their USFs under independent control (ITU, 2013, pp. 90, 106 & 111), but this was almost entirely for accountability's sake, without any of the advocacy and quasi-regulatory functions assigned to the USA. The imposition of USOs on the fixed-line operator was in accordance with existing international good practice, albeit that the legislators did not recognise that such USOs had already been extended *de facto* to the mobile operators as per their licences issued in 1993. The creation of the USF, its source of funding, and its envisaged areas of expenditure were likewise in accordance with international good practice.

3.8 Conclusion

The process of adopting, adapting and implementing international telecomms reform good practice in South Africa, and its UAS precepts in particular, is characterised by several key features.

The first of these is the primacy of UAS within the process of telecomms reform. From the outset, the ANC was preoccupied with addressing the legacy that *apartheid's* telecommunications deprivation had inflicted upon the country's 'black' majority, with healing its 'digital *donga*'. No analysis of the sector could fail to chart the country's starkly racialised gap in access to telecommunications services that had been created by the legacy of *apartheid*. As a result, UAS became a fully legitimated, central *raison d'être* for ICT sector policy implementation.

The second major feature of the period is a partially unresolved question, namely the extent to which policy diffusion took place. There was certainly a degree of unacknowledged policy emulation in the early reform forays of the *apartheid* government as it neared the end of its lifespan. The uniquely embedded position of the ANC's head of ICT policy, Andile

Ngcaba, within the global ICT policy regime and its epistemic community, meant that any policy reforms were consciously framed in relation to global telecomms reform good practice, thereby ensuring a degree of policy diffusion.

But, equally, the ANC sought a model of telecomms reform that tailored to the country-specific circumstances of South Africa. There was thus a substantial degree of policy learning as Ngcaba and his cohorts sought to adapt the precepts of reform in order to address the imperatives of UAS. Their fixation, however, on fixed-line service as the path to UAS—ironically just as mobile was beginning to change the nature of the game—was to result in a blinkered approach to UAS. As a result, sector reform in South Africa embraced the protection of Telkom's state-owned exclusivity, and ended up sheltering behind the same monopoly fig leaf that the proponents of telecomms reform had attacked internationally.

The course of reform in South Africa was also marked by substantive shifts in the policy and culture of the ANC, as the organisation shifted its position from the radicalism of liberation politics to the embrace of neoliberal, Washington Consensus positions, and from the participatory culture of the mass democratic movement to the top-down neo-authoritarianism of a political bureaucracy.

It is indeed ironic that ANC ended up embracing the very privatisation paradigm (albeit under the euphemistic rubric of 'strategic equity partnership') that they had attacked so vociferously when it came from the hand of the National Party government. Some of that is accounted for by an ideological shift within the ANC, but it is also due to the ANC becoming protagonists within the structures of governance: reform looks very different from within the confines of a civil service office than it does from behind protesting placards in the streets below.

By the end of 1996, however, a new Telecommunications Act was in place. It represented the stamp of the new, democratically elected ANC government upon the face of the ICT sector, and was to govern the sector for the next ten years. It had been the outcome of a uniquely participatory process, albeit one that had its limitations, and one that had become beset by controversy and contestation towards its end.

But the Act was nonetheless a piece of legislation that embodied many of the major components of the global telecommunications regime. It created an independent regulator. It embodied a structured transition towards a competitive ICT market structure, albeit a very tightly managed one. And, importantly, it contained extensive provisions intended to ensure universal access and service.

If the provision of universal, affordable access to telecommunications services was the heartbeat of ICT sector reform in South Africa and the primary objective of the new Act, then its cardiograph must surely be taken by monitoring the performance of the various initiatives and interventions it set in motion.

The 1993 licences of Vodacom and MTN had decreed both network rollout requirements and a series of community service obligation commitments. Telkom had been committed to extending its network and services to areas and communities that were either unserved or under-served. A Universal Service Agency had been created to champion and oversee progress towards universal access. A Universal Service Fund had been established, funded through contributions from licensees and designed to underwrite the extension of the network and to assist needy persons to gain access to telecommunications service. And, some years later, a cluster of small-scale, rural telecommunications licences were to be issued to provide services in areas with minimal access to Telkom's network.

Important lessons are to be learned from those initiatives and their outcomes, from their relative success and failure. How these UAS interventions played themselves out is the subject of the next four chapters.

References

Akhtar, S. (1995, January 10). *Fax to Willie Currie*. Ottawa: International Development Research Centre.

Akhtar, S., Melody, W., & Naidoo, D. (1994). *National Information Project South Africa*. Ottawa: International Development Research Centre. Retrieved from https://idl-bnc.idrc.ca/dspace/bitstream/10625/16597/1/101313.pdf.

ANC. (1992). *Ready to govern: ANC policy guidelines for a democratic South Africa*. Johannesburg: African National Congress. Retrieved from http://www.anc.org.za/show.php?id=227.

ANC. (1993, Third Quarter). Reconstruction and development programme (Fourth Draft). *African Communist*, pp. 15–29.

ANC. (1994a). *The ANC policy for equity and efficiency in the telecommunications sector*. Johannesburg: African National Congress.

ANC. (1994b). *The reconstruction and development programme: A policy framework*. Johannesburg: African National Congress.

ANC. (1996). *Growth, employment and redistribution—A macroeconomic strategy*. Pretoria: Department of Finance, Republic of South Africa. Retrieved from http://www.treasury.gov.za/publications/other/gear/chapters.pdf.

Anonymous. (1995, May 11). Strictly confidential.

Bidoli, M. (1993a, April 2). Telecommunications: Scrambling for cellular licences. *Financial Mail.*

Bidoli, M. (1993b, April 16). Telecommunications: Squeezing the cellular-phone industry. *Financial Mail.*

Blake, E. (1996, November 27). *Information society and development conference—What was and is happening?* Cape Town: Department of Computer Science, University of Cape Town. Retrieved from http://people.cs.uct.ac.za/~edwin/OldWeb/isad-pm/isad-pm.html.

Boyle, B. (1996, August 25). Telkom sets privatisation date. *Business Time.*

Brummer, S. (1996, June 28). Naidoo caught in Telkom controversy. *Mail & Guardian.*

Bulger, P. (1993, September 22). ANC-linked Thebe in group calling for rethink on cellular phones. *Business Day.*

Business Day. (1991, November 7). Conference remarks not by ANC's Ngcaba. *Business Day.*

Business Day. (1992, November 19). 'Strong feelings' on telecommunications. *Business Day.*

Business Report. (1993, February 15). Telecommunications shake-up. *Business Report.*

Cape Times. (1993a, September 15). Deadlock over cellular phone licences. *Cape Times.*

Cape Times. (1993b, October 23). ANC, govt settle cellular phone row. *Cape Times.*

Cape Times. (1995, May 16). Communications team named.

Cavill, J. (1996, January 12). US bank to find Telkom partner. *Business Day.*

CDITP. (1995). *CDITP—The Centre for the Development of Information and Telecommunication Policy: A summary of activities.* Johannesburg: Centre for the Development of Information and Telecommunication Policy.

Chalmers, R. (1993, December 1). Phones' countertrade bonus. *Business Day.*

Chalmers, R. (1996a, May 8). Jay Naidoo sets his sights on shake-up. *Business Day.*

Chalmers, R. (1996b, June 20). Cabinet approves draft telecommunications bill. *Business Day.*

Chester, M. (1993, June 25). On a hot line to controversy. *The Star.*

CODESA. (1992). *Working documents for CODESA 2, 15 & 16 May 1992:* (Vol. 1). Johannesburg: Convention for a Democratic South Africa.

Coopers & Lybrand. (1992). *Telecommunications sector strategy study for the Department of Posts and Telecommunications.* Pretoria: Department of Posts and Telecommunications.

COSATU. (1996, July 22). *Decisions of COSATU executive*. Johannesburg: Congress of South African Trade Unions. Retrieved from http://www.cosatu.org.za/show.php?ID=694.

Currie, W. (1994, December 14). *Towards a public process for formulating telecommunications policy and regulation.*

Currie, W. (1995, February 1995). *South Africans for technical study team.*

Currie, W. (1996a). *A rough guide to the national telecommunications policy process.*

Currie, W. (1996b, June 24). *Fax to Jay Naidoo.*

Davis, G. (1996, March 4). Crossing Madiba cost Jordan his job. *Mail & Guardian.*

de Villiers, W. (1989). *Summarised report on the study by Dr. W. J. De Villiers concerning the strategy, policy, control structure and organisation of posts and telecommunications.* Pretoria: Department of Posts and Telecommunications.

Dison, D., & Markovitz, M. (1995, August 4). Telkom's solution lies in regulated competition. *Business Day.*

DPT. (1993, October 29). Issue of licences to provide national cellular telecommunication services. *Government Gazette.*

DPTB. (1995). *Report on the proceedings of the National Colloquium on Telecommunications Policy, Mount Grace Hotel, Magaliesburg, 20–23 November 1995* (M. Andersson, Ed.). Pretoria: Department of Posts, Telecommunications & Broadcasting.

DPTB. (1996a, May 3). *Telecommunications bill.* Pretoria: Department of Posts, Telecommunications and Broadcasting.

DPTB. (1996b, May 27). *Points discussed at the EPG/legislative team meeting on the department of state expenditure's response to the draft telecommunications bill.* Pretoria.

DPTB. (1996c, June 5). *Telecommunications bill.* Pretoria: Department of Posts, Telecommunications and Broadcasting.

DSE. (1996, May 20). *Draft telecommunications bill.* Pretoria: Department of State Expenditure.

Fine, B. (1995). Privatisation and the RDP: A critical assessment. *Transformation* (27), 1–23.

Financial Mail. (1983, April 29). Future office shapes up. *Financial Mail.*

Financial Mail. (1989, March 24). De Villiers report: More bad points than good. *Financial Mail.*

Financial Mail. (1990, August 24). Post office: Testing time. *Financial Mail.*

Financial Mail. (1991, March 29). Post office: The commercialisation battle. *Financial Mail.*

Financial Mail. (1993a, August 6). Telecommunications: Hot-wire policy. *Financial Mail.*

Financial Mail. (1993b, October 29). *Cellular phones: Dividing the spoils.*

Financial Mail. (1993c, November 26). Cellular telephones: Free to shop around. *Financial Mail.*

Financial Mail. (1995a, March 31). Telkom: Strangled by red tape. *Financial Mail.*

Financial Mail. (1995b, July 14). Telecommunications policy: Green Paper, but pallid prospects. *Financial Mail.*

Financial Mail. (1995c, August 25). Telkom: Global pressures force change. *Financial Mail.*

Financial Mail. (1995d, August 25). MinZPallo on the rack. *Financial Mail.*

Financial Mail. (1996a, January 19). Telkom: Fear of the unknown. *Financial Mail.*

Financial Mail. (1996b, February 16). Telkom: Plugging into a faulty switchboard. *Financial Mail.*

Financial Mail. (1996c, March 22). Pallo blots his own White Paper. *Financial Mail.*

Financial Mail. (1996d, July 5). Protecting a monopoly compounds the problem. *Financial Mail.*

Franks, C. (2006). Green Paper. *The Canadian Encyclopedia.* Toronto: Historica Canada. Retrieved from http://www.thecanadianencyclopedia.com/en/article/green-paper/.

Gillwald, A. (2002). Experimenting with institutional arrangements for communications policy and regulation: The case of telecommunications and broadcasting in South Africa. *Southern African Journal of Information and Communication, 2*(1).

Golding-Duffy, J. (1996, February 9). Telkom's gargantuan task. *Mail & Guardian.*

Grawitzky, R., & Soggott, M. (1995, December 21). Telkom bears brunt of stoppages to protest against privatisation. *Business Day.*

Gumede, W. (2005). *Thabo Mbeki and the battle for the soul of the ANC.* Cape Town: Struik.

Habib, A. (1997). From pluralism to corporatism: South Africa's labour relations in transition. *Politikon: South African Journal of Political Studies, 24*(1), 57–75. https://doi.org/10.1080/02589349708705041.

Harfoush, N., & Wild, K. (1994). *National information management project, South Africa.* Ottawa: International Development Research Centre. Retrieved from http://www.africa.upenn.edu/Articles_Gen/nim_anc.html.

Herbert, R. (1995, July 10). Competition will succeed where Telkom falls down. *Cape Times.*

Horwitz, R. (2001). *Communication and democratic reform in South Africa.* Cambridge: Cambridge University Press.

Horwitz, R., & Currie, W. (2007). Another instance where privatization trumped liberalization: The politics of telecommunications reform in South Africa—A ten-year retrospective. *Telecommunications Policy* (31), 445–462.

ICASA. (2004, December 9). Licence to provide a national mobile cellular telecommunication service, Issued to Mobile Telephone Networks (Pty) Ltd in terms of Section 37(1), and as amended in terms of Section 48 of the Telecommunications Act, No 103 of 1996. *Government Gazette, 474*(27088).

IOL. (2000, July 16). Nail hangs on MTN prospects. *Independent Online*. Retrieved from https://www.iol.co.za/business-report/companies/nail-hangs-on-mtn-prospects-795028.

ITU. (1998). *World telecommunication development report 1998: Universal access.* Geneva: International Telecommunication Union. Retrieved from http://www.itu.int/ITU-D/ict/publications/wtdr_98/.

ITU. (2013). *Universal service funds and digital inclusion for all.* Geneva: International Telecommunication Union. Retrieved from http://www.itu.int/en/ITU-D/Regulatory-Market/Documents/USF_final-en.pdf.

Johannes, G., & du Plessis, W. (1995, August 14). For whom the bell rings. *The Argus.*

kaNkosi, S. (1997, September 19). Solidarity in opposition to Gear. *Mail & Guardian*. Retrieved from http://madiba.mg.co.za/article/1997-09-19-solidarity-in-opposition-to-gear.

Kaplan, D. (1990). *The crossed line: The South African telecommunications industry in transition*. Johannesburg: Witwatersrand University Press.

Khumalo, F. (2001). National telecommunications forum. In T. James (Ed.), *An information policy handbook for Southern Africa—A knowledge base for decision-makers* (p. 184). Ottawa: International Development Research Centre.

Knott-Craig, A., & Afonso, E. (2009). *Second is nothing: Creating a multi-billion rand cellular industry.* Johannesburg: Pan Macmillan.

Lambert, L. (1990, May 18). Bill recommends that P & T be split in two. *Business Day.*

Lamont, J. (1996, June 7). Union may accept Telkom sale. *Business Report.*

Leney, F. (1996, May 8). Naidoo seeks urgent sale of Telkom stake. *Business Report.*

Leshilo, T. (1996, February 6). Jordan insists on selling part of Telkom. *Business Report.*

Limpitlaw, J. (2014). South Africa. In C. Long & P. Brisby (Eds.), *Global telecommunications law and practice.* London: Sweet & Maxwell.

Lodge, T. (1999). Policy processes within the African National Congress and the Tripartite Alliance. *Politikon: South African Journal of Political Studies, 26*(1), 5–32. https://doi.org/10.1080/02589349908705068.

Lunsche, S. (1995, July 9). Jordan hangs up the phone on Telkom's foreign callers. *Sunday Times.*

Lunsche, S. (1996a, June 2). Telkom's grand RDP plans hit by shortage of cash. *Business Times.*

Lunsche, S. (1996b, June 23). Cabinet backs Naidoo's stance. *Business Times.*

Makhanya, M. (1993, September 17). Playing broken telephones. *Weekly Mail.*

Mandela, N. (1995). Address by President Nelson Mandela at the opening ceremony of Telecom 95, the 7th World Telecommunications Forum and Exhibition. *Telecom 95, the 7th World Telecommunications Forum and Exhibition.* Geneva: International Telecommunication Union. Retrieved from http://v1.sahistory.org.za/pages/people/special%20projects/mandela/speeches/1990s/1995/1995_opening_telecom95_WTFE.htm.

Maphunye, K. (2002). The features of South Africa's post-1994 civil service and the challenges it faces in the new dispensation. *African Administrative Studies, 58*, 1–9.

Marais, H. (1996, Third Quarter). All GEARed up. *African Communist, 145.* Retrieved from http://www.sacp.org.za/main.php?ID=2375#STORY6.

Morris, M., & Stavrou, S. (1993, September/October). Telecommunication needs and provision to underdeveloped black areas in South Africa. *Telecommunications Policy*, 529–539.

Msimang, M. (2006). Universal service and universal access. In L. Thornton, Y. Carrim, P. Mtshaulana, & P. Reyburn (Eds.), *Telecommunications law in South Africa.* Johannesburg: STE Publishers. Retrieved from http://www.wits.ac.za/files/buads_542496001393429228.pdf.

Muriu, D. (2002). Paying lip-service to the principles of regulation: A comparative critique of Kenya's telecommunications law. *Journal of African Law, 46*(1), 14–30.

Naidoo, J. (1993, August 31). Cellular telephone proposals ring impractical. *Business Day.*

Naidoo, J. (2010). *Fighting for justice: A lifetime of political and social activism.* Johannesburg: Picador Africa.

Ngcaba, A. (1993, September 17–23). Hah! government caught in the Act! *Weekly Mail.*

Ngcaba, A. (2001, February 2). *Speech by the director general of communications, Andile Ngcaba, at the telecommunications colloquium.* Retrieved from http://www.polity.org.za/polity/govdocs/speeches/2001/sp0204.html.

NP. (1996, May 9). *Statement by Mr. F. W. De Klerk, leader of the National Party.* Retrieved from https://www.nelsonmandela.org/omalley/index.php/site/q/03lv02039/04lv02046/05lv02047/06lv02049/07lv02064.htm.

Ó Siochrú, S. (1996). *Telecommunications and universal service: International experience in the context of South African policy reform*. Ottawa: International Development Research Centre. Retrieved from http://web.idrc.ca/openebooks/321-6/.

Ofir, Z. (2003). *Information & Communication Technologies for Development (Acacia): The case of South Africa*. Johannesburg: Evalnet.

Payne, B. (1995, November 8). Telkom's privatisation gets a nod. *Business Day*.

Perlman, L. (1995a, October 20). Strategies shift in telecom arena. *Mail & Guardian*.

Perlman, L. (1995b, December 1). 'All shall call' is the message for SA. *Mail & Guardian*.

Ramaphosa, C. (1993, October 27). Mixed economy the right solution for telecommunications. *Business Day*.

Reuters. (1996, June 12). *South Africa accelerates privatisation moves*. Cape Town. Retrieved from http://www.hartford-hwp.com/archives/37a/068.html.

Rohan, R. (1995, July 9). Let SA Ring! Jordan's phone call just needs unscrambling .... *City Press*.

RSA. (1987). *White Paper on privatisation and deregulation in the Republic of South Africa*. Pretoria: Republic of South Africa.

RSA. (1991, June 19). Post Office Amendment Act, 1991. *Government Gazette, 312*(13310).

RSA. (1993). *Constitution of the Republic of South Africa, Act 200 of 1993*. Pretoria: Republic of South Africa.

RSA. (1995). *Telecommunications Green Paper*. Pretoria: Ministry of Posts, Telecommunications and Broadcasting. Retrieved from http://www.polity.org.za/html/govdocs/green_papers/telecomms.html.

RSA. (1996a). *White Paper on telecommunications policy*. Pretoria: Ministry for Posts, Telecommunications and Broadcasting.

RSA. (1996b). *Telecommunications Act, 1996* [*No. 103 of 1996*]. Pretoria: Republic of South Africa.

RSA. (2005). *Electronic Communications Act* [*No. 36 of 2005*]. Pretoria: Republic of South Africa.

Sergeant, M. (1992, November 5). Rejection of report on telecommunications. *Business Day*.

Sergeant, M. (1993a, February 26). ANC slates decision on cellular phones. *Business Day*.

Sergeant, M. (1993b, April 5). Govt fees threaten cellular networks. *Business Day*.

Sergeant, M. (1993c, April 13). Govt resolute on cellular phone plans. *Business Day*.

Sergeant, M. (1993d, May 6). Information technology: Telkom picks UK cellular phone firm. *Business Day*.

Sergeant, M. (1993e, June 10). ANC to act on 'corrupt' telephone deregulation. *Business Day*.

Sergeant, M. (1993f, June 16). Cellular phone tender row grows. *Business Day*.

Sergeant, M. (1993g, July 8). US bid to delay tenders for cellular network fails. *Business Day*.

Sergeant, M. (1993h, September 23). Defiant government issues cellular phone licences. *Business Day*.

Sergeant, M. (1996, February 7). Labour and business clash over telecommunications strategy. *Business Day*.

Shopsteward. (1996, June/July). New union to tackle restructuring. *The Shopsteward*, *5*(3). Retrieved from http://www.cosatu.org.za/show.php?ID=2080#SECTOR3.

Snyman, J. (1998). *Voice network management from a business perspective*. Johannesburg: Rand Afrikaans University. Retrieved from https://ujdigispace.uj.ac.za/bitstream/handle/10210/6371/J.J.%20SNYMAN_1998_MA.pdf.

Song, S., & Akhtar, S. (1995). Communication for reconstruction and development: The information highway as basic infrastructure in the New South Africa. *Information Technology for Development* (6), 53–65.

Sowetan. (1993, August 12). ANC at odds with network operators. *Sowetan*.

Sowetan. (1995, December 15). 50 POTWA members stage a sit-in. *Sowetan*.

Sparks, A. (1994). *Tomorrow is another country*. Struik.

Stavrou, A., Whitehead, A., Wilson, M., Seloane, M., & Benjamin, P. (2001). *Presentation notes: Of recommendations on the future of the Universal Service Agency*. Pretoria: Universal Service Agency—Conference Convening Committee.

The Star. (1993, June 25). On a hot line to controversy. *The Star*.

UNDP/ITU. (1995). *Sector study: Telecommunications and broadcasting in South Africa*. New York & Geneva: United Nations Development Programme & International Telecommunication Union.

Volschenk, C. (1996, April 12). It's business as usual says Naidoo. *Business Report*.

von Holdt, K. (2004, December). Towards transforming SA industry: A 'reconstruction accord' between unions and the ANC? *South African Labour Bulletin*, *28*(6).

West, E. (1996, October 15). Too little time to study bill—Claim. *Business Day*.

CHAPTER 4

Universal Service Obligations

Imposing universal service obligations (USOs) on licensees is standard international good regulatory practice (infoDev, 2009, p. 37; Intven, 2000, pp. 6–19; Maddens, 2009, p. 6), either as a trade-off for a period of exclusivity (possibly combined with privatisation) or as a *quid quo pro* when a new licence is awarded under competition.

In either case, such obligations may include: extension of the network; the installation of payphones or telecentres; and the provision of services to targeted groups of customers. Exclusivity offers protection from competitive market dynamics and allows cross-subsidisation from lucrative market segments to non-profitable ones. When privatisation or competition is involved, USOs prevent operators from 'cherry-picking'—the practice of focusing narrowly on lower-cost, higher-revenue segments of the market.

In South Africa, all of these dynamics were at play. The discretionary period of exclusivity afforded to Telkom was designed to allow the company to rebalance its tariffs—and to roll out connectivity and services to those areas and customers historically ignored under *apartheid*. In the years leading up to the 1996 Telecommunications Act, Telkom had already unveiled a number of ambitious plans to do just that. These included the 1995 'Megaline tender' to roll out "1-million new phone lines covering vast tracts of… rural areas where phone density is below 5%" (*Business Day*, 1995), which then evolved into a far more comprehensive Vision 2000 network expansion project, which in turn envisaged both

C. Lewis, *Regulating Telecommunications in South Africa*,
Information Technology and Global Governance,
https://doi.org/10.1007/978-3-030-43527-1_4

replacing one million "obsolete lines" and adding two million new lines in "rural and urban underserved areas", along with digitising all exchanges (*Financial Mail*, 1995). Neither project was ever finalised.

Both may indeed have been kite-flying. They did, however, demonstrate the need for an equity injection to fund such an ambitious universal service rollout, estimated to cost between R16 and R30 billion (USD 2.5 - 4 billion) (Horwitz, 1999, p. 233). Such areas, where the cost of extending the network was high, and where the likely returns on investment from call traffic were low, would be a very unattractive to a foreign investor seeking a high return on capital.

Equally, in the mobile sector, which had been envisaged as a luxury service with a limited subscriber uptake, USOs were also a reasonable *quid pro quo* for allowing the new licensees to focus on areas already served by Telkom and to target a customer base at the upper end of the income spectrum.

The attention of the policy-makers, however, remained on Telkom and on a fixed-line approach to addressing the access gap, with the Act imposing USOs only on PSTS licensees (i.e. Telkom, in the short to medium term), each of which would be required to

> comply with conditions specified in the licence in question relating to the extension of its public switched telecommunication service to areas and communities which are not served or not adequately served by telecommunication services, with a view to the achievement of universal service. (RSA, 1996, Section 36 (2))

The Act makes no corresponding USO provision for mobile services, nor indeed for any other of the six licence categories. The oversight in respect of mobile is surprising in view of the mooted introduction of one or more additional competitors in this sub-sector, and given that Vodacom and MTN already had coverage and community service telephone obligations in their licences.[1] But what it does again suggest is that government's approach to UAS was largely limited to fixed-line telephony, with mobile seen as a luxury service having a small potential market and negligible universal access role.

[1] The omission did have the unintended effect of leaving the USOs in the existing mobile licences without formal legal backing.

The USOs were to be specified in the licence (as in the case of Vodacom and MTN) rather than by regulation, in accordance with general practice at the time,[2] as codified a few years later (Intven, 2000, pp. 6–11). However, because a licence is a long-term (typically in the order of 25 years) legal contract, subject only to negotiated changes, this provides very limited scope for the regulator to adjust USOs in accordance with changing circumstances and market trends. In the case of the mobile licensees, this was to hamstring the regulator, which was largely locked into the limited original USOs specified in their licences, even as the uptake of their services burgeoned and overtook Telkom's customer base.[3]

4.1 Telkom's Targets

The fixed-line services of Telkom were, as we have seen, the focus for achieving universal access and service. The company had originally envisaged an "ambitious network expansion and modernisation programme" which aimed at installing 3 million lines, 2 million of them in "underserviced areas" (Telkom, 1996, p. 21). But there seems to have been considerable back-pedalling on these ambitious targets. By the time the draft licence was published for public comment in early 1997, it provided for a "much more modest 1.8 million lines in five years" (Horwitz, 2001, p. 277). This was likely due to pressure from potential strategic equity partnership bidders seeking to trade off USOs against the price of their stake (Lunsche, 1997).

By the time the strategic equity partnership agreement was concluded with the preferred bidders, SBC and Telekom Malaysia,[4] the USO targets had been pushed back upwards again. The R5.5 billion agreement[5] now

[2] The introduction of licensing in telecommunications was a relatively recent phenomenon in most jurisdictions, usually consequent on the introduction of sector reform, often in the absence of, or along with the creation of, a sector regulator.

[3] ICASA appears also to have been constrained by its own lack of vision in respect of USOs.

[4] Of the other potential bidders, Deutsche Telekom did not submit a final bid, and France Telecom was excluded from the final negotiations (Argus, 1997).

[5] This is close to initial estimates, suggesting no significant discount in return for more aggressive rollout targets.

provided for 2.8 million new lines, 120,000 payphones and the digitisation of 1.25 million analogue lines (Chalmers, 1997). Minister Naidoo reportedly described the rollout plan as follows:

> priority areas would be underserviced provinces, with KwaZulu-Natal and the Eastern Cape receiving more than half the new lines in the first year. Northern Province would see the greatest increase in telephone density over five years. Other priority customers were educational and medical establishments, libraries, local authorities and 3 200 villages. (Chalmers, 1997)

Telkom's final licence was issued by the Minister in May 1997 (DoC, 1997)[6] and sets down rollout targets very close to the numbers reported by Chalmers. Telkom's USOs were listed in great detail, taking up just over half of the licence's 126 pages.[7]

The licence specified a total USO of 2.69 million new lines over the five-year period of guaranteed exclusivity, of which somewhat under two-thirds were required to be in "under-serviced areas", as well as 120,000 payphones. Included in the line rollout totals were a number of "priority customers", mostly schools,[8] and just over 3200 villages (DoC, 1997, p. Schedule A) (see Table 4.1).

Thankfully, the list of the schools, hospitals, libraries, local authorities and villages to be covered was not included.

With the important exception of its payphone targets, Telkom's obligations (see Table 4.1) were essentially aimed at boosting universal service (telephony to the household) rather than universal access (shared or public access). Further, the model is essentially a market-orientated one: although subsidies are not specifically excluded, the approach assumes pent-up demand would be sufficient to sustain uptake at market prices.

[6] The Department of Posts, Telecommunications and Broadcasting had been renamed the Department of Communications earlier that year.

[7] The Act, you may recall, only specified USOs in respect of a PSTS licence.

[8] 19,270 schools to be precise, plus 627 hospitals, 268 libraries and 81 local authorities (DoC, 1997, p. Schedule D).

Table 4.1 Telkom's rollout targets

Category	*1997/1998*	*1998/1999*	*1999/2000*	*2000/2001*	*2001/2002*	*Total*
1. New lines (excl payphones) 'Total line target'	340,000	435,000	575,000	675,000	665,000	2,690,000
2. Sub-target: New lines in under-serviced areas 'Under-serviced line target'	265,000	318,000	359,000	357,000	378,000	1,676,000[a]
3. Sub-target: New lines for priority customers 'Priority customer target'	3240	3845	4055	5060	4046	20,246
4. Sub-target: No of villages in under-serviced areas 'Village target'	510	610	640	800	644	3204
5. Additional target: No of public payphones 'Public payphone target'	20,000	25,000	25,000	25,000	25,000	120,000
6. Additional target: No of replacement lines 'Replacement line target'	20,000	13,000	65,000	551,000	603,000	1,252,000

[a]There is an error of arithmetic in the original licence. The correct total is 1,677,000

4.2 Mobile Coverage and Community Service

The USOs imposed on the mobile licensees, paradoxically, constituted far more of a universal access approach. Originating from the furore surrounding the tender and the award of the licences (see Chapter 3), they comprised two aspects, namely geographic coverage and community service obligations.

The first of these, the geographic rollout obligations, were specified in a "Network Implementation Timetable" which was attached to the Multiparty Implementation Agreement between the National Party government and the ANC (RSA, 1993, p. 32) that had allowed the licensing of Vodacom and MTN to proceed.

Overall, this specified that 60% of the country's population should have coverage at a specified minimum signal strength within 2 years, increasing to 70% by the end of four years (RSA, 1993, p. 11). Additional, detailed, licensee-specific network implementation timetables were also imposed.

For Vodacom, this required coverage of the major urban centres of "Johannesburg, Pretoria, Durban and Cape Town core areas" at commercial launch (ICASA, 2002b, pp. 36ff.),[9] along with a further 19 localities, where coverage was defined by radius (20 km or 40 km) and signal strength (between 2 and 8 watts). Within 5 months, this had to be extended to the "Greater PWV[10] area, Cape Peninsula, Durban, Pietermaritzburg and Port Elizabeth-Uitenhage metropolitan areas", comprising an additional 59 defined localities and 9 sections of the road network. By the end of 48 months of commercial launch, a further 14 road network routes and 68 adjacent towns were to be added.

For MTN coverage obligations comprised a detailed list of 261 towns and 146 townships,[11] with an additional 54 towns and 56 townships added in annual increments over the following four years (ICASA, 2002a, pp. 78ff.). Although wattage requirements were included, roads and coverage radius were not.

Vodacom's rollout requirements were heavily weighted in favour of the country's major urban and industrial centres and the road links between them, in other words, centred around affluent, 'white' communities. It is ironic, in the light of these obligations, that then Vodacom CEO, Alan Knott-Craig, was later with some hubris to claim personal credit for the innovative "idea of extending network coverage to include thousands of kilometres of national highways" (Knott-Craig & Afonso, 2009, p. 85).

[9]The Schedules appended to the Multiparty Implementation Agreement were not included in the relevant Government Gazette, and are no longer publicly available. They are, however, reproduced in the licences gazetted by ICASA in 2002.

[10]Pretoria-Witwatersrand-Vaal, South Africa's economic heartland, substantially the same area that today comprises the province of Gauteng.

[11]In South Africa, the term 'township' usually refers to a peri-urban dormitory settlement, often underdeveloped and poverty-stricken, set aside under *apartheid*'s racially segregated strictures, for 'Africans', or 'Coloureds', or 'Indians'.

Nevertheless, it was a set of obligations that impelled Vodacom's mobile offering from niche to a valuable communications tool for the affluent.

MTN's requirements also included urban and industrial centres, but comprise in addition a large number of poor, 'black' townships. To this day, its offerings have targeted less affluent consumers.

The second, "Community Service Telephone" (CST) obligation also originated from the Multiparty Implementation Agreement, albeit somewhat embryonically (RSA, 1993, p. 4). A CST was defined as a handset ("Terminal Equipment"), available for use and "freely accessible" by the "general public", and "located in an Under-serviced Area or in a Community Centre", with calls priced in accordance with a specified "Community Service Telephone Tariff" (RSA, 1993, p. 4). An under-serviced area was defined, in turn, as a "city, town, township, shantytown, location, village or human settlement… as prescribed by the Postmaster General", and community centres were defined as including "schools [and] railway stations" (RSA, 1993, pp. 4 and 8).

Behind the legalese, the concepts of availability, accessibility and affordability that were already central to the notion of universal access and service (OECD, 1991, p. 26) are clearly discernible. But the lack of clarity in specifying CSTs and their rollout suggests policy-makers were somewhat fumbling in the dark.

For its part, Vodacom was required to have 500 CSTs at commercial launch, increasing annually to a total of 22,000 such handsets at the end of five years (ICASA, 2002b, p. 42). Distribution of these CSTs was broken down by the then provinces, with 50% earmarked for the Transvaal, 30% for Natal and the remaining 20% for the Cape and the Orange Free State.[12] In addition, the schedule listed some 62 under-serviced areas, ranging from Johannesburg's Alexandra township to Zwide township in Port Elizabeth (ICASA, 2002b, pp. 42–43).

MTN's CST obligations required 300 such handsets at commercial launch, increasing to 7500 by the end of 5 years, but without any earmarked provincial breakdown or specification of under-serviced areas (ICASA, 2002a, p. 85). There has been some speculation as to why MTN's CST obligation was lesser than that imposed on Vodacom. Matthysen suggests that this differential treatment was due to a greater level of offset commitments made by MTN under its Joint Economic

[12]The subsequent 1994 Interim Constitution broke the four existing provinces into 9 regions.

Development Plan (Open University, 2002, p. 5). MTN's Karel Pienaar offers a rather more prosaic interpretation, suggesting Vodacom simply copied the idea from MTN's bid and "just upped the numbers" (interview, 6 February 2015).

By the time the third mobile licence was awarded to Cell C in 2001, with Vodacom and MTN a well-established duopoly, rather different USOs were imposed (ICASA, 2001a). Subject to the conclusion of a roaming agreement,[13] seen as a key enabler of its successful market entry, stringent geographic (40%) and population (80%) coverage requirements were to be enforced within the first year. Cell C's own network was, by contrast, only required to cover 8% of the country and 60% of the population—and that within a much longer 5 years. In both cases, this was subject to a rollout plan agreed with the regulator.

Cell C was also required to roll out 52,000 CSTs within 7 years to under-serviced areas—which now included clinics and police stations, with an additional requirement that an under-serviced area should have less than 10% fixed-line penetration and be one "where it is necessary to roll out Community Service" (ICASA, 2001a).

Further additions were subsequently made to this initial set of USOs.

In 2003, additional obligations were imposed on both Vodacom and MTN by Minister Matsepe-Casaburri in return for access to spectrum in the more desirable 1800 MHz frequency band (Weidemann, 2003)—something that had been enjoyed by Cell C from the outset—and comprised the provision and delivery in each case of:

1. 2,500,000 "SIM Card Connection Packages", subject to an "Implementation Plan" targeting "under-serviced/un-served areas", with access to free emergency calls, voicemail, directory services and three free SMSs daily, with additional usage priced at "non-competitive pre-paid" rates (ICASA, 2004, pp. 49–50);

[13] Such an agreement, allowing Cell C subscribers to 'roam' on Vodacom's network, in areas where Cell C did not have network coverage, was struck in July 2001 and remains in force today. In 2015, it was extended to include 3G roaming.

2. 125,000 items of "Terminal Equipment",[14] again according to an approved "implementation time-table", with the explicit requirement that this assist in the "promotion of Universal Service and Universal Access" (ICASA, 2004, pp. 52–54).

The updated licences, however, went further than the original announcement and included access to 3G spectrum in the 2100 MHz band—in return for further USOs, entailing the provision of:

1. "Internet Access" plus a "minimum" of 10 handsets to each of 140 learning "Institutions for Persons with Disabilities" within 3 years;
2. "Internet access" to 5000 "public schools" within 8 years (ICASA, 2004, pp. 57–64).

In both cases, Internet service was to be discounted by 50%, with rollout in accordance with an implementation timetable specified in the licence and subject to an approved "roll-out plan" (ICASA, 2004, pp. 57–64).

The above set of provisions was subsequently extended to Cell C (ICASA, 2009)—at the licensee's own request, because it was concerned about what an additional two and a half million subscribers for each of its two larger rivals would mean for its market share and competitive position (Leona Mentz, former Cell C regulatory staffer, personal communication). In addition, this obligation would have allowed the smallest of the three operators almost to double its subscriber base, then just 3 million (2014, pp. 1v1–35). This suggests that the market impact and market dynamics of USOs needs to be given more careful consideration.

The USOs for the mobile licensees are summarised in Table 4.2.

USOs were also imposed on the 'second network operator', Neotel, when it was licensed at the end of 2005, as a fixed-line entrant following the 2002 lapsing of Telkom's exclusivity period—but it has remained a marginal player, and these are not considered here.

[14] A handset or data modem, formally defined as a "GSM terminal" (ICASA, 2004, p. 11).

Table 4.2 Mobile licensees' USOs

Operator	*Coverage*	*Community service telephones*	*Additional obligations*
Vodacom	– 146 localities and 23 arterial roads over 4 years – 60% of population within 2 years – 70% of population within 4 years	– 22,000 CSTs in 62 specified areas over 5 years (50% in the Transvaal, 30% in Natal, 20% in the Cape and the Orange Free State)	– 2,500,000 SIM card connection packages – 125,000 handsets – 140 institutions for people with disabilities over 3 years (Internet access and 10 terminals each) – 5000[a] public schools over 8 years (Internet access) (subject to approved implementation plan)
MTN (Mobile)	– 315 towns and 202 'townships' over 4 years – 60% of population within 2 years – 70% of population within 4 years	– 7500 CSTs over 5 years	– 2,500,000 SIM card connection packages – 125,000 handsets – 140 institutions for people with disabilities over 3 years (Internet access and 10 terminals each) – 5000 public schools over 8 years (Internet access) (subject to approved implementation plan)
Cell C (Mobile)	– Own network only: – 8% of country within 5 years – 60% of population within 5 years – With roaming agreement: – 40% of area within 1 year – 80% of population within 1 year	– 52,000 CSTs in under-serviced areas (with less than 10% fixed teledensity)	– 2,500,000 SIM card connection packages – 125,000 handsets – 140 institutions for people with disabilities over 3 years (Internet access and 10 terminals each) – 5000 public schools over 8 years (Internet access) (subject to approved implementation plan)

[a]Reduced in 2014 to 1500 schools, as were the figures for MTN and Cell C

4.3 Telkom's Access Line Rollout

As we can see, the fixed-line mindset of policy-makers and the regulator meant that primary burden of the USOs fell to Telkom.

Initially, the company moved aggressively to meet its obligations. During the first three years (1997–2000), the number of mainlines in operation increased from 4.3 million to 5.5 million (Telkom, 2000, p. 73). This impressive increase in penetration (of some 30%, or just over 1.2 million lines) was nonetheless still short of Telkom's total line target (1.47 million lines).

Telkom was soon, however, forced to reappraise its initial gung-ho attitude towards rolling out new lines in order to meet its USO targets. Telkom had, unaccountably, failed to anticipate that large numbers of the poor customers thus connected would be unable to pay their bills (Benjamin, 2001, p. 109; Hodge, 2004, p. 209). The impact of this on the company's financial bottom line[15] led to a "complete review of non-paying customers and a crackdown on commercial fraud" (Telkom, 2001, p. 8)). The ensuing disconnections of these defaulting recipients of USO largesse led to a nearly 10% nett shrinkage (by over half a million) in Telkom's installed customer base.

In fact, the actual rate of disconnections was even more dramatic—and substantially masked by ongoing new connections. Hodge, for example, reports 1.16 million disconnections in 2001—offset by 630,000 new connections (2004, p. 209).[16] As a result, the number of lines disconnected in 2001 amounted to over 90% of the lines so painstakingly previously connected as part of Telkom's total line target. Similarly, Benjamin reports a rate of churn of 50–70%, meaning that most USO lines were subsequently disconnected (Benjamin, 2001, p. 109), vitiating the entire initiative.

Telkom's rollout of the necessary access lines to meet its target had been, it is true, beset by a number of countervailing factors. Telkom's foreign investment partners, particularly SBC, appear to have had a cavalier lack of understanding of the South African economic and cultural

[15] Telkom was later to report bad debts of R560 million in 2000, rising to R965 million in 2002 (2003, p. 18).

[16] Hodge goes on to report the disconnection of a further 606,000 lines in 2002, once again largely offset by the installation of 570,000 new lines (2004, p. 209).

context into which the new lines were being rolled out.[17] The levels of poverty, along with the gap between rich and poor, are dire. Coupled with a 'culture of non-payment' for the delivery of services that had its origins in the anti-*apartheid* boycotts of the late 1980s (Fjeldstad, 2004), and the lack of experience in managing accounts—getting a Telkom line was once described as the "only unlimited credit poor people get" (Benjamin, 2003)—this led to a situation where the non-payment of telephone bills was rife, particularly in the very under-serviced areas targeted by the USOs (Telkom, 2003, p. 18). Further, the DECT wireless local loop system introduced by Telkom into rural areas, and targeted to cover some 420,000 customers, ran into a number of problems (Baker, 1999, p. 1), amongst which was the unanticipated theft of its solar panels (Dyani, n.d.).[18]

Worse, the point when Telkom decided to embark on its campaign of disconnections also coincided with the very point when mainline penetration was overtaken by mobile subscriptions. By early 2000, Vodacom and MTN had 5,369,000 subscribers between them, a figure nipping at the heels of Telkom's 5,492,838 mainlines. A year later, the number of mobile subscribers had topped 8 million.[19] This was due to a number of factors, most notably the introduction of prepaid mobile (ITU, 2003, pp. 35ff.; Melody, 2001, p. 5), which dramatically eased access to the telephony market for consumers, and substantially reconfigured the affordability threshold (Barrantes & Galperin, 2008; Hodge, 2005). Hodge's analysis is of particular relevance to the South Africa market, showing that for low-volume users, it was actually *cheaper* to be on prepaid mobile as opposed to Telkom's post-paid fixed-line service (2005). And there were factors other than affordability—including lack of the need for a credit

[17] For example, Horwitz and Currie have labelled SBC's approach to its customers under the rollout as "sociologically inappropriate" (2007, p. 446).

[18] Anecdotal accounts suggest they made excellent and attractive table-tops.

[19] The comparison is a pyrrhic one, since mainlines and mobile subscribers (effectively 'active SIM cards) are not truly comparable statistics (Sutherland, 2009).

record or a permanent fixed abode, the ability to exploit cheaper communications options such as missed calls[20] or the use of SMS services—that added further impetus to the ongoing swing to mobile.[21]

Telkom's response to this erosion of its customer base was both tardy and clumsy. It finally launched its own 'prepaid' offering, 'PrepaidFone', towards the end of 1999 (ITWeb, 1999). Although Telkom claimed some 480,000 users of the service a year later (2001, pp. 19–20), the offering lacked crucial features which might have enabled it to compete with those of the mobile operators: for example, it still required a monthly rental (mobile prepaid users paid only for actual usage) and it offered limited value-added services (it charged for voicemail, a free service to mobile customers) (ITWeb, 2001). Further, Telkom's disconnections cut off incoming, revenue-generating calls[22] along with the outgoing calls that were the likely cause of the unpaid bill in the first place—this despite a 1998 study for the regulator into 'needy persons' which was already recommending 'staggered disconnection' (blocking of outgoing, billable calls) for households unable to pay their monthly bills (1998, pp. 22 and 35). Telkom did eventually adopt a policy of partial disconnection (News24, 2002), but by then its subscriber base was already in terminal decline (see the graph below). It may have taken another 10 years before the number of mainlines in service fell below the number at the start of its universal service rollout obligation, but the trend from 2001 has been irreversible. And, as a result, many former, disconnected Telkom customers were lost from fixed-line services forever, becoming instead prepaid customers of MTN and Vodacom (Fig. 4.1).

Critically, despite Telkom's campaign of disconnecting defaulting customers, coupled with the swing to mobile, and the consequent significant negative impact on the number of lines, Telkom continued to claim that it was meeting its licence USOs. Witness its 2001 annual report:

[20] Because of mobile calling line identification (CLI), an unanswered call can be used to send an agreed signal to the recipient, such as 'I have arrived home safely' or 'Please call me back'.

[21] Prepaid mobile was also beneficial to operators because of the termination revenue via incoming calls (hence the provision of a daily allocation of free 'Please Call Me' SMSs to prepaid subscribers). Operators also saved on the cost of issuing monthly accounts and on the expense of debt collections.

[22] At the time, in 2000, Telkom was charging the mobile operators between R0.45 (off-peak) and R0.80 (peak) per minute to terminate their traffic on its network. Telkom was seemingly oblivious to this considerable source of revenue.

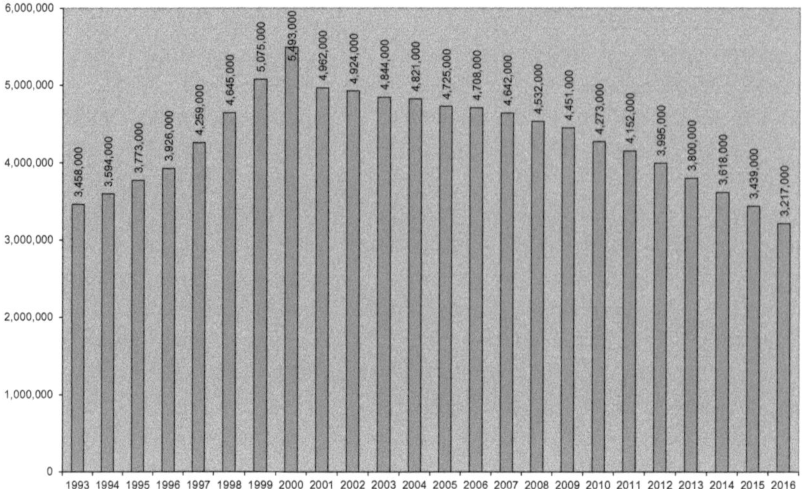

Fig. 4.1 Telkom mainlines in service (1993–2016) (*Source* Telkom annual reports)

> It is extremely pleasing to report that Telkom has met or exceeded all line rollouts for the first four years of its licence. During this period, Telkom has installed over 2.1 million lines taking the total to 4.9 million. Of these, 1.4 million were installed in under-serviced areas. We have quite literally connected whole communities to the network with 2692 villages "wired-up" and over 108,874 payphones installed. (2001, p. 11)

It is clear from the assertion above that Telkom was counting towards its USO obligation—in contravention of its licence—lines that had been installed but subsequently disconnected for one or other reason.

The wording of the relevant sections of the licence is complex and opaque, but it appears clear that it was intended that Telkom's USO lines should remain in service. It states that

> for the avoidance of doubt, any new Exchange Line brought into service in a relevant financial year in respect of the Roll-out Targets and the New Line Roll-out Targets, if disconnected in accordance with condition 13.4.3 [which deals with breach of contract, failure to pay, illegal usage etc.], shall be discounted from the measurement referred to. (DoC, 1997, p. 52)

Table 4.3 Telkom's access line targets vs rollout

Year	*1996/1997*	*1997/1998*	*1998/1999*	*1999/2000*	*2000/2001*	*2001/2002*
New access line target		340,000	435,000	575,000	675,000	665,000
Total lines intended		4,598,639	5,033,639	5,608,639	6,283,639	6,948,639
Total Lines Actual	4,258,639	4,645,065	5,075,417	5,492,838	4,961,743	4,924,458
Actual net line growth		386,426	430,352	417,421	−531,095	−37,285

New access line target as per Telkom's licence (DoC, 1997)
All other figures calculated from Telkom's annual reports

The wording seems clearly designed to prevent phones disconnected for non-payment or breach of contract being counted towards Telkom's USO rollout targets. Yet Telkom unapologetically did just this, stating as much in its final report on its licence obligations: "lines disconnected because of non-payment are also counted in the totals" (Telkom, 2002b, p. 6).

And it was only by arguing that disconnected lines could be included in the totals that Telkom could claim that it fell a mere 16,448 lines short (a variance of 6%) of its overall new access line target (Telkom, 2002b, p. 6). In fact, the total number of lines in service only grew by a mere 665,000 over the entire period (see Table 4.3).

Strangely, there seems to have been no attempt by the regulator to challenge this report, or indeed any previous compliance reports,[23] where Telkom's line of argument must have already been apparent. Andries Matthysen, ICASA's Head of Licensing at the time, is quoted as confirming this failure, stating that "while the regulator was tasked with such monitoring, it failed to do so and relied on annual accounting for targets by Telkom" (Hodge, 2004, p. 218). This despite the fact that ICASA's annual reports for the period note its duty to "check compliance of

[23]The report is marked as report no. 7, but is the only one the author has been able to source.

licensees against [*inter alia*]... delivery on universal service obligations" (ICASA, 2003, p. 17).

4.4 Telkom's Payphones

Telkom's approach to the 120,000 payphone USO target set out in its licence proceeded in similar gung-ho fashion to its access line rollout, as can be seen below. Their licence required them to install payphones at a rate of 25,000 per year (20,000 in the first year) (DoC, 1997, p. 59).

But it was soon clear that the operation to roll out payphones was in trouble. Theft of cash from coin-operated payphones was rife, vandalism was prevalent, and there were even counterfeit cards for card-operated phones in circulation (Steenkamp, 1998a, 1998b). However, Telkom pressed on, "continuing to install payphones in areas defined in [its] licence, including underserviced communities, schools, hospitals, as well as to mass transport routes such as taxi ranks, train stations and airports" (Telkom, 2001, p. 9).

However, the nett annual increase in payphones fell well short of rollout targets. Only in 1998/1999, when the numbers of payphones in operation grew by 26,204, was the USO target breached. But, over the same period, Telkom claimed to have installed more than 27,000 new payphones (Chalmers, 1999), meaning that at least some vandalised or stolen payphones were not being replaced. And, by 2001, when the total number of payphones had grown by only 66,000, Telkom was claiming to have rolled out 108,874 payphones "as per license [sic] requirements" (2001, p. 20). Although Telkom continued to allude to the problem of vandalism, reporting that it "frequently repairs or replaces a large number of vandalised payphones" (2001, p. 20), it never stated that large numbers of payphones were being decommissioned for these or other reasons. However, Fig. 4.2 suggests a different story, and follows the same pattern as Telkom's fixed-line rollout.

It further appears that Telkom payphones were destroyed for reasons other than raw vandalism. Andries Matthysen claims that Telkom payphones were being destroyed because they were a cheaper alternative to the mobile CST phones: "The minutes stopped flowing. Individuals vandalised Telkom's payphones so they could offer calls at R 2,80 a minute" (interview, 9 January 2015). As a result Telkom began to introduce "containerised semi-public fixed-line telephones", and embarked on

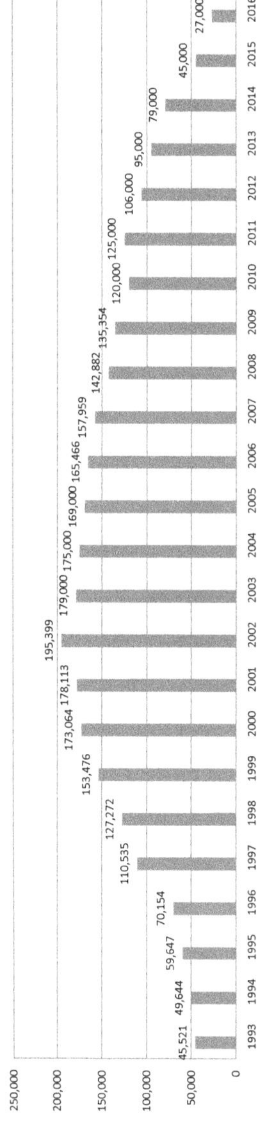

Fig. 4.2 Telkom payphones (1993–2016) (*Source* Telkom, annual reports)

a campaign of consultation with rural communities designed to reduce vandalism (Telkom, 2002a, p. 25).

The fact that Telkom's payphone USO was vitiated by the arbitrage disparities between its model and that of the mobile CSTs, points to a bitterly ironic policy inconsistency. The problem would have been exacerbated by the upsurge in mobile subscribers and by the arrival of Cell's 52,000 CSTs into the market.

Once Telkom was able to claim it had met its payphone USO, the roll-out of payphones rapidly gave way to a programme of disconnection and decommissioning. Between 2002 and 2003, the number of payphones in operation fell by over 16,000, and has continued to decline ever since. By 2016, Telkom was itching to do away with payphones entirely (McLeod, 2016).

4.5 Monitoring Telkom's USOs

There seems to have been no attempt whatsoever by the regulator to assess Telkom's compliance with its USOs. While there were some efforts by the then Universal Service Agency, they lacked the legal authority to compel operator compliance (Ngubane, 1999; Stavrou, Whitehead, Wilson, Seloane, & Benjamin, 2001) and were thus unable to compile the necessary data (Katharina Pillay, interview, 13 January 2015). As a result, there exists no independent, third-party assessment of Telkom's compliance with its licensed USOs.

All this is available in Telkom's own reporting to the regulator (see Table 4.4).

Table 4.4 Telkom's assessment of its access line compliance (1997–2002)

Category	*Target*	*Achieved*	*Variance (%)*
Total lines	2,690,000	2,673,552	−0.6
Under-serviced area lines	1,677,000	1,787,968	6.6
Priority customers	20,246	25,577	26.3
• Schools *(as calculated)*	17,272	18,294	5.9
• other	2974	7283	144.9
Villages	3204	2699	−15.8

Source Telkom (2002b, p. 6)

The claims in respect of Telkom's 'Total line' target have already been discussed above. As we saw, the 2.67 million line rollout claimed as 'achieved' clearly includes large numbers of lines subsequently disconnected. The claim to have installed nearly 1.8 million new lines in under-serviced areas—likely to have been disproportionally affected by problems of affordability and non-payment—is equally suspect.

Similar doubts apply in respect of Telkom's claim to have exceeded its 'Priority customers' targets. Further, Telkom seems to have mis-stated at least one of the targets in order to avoid a financial penalty: the 'schools' target as stated in Telkom's licence is 19,270 (DoC, 1997, p. 67)[24]—not the considerably lower "calculated" 17,272 given in Table 4.4. In fact, Telkom was 976 schools short and should have been fined R878,400 (USD 120,000).[25]

Telkom further claimed to have exceeded its payphone target (120,000) by rolling out 132,990 new payphones (Telkom, 2002b, p. 18). This clearly also includes payphones subsequently disconnected, since the nett increase in payphones by 2002 was only some 85,000 (see figure above). Telkom offered no explanation for its calculation, which again was never challenged by ICASA (which had access to Telkom's annual payphone figures). Had Telkom been assessed on the correct payphone rollout number, it would have been fined R78 million (USD 10 million).[26]

It appears, therefore, that Telkom at best manipulated its submissions to ICASA, using the definitional sleight of hand described above to claim that it met its overall rollout target. Indeed, had the company been disallowed from counting any of the disconnected lines, it could have been liable for a fine of as much as R1.8 billion (USD 250 million).[27]

Telkom was thus able to concede a fine of R10,183,285 (USD 1,4 million) for failing to achieve its USO targets, the overwhelming majority (93%) due to the shortfall in the overall number of access lines (Telkom, 2002b, p. 6). A proper audit by the regulator, backed by a far clearer specification of those USOs and of what constituted compliance, might have increased this fine by several orders of magnitude.

[24] Telkom incorrectly claims that "no specific target is set in the licence for schools" (Telkom, 2002b, p. 18).

[25] At R900 per school short.

[26] At R2,250 per payphone short.

[27] A fine of R225 for each of the first 100,000 lines in the shortfall, plus a fine of R900 for each of the remaining lines (DoC, 1997, p. 53). Significantly, the number by which Telkom conceded having missed its overall rollout target fell within the former bracket.

4.6 Rolling Out Mobile CSTs

The initial phases of the rollout of the mobile CSTs are not well documented. In addition, the definition of what comprises a CST offers only the vaguest of indications to the operators as to how to proceed.

Rolling out handsets "freely accessible" to the "general public" and "located in an Under-serviced Area or in a Community Centre" (RSA, 1993, p. 4) appears to imply some form of payphone rollout. Underserviced areas were defined vaguely as including any "city, town, township, shantytown, location, village or human settlement… as prescribed by the Postmaster General from time to time", including specifically the coverage areas listed in each licence under the "Implementation Timetable" (RSA, 1993, p. 4). This was a definition with considerable leeway for creative application by the licensees, covering both major urban centres and their neighbouring disadvantaged 'black' townships, but with no rural areas specified at all.

Vodacom chose to adopt a two-pronged interpretation, involving both mobile handsets issued to individuals (which it dubbed "transportables") and 'mobile' phones housed in refurbished shipping containers ("phone shops") (SATRA, 1998, p. 24), with the former the company's primary initial strategy towards meeting its USOs (Karel Pienaar, interview, 6 February 2015).

'Transportable' mobile handsets were accordingly handed over to "faculty and administrators at universities and technical colleges in disadvantaged areas" (Kaul, Ati, Janakiram, & Wattenstrom, 2008, p. 19) with the intention that they be made available to students to make and receive phone calls (Andries Matthysen, interview, 6 January 2015). This approach was, hardly surprisingly, ineffective, as the lecturers merely appropriated the handsets for personal use without making them available to their students (Kaul, Ati, Janakiram, & Wattenstrom, 2008, p. 19; Open University, 2002, p. 6; SATRA, 1998, pp. 264–265)[28]—this despite signed agreements to the contrary (SATRA, 1998, p. 134).

Despite the manifest shortcomings of the model, Vodacom persisted with 'transportable' CST phones for a number of years. The model was "easier and faster to roll out", and was only phased out in late 2003 (Kaul et al., 2008, p. 19).

[28] The SATRA audit lists numerous quotations from interviewees attesting to the frequent misappropriation of these 'transportables' for personal use.

Table 4.5 Vodacom's "transportable" CST rollout (1998)

Province	*Transportable phones*	*% of total*
Kwa Zulu Natal	1217	11
Gauteng	705	6.5
Eastern Cape	2713	25
Northern Province	2196	20
Western Cape	1805	16.5
North West	685	6
Mpumalanga	0	0
Free State	1396	13
Northern Cape	180	2
Total	**10,897**	**100**

Source SATRA (1998, p. 239)

By 1998, Vodacom was reporting 11,000 such phones in place, predominantly in the poorer provinces of the Eastern Cape and Northern Province (now Limpopo), but with the curious exclusion of Mpumalanga (see Table 4.5). This geographic spread also failed to meet the requirements specified in the licence, with a mere 32.5% in the former Transvaal[29] as opposed to the required 50%, and a mere 11% in KwaZulu-Natal as opposed to the required 30%. The Cape[30] and Free State, by contrast, were heavily over-represented at 56.5% as opposed to the required 20%.

Vodacom's other model, the fixed-location containerised 'phone shops', was also implemented from the outset. Despite some 2000 claimed to be in place by early 1995 (Hack, 1995), the rollout in fact proceeded far more slowly than the company's 'transportables' (see Table 4.5). The phone shops were initially housed in Vodacom-branded refurbished shipping containers, franchised out to local entrepreneurs, each containing between 5 and 10 GSM phones with per-call billing facilities (Chonco, 2002).

The numbers of these phone shops grew rapidly, from 700 containers, housing just under 5000 phones in 1998 (SATRA, 1998, p. 240), through over 2000 phone shops in 2001(Benjamin, 2001, p. 143), and 4102 phone shops (Chonco, 2002) to "27,884 payphone units" the

[29] Now split into Gauteng, Mpumalanga, Northern Province (now Limpopo) and North West Province.

[30] Now split into Western Cape, Eastern Cape and Northern Cape.

Table 4.6 Vodacom's "phone shop" CST rollout (1998)

Province	*Phone shops*	*% of total*	*Phones*	*Ave phones/shop*
Kwa Zulu Natal	122	17.5	915	7.5
Gauteng	171	24.5	1101	6.4
Eastern Cape	67	9.5	424	6.3
Northern Province	91	13	434	4.8
Western Cape	38	5.5	263	6.9
North West	109	15.5	611	5.6
Mpumalanga	39	5.5	268	6.9
Free State	50	7	824	16.5
Northern Cape	11	1.5	85	7.7
Total	**698**	**100**	**4925**	**7.1**

Source SATRA (1998, p. 240)

following year (Telkom, 2002a, p. 14). By late 2003, Reck and Wood were suggesting some 30,000 community service lines in service (2003, p. 5).[31]

The picture that emerges shows a gradual shift to the phone shop model, likely in response to the failures of the 'transportables' model (Katharina Pillay, interview, 13 January 2015). By the time of ICASA's 2010 review of the USOs of the operators, Vodacom's community service line portfolio had grown to 115,713 lines (BMI-T, 2010, p. 6), reaching "over" 118,000 a year or two later (ICASA, 2014b, p. 4)—with the 'transportable' model having been abandoned. The geographical distribution of these phone shops remained far from equitable, with a heavy concentration in the populous but richer Gauteng province, and far fewer located in the poorer, more under-served Mpumalanga. The geographic spread again failed to meet the requirements of the licence—with only 23.7% in the former Transvaal (required to be 50%), 7.5% for KwaZulu-Natal (30% required) and once again the former Cape and the Free State over-represented at 37.4% (20% required) (Table 4.6).

The phone shop approach represented a greatly superior model, based on sound entrepreneurial principles and a clear business model, rather than one that flew in the face of self-interest. Benjamin points to "clear

[31] The figures are not properly comparable. Benjamin's unsourced figure seems rather high for the time, and the figures from Telkom clearly still include numbers of 'transportables'.

business plans" and repeatedly refers to the success of the model, citing "stories of these people buying Mercedes cars within a few months of starting operation" (2001, p. 143). It is not hard to see why. Vodacom itself began to punt the model, citing traffic figures of 124 million minutes a month, and monthly revenue of R86.9 million, generating monthly commission of R28.5 million or an average of R17,818 per phone shop (Chonco, 2002, pp. 5–6). Some of the accounts verge on the hagiographic (Reck & Wood, 2003), but the success of the community phone shop model seems clear and undeniable (Coetzer, 2008; Hamilton, 2003).

MTN, on the other hand, took a different approach to meeting its CST commitments, rolling out card-operated GSM payphones (Hack, 1995; Open University, 2002, pp. 6–7; SATRA, 1998),[32] along the lines of the payphone model favoured by Telkom at the time. Based on a partnership with a local payphone manufacturer and the development of what it claimed was the "first fully integrated GSM pay phone in Africa", the model was first unveiled in the urban ghetto township of Alexandra, Johannesburg in June 1994 (Gregson, 2000). These GSM call boxes were of "rugged" design, operating on a "debit-card system", and are described as follows:

> [They] resemble conventional pay phones and run off any 12-volt power source, [and] are set up on the outside walls of existing businesses. The cost and duration of each call are displayed on the phone's display screen. The adjacent businesses sell the… debit cards, with a pre-paid number of minutes, at a small profit. (Hack, 1995)

By early 1995, some 500 of these units had reportedly been installed in 32 townships around the country (Hack, 1995). Three years later, this number had increased tenfold, as shown in Table 4.7.

As with Vodacom, the distribution of these CSTs reveals an uneven focus on those disadvantaged areas most in need of connectivity: MTN's GSM payphones are disproportionally located in the more advantaged Gauteng, with almost none in the provinces of Free State and Northern Cape.

The GSM payphone model had considerable advantages. In particular, these CSTs offered 24-hour availability, in contrast to being dependent on the opening hours of Vodacom's phone shops and the whims of the

[32] MTN's Karel Pienaar claims that MTN's model involved entrepreneurs and containers from the outset (interview, 6 February 2015), but is surely the product of hindsight.

Table 4.7 MTN's GSM payphone rollout (1998)

Province	*GSM payphones*	*% of total*
Kwa Zulu Natal	691	12.5
Gauteng	1171	21.5
Eastern Cape	587	11
Northern Province	731	13.5
Western Cape	478	9
North West	1121	20.5
Mpumalanga	654	12
Free State	3	0
Northern Cape	5	0
Total	**5441**	**100**

Source SATRA (1998, p. 178)

owners of its 'transportables'. However, mounting them in public spaces exposed them to "substantial vandalism" with criminals prepared to "actually break these phones open, hoping to get hold of a handset" (Open University, 2002, p. 6). Vandalism of these phones to get hold of the SIM cards was widely reported (Gregson, 2000; M-Cell, 2002, p. 48; SATRA, 1998, p. 61)[33], and MTN's Karel Pienaar and has one in his office with a bullet hole in it (interview, 6 February 2015). To combat these problems, the payphone was redesigned to make it more secure, with the handset and SIM card removed, and many were moved inside spaza shops (thus reducing their accessibility quite dramatically, to users as well as thieves) (SATRA, 1998, p. 61). This in turn created a new challenge of winning the trust of spaza shop owners, since MTN was "still often viewed with suspicion" as a 'white' company out to exploit 'blacks' (Hack, 1995).

There were other problems. Both Pienaar and Matthysen report a high incidence of hoax calls (up to 20%) to emergency service numbers (interview, 6 February 2015; Open University, 2002 p. 6). As a result, emergency calls were made dependent on the insertion of a phone card (Open University, 2002, p. 6), creating obvious accessibility problems. There were also considerable supply chain problems. Many such payphones were effectively unusable to nearby users because there were no phone card outlets nearby, or because outlets (typically spaza shops, for whom the

[33] SATRA reports around 900 of MTN's over 5000 phones as having been vandalised.

cards were low-profit margin items (SATRA, 1998, p. 62).) were out of stock (SATRA, 1998, pp. 75 and 81; Open University, 2002, pp. 6–7).

Because of the problematic nature of the GSM payphone model, particularly the rate of vandalism, with the escalating costs for replacement, prompted by an internal evaluation, MTN opted to move towards the much more viable phone shop model that had been adopted by Vodacom (Katharina Pillay, interview, 13 January 2015). The move was formally announced somewhat later:

> As a result of vandalism, MTN is currently replacing in the order of 3000 of these phones under a revised business model. This model includes the installation of phoneshops [sic] / telecentres, each equipped with six to eight phones, in underserviced areas and forms the basis of stimulating rural entrepreneurship. (M-Cell, 2002, p. 48)

The viability issues with the GSM payphone model mean that it has been less widely reported, and the extent of its rollout less accurately tracked. The numbers rose from 5441 GSM payphones in 1998 (SATRA, 1998, p. 178) to more than 8500 such payphones in 2002 (M-Cell, 2002, p. 48). No further figures are available. The 22,000 community service lines reported in 2010 (BMI-T, 2010, p. 6) were likely mostly housed in phone shops. The model has, however, been continued, with modifications based on the lessons learned in South Africa, in other jurisdictions where MTN operates, including Nigeria, Rwanda and Uganda.

4.7 Monitoring the Mobile CSTs

There were several attempts over the years to monitor the USOs of the mobile operators, only the most recent of which saw the formal light of day, leading the authors to conclude—incorrectly—that "it does not appear that monitoring and evaluation of the operators' compliance with the [USOs] was ever done" (BMI-T, 2010, p. 4).

4.7.1 Community Services Audit Report (1996)

The first such attempted audit appears to have been conducted by the Department[34] in around 1996. This is referred to in a number of other

[34] Then still the Department of Posts and Telecommunications.

reports (SATRA, 1998; Stavrou et al., 2001, p. 2), but the details of what it found are not known, as it was never released and it is not part of the public record.

The audit had been commissioned in February 1996[35] (Joffe, 1996) and ran for six months. Its findings were leaked by one of the members of the audit team, Sudheer Sukumaran, in a conference paper towards the end of the year, and make damning reading. Sukumaran is quoted as alleging that "many of the community phones installed by the operators [70% in the case of MTN] were no longer functional" and that "many of the phones installed by the two operators were outside the designated rural [sic] areas" (Rosenthal & Volschenk, 1996) and hence did not qualify.[36]

It was an audit predictably roundly rejected by the operators. MTN, for example, criticised the report for "inconsistency, vagueness and faulted methodology" and accused the Department of acting as "policeman, judge, jury and hangman" (cited in SATRA, 1998, pp. 67–68).

Sukumaran is further quoted as alleging that numbers of Vodacom's 'transportables' were simply "distributed in bulk, to lecturers at the universities of Fort Hare and Grahamstown - both outside the rural [sic] areas defined in the licence agreement" and that again these did not meet the CST criteria (Rosenthal & Volschenk, 1996).

Having been found sorely wanting by the audit, the operators reportedly "questioned the methodology" and claimed that the audit team were "unable to distinguish between phones which were busy, switched off by the operators, or not operational" (Rosenthal & Volschenk, 1996). In much later subsequent correspondence with SATRA, MTN continued to attack both methodology and findings of the Audit Report (SATRA, 1998, pp. 67–68).

Unfortunately, full official details of this first audit, either in respect of methodology or findings, were never released into the public record, and the documentation appears to have disappeared.

[35] The audit preceded the 1996 Telecommunications Act and the consequent creation of SATRA and may have been commissioned as input into the Green and White Paper process.

[36] Rosenthal and Volschenk appear to have misinterpreted the USO requirement here. It was in fact 'under-serviced areas' and 'community centres' that had been specified, which were largely but by no means exclusively rural.

4.7.2 SATRA Community Service Obligations Audit (1998)

Findings similarly damning emerged from a different source in 1998, when the new regulator, SATRA, commissioned a second audit of the CST obligations of the mobile operators in preparation to reissuing their licences under the 1996 Telecommunications Act (SATRA, 1998). This second audit appears to have been far more comprehensive and methodologically robust than its predecessor, employing a comprehensive mix of both qualitative and quantitative methodologies, including random sampling of operator-supplied databases in the latter case (SATRA, 1998, pp. 14–19).

What emerged was a damning indictment of the rollout of the CSTs, its findings categorised as "disastrous" and a "catastrophe of deprivation" for needy persons (SATRA, 1998, pp. 198 and 273).

The audit sought to verify whether:

- The "Mobile Telephone Operators have achieved the deployment of the required number of Community Service phones";
- These CST phones are all located in "Under-Serviced areas";
- These CST phones "fundamentally operate";
- The "community has ready access to the phones";
- The CSTs "operate under the approved tariffs";
- "Phone Cards [in the case of MTN] are readily available" (SATRA, 1998, p. 17).

Firstly, a random sample of phones from the databases supplied by the operators was tested to see if the phones could be located (the 'locational integrity' test). A probability sampling approach was used, segmented by service type ('transportables'/phone shops/GSM payphones) and by province, and with the actual sample size in each of the 27 segments adjusted in order to ensure 95% accuracy (SATRA, 1998, pp. 27–30).

The phones thus located were then tested for: 'fundamental operation' (ability to make and receive calls of "conversation quality"); for 'public accessibility' (whether the "general community has access"); in relation to 'service tariffs' ("whether the approved [discounted] Community Service tariffs" were being applied); and, in the case of the MTN payphones, for 'card availability' ("whether phone cards could be readily purchased, in the general locality of the Community Service phone") (SATRA, 1998, pp. 24–25).

The audit team recognised that in the absence of an official list, a "more usable definition of 'under-serviced areas'" was needed, but resolved "in the interim... without prejudice to any future audits" to use the definition from Telkom's licence[37] (SATRA, 1998, p. 24).

Although the licences also specified precise availability and quality of service parameters, the SATRA team[38] elected not to audit these "at this time, without prejudice to future audits" (SATRA, 1998, p. 16).

The audit was particularly harsh on Vodacom's rollout of its 'transportable' phones. Only 24% of the 'transportable' phones in Vodacom's database could be traced, 10% of which did not work properly (SATRA, 1998, pp. 275–276). The report further notes the skewed distribution of 'transportables', querying in particular why there were none in Mpumalanga (SATRA, 1998, p. 283). Only a mere 10% of 'transportable' phones (some 44% of the phones that were located) were accessible for 8 or more hours a day (SATRA, 1998, p. 254). The report goes on to suggest that the educational institutions targeted did not qualify as 'underserviced areas' and that the choice of "professors,[39] who are rarely available" as holders of such phones was a fundamental problem (SATRA, 1998, p. 283). Coupled with the fact that the 'transportable' phone service was not properly advertised, these findings led the report to conclude that there are "little [sic], if any, redeeming features" in the 'transportable' "delivery mode, which does not work" (SATRA, 1998, p. 283).

Vodacom's phone shop model fared rather better. In this case, 51% of those listed on the database could be located. But, with some 15% of those not working, only 43% of phone shop phones were considered to be operational (SATRA, 1998, pp. 275–276). The accessibility of phone shops was far higher, with 94% of those located being open 8 or more hours a day (SATRA, 1998, p. 255).

Overall only 2% of Vodacom's community service phones passed all the tests (SATRA, 1998, p. 278). Some of the problems, particularly the difficulties in tracking down CST phones, were due to Vodacom's

[37]This comprised all local exchange areas with less than 50% fixed-line teledensity as at June 1996, as well as any area "inhabited by communities historically discriminated against on the basis of race".

[38]The project ran under the overall direction of Councillor Noluthando Gosa, but was led by newly appointed SATRA staffer Andries Matthysen, supported by international consultant Doug Rowell.

[39]These phones had been handed out to lecturers at Rhodes University and the University of Fort Hare, with the misplaced and widely ignored proviso that they should be made available for use by students.

own database inadequacies—but this in turn affected all the subsequent tests. SATRA comments that "it is difficult to determine how Vodacom efficiently maintains and manages these phones, when they don't know where they are" (1998, p. 133).

MTN's GSM payphone model came in for similarly stinging criticism (SATRA, 1998, pp. 199–202). As in the case of Vodacom, a high proportion (41%) of MTN's payphones could not be located. With a mere 29% of the payphones located, found to be in working order, the report calls for a "more concerted approach to maintenance". The report notes that the "bulk" (60%) of MTN's payphones were accessible for 8 or more hours per day. A major cause for concern raised by the audit was the lack of availability of the phone cards necessary for people to utilise the payphones, with a mere 29% of located phones having a nearby source of phone cards. Overall, only 1.5% of MTN's community service phones passed all the tests.

A summary of the audit results is given in Table 4.8.

What is clear from the table above is that the phone shop model adopted by Vodacom was the most successful approach to CSTs, with high percentages being operational (85%), accessible for more than 8 hours a day (94%), and charging correct community service tariffs (96%).

By contrast, the 'transportable' model was clearly a failure. A disproportionate number (76%) of Vodacom's 'transportables' were untraceable, with a dismally low proportion of those that could be found (44%) being accessible for 8 or more hours a day.

MTN's GSM payphones were again shown to be particularly vulnerable to damage or vandalism, with only 29% of the phones that were located actually in working order. Problems with the supply chain for phone cards also undermined the viability of the model.[40]

It is, therefore, hardly surprising that Vodacom discontinued its 'transportable' model and that MTN switched to the phone shop model. What is surprising is that it took the two companies so long to react to the obvious lessons of the 1998 SATRA audit.

The report voices a specific concern over the uneven distribution of the CST rollout. The concluding comment in respect of each of the two

[40]The report does not indicate which working GSM payphones also had a ready local supply of phone cards. That missing data could have pushed the effectively working payphone percentage below 10%.

Table 4.8 Community service telephone audit summary

	Vodacom			*Vodacom*			*MTN*		
	Transportables	*% of claimed*	*%[a] of located*	*Phone Shops*	*% of claimed*	*% of located*	*Pay-phones*	*% of claimed*	*% of located*
Claimed	10,897			4925			5441		
Located[b]	2618	24		2502	51		3196	59	
Working[c]	2451	23	94	2125	43	85	914	17	29
Accessible[d]	1139	11	44	2355	48	94	1909	35	60
Tariffing[e]	2406	22	92	2389	49	96	3238	60	101
Cards[f]							934	17	29

[a]Only those phones that could be located were assessed for operational status, accessibility and community service tariffs. It is therefore important to assess these attributes as a proportion of the phones actually tested
[b]Number of phones passing 'locational integrity' test
[c]Number of phones passing 'operational integrity' test
[d]Number of phones accessible 8 or more hours per day
[e]Number of phones where approved community service tariffs were being applied
[f]Only applicable in the case of MTN's GSM payphones
Compiled from SATRA (1998)

licensees that "there does not appear any clear correlation between distribution and need" implies that neither Vodacom nor MTN paid much attention to ensuring that their CST rollout targeted under-serviced areas (however ill-defined these were) (SATRA, 1998, pp. 200 and 275).

The report also raises, albeit indirectly, the question of how long a CST needed to remain in place before it could be counted towards USO targets. MTN argued that the high rate of vandalism meant that any "community payphones that are stolen, or damaged beyond repair… [should still be regarded as] constituting part of MTN's Community Service Obligations" (SATRA, 1998, p. 67).[41] The audit team was clearly unsympathetic to such pleadings and expected all CST phones to be in place and compliant with the audit criteria.

The report makes much of the issue of accessibility, expecting all CST phones to be accessible 24 hours a day, seven days a week. Based on these concerns, it proposes that CST obligations be adjusted according to an "accessibility equivalence" index, weighted from "Class A" CST phones ("available 24 hours a day, 7 days a week") down to "Class E" (20% availability)[42] (SATRA, 1998, pp. 83, 136 and 356ff.).

The report includes a complex series of conclusions and recommendations, noting that the dismal "audit results are the consequence of management policies and practices, which have been endemic to the system of corporate behaviour, of both MTN and Vodacom, from the outset of their licences". The report includes calls to:

- "Impose punitive financial measures" on both MTN and Vodacom;
- Develop a "National Telecommunications Community Services Development Strategy Plan, with the co-operation and involvement of the Mobile Operators, Telkom and the Universal Service Agency (USA)" to guide co-ordinated rollout of the CST obligations;
- Establish a "Telecommunications Community Services Consultative Committee (TCSC), involving the Mobile Operators, Telkom, [SATRA] and the USA" (SATRA, 1998, p. 342).

[41] This mirrors Telkom's claim that its fixed-line still be counted even if disconnected for non-payment.

[42] For example, an operator would need to roll out 5 Class E phones (i.e. with 20% availability) to meet the requirement of one CST phone.

4.7.3 *Impact of the SATRA Audit*

Strangely, SATRA's audit of the USOs of the two mobile operators seems to have gone unremarked in the press. It was equally overlooked in ICAS-A's first annual report, which covered the period (SATRA, 2000b) during which attempts to finalise the report were under way. To the contrary the latter states that no "audit into community service obligations of Vodacom and MTN [was possible] due to lack of financial and human resources" (ICASA, 2001b, p. 22).

The report was certainly not unremarked by the licensees, who, for obvious reasons, mounted a concerted challenge to its findings and its validity. Little of the correspondence is available, but the disputation dragged on for several years. The operators were able to attack the report on a technicality—its methodology of "sampling without replacement instead of sampling with replacement", which increased the margin of error—and to expose weaknesses in the field survey questionnaires (SATRA, 2000a, pp. 4–5).

While holding firm to the conclusion that the audit had "revealed that there was a significant shortfall in the delivery of community services by the cellular operators", SATRA was unable to repair the data and was hence forced to concede that the "statistical base of the audit conducted by SATRA is fundamentally and irreparable [sic] flawed" (SATRA, 2000b, pp. 2–3).

As a result, SATRA moved to withdraw the field survey sections of the report, where the substance of the CST shortfall by Vodacom and MTN was starkly revealed, before finally shelving the entire audit.

Although the report never saw the official light of day, drafts were seen by some. Benjamin, for example, characterises the methodology as "weak", but confirms that the report "showed that both MTN and Vodacom were greatly under-performing in their obligations" (2001, p. 108). Rather more forcefully, Aki Stavrou says that the report showed the operator CSTs to be "absolutely crap" and complains that "they were basically let off the hook" (interview, 17 October 2014). Similarly, Matthysen also continued to defend the high-level findings of the report, reiterating several years later the problems it had exposed with the 'transportable' and payphone models (Open University, 2002, pp. 5–7). Despite the problems with the statistical methodology and some of the fieldwork, it was "clear that the end-user experience of CSTs was not good" (interview, 6 January 2015).

Nevertheless, the exercise was not altogether without positive impact. In its final briefing to the ICASA Council, in which it sought to get at least some parts of the audit report adopted and released, the team noted that:

> Vodacom has undertaken to do away with transportable community service phones as a mode of delivery of community service. They have also embarked on a further effort to make community service phones accessible 24 hours a day by mounting a phone outside their phone shops.
>
> MTN have been re-evaluating its placement of community service phones and have reflected its intentions to the Universal Service Agency and ICASA to provide or place these community services phones in tele-centres, which will assist in curbing vandalism of their phones. In so doing they will also be placing these phones on the outside of these tele-centre containers to improve 24 hours accessibility. (SATRA, 2000b, p. 3)

The team also emphasised the need for ICASA to use the audit to establish "relevant performance indicators for community service delivery in future" in order to obviate ongoing "problems when trying to impose punitive measures on the operators for non-compliance of their CSOs" (SATRA, 2000b, pp. 3–4).

4.7.4 ICASA USAO Audit (2010)

A third USO compliance audit of the mobile licensees (now three in number, with the advent of Cell C) took place some ten years later, amidst a series of engagements from the regulator on UAS issues at the time.

It was kicked off with the launch of a Discussion Document on the USOs imposed on both fixed and mobile operators (ICASA, 2010). Although the review was a far broader examination of the entire USO framework—including broadcasting, the USF and the e-rate—it also reviewed licensee compliance with the existing USOs. Conducted by consultancy firm BMI-Tech, this report (BMI-T, 2010) focused on 7 of the major licensees (including broadcast signal distributor, Sentech), but suffers from a number of key limitations.

Firstly, the consultants were not made aware of either of the previous two audits and believed that no previous "monitoring and evaluation of the operators' compliance with the USAOs [had] ever [been] done" (BMI-T, 2010, p. 4). Secondly, and more tellingly, there was no attempt to audit or verify the results. The report was "based solely on the answers provided by the licensees" (BMI-T, 2010, p. 5) to a self-completed questionnaire. The quality of the licensees' responses varied from detailed, to short, to non-existent, with no supporting documentation. The consultants were also not given access to licensee compliance reports previously submitted to ICASA. In short, and especially in the light of what its predecessors seem to have uncovered, the report is likely to have been heavily whitewashed and reveals little that the operators did not wish to be made public.

Telkom's USO compliance has been dealt with extensively above: it is therefore only the compliance of Vodacom, MTN and Cell C that will be discussed—albeit that these licensees declined or omitted to respond to certain of the questions in the questionnaire.[43]

All three licensees claimed to have met or exceeded their CST targets. Vodacom claimed 115,713 "active" CSTs (against its licence USO of 22,000); MTN claimed 20,000 (against 7,500); and Cell C merely asserted it had complied with its target of 52,000 (BMI-T, 2010, pp. 6–9). Cell C's bland declaration of compliance must be viewed as a fudge, in the shadow of 2008 litigation from MTN, in which it emerged that Cell C had already rolled out 100,000 CSTs (Jones, 2008).[44]

While the unpublished findings of the previous two audits show that operator CST figures are not to be trusted, the MTN court case shows that, once the operators had settled on Vodacom's phone shop model, at least some of them were quick to capitalise on it. This was because there were opportunities for arbitrage on the termination rate differential between normal mobile calls and those made from CST phones. Simply put, a CST termination fee of R0.06 per minute as opposed to the standard R1.25 (at the time) allowed for much higher profit margins on CST calls, creating phone shop business opportunities, and an incentive to classify as CSTs many phones outside under-serviced areas and in excess of the licence requirements. It was this perverse incentive that lay at the

[43]Vodacom was "silent" on five of the questions; MTN did not answer one of the questions; Cell C did not answer four of the questions (BMI-T, 2010, pp. 6–9). BMI-Tech's terms of reference did not allow them to pursue these lacunae further.

[44]The neatly rounded numbers of MTN (possibly derived from their allocated CST number ranges [083,106 xxxx and 083,109 xxxx] which would have catered for 20,000 CST lines) and Cell C invite disbelief.

heart of MTN's litigation against Cell C (Jones, 2008).[45] The dispute resulted in a court ruling which forced ICASA to reconsider its acceptance of Cell C's definition of under-serviced areas (ICASA, 2008a), but was ultimately settled out-of-court and confidentially (Muller, 2009).

Very disappointing answers were received in respect of compliance with the additional USOs imposed in return for access to 1800 MHz spectrum: namely distributing SIM cards and handsets and providing access to persons with disabilities. Most either did not answer the questions, or simply stated that they had not complied (BMI-T, 2010, pp. 6–9), with a range of excuses.[46]

The USOs covering a total of 20,500 schools elicited rather more detail. Vodacom and MTN both claimed partial compliance (the former reporting connections to 706 out of 713 "imposed" by ICASA,[47] and the latter reporting 486 schools), while Cell C gave no details (BMI-T, 2010, pp. 6–9). These assertions contrast markedly with ICASA's much earlier assertion that it had "approved… implementation plans" from Vodacom, MTN and Cell C for 716, 719 and 718 "public schools", respectively (ICASA, 2008b, p. 25).

The licensees gave various reasons for their failure to comply. Vodacom claimed these USOs had lapsed because they had "not been carried over into its ECNS licence" issued under the 2005 ECA (BMI-T, 2010, p. 6). All three licensees pointed to numerous problems with the rollout to public schools in particular. Identifying target schools seems to have been especially problematic, with delays and confusion blamed on both ICASA and the Department of Education, and on the lack of co-ordination between them. It certainly seems that whatever lists there were fell well short of the 20,500 schools envisaged.[48] Vodacom, in particular, pointed to a range of additional problems, including duplicated allocations, along with failure to take coverage areas into account (BMI-T, 2010, pp. 6–9). Vodacom also pointed to additional problems with the

[45] One of several litigious engagements between Cell C and MTN on the question of CSTs and their associated call tariffs.

[46] Vodacom said it believed this USO had "lapsed", while MTN blamed lack of feedback from DoC for its non-compliance (BMI-T, 2010, pp. 6 and 8).

[47] Vodacom claimed, on an unstated and entirely unclear basis, that its licence only required it to connect 625 schools.

[48] 20,500 would have been more than 80% of the 24,451 public schools then believed to exist and thus would clearly have included some already online.

public schools USO, including lack of skills and teacher training, lack of electricity in some designated schools, while others already had Internet access (BMI-T, 2010, pp. 6–7). Further, it was an intervention bedevilled by being a centrally imposed, top-down initiative without consultation with, or involvement of, its intended beneficiaries (USAASA, 2014, pp. 1v1–36).

The problems besetting this USO led to a 'Project Implementation Team' being appointed in late 2010 by then Minister Siphiwe Nyanda in an attempt to "seek a sustainable solution to ensure that these essential obligations are implemented" (2010b). This rescue attempt, however, sank without trace.

In 2014, the schools' targets were substantially revised downwards, presumably because of the failures of implementation and monitoring discussed above, to 1,500 for each of the mobile licensees (ICASA, 2014a). What counted as connectivity for each school was also specified in far greater detail, including hardware, software and connectivity QoS parameters, along with a detailed table at last specifying co-ordination responsibilities (ICASA, 2014a).

This rescue attempt appears to have been subsumed in 2015 under one of the arms of Operation Phakisa, an initiative launched under the Department of Planning, Monitoring and Evaluation to "fast track the implementation of solutions on critical delivery issues highlighted in the National Development Plan" (Phakisa, 2016). But, by late 2016, Operation Phakisa was claiming some 2,430 (75%) of the 3,250 schools had been connected (Phakisa, 2016)[49]—still far short of the original targets.

The schools USO obligation, therefore, appears to have been ill-considered, badly informed, poorly planned and incompetently executed—reaching under 10% of its targets.[50] The other 1800 MHz spectrum USOs appear to have fared even worse, never even getting out of the starting blocks.

Similarly, there were problems with the SIM card initiative. Once again, what appeared to be an innovative initiative appears not to have been thought through in respect of implementation shortfalls or perverse

[49] These figures look to be accurate, although the quality of the document leaves much to be desired.

[50] Cell C did report some rollout, but this appears to have been limited and no numbers were provided.

incentives it might create. Muller suggests it "failed to fly" because it became

> bogged down by administrative and technical hitches. The cards were useless without a handset, so the owner had to borrow a phone. Though the cards gave the recipient a cellular number, they were not loaded with airtime so users still had to pay the high retail rates for prepaid airtime. (2008)

Anecdotal accounts further suggest that, beyond the borrowing of handsets, the initiative opened up a market in stolen handsets.

The handset obligation mentioned previously was later abused in a barely reported minor scandal, which saw this USO hijacked in the cause of the 2010 soccer World Cup, hosted by South Africa. In his budget vote speech, Minister Siphiwe Nyanda reported an "agreement with the mobile operators to avail 80 000 mobile units by May 2010, which will be distributed to the Police, Safety and Security agencies, and Emergency Officers who will be deployed at the various FIFA 2010 stadia" (2010a). The handsets concerned, a little over 20% of the overall commitment, were duly handed over at a public ceremony a few months later (Nyanda, 2010b), and trumpeted as "part of [the operators'] universal service obligations". In the event, the actual rollout was just under 80,000, broken town as 26,666 (Cell C), 25,068 (MTN) and 26,667 (Vodacom) (Odendaal, 2013). And this deviation from the intention behind the USOs—to provide access for under-serviced areas and communities—passed quite unremarked in the media (Rasool, 2010).

Not only were the soccer World Cup handsets a perversion of the USOs in the licences of the mobile operators, it appears that these handsets simply disappeared without trace. Ngcobo lists them as an example of the "abuse" of USOs, suggesting they "seem to have never been distributed appropriately" (2012, pp. 122–123). None of the operators thought them worthy of mention when they reported their USO compliance to ICASA in 2010. Nor did ICASA's 2011 annual report, which deals extensively with the regulator's contribution to a successful World Cup (pp. 33–34) think these USO handsets worth mentioning. Perhaps they recognised that dodgy deals were best left unreported.

It remains unclear what actually happened to these 80,000 phones. They may have ended up in the private pockets of the lucky recipients.

Worse, some or all of the entire shipment may have been misappropriated and sold.

4.8 Universal Service: From Obligation to Obfuscation

Despite the fact that imposing USOs on the mobile operators was an innovative step, one motivated by firm universal access and service objectives, the full set of USOs was poorly thought-out, haphazard and ineffective in implementation. The models were fumbling and poorly formulated, with both operators and the regulator slow to react to market change and technological development.

Audits with any depth, detail and rigour came up with findings that were damning, and had their publication strenuously resisted by the mobile licensees. The only 'audit' (BMI-T, 2010) ever to see the public light of day was perfunctory at best.

Further, rollout was disproportionately urban, with little, if any, co-ordination between operators, or with USAASA or ICASA, a failure ascribed by Benjamin to lack of "political will" (2001, p. 115). As the Universal Service Agency itself noted:

> most significantly the co-ordination of community service obligations among the mobile operators and Telkom has not been achieved despite several efforts, resulting in multiple operators fulfilling the obligations in the same market rather than dispersing these across under serviced areas across the country. (USA, 2005, p. 98)

The licensees appear to have treated their USOs as a necessary evil that came bundled with their licences—something to be complied with, but on which the least possible effort should be expended, and where corners were to be cut at every turn. As a result, the social imperative to provide universal, affordable access to telecommunications services shifted from the adoption of international good practice in the service of post-*apartheid* redress and equity to mere outward observance of empty formulas.

References

Argus. (1997, March 4). Foreign billions scoop 30% of Telkom. *Argus*.

Baker, N. (1999). *Telkom South Africa: Case study in WLL deployment*. Boston MA: Pyramid Research. Retrieved from http://www.itu.int/ITU-D/fg7/case_library/documents/pyr001.doc.

Barrantes, R., & Galperin, H. (2008). Can the poor afford mobile telephony? Evidence from Latin America. *Telecommunications Policy, 32*, 521–530. https://doi.org/10.1016/j.telpol.2008.06.002.

Benjamin, P. (2001). *Telecentres and universal capability: A study of the telecentre programme of the Universal Service Agency in South Africa, 1996–2000*. PhD thesis.

Benjamin, P. (2003, August 5). *Universality & telecentres*.

BMI-T. (2010). *USAO compliance review of licensees for ICASA*. Johannesburg: BMI-TechKnowledge, and Mkhabela Huntley Adekeye Inc. Retrieved from http://www.ellipsis.co.za/wp-content/uploads/2010/12/USAO-Compliance-Review-Report.pdf.

Business Day. (1995, March 23). Telkom makes call for help. *Business Day*.

Chalmers, R. (1997, March 27). Telekom Malaysia, SBC get Telkom slice. *Business Day*.

Chalmers, R. (1999, July 2). Telkom tightens belt ahead of deregulation. *Business Day*.

Chonco, N. (2002, December 12). Empowering Communities Through Telecommunications: It works, It's Sustainable, presentation to Workshop on Empowering the Poor. World Bank. Retrieved from http://siteresources.worldbank.org/FINTGENDER/Resources/4pptVodacomPhone.ppt.

Coetzer, P. (2008). *Low income does not mean no income—A Vodacom initiative*. Cape Town: Reciprocity. Retrieved from http://www.bop.org.za/BoP_Lab/Publications_files/Vodacom08.pdf.

DoC. (1997, May 7). Licence issued to Telkom SA Limited to provide telecommunication services under section 36 of the Telecommunications Act, 1996. *Government Gazette* (17984).

Dyani, P. (n.d.). *Telkom South Africa's TDMA/DECT wireless local loop deployment*. Pretoria: Telkom SA Limited. Retrieved from http://www.itu.int/ITU-D/fg7/case_library/documents/saf001.doc.

Financial Mail. (1995, November 10). Strategic partner in the wings? *Financial Mail*.

Fjeldstad, O. (2004). What's trust got to do with it? Non-payment of service charges in local authorities in South Africa. *Journal of Modern African Studies, 42*(4), 539–562. https://doi.org/10.1017/S0022278X04000394.

Gregson, R. (2000, November 1). GSM pay phones provide telecom option to rural Africa. *RCR Wireless News*. Retrieved from http://www.rcrwireless.

com/20001101/carriers/gsm-pay-phones-provide-telecom-option-to-rural-africa.

Hack, S. (1995, March 20). $200 a day. So. Africans mistrust new phones. *Advertising Age*. Retrieved from http://adage.com/article/news/200-a-day-africans-mistrust-phones/83152/.

Hamilton, R. (2003, December 2). Community phones connect SA townships. *BBC News*. Retrieved from http://news.bbc.co.uk/2/hi/technology/3246732.stm.

Hodge, J. (2004, March). Universal service through roll-out targets and licence conditions: lessons from telecommunications in South Africa. *Development Southern Africa, 21*(1), 205–225.

Hodge, J. (2005). Tariff structures and access substitution of mobile cellular for fixed line in South Africa. *Telecommunications Policy, 29,* 493–505. https://doi.org/10.1016/j.telpol.2005.05.001.

Horwitz, R. (1999). South African Telecommunications: History and Prospects. In E. Noam (Ed.), *Telecommunications in Africa* (pp. 205–248). Oxford: Oxford University Press.

Horwitz, R. (2001). *Communication and democratic reform in South Africa*. Cambridge: Cambridge University Press.

Horwitz, R., & Currie, W. (2007). Another instance where privatization trumped liberalization: The politics of telecommunications reform in South Africa—A ten-year retrospective. *Telecommunications Policy, 31,* 445–462.

ICASA. (2001a, June 29). Mobile cellular telecommunication service licence, issued to Cell C (Proprietary) Limited. *Government Gazette* (22429). Retrieved from http://www.icasa.org.za/Manager/ClientFiles/Documents/cell_c_licence.pdf.

ICASA. (2001b). *Annual report 2000–2001.* Johannesburg: Independent Communications Authority of South Africa.

ICASA. (2002a, August 19). Licence to provide a national mobile cellular telecommunication service, issued to Mobile Telephone Networks (Pty) Ltd in terms of section 37(1) of the Telecommunications Act, No. 103 of 1996. *Government Gazette, 446*(23760). Retrieved from http://www.gov.za/sites/www.gov.za/files/23760b_0.pdf.

ICASA. (2002b, August 19). Licence to provide a national mobile cellular telecommunication service, issued to Vodacom (Pty) Ltd in terms of section 37(1) of the Telecommunications Act, No. 103 of 1996. *Government Gazette, 446*(23760). Retrieved from http://www.gov.za/sites/www.gov.za/files/23760a_0.pdf.

ICASA. (2003). *Annual report 2003.* Johannesburg: Independent Communications Authority of South Africa.

ICASA. (2004, December 9). Licence to provide a national mobile cellular telecommunication service, issued to Vodacom (Pty) Ltd in terms of section 37(1) and as amended in terms of section 48 of the Telecommunications Act, No. 103 of 1996. *Government Gazette* (27089).

ICASA. (2008a, May 6). Notice in terms of section 4B of the Independent Communications Authority of South Africa Act. *Government Gazette, 515*(31031).

ICASA. (2008b). *Annual report 2007/8.* Johannesburg: Independent Communications Authority of South Africa.

ICASA. (2009). *Radio frequency spectrum licence no 00-476-898-6 granted and issued to Cell C (Pty) Ltd for the use of 900 & 1800 MHz radio frequency spectrum.* Johannesburg: Independent Communications Authority of South Africa.

ICASA. (2010, August 17). ICASA discussion paper: Review of Universal Service and Access Obligations framework (USAOs). *Government Gazette, 542*(33467).

ICASA. (2011). *Annual report 2010/2011.* Johannesburg: Independent Communications Authority of South Africa. Retrieved from https://www.icasa.org.za/Portals/0/Regulations/Annual%20Reports/ICASA%20Annual%20Report%202011.pdf.

ICASA. (2014a, June 4). General notice—MTN amended universal service obligations; General notice—Vodacom amended universal service obligations; General notice—Cell C amended universal service obligations; General notice—NeoTel amended universal service obligations. *Government Gazette* (37718).

ICASA. (2014b). *Vodacom (Pty) Ltd annual compliance report 2012/2013.* Johannesburg: Independent Communications Authority of South Africa.

infoDev. (2009). *Universal access and service: Executive summary.* Washington, DC and Geneva: infoDev & International Telecommunication Union. Retrieved from http://www.ictregulationtoolkit.org//Mod4ExecSummary.

Intven, H. (2000). Universal service. In H. Intven (Ed.), *Telecommunications regulation handbook.* Washington, DC: infoDev. Retrieved from http://www.infoDev.org/projects/314regulationhandbook/module6.pdf.

ITU. (2003, December 8–9). *Universal access regulatory best practice guidelines.* Global Symposium for Regulators, Geneva, Switzerland. Geneva: International Telecommunication Union. Retrieved from http://www.itu.int/ITU-D/treg/bestpractice/2003/BestPractices_E_31.pdf.

ITWeb. (1999, June 22). Telkom prepaid set to kick off. *ITWeb.* Retrieved from http://www.itweb.co.za/index.php?option=com_content&view=article&id=132385:telkom-prepaid-set-to-kick-off&catid=260.

ITWeb. (2001, April 30). Value-added services in store for Telkom's PrepaidFone users. *ITWeb.* Retrieved from http://www.itweb.co.za/index.php?option=com_content&view=article&id=96572.

Joffe, H. (1996, May 30). Wrinkles to iron out in the cellphone sector. *Business Day.*

Jones, C. (2008, October 9). Cell C, MTN lock horns. *ITWeb*. Retrieved from http://www.itweb.co.za/sections/quickprint/print.asp?StoryID=190252.

Kaul, S., Ati, F., Janakiram, S., & Wattenstrom, B. (2008). *Business models for sustainable telecoms growth in developing economies*. Hoboken, NJ: Wiley.

Knott-Craig, A., & Afonso, E. (2009). *Second is nothing: Creating a multi-billion rand cellular industry*. Johannesburg: Pan Macmillan.

Lunsche, S. (1997, February 9). Stringent Telkom targets set to lower privatisation profit. *Business Times*.

Maddens, S. (2009). *Trends in universal access and service policies: Changing policies to accommodate competition and convergence*. Geneva: International Telecommunication Union. Retrieved from http://www.itu.int/ITU-D/treg/Events/Seminars/GSR/GSR09/doc/USPolicy_ITUEC.pdf.

M-Cell. (2002). *M-Cell Limited annual report 2002*. Johannesburg: M-Cell.

McLeod, D. (2016, November 16). Telkom wants to get rid of payphones. *TechCentral*. Retrieved from ttps://www.techcentral.co.za/telkom-wants-to-get-rid-of-payphones/70095/.

Melody, W. (2001). *Issues for consideration by South Africa in developing the new policy for universal access/service in a changing national, regional and international environment*. Delft: Lirne. Retrieved from http://lirne.net/resources/papers/UnivS-SA.pdf.

Muller, R. (2008, April 22). Free cellphone numbers. *MyBroadband*. Johannesburg. Retrieved from http://mybroadband.co.za/news/cellular/3566-free-cellphone-numbers.html.

Muller, R. (2009, June 24). Cell C challenges Icasa on licencing [sic] obligations. *MyBroadband*. Retrieved from http://mybroadband.co.za/news/cellular/8530-cell-c-challenges-icasa-on-licencing-obligations.html.

News24. (2002, June 6). End to Telkom, Icasa squabble. *News24*. Retrieved from http://www.fin24.com/Economy/End-to-Telkom-Icasa-squabble-20020606.

Ngcobo, M. (2012). *Monitoring and evaluation of universal service obligations for mobile network operators in South Africa*. Johannesburg: University of the Witwatersrand. Retrieved from https://www.google.com/search?q=ngcobo+Monitoring+and+evaluation+of+Universal+Service+Obligations+for+mobile+network+operators+in+South+Africa&ie=utf-8&oe=utf-8.

Ngubane, P. (1999, September 7). Phones for all—First phase before December. *Cape Times*.

Nyanda, S. (2010a, April 20). Budget vote speech by the Communications Minister, National Assembly. Pretoria: Department of Communications. Retrieved from http://www.polity.org.za/article/sa-nyanda-budget-vote-speech-by-the-communications-minister-national-assembly-20042010-2010-04-20.

Nyanda, S. (2010b, June 8). Address by the Minister of Communications, at the presentation of mobile phones to the Ministers of Health and Police, Pretoria. Pretoria: Department of Communications. Retrieved from http://www.polity.org.za/article/sa-nyanda-address-by-the-minister-of-communications-atthe-presentation-of-mobile-phones-to-the-ministers-of-health-and-police-pretoria-08062010-2010-06-08.

Odendaal, N. (2013, November 29). Icasa proposes reduction to network operators' universal access obligations. *Engineering News*. Retrieved from http://www.engineeringnews.co.za/article/icasa-proposes-reduction-to-network-operators-universal-access-obligations-2013-11-29.

OECD. (1991). Universal service and rate restructuring in telecommunications, No. 23. *OECD Digital Economy* (4). https://doi.org/10.1787/237454868255.

Open University. (2002). *BBC final transcript—Universal service obligation*. Retrieved from htp://www.open.ac.uk/StudentWeb/t305/scripts/audio5.rtf.

Phakisa. (2016, September 7). *Operation Phakisa: ICT in education*. Department of Planning, Monitoring & Evaluation. Retrieved from http://www.operationphakisa.gov.za/operations/Education%20Lab/pages/default.aspx.

Rasool, F. (2010, June 8). DOC bears mobile gifts. *ITWeb*. Retrieved from http://www.itweb.co.za/index.php?option=com_content&view=article&id=33826:doc-bears-mobile-gifts&catid=260.

Reck, J., & Wood, B. (2003). *What works: Vodacom's community services phone shops*. Washington, DC: United States Agency for International Development. Retrieved from http://www.wri.org/sites/default/files/pdf/dd_vodacom.pdf.

Rosenthal, J., & Volschenk, C. (1996, October 11). Row brewing over cellphone report. *Business Report*.

RSA. (1993, October 29). Multiparty implementation agreement. *Government Gazette* (15232). Retrieved from https://secure1.telkom.co.za/apps_static/ir/pdf/financial/pdf/exhibit10_5.pdf.

RSA. (1996). *Telecommunications Act, 1996. No. 103 of 1996*. Pretoria: Republic of South Africa.

SATRA. (1998). *Mobile telephone services community service audit project*. Johannesburg: South African Telecommunications Regulatory Authority.

SATRA. (2000a). *1998 CSO audit report: Response analysis report*. Johannesburg: South African Telecommunications Regulatory Authority.

SATRA. (2000b, August 8). *Council brief on 1998 CSO audit report* (A. Matthysen, Compiler). South African Telecommunications Regulatory Authority.

Stavrou, S., & Mkhize, K. (1998). *A telecommunications universal service policy framework for defining categories of needy people in South Africa*. Johannesburg: South African Telecommunications Regulatory Authority.

Stavrou, A., Whitehead, A., Wilson, M., Seloane, M., & Benjamin, P. (2001). *Presentation notes: Of recommendations on the future of the Universal Service Agency*. Pretoria: Universal Service Agency—Conference Convening Committee.

Steenkamp, W. (1998a, March 12). Make that call, keep a thief happy. *Cape Times*.

Steenkamp, W. (1998b, March 12). New methods to combat scams. *Cape Times*.

Sutherland, E. (2009). Counting customers, subscribers and mobile phone numbers. *info, 11*(9), 6–23.

Telkom. (1996). *Annual report 1996*. Pretoria: Telkom.

Telkom. (2000). *Telkom annual report 1999/2000*. Pretoria: Telkom.

Telkom. (2001). *2001 annual report Telkom Group*. Pretoria: Telkom.

Telkom. (2002a). *Telkom Group annual report 2002*. Pretoria: Telkom.

Telkom. (2002b). *Telkom Report on licence obligations 2002*. Pretoria: Telkom.

Telkom. (2003). *Prospectus*. Pretoria: Telkom. Retrieved from https://secure1.telkom.co.za/apps_static/ir/pdf/financial/pdf/prospectus.pdf.

USA. (2005). *Universal Service Agency impact document*. Johannesburg: Universal Service Agency.

USAASA. (2014). *The national strategy on universal service & access report*. Johannesburg: Universal Service and Access Agency of South Africa.

Weidemann, R. (2003, June 2). Opening of 1800 MHz a win-win situation. *ITWeb*. Retrieved from http://www.itweb.co.za/index.php?option=com_content&view=article&id=80038:opening-of-1800mhz-a-win-win-situation&catid=260.

CHAPTER 5

The Universal Service Fund

South Africa's Universal Service Fund (USF) was created by the 1996 Telecommunications Act, along with the Universal Service Agency (USA), which was to exercise the necessary financial control. The USF was to be funded through a levy to be imposed upon all licensees (with an added provision for inflows via "money accruing… from any other source") (RSA, 1996, Section 65(1)(b)). Although the name of the fund was later changed to become the Universal Access and Service Fund (USAF), under the 2005 Electronic Communications Act (ECA), it remains in place, still under the control of what is now the Universal Service and Access Agency of South Africa (USAASA).

5.1 Contributions to the Fund

Conceived and formulated in accordance with international good practice (ITU, 1998, p. 89; 2003, pp. 67–83), the USF has formally been in existence since 1 April 1999 (DoC, 1999b).

The current regime for contributions to the USAF involves a complex formulation under the ECA, requiring ICT sector licensees to contribute a percentage of "annual turnover" (RSA, 2005, Section 89). The precise formulation of the contributions, their due dates and the manner of payment are regulated by ICASA, albeit constrained by a legislated ceiling of 1%.

C. Lewis, *Regulating Telecommunications in South Africa*,
Information Technology and Global Governance,
https://doi.org/10.1007/978-3-030-43527-1_5

The regulations currently in force were promulgated by ICASA in 2011 and require all licensees (except community broadcasting licensees[1]) to contribute 0.2% of annual turnover derived from their licensed activities to the USAF. Licensees may further deduct "service provider discounts, agency fees, interconnection and facilities leasing charges, government grants and subsidies" from their annual turnover before calculating their contribution (ICASA, 2011a).

5.1.1 The Evolving Universal Service Levy

The imposition of a levy to create the USF was to be labyrinthine and ineffectual.

Despite both the regulator and the Agency being established early in 1997, the initial implementation of the USF levy was a disappointingly slow process, especially given the fact that UAS had been the centrepiece of telecommunications policy: it took nearly two and a half years to complete the first set of regulations.

Although the Act left the "basis and manner of determination of such contributions" (RSA, 1996, Section 67(2)(a)) entirely at the discretion of the regulator, the first intervention came through a Ministerial Policy Direction. In a strangely contrary move, Minister Naidoo capped the annual contribution to the Fund at R20 million—R10 million for Telkom and R10 million in "aggregate" for all other applicable licensees (1997)—in a move possibly intended to make Telkom a more attractive proposition to potential foreign investors (USA, 2005, p. 68), but one that simply circumscribed the monies available for this critically important fund.

Shortly thereafter, SATRA developed draft contribution regulations, envisaging a fixed amount (R10 million) to be levied on Telkom, with percentage levies applicable to the other licensees, up to the R10 million "aggregate" (SATRA, 1997). But it took more than a year for the regulations to be finalised, with several errors (DoC, 1999a, 1999b) along the way. The rather complex formula adopted—fixed amounts for smaller licensees and a percentage of revenue for the others (Vodacom, MTN)—echoes the approach espoused by the ITU in the following year, which

[1]Other categories of broadcasting licensee may offset contributions to another, broadcast-specific, fund run by the Media Development and Diversity Agency (MDDA).

favoured a percentage levy (ITU, 1998, pp. 86–89). Subject to the Ministerial Policy Direction, and hence to caps, this was to remain the regulation in force for the next five years (although the caps were either ignored or proved impossible to implement[2]).

Subsequent attempts by the regulator to standardise and streamline the levy regulations proceeded by fits and starts (ICASA, 2000, 2002) interrupted by a volley of Ministerial Policy Directions emanating from the 2001 colloquium to prepare for the imminent end of Telkom's period of exclusivity (DoC, 2001a, 2001b, 2001c). The regulations, then, took over a year to finalise (ICASA, 2003). By then, the formulation had been dramatically simplified in favour of a single rate applicable to all operators, and the planned steep hike in the rate had been dropped, with ICASA settling instead on a far more modest increase to 0.2% of turnover.

Further amendments followed the promulgation of the 2005 ECA, albeit tardily. The changes were relatively straightforward and largely concerned with widening the scope of contributors to include broadcasters, and with providing for the deduction of MDDA contributions by them. The rate was left unchanged at 0.2% of annual turnover.

The revised regulations unfortunately, however, created an anomalous situation for the non-profit community broadcasters, many dependent on subsidies from the MDDA, who suddenly found themselves required to contribute to the USF, a problem which ICASA claimed it had no power to resolve (ICASA, 2010, pp. 10, 11). The Act was later amended to exempt community broadcasters in 2014, but this has yet to be incorporated into the regulations.

ICASA was, however, induced to make a key change in 2011 that had the effect of substantially reducing income to the Fund: licensees are now allowed a range of deductions from their annual turnover before calculating the levy. These include "service provider discounts, agency fees, interconnection and facilities leasing charges, government grants and subsidies" (ICASA, 2011a). Allowing deductions came as a result of pressure from licensees, who alleged "double taxation" (ISPA, 2007, p. 5) on facilities leased from other licensees. These amounts can be very substantial (with inter-operator interconnection fees estimated in 2009 as running in the order of R16 billion annually [My Broadband, 2009]).

[2] The workability of the calculation is dubious at best, given differing financial year-ends for the licensees.

Table 5.1 Regulating contributions to the Universal Service Fund

Effective date	*Applicable to*	*Rate*	*Calculated on*
1 April 1999	Telecomms, VANS, PTN licensees	0.16%/R1500/R1000[a]	Annual turnover
1 July 2004	Telecomms service licensees	0.2%[b]	Annual turnover
1 April 2009	All ECNS, ECS & broadcasting[c] licensees	0.2%	Annual turnover
9 February 2011	All ECNS, ECS & BS licensees	0.2%	Annual turnover (less deductions)

[a]Differentiated by licence category
[b]USAL and PTN licensees were levied a nominal R1 per annum
[c]Subject to deductions of broadcasters' contributions to the MDDA Fund

However valid the double taxation argument may be, it opens the door to the manipulation of licensee accounts in order to secure the maximum possible deduction for the purposes of calculating the levy to be paid. It is true that turnover may involve double taxation, but is far easier to calculate, administer and monitor.

Further, there seems to have been a failure on the part of the regulator to anticipate the impact of the changes upon revenue to the Fund. The first year under the new regulations saw contributions to the Fund plummet by 70% to a level from which they have never recovered.

The effective date of the new regulations (9 February 2011) seems also to have been a blunder, creating considerable legal confusion. The financial year-end of some licensees (e.g. MTN, on 31 December) had already passed, implying they could not claim the deductions. Conversely, the financial year-end of others (e.g. Cell C, Telkom, Vodacom, on 31 March) made the deductions at least partially applicable. Worse, there was no pro rata provision in the regulations. In practice, all, except Vodacom, seem to have taken advantage of the legal lacuna and slashed their contributions.

Table 5.1 summarises the changing basis, scope and nature of the levy as officially applicable over the years.

5.2 UAS Levy Trends

The widening scope of the levy's application since its inception is not especially remarkable in the light of the phenomenon of convergence and South Africa's move to a converged regulator. Originally applicable only to holders of telecommunications service licences, including VANS and PTN licensees (RSA, 1996, Section 67), the funding base was broadened under the 2005 ECA to include all infrastructure and service licensees[3] (RSA, 2005, Section 89).

A greater challenge lies in determining the basis of calculation for the levy. A specified percentage of 'annual turnover' seems straightforward and is reasonably simple in a small market with limited competition, dominated by a small number of vertically integrated players. Indeed, 'annual turnover' and 'licensed activity' were never formally defined in either legislation or regulation, creating potential problems with the "proper calculation and payment of USAF contributions" by licensees, and making "proper compliance nigh-on impossible" (ISPA, 2007, pp. 5, 6). 'Annual turnover' is now defined in the regulation (ICASA, 2011a, p. 5), but 'licensed activity' still not. Further, the calculation may require an onerous separation of accounts for any licensee whose income includes revenue from non-licensed activities and appears to impose a formal audit on even the smallest of players for whom no such statutory requirement otherwise exists (ISPA, 2007, p. 8).

Recent sets of regulations introduce hefty penalties (25%, plus penalty interest) on late payments (ICASA, 2008, Section 4), suggesting substantial problems with late payment and non-payment of the required contributions. Penalty and interest charges are retained in the current regulations, although they are now slightly less punitive in the light of "recent developments in drafting principles" and to ensure alignment with the 1999 Public Finance Management Act (ICASA, 2011a).

Finally, the recent ICT Policy Review Panel recommended that the levy be increased, potentially up to the legislated maximum of 1%, subject to a "study to ascertain the quantum of funding that will be required", partly in order to fund the wider scope and mandate of Digital Development Fund it proposed as replacement to the USF (DTPS, 2015, pp. 42–46). Government's ensuing White Paper controversially goes further, adopting (without undertaking the recommended study) a figure of "at least one per cent" as the new benchmark (DTPS, 2015, p. 45). In addition, it hands the Minister "responsibility for setting and reviewing the Fund

[3]With the legislated exclusion of not-for-profit community broadcasters.

levy" (DTPS, 2016, p. 40). Both changes are, however, ultra vires the current Act, with no legislative amendment currently on the table.

5.3 How Contributions to the Fund Are Made

Throughout the lifespan of the Fund, licensees have made payment of their contributions to ICASA, which in turn, passes those contributions to the National Revenue Fund (NRF) under the control of Treasury (RSA, 2005, Section 87).

This has created considerable difficulties in respect of determining the total of licensee contributions to the Fund, with no complete, accurate figures available from either ICASA or USAASA. Estimates range from Perry's rather speculative R1 billion (2010, p. 19), through SACF's loosely calculated R1.5 billion (SACF, 2013, p. 25), to USAASA's own—incorrect—assertion that "there is no publicly available record of the value of annual USAF contributions by operators into the National Revenue Fund" (USAASA, 2014a, p. 70).

Such uncertainty arises from the failure of ICASA and USAASA to put in place the necessary co-ordination and transparency mechanisms to give effect to the legislative provision requiring that "all money received, the amounts of which in terms of subsection (1) must be credited to to [sic] the Universal Service and Access Fund in the books of the Agency, must be paid into the National Revenue Fund" (RSA, 2005, Section 87(2)). This speaks to USAASA's lack of political will to determine how much money is potentially available to fund UAS interventions.

Attempts to address this problem via a 2014 amendment to the ECA may in fact have created additional problems. On the one hand, USAASA is still required to "keep account of the Fund in its books" and to "collect [and credit] all money that is due and payable to the Universal Service and Access Fund from the Authority [ICASA]" (RSA, 2005, Sections 87(2), 87(1) and 89(4)). But on the other, ICASA is also still required to pay the contributions of licensees into the NRF. While ICASA is now obliged to provide USAASA with a detailed breakdown of the contributions it receives towards the Fund, quite how the mutually contradictory destinations of the payments (the NRF vs USAASA) will be resolved remains to be seen.

As Table 5.2 indicates, a substantially accurate assessment of the contributions to the Fund is in fact available—see right-hand column (figures sourced from USAASA and ICASA are included for comparative purposes

Table 5.2 Universal Service Fund: licensee contributions

	USAASA[a]	*ICASA*[b]	*Treasury*[c]
1998/1999			R482,000
1999/2000	R10,000,000		R19,508,000
2000/2001	R10,220,000		R24, 349,000
2001/2002	R10,935,400		R33,575,000
2002/2003	R11,438,428		R29,565,000
2003/2004	R26,171,122		R26,745,000
2004/2005	R92,052,881		R99,848,000
2005/2006	R142,229,746	R142,033,677	R142,034,000
2006/2007	R151,993,963	R153,438,706	R152,120,000
2007/2008	R180,962,588	R182,673,416	R181,085,000
2008/2009		R206,313,581	R207,167,000
2009/2010		R219,099,054	R224,773,813
2010/2011		R181,205,854	R255,341,290
2011/2012		R176,053,541	R75,088,737
2012/2013		R192,389,253	R155,083,589
2013/2014		R196,071,924	R126,852,000
2014/2015		R201,862,357	R176,681,000
2015/2016		R209,541,652	R198,612,000
Total			**USD305 million**

[a]USAASA only once ever recorded the figures in its annual report (2008a, p. 14). Repeated attempts to obtain more recent figures from USAASA proved fruitless

[b]Repeated attempts to obtain a comprehensive set of figures from ICASA also proved fruitless. Partial figures were sourced from some annual reports, some licensee compliance reports, and via email correspondence

[c]Figures sourced from annual Budget Review reports issued by Treasury

and show that their records only tally approximately, especially in the early years, with each other, and with the official figures). The figures show that licensees have in fact contributed more than R2.1 billion to the Fund since its inception.

Although the contributions to the Fund remained relatively low in the years for which the contribution cap was in place (up until 2003/2004), they did not remain within the ceiling established in the regulations. It seems likely that this was due to the difficulties of managing a cap at all, let alone equitably, between multiple contributors with differing financial year-ends. Collections soared once the cap was removed. Even more dramatically, they plummeted after 2010/2011, once allowable deductions were introduced, before slowly climbing again (Fig. 5.1). It is unclear why the Treasury figures are so wildly different in 2010/2011

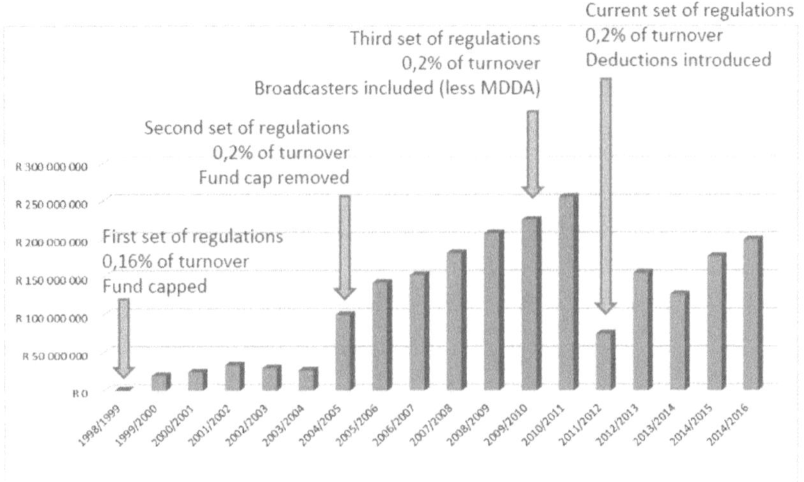

Fig. 5.1 Universal Service Fund: licensee contributions (Treasury figures)

and 2011/2012, perhaps because of accounting differences.[4] It is also unclear why the ICASA figures are consistently so much higher than those reported by Treasury (over R150 million more since 2009/2010).

Contributions to the Fund are almost exclusively sourced from telecommunications licensees. With the exception of Primedia, broadcasting licensees have preferred rather contribute to the MDDA, presumably because of that fund's more specific broadcasting focus and because of its better disbursement record. As soon as they were required to contribute (i.e. from 2009/2010), inflows from broadcasters to the MDDA fund more than trebled from R5.3 million to R17.9 million (MDDA, 2010, p. 86), reaching R32 million in 2013/2014 (MDDA, 2015, p. 53).

[4] ICASA accounts for the contribution according to the licensee financial year to which it is applicable. Treasury accounts for the contribution according to when it actually receives the money.

Extending the scope of the USAF to include broadcasters, therefore, achieved almost nothing. Given the choice of where to place their universal service liability, the broadcasters voted overwhelmingly in favour of the MDDA.

5.4 Monitoring: ICASA vs Licensees

Verification of USF compliance by the licensees is currently undertaken in terms of the standard annual compliance reports that all licensees are required to submit, which have been made publicly available since 2009/2010.

But ICASA has difficulties collecting these reports in the first place. Although the number of published reports rose from 25 for 2009/2010 to 89 for 2012/2013, this is still a small proportion of the total number of licensees—albeit that the listing does contain all the major players.

Assessment of the compliance reports is undertaken separately for broadcasting licensees and ECNS and ECS licensees. ICASA's Head of Broadcasting Compliance, Fikile Hlongwane, assures that "verification" of "USAF calculations [which would require audited financial statements] as well as the MDDA proof of payment" takes place, and that "in the event of any short fall [sic] in the contributions, finance takes the matter up with the relevant licensee/s" (personal communication, 19 February 2015). It is hard, however, to believe that there are neither defaulters nor errors. But there is no independent verification of ICASA's ability to do this, and no publicly available report assessing the state of compliance.

The compliance reports covering the earlier years make interesting reading, since they are relatively unsanitised. Most detail has been excised in recent years, following operator demands for confidentiality (Godfree Maulana, personal correspondence, 9 February 2015). However, ICASA's own assessment of the early compliance reports of seven of the major contributors to the Fund (viz. Cell C, iBurst/WBS, Internet Solutions, MTN, Neotel, Telkom, Vodacom) reveals that monitoring and enforcement difficulties have been quite substantial (ICASA, 2011b).

One of these has been late submission of payments to the USAF. Only Telkom and Vodacom seem to have paid within the prescribed 3 months after financial year end. Most of the others took up to 6 months to pay, with ICASA deciding to waive penalties and interest, because the incoming 2011 regulations (albeit, not then in force) had moved to a 6-month window. Only, in the case of Internet Solutions, where the payment was 8 months late, were enforcement of penalties and interest recommended.[5]

The second major problem area involved calculation errors, either by accident or design. MTN and Sentech used "adjusted gross revenue"[6] (rather than "annual turnover" without any adjustment, as required) as the basis of their calculation. In MTN's case, correcting the calculation added R22 million to the bill, nearly doubling their contribution to the Fund. In addition, both payments were late, which led ICASA to seek, over the objections of MTN, to levy penalties and interest amounting to a further R10 million.

Worryingly, not a single broadcast licensee[7] was assessed in either 2009/2010 or 2010/2011 in respect of their contribution to the USAF in any of the over 50 published compliance reports.

Further, ICASA's ability to follow through on or interrogate the substance of the reports seems lacking. For example, the outcome of penalty fees and interest levied on MTN in 2009/2010 is never mentioned again by ICASA. In a related vein, the degree of compliance by Internet Solutions remains highly unclear. Each of their compliance reports subsequent to 2009/2010 merely states that their USAF payment is not yet due. As a result, their contribution to the fund remains seemingly unaudited in recent years. Attempts to gain clarity from ICASA on the matter elicited a firm 'no comment' on the grounds that this was a "compliance matter" (personal communication, 11 February 2015).

Importantly, the contributions of all four major operators fell substantially between 2009/2010 and 2010/2011,[8] this despite all except Telkom reporting increased revenues (Cell C, 2011; MTN, 2011, p. 46; Telkom, 2011, p. 144; Vodacom, 2011, p. 9). It is therefore surprising that ICASA's compliance reporting makes no comment on the substantial fall in payments to the Fund on the part of its four largest contributors. Basing contributions on 'annual turnover derived from the licensee's licence activity' seems, however, to have offered licensees unexplained ways of reducing their financial commitments to the USF.

[5] There is no report of Internet Solutions having paid, and a request for an update on the matter, received an evasive answer.

[6] A definition erroneously included in the regulation, but never used.

[7] Excluding MultiChoice, likely in respect of its ISP subsidiary, MWeb.

[8] The drop was 55% in the case of Cell C, 29% in the case of Telkom, 26% in the case of MTN and 5% in the case of Vodacom.

Taken together, the issues highlighted above suggest a worrying inability on the part of ICASA to monitor, enforce and follow through on USF payment compliance year on year.

Policy implementation difficulties are, therefore, clearly evident, as regards contributions by licensees towards the USF, with serious institutional difficulties thus undermining the effectiveness of the fundraising for UAS projects. ICASA seems to have been unable to keep track of contributions or to align its reporting with that of Treasury. USAASA seems to have had only the vaguest of notions as how much funding was potentially available to increase levels of ICT access. There seems to have been no communications structure between the two.

As a result, there is no single, publicly available, reliable and accurate set of figures for the amounts of money contributed towards the Fund over the years. Treasury officials report that neither ICASA nor USAASA ever consulted them on the status or amount of contributions to the Fund; nor was there ever a structured relationship or formal consultation framework between ICASA and USAASA on the issue (Mandla Msimang, interview, 7 November 2014). This belies the provisions of the original 1996 Act requiring "all money received [via ICASA to] be credited to the Universal Service Fund in the books of the Agency" (RSA, 1996, Section 65(2)). As a result, in the absence of a clear record of contributions, planning for expenditure is severely hamstrung.

The second major issue bedevilling contributions to the Fund has been the lack of a clearly defined basis for calculating contributions. The lack of adequate definitions for key concepts such as 'annual turnover' and 'licensed activity', coupled with the introduction of a range of allowable discounts for items such as 'interconnection', 'agency fees' and 'facilities leasing charges', creates a highly complex compliance environment. On the one hand, it is a recipe for confusion by licensees attempting to comply, as well as an opportunity for the unscrupulous to obfuscate or under-pay. On the other, it ensures a monitoring and enforcement nightmare for ICASA. Further, perhaps in consequence, there appear to be a number of question marks over ICASA's capacity to monitor, verify and ensure licensee compliance with the USAF levy regulations.

Nevertheless, while far from perfect, the USF levy imposed on licensees over the last 15 or so years has been able to accumulate a substantial financial resource potentially at the disposal of interventions intended to promote the cause of UAS.

5.5 Spending the Universal Service Fund

Expenditure by USAASA from the Fund follows a convoluted process, inversely akin to that of the contributions discussed above. Access to funding for UAS interventions proceeds via the annual budget allocation to the Department from the National Revenue Fund, and is formalised once the annual Appropriation Act is adopted by Parliament. USAASA's ability to access the full amount of the contributions to the USAF has been hampered by its lack of information in respect of these amounts, and by Treasury's reluctance to release the money in the absence of proper business planning or an effective track record in deploying the funds at its disposal (Mandla Msimang, interview, 7 November 2014).

5.5.1 Funds Available to the Agency

Similar difficulties exist in establishing exactly how much money has been allocated to the USF, particularly in the early years. Expenditure from the fund has been widely (and correctly) speculated to be far below the amounts paid in by the licensees over the years (see above), but no authoritatively accurate numbers have been available (Lewis, 2013, p. 102) before now. Table 5.3 represents an attempt to quantify the funds actually made available to the Agency over the years, but is beset by several challenges—hence the inclusion of figures from different sources.

Figures are reflected in the annual reports of the Agency, but most of these are no longer in the public domain. Worse, USAASA itself no longer has copies of many of the earlier ones. A recent USAASA strategy (2014a, pp. lvl–71) attempts to provide a breakdown, but is bedevilled by the fact that its figures are drawn from an earlier, but partially incorrect, SACF report (2013, pp. 6, 25).[9] The figures from the full set of annual reports of the Agency, however, must be considered authoritative, since they have been independently audited. Where the figures from the corresponding Appropriation Act differ, this usually means funds have been appropriated, but not drawn down into the USF account.

The figures show earmarked allocations to the Fund since its inception have amounted to just over R2.8 billion and are illustrated in Fig. 5.2. The towering spike from 2011/2012 onwards (light blue) marks the

[9] Aside from some typographical errors, several early numbers—incorrectly—simply reproduce the legislated cap on the fund.

Table 5.3 Universal Service Fund appropriations

	SACF report[a]	*Appropriation Acts*[b]	*USAASA annual reports*
1997/1998	R3,599,000	R3,000,000	Nil
1998/1999	R20,000,000	R10,000,000	R482,000
1999/2000	R20,000,000	R11,295,000	R11,295,000
2000/2001	R20,000,000	R21,100,000	R25,595,324
2001/2002	R22,496,000	R22,486,000	R22,486,000
2002/2003		R23,679,000	R23,679,000
2003/2004	R24,500,000	R24,745,000	R24,745,000
2004/2005	R26,230,000	R26,230,000	R26,230,000
2005/2006	R29,400,000	R29,400,000	R29,400,000
2006/2007	R31,164,000	R31,164,000	R31,164,000
2007/2008	R32,722,000	R32,722,000	R32,722,000
2008/2009	R34,581,000	R34,581,000	R34,581,000
2009/2010	R36,427,000	R36,427,000	R36,427,000
2010/2011	R218,613,000	R218,613,000	R38,613,000
2011/2012	R260,930,000	R260,930,000	R260,930,000
2012/2013		R273,977,000	R273,977,000
2013/2014		R285,046,000	R285,046,000
2014/2015		R840,988,000	R840,988,000
2015/2016		R233,540,000	R233,540,000
2016/2017		R644,540,000	R644,540,000
Total	**R780,662,000**	**R3,064,463,000**	**R2,876,440,324**

[a]SACF (2013, pp. 6, 25)

[b]Figures from 2010/2011 include specific allocations for the migration to digital terrestrial television, mostly earmarked for subsidised set-top boxes

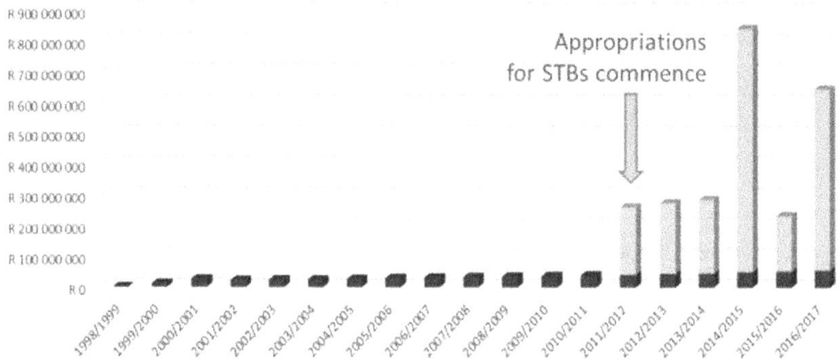

Fig. 5.2 Universal Service Fund: appropriations to USAASA

inclusion of set-asides to finance the distribution of subsidised set-top boxes (STBs) for poor households as part of the migration to digital terrestrial television (DTT), which process itself remains largely stalled. These amounts total nearly R2.3 billion, almost all of it so far unspent, leaving the fund carrying a surplus of some R2.5 billion by the end of the 2016/2017 financial year (USAASA, 2017, p. 51).

Allocations earmarked for core UAS interventions have, however, meandered along at much the same level throughout, reaching a mere R55 million in 2016/2017, and totalling some R625 million overall. Meanwhile, telecommunications licensees (in the main) have contributed nearly four times as much as their sub-sector received over the same period, over R1.9 billion in all.

Some of the confusion as to exactly how much money was available to the Agency to fund UAS interventions derives from the popular misconception that levies contributed by the (mostly telecommunications) licensees had been set aside and reserved for the USF, a misperception shared by the Agency's own CEO, who claimed that the "money had been ringfenced by National Treasury and should still be available once it is needed" (Vecchiatto, 2008a). Instead, the levies went into the "large pot" of the National Revenue Fund and were hence "treated like an ordinary tax rather than a levy designated for a specific purpose" (Vecchiatto, 2008b).

It is worth recalling that early drafts of the original Telecommunications Bill had envisaged the Fund as a ring-fenced entity into which operators would contribute directly (DPTB, 1996, Section 68). This provision was removed at the insistence of the Department of State Expenditure, which sought to enforce a Cabinet decision to incorporate the Department of Posts, Telecommunications and Broadcasting within South Africa's main Budget, and sought to align the USF with the recommendations of the Katz Commission on Taxation (DSE, 1996).

5.6 Beneficiaries of the Fund

The intended target beneficiaries of the USF have undergone some changes over the years.

In terms of the 1996 Telecommunications Act, the USF was to be "utilised exclusively for the payment of [two types of] subsidies"—intended, on the one hand, to provide support for "needy persons" to gain access to telecommunications services, and, on the other, to subsidise

PSTS licensees (i.e. Telkom) to meet their USOs for the "extension of… service to areas and communities which are not served or not adequately served by telecommunication services" (RSA, 1996, Section 66).[10]

The regulator was assigned overall "control" and direction over how the Agency should expend the Fund, along with determining the "categories of needy persons" eligible for support, how such needy persons should apply and how the subsidies should be disbursed. As the Fund was being established, the Minister directed that 99% of USF expenditure should be directed to needy persons (DoC, 1999b). In the light of the high priority thus accorded to providing telephony access to the poor, it is indeed ironic that, as will be shown, no needy person has ever received such a subsidy.[11]

A number of additional beneficiary categories were added some years later, when the Act was amended in 2001, viz. providing Internet access to public schools and colleges; establishing telecentres[12] and "public information terminals"; support for "small businesses and cooperatives to acquire and construct [telecommunications] infrastructure" in under-serviced areas[13]; and the "provision of multimedia services" (RSA, 2001). At the same time, the Minister assumed overall direction of the Fund and everything pertaining to 'needy persons'.

The passage of the current ECA in 2005 saw relatively few changes to this funding regime. Disbursements from the Fund remain earmarked exclusively for the payment of subsidies to further UAS in respect of ICT services. Subsidies now include:

- assistance for needy persons to acquire broadcasting, electronic communications network and electronic communications services;
- financial support for the construction or extension of electronic communications networks in under-serviced areas by any ECNS (infrastructure) licensee;

[10]This latter proviso (dropped in 2001) was intended to fall away once Telkom's rates had been rebalanced.

[11]The provision has, however, recently been used for distributing subsidised DTT set-top boxes to poor households.

[12]Likely a post hoc legitimation of the Agency's long-standing telecentre programme, *ultra vires* the original Act.

[13]To cater for subsidies to the Under-serviced Area Licensees, introduced at the same time.

- procurement of broadcasting, electronic communications and electronic communications network services by public schools and FET colleges;
- establishment and operation of community centres providing access to electronic communications network services, electronic communication services and broadcasting services (RSA, 2005, Section 88).

A final catch-all clause was added when the ECA was amended in 2014. This wide-ranging, open-ended provision allows the Minister to prescribe, with the agreement of the Minister of Finance, how the subsidies should be directed (RSA, 2005, Section 88(f)) and may have had subsidised set-top boxes for digital terrestrial television in mind.

5.6.1 Telecentres

Telecentre delivery was the first area of support under the Fund, and one of its longest standing project areas. Without any specific legal mandate under either category of subsidies outlined above, they were being extensively punted at the time by both the IDRC (Fuchs, 1998; Ofir, 2003, pp. 41 and 46) and the ITU (ITU, 1994, p. 18; Townsend, 2002) as a vehicle for the promotion of universal access. This enthusiasm for the telecentre model was shared by Jay Naidoo: shortly before introducing the Telecommunications Bill into Parliament, he was quoted as saying:

> I want to see every community with a multi-purpose communications and information centre… [with] access to the Internet and on-line government information – everything from what government tenders were available to how you could apply for a pension, or get a drivers' licence. (Randall, 1996)

Following its establishment in February 1997, the Agency moved ambitiously to roll out telecentres, seemingly without any justification other than enthusiasm. Its inaugural head Mlungisi Hlongwane had declared that the USA would "facilitate the establishment of a pilot project, the 'telecentres', throughout the country" (Malunga, 1997). Benjamin points to a direct instruction from Director General Ngcaba and Minister Naidoo to the fledgling Agency (2001, pp. 99–100), noting that Ngcaba saw telecentres as "prestige projects, with high quality equipment and facilities", and describing how the Department put "pressure" on the Agency to "deliver quickly" (2001, pp. 2, 121).

As a result, the first telecentre was launched with some fanfare in under-serviced Ga-Seleka, a poor, arid rural settlement, near the remote Botswana border, in early 1998 (Allchurch, 1998; Benjamin, 2001, p. 149). A further five telecentres in various under-serviced settlements across the country followed over the short space of the next two months (Khumalo, 1998), with a dozen more added by March 1999 (USA, 2005, p. 77).

This initial cluster of telecentres was part of a small IDRC-funded pilot project covering 12 such centres (Benjamin, 2001, p. 121; James, 2001, p. 67). It was a pilot that soon escalated into something "very ambitious" (Khumalo, 1998), a grandiose vision that projected a rollout totalling 4000 (USA, 2005, p. 77).

Few at the time questioned the notion of telecentres as being at the forefront of UAS projects to be funded from the USF. The acting head of the Agency at the time, Fikile Khumalo, spoke publicly and ambitiously of the future of the intervention (1998). Tina James, then a senior IDRC staffer, described the telecentre programme as being at the core of the Agency's UAS interventions "with funding provided by the Universal Service Fund and augmented by donor funding from the international community" (2001, p. 67). It was only rather later that the programme was recognised as problematic, outside the scope provided for in the Act (Benjamin, 2001, p. 99; USA, 2005, p. 65).[14]

The USA's pilot telecentre rollout almost immediately ran into difficulties. The very first telecentre only received its telephone line just in time to make the official launch, following what seems to have been a mix of foot-dragging and incompetence on the part of Telkom (Benjamin, 2001, p. 149). In August 1998, the USA's acting head Fikile Khumalo was to report that two of the initial six telecentres (Thaba Nchu—no electricity, and Winterveldt—equipment theft) were "not operational" (1998).

It took a little longer for the extent of the problems to become apparent to the IDRC. The crisis broke at the May 1999 launch of an IDRC-funded school-based telecentre in Bulwer, a small country town in KwaZulu-Natal. The event was variously described as a "circus" (Tina

[14] Some of the Agency's other programmes—its "Teacher's E-Readiness Training Programme" and the "Intern Programme… for young people studying in the ICT field" (USA, 2004, p. 5)—equally rested on dubious legal foundations.

James, interview, 27 November 2014) and a “disaster” (Benjamin, 2001, p. 123). The telecentre had been claimed by the USA as operational, but when the Minister arrived for the official launch, the Agency staffer was still frantically trying to get phone lines reconnected (they had been appropriated by the school principal, and then disconnected by Telkom for non-payment), and the IDRC’s Tina James was unpacking computers from their boxes and setting them up (no-one else there knew how to do this) (Tina James, interview, 27 November 2014).

As a result of this fiasco, the IDRC instituted a formal audit into the telecentre programme, which uncovered widespread misreporting, maladministration and fraud. The malpractices thus exposed included:

- Inflated and fraudulent tenders;
- Wasteful expenditure;
- Ghost workers;
- Lack of book-keeping and record-keeping;
- Theft and disappearance of equipment (Tina James, interview, 27 November 2014).

The situation was deemed so serious that the IDRC called an urgent meeting with Director General Ngcaba, at which it formally advised that the USA and its entire telecentre programme should be closed down. But nothing was done, and, as a consequence, the IDRC withdrew its funding the following year (Benjamin, 2001, p. 123).

James attributes much of the debacle to “incompetence” on the part of the staff at the Agency rather than the kind of deliberate, collusive fraud that was later to surface. In her words: the USA staff, many of whom had been appointed on the basis of their trade union backgrounds, just “didn’t have the right background; they didn’t have the right skills; they didn’t understand tender processes” (Tina James, interview, 27 November 2014).

In the meantime, the Agency continued to steam ahead with its telecentre rollout, apparently oblivious to the all the problems, possibly under pressure from both DG Ngcaba and Minister Naidoo (Benjamin, 2001, pp. 99 and 123). Tenders were awarded to establish a further 35 telecentres in “townships, informal settlements and rural areas” by the end of 1999 (Ngubane, 1999).

Reports that the telecentre project was in trouble began to filter through into the press (Eveleth, 1999), but the warning signs went unheeded.

International consultants had been brought in to draft an ambitious five-year telecentre rollout programme. Tabled in mid-1999, the report proposed a more differentiated model, ranging from small-scale "Tele-shops" (to be contracted out to Vodacom, and based on its CST phone shops and the Grameen phone model), through "Mini-Telecentres",[15] up to top-of-the-range "Multipurpose Community Telecentres" (DNTA, 1999a, pp. 13–14 and 35–37). The plan's emphasis on the more modest forms of telecentre—some 70% of its proposed 2128 telecentres were to be tele-shops, with only 14% to be full-on MPCCs—likely did not sit well with the grandiose telecentre visions of government.

In the event, neither vision came anywhere close to being realised. By 2001, a mere 65 telecentres had been set up. Benjamin's gloomy, but realistic, assessment of these revealed a dismal picture: less than half were functional, offering telephony and computer facilities, but less than one in five of these enjoyed Internet access; nearly a third were no longer operating; another fifth did not even have telephone access (2001, pp. 127–129).

An annual report of the Agency gives some assessment of the programme. Despite recording some of the problems—including burglaries, difficulties of technical support, lack of capacity and management skills[16]—it gives no figures for the telecentre rollout and asserts a determination to press ahead with model (USA, 2002, pp. 10, 11). An audit and an evaluation of the telecentres were commissioned in late 2001, and a national telecentre meeting early the following year resulted in another implementation plan (USA, 2002, pp. 10 and 13)—but neither document was ever made public. Meanwhile, the Agency continued to spend intensively on telecentres—some R23 million in 2000/2001 and nearly R4 million in 2001/2002 (USA, 2002, p. 33).

Subsequent annual reports continue to cite numbers of telecentres rolled out—24 in 2003/2004, 50 more in 2005/2006, another 14 in 2006/2007—without any reference to the operational status of those

[15] A modest micro-enterprise comprising up to 2 phone lines, one dial-up Internet-connected PC, and a multi-function printer/scanner/copier/fax.

[16] It fails to mention Telkom's high levels of pricing, which left little margin for profitability (Ngubane, 1999).

rolled out in previous years. However, the Agency's numbers game seems to have ceased from 2008/2009, after which no further specific numbers are available. However, best estimates suggest that a total of 154 telecentres and 362 cyber-labs[17] had been rolled out by the end of 2009/2010. Even assuming all telecentres were operational, the rollout was proceeding at a glacial average rate of some 10 telecentres a year.

The telecentre deployment was further complicated by the introduction of a number of competing initiatives. These included: a 1998 Post Office programme to roll out self-service Internet-connected kiosks, called Public Information Terminals (PITs), as well as another Multipurpose Community Centre (MPCC) programme via the oddly named Government Communication and Information System (GCIS) (RSA, 2000). These GCIS MPCCs were later renamed 'Thusong Community Service Centres' and combined with the Agency's own telecentre programme (USAASA, 2007, p. 7). The Agency's telecentre programme also underwent a number of name changes. Aside from 'Thusong Service Centres', other terms in use in the documentation include 'digital hubs' and 'community access centres', all of which were later subsumed under a programme for the 'Rapid Deployment of Public Access Facilities in Under-Serviced Areas' (USAASA, 2009a, p. 51). The shifts in nomenclature may have been occasioned by the rapid turnover of personnel at the Agency, but could also have been motivated by a desire to camouflage the manifest failures of the deployment, and possibly later to cover up corruption and the looting of the Fund.

Alongside the shifting vocabulary, there were ongoing efforts on the part of the Agency to remedy the manifest problems of the programme. A 'Rehabilitation of Telecentres Programme', was launched in 2003/2004, which saw the installation of new equipment in some 20 telecentres (USA, 2004, p. 11). 'Rehabilitation' of existing telecentres and cyber-labs was still continuing to engage the Agency as late as 2010, even as it sought to hand over its responsibility for them to other entities (USAASA, 2010, p. 12).

The most recently available estimate counts 103 telecentres and 186 cyber-labs, but cites no sources for these figures (USAASA, 2014a, pp. 1v1–63). Taken together, these figures suggest a rollout drastically

[17] Figures compiled from annual and other Agency reports.

short of the original five-year target of 2128—despite more than 15 years having elapsed.

The Agency's telecentre programme has continued to be dogged by allegations of corruption and mismanagement. Former USAASA Board member Shaun Pather describes how a nest of maladministration, misappropriation and corruption—many of the same issues that the early IDRC audit had uncovered, but now writ large and on an organised scale—was uncovered in mid-2011 during his tenure (interview, 27 March 2015).

Suspicions were aroused by the inflated prices on recommended bids for the 'Rapid Deployment Project'. Random site visits revealed that most of the telecentres were "empty shells" with a "few tables". Only two of the telecentres, Impendle in rural KwaZulu-Natal and Ulwazi in an informal settlement close to Cape Town, were reported to be working. Both had been amongst the flurry of telecentres and cyber-labs opened with public fanfare by the Minister and his deputy in the run-up to the May 2011 local government elections (Bapela, 2011; Padayachie, 2011). Similar problems appear to have surfaced at around the same time in relation to the uMsinga 'broadband project', which had been intended as a "flagship to demonstrate that with community support and with appropriate technology, you could make a difference" (Shaun Pather, interview, 27 March 2015). The appointed contractor, Umzinyathi Telecommunications (aka former USAL Umzitel), appears to have been paid much, but delivered little in the way of functioning telecentres.

In consequence, a number of Board members approached Minister Padayachie, who agreed to a forensic audit (GFIA, 2012), which led in turn to the suspension, dismissal and the laying of criminal charges against a number of senior USAASA staff, including the CEO and the CFO, and external suppliers, all allegedly implicated in corruption to the tune of some R30 million (GFIA, 2012; Malefane & Ncana, 2011; USAASA, 2013a, p. 34).

Despite the forensic audit, its findings and the consequent sanctions against USAASA staff implicated, a similar set of allegations of corruption was to surface barely two years later, this time via opposition MP Bantu Holomisa. In an open letter to President Zuma, Holomisa alleged that Mthinte Communications had been dramatically overpaid (an initial R7 million contract had been improperly escalated to over R33 million) and had equally dramatically under-delivered (with only 9 of the contracted 120 telecentres in operation) (Holomisa, 2013).

Holomisa went on to allege "ethnic" bias in the project, pointing out that almost all of the 'Rapid Deployment' telecentres were to be located in the home provinces of the Minister and then President Zuma.

The resultant furore led to further forensic investigations (USAASA, 2013a, p. 106) and the initiation of an investigation under the Special Investigation Unit (SIU) (RSA, 2014). One of the specific areas targeted by the SIU investigation was the 'Rapid Deployment of Public Access Facilities Programme', in other words, the telecentre rollout outlined above. The investigation was to cover both the Rapid Deployment tender process and whether any "unauthorised, irregular or fruitless and wasteful expenditure" had been incurred by the Agency. As of early 2017, the SIU lists the status of this investigation as "Final Report Being Prepared"[18] (SIU, 2017).

It is hard, therefore, to describe the telecentre programme as anything other than an abject failure. The Agency's own report questions whether the telecentre model is an appropriate vehicle for the provision of UAS and goes on to describe the entire intervention as "misdirected" (USA, 2005, pp. 52–53 and 58). Similarly, Benjamin's early (2001) conclusion that the first telecentres were neither effective nor sustainable—undermined by lack of skills and capacity, by poor financial management, and beset by technical challenges and theft—is echoed in more recent studies. James describes working on a 2007 audit of telecentres in KwaZulu-Natal which

> showed that 99% of the IDRC funding had gone to waste, that hardly a single USA telecentre was still functioning. Most of them were completely dysfunctional or closed down, but there were still people working there, being paid by the USA, with nothing to do. (interview, 27 November 2014)

Similarly, Attwood and Braathen suggest that the percentage of operational telecentres may be very low (Attwood & Braathen, 2010). Others conclude equally gloomily that little has changed since Benjamin's study, which in turn leads them to question the viability of the telecentre

[18] A late 2019 answer by the Minister to a Parliamentary question, as this book was in press, gives some glimpse into the findings of the still-unpublished SIU report. It refers to numerous irregularities surrounding the contract with Mthinthe Communications, amounting to "financial misconduct", for which prosecution was recommended.

model itself (Gomez, Pather, & Dosono, 2012). A number of academic and other studies over the years have echoed similar concerns (Hulbert & Snyman, 2007; Parkinson, 2005, pp. 29–30; Stavrou, Whitehead, Wilson, Seloane, & Benjamin, 2001; Sumbwanyambe, Nel, & Clarke, 2011) over what UAS researcher Andrew Dymond has described as "un-telecentres… the famous telecentres without any tele connection" (personal communication, 20 November 2014).

The causes for the failure of the Agency's telecentre programme are manifold and complex, but a number of key problems stand out.

The first of these lies on the slippery slope between pilot project and full-scale implementation. As James points out, the "original intention that *pilot* telecentres would be run by the USA, was overtaken by the intention to launch a full-scale national rollout plan" (2001, p. 79). Under political pressure for urgent, high-profile demonstration telecentre projects (Aki Stavrou, interview, 17 October 2014), the USA never paused to evaluate the lessons of the initial rollout, some of which were readily apparent, or to apply the lessons learned. As a result, there was no viable, sustainable telecentre rollout model, based on a more realistic, less "sophisticated" (James, 2001, p. 79), and hence more scalable approach.

Lack of financial viability of the individual telecentres was clearly also a serious problem. For example, Benjamin estimates that barely a "quarter appeared to have a chance of sustainable operation" in the medium term (2003, p. 7). The problem appears to have been compounded by the fact that the majority of the telecentres were 'community-owned', a structure that mitigates against entrepreneurship and business acumen, and allows internal conflicts to fester.

The adherence to a 'community ownership' approach, in the face of countervailing evidence and recommendations available at the time of the success of the Vodacom entrepreneurial model (Benjamin, Stavrou, McCarthy, & Burton, 2000), is perhaps a spillover of the stakeholder-based approach prevalent at the time (see Chapter 3). But it is likely that the ideological influence of those driving the rollout from the USA at the time, many of whom had come from the labour unions and the SA National Civic Organisation, also played a role.

Lack of administrative, technical and managerial skills seems also to have been a challenge. This was identified by Benjamin, both as necessary for success, and, conversely, as a cause of telecentre failure (2003, pp. 4 and 8). Stavrou concurs: "there was no management training, no basic accounting training, no control over stocks" coupled with a "serious lack of marketing skills, understanding... how to promote telecentre services" (interview, 17 October 2014). In addition, training was often poorly timed, taking place "up to one year before the telecentre was ready which meant that most of the learning had been forgotten" (Tina James, personal communication, 31 March 2017). Even the annual reports of the Agency in the early period are replete with references to the need for training provision to telecentre staff and managers (USA, 2002, p. 11).

A range of technical support problems plagued the early telecentres, in particular lack of access to electricity and telephone lines (Benjamin, 2003, pp. 4 and 7). There were also considerable difficulties in securing technical support for ICT equipment in remote, rural communities (Benjamin et al., 2000, p. 26). This was coupled a failure to co-ordinate with Telkom's own rollout plans (Tina James, personal communication, 31 March 2017), placing many telecentres in areas without any prospect of access to telephony. Similar problems continue to plague telecentres today (Attwood, Diga, Braathen, & May, 2013, p. 9).

Undoubtedly, the penchant of the USA for getting involved in the actual delivery of telecentres on the ground—an area for which its staff was ill-equipped and in which they had little if any experience (Tina James, interview, 27 November 2014)—contributed to the early fiascos. The role of the Agency in relation to the USF was clearly intended to be one of the management and disbursement of funds, rather than that of implementation. Consultants engaged in 'institutional strengthening' for the Agency at the time were equally forthright:

> It is not the job of the USA to implement telecentres nor to do any other type of specific project implementation, unless it is on a pilot project basis. Long terms [sic] project implementation by the USA is contrary to the spirit of the Telecommunications Act and inconsistent with the use of the USF resources. (DNTA, 1999b, p. 22)

Worse, undertaking telecentre implementation landed the Agency with the responsibility for ongoing support and maintenance of the centres, and hence with the need, alluded to above, to undertake 'rehabilitation' on an ongoing basis.

Finally, corruption was clearly a factor in the ineffectiveness of the telecentre rollout. Misappropriation and maladministration of monies from the Fund seem to have been endemic and actively driven by Agency staff, as can be seen from the 2012 forensic audit and the allegations made by Holomisa (2013).

5.6.2 *Needy Persons*

In contrast to USAASA's gung-ho approach to telecentres, the provision of subsidies to 'needy persons' remained mired in bureaucratic inefficiency and overlapping mandates for some twenty years.

It seems clear that government intended support for the needy in securing access to telecommunications services to be the key priority for expenditure from the USF (DoC, 1999b). The responsibility for defining the categories of needy persons, however, lay with the regulator, SATRA at the time. SATRA, in turn, commissioned consultants to make recommendations on how to proceed. Their final report analyses levels of poverty, telecommunications penetration and affordability across South Africa, concluding, for instance, that "39% of all households are unlikely to be able to afford a telephone in the near future" (Stavrou & Mkhize, 1998, p. 22). It goes on to make a series of recommendations covering: people with disabilities; the aged; households that cannot afford to pay their bills; schools, preschool and adult education centres; hospitals and clinics; multi-purpose community centres and telecentres. It is, however, leery of committing large sums of money from the USF to support poor households and individuals.

Subsequently, the USA initiated a separate process to determine appropriate definitions for 'universal access' and 'universal service'. Bizarrely, these two definitions fell under the purview of the USA, while the that of 'needy persons', clearly intimately related, was assigned to SATRA (RSA, 1996, Sections 9(2) and 66(4)). Such a complicated web of interlocking responsibilities between the Minister, the regulator and the Agency can only have served to muddy the process.

Nevertheless, a joint task team, bringing together representatives of both the USA and SATRA, was established in mid-1998. A series of discussion papers resulted in a set of recommendations on UAS to the Minister in late 1999 (USA, 1999b). The three documents all do make reference to the question of 'needy persons', but are increasingly less specific, presumably because this was an issue outside the mandate of the USA, which was leading the process. The first discussion paper deals with:

- the challenges of affordability;

- the problem of 'churn'[19];
- the question of whether telecommunications is a "right" or a "privilege";
- a series of tiered options for "Universal Service Packages" to ensure users do not "'fall out of' the network", ranging from a "full basic package" to an "essential services" package (incoming calls, plus only emergency and operator outgoing calls);
- options for "flexible billing" and "low user schemes" (USA, 1998, pp. 13–17).

The Agency was, however, hamstrung by the inability to deal fully with the definition of 'needy persons. The final submission to the Minister, accordingly, deals only with recommended definitions for 'Universal Access' and 'Universal Service', along with a fairly general discussion of the question of 'Affordability'.

The SATRA process was never formally and publicly completed, despite a public consultation in early 1998 (Chalmers, 1998). After SATRA was subsumed under the new, converged regulator, ICASA, a draft regulation dealing with "categories of needy people" was sent to the Minister for approval, but was returned to be revised (ICASA, 2001, p. 22). But neither ICASA nor the Minister appears to have taken any further steps to complete the process, leaving 'needy persons' in an ongoing state of limbo.

The question of definitions for UAS lingered on the agenda of the Agency, albeit without any concrete attempt to have them finalised, until a good few years later, when in 2005, in the process leading up to the adoption of the ECA, the Agency commissioned a series of studies, on which it spent a little over R3 million (USA, 2006b, p. 9). One of these looked at the question of the affordability of telecommunications services and the question of 'needy persons' (USA, 2006a). It is again not clear what triggered this study, since the Minister was to retain responsibility for 'needy persons' under the soon-to-be-passed ECA (RSA, 2005, Section 88(4)).

[19] Telecommunications subscribers discontinuing their subscriptions, usually because of their inability to afford the service.

Completed in early 2006, the study is a relatively generic (and sometimes wildly incorrect[20]) desk analysis of UAS in South Africa, containing a series of generalised recommendations, covering affordability, definitions of universal access and universal service and under-serviced areas, 'needy persons' and the mandate of the Agency in general. It defined low-income users as those earning less than R1800 per month and proposed the following definition of 'needy persons':

> low-income users that cannot obtain communication services at commercial rates - including vulnerable groups of users such as the elderly, those with disabilities, or those with special social needs and users to whom the provision of communication services is not commercially viable. (USA, 2006a, pp. 58 and 60)

The various reports were subsequently consolidated into a single discussion document (Sipho Mngqibisa, personal communication, 14 February 2017), which was issued some two years later (USAASA, 2008b) as part of a formal public 'notice-and-comment' procedure, leading in rather convoluted steps to a formal recommendation and implementation plan that was tabled to the Minister (USAASA, 2009c). The recommended definition of 'needy persons' specified:

- persons (either collective or individual) who qualify through the application of a means test, considering a combination of factors, such as financial means, disability, age or other vulnerabilities (USAASA, 2009c, p. 7).

Some of the debate during the process centred around which criteria to be considered when determining whether someone is 'needy', whether to apply a financial 'means test', as well as how the subsidies would be implemented. Reference to geography or location as a criterion was omitted from the final recommendation, despite being a contentious issue. Likewise, reference to the specific services in relation to which a person is to be considered 'needy' (i.e. electronic communications and broadcasting) was omitted, presumably because of the voiced intention by the

[20] For example, it states that 'access deficit charges' and 'network externality surcharges' have been applied in South Africa (USA, 2006a, pp. 71–72).

Minister to use the Fund to subsidise set-top boxes (STBs) for the broadcasting digital migration (Vecchiatto & du Toit, 2008).

Illustrating a degree of tardiness hard to surpass, the recommendation languished for over a year, before the new Minister finally gazetted a set of definitions (DoC, 2010). Inexplicably and bizarrely, 'needy persons' (along with 'under-serviced areas') was omitted from the Gazette, despite being the specific responsibility of the Minister.

As a result of this, South Africa has never, in over 20 years, had a formal definition of 'needy persons'. No subsidies for ICT services have, therefore, ever been paid out to those unable to afford access to ICT services.

5.6.3 *Schools and Colleges*

Alongside the rollout of telecentres, the Agency had, from very early on, also been deploying school and university computer laboratories, under the funky rubric of 'cyber-labs' (Benjamin, 2001, p. 123; USA, 2002). Support from the USF for "public schools and public further education and training institutions" to finance the "procurement of internet services and equipment", subject to an 'e-rate',[21] was added via the 2001 amendment to the Act (RSA, 1996, Section 66(1)(c)).

This provision was left essentially unchanged when the 2005 ECA was passed. The definition of eligible "schools and colleges" was, however, slightly expanded to include many "independent schools and private colleges", while the range of applicable procurement areas was made more technologically neutral ("broadcasting and electronic communications services and access to electronic communications networks"), and reference the e-rate (which had been a non-starter (Vecchiatto, 2010)) was dropped (RSA, 2005, p. Section 88(1)(d)).

The Agency appears to have begun providing subsidised access to schools from around 2003 (alongside the provision of computers and training to some 69 teachers) (USA, 2004, p. 9). Expenditure on Internet access and services for schools and colleges rose rapidly, topping R9 million in 2004/2005 and reaching over R20 million in 2005/2006 (USA, 2006b, p. 14). The Agency subsequently spoke of the important work "being done with ICASA and the operators to integrate the e-rate and

[21] A mandatory 50% discount on ISP charges applicable to educational institutions.

USAASA subsidies in an ambitious programme to connect the schools, beginning with those schools in the lowest quintiles" (USAASA, 2007, p. 7). The programme, which covered 89 subsidised sites by 2007, seems to have overlapped with the Agency's 'cyber-labs' programme, and the refurbishment of old PCs (243 in 2006/2007), as well as the provision of e-mail and the promotion of open-source software in schools (USAASA, 2007, p. 17). In 2007/2008, it was extended to some 18 Further Education and Training colleges (USAASA, 2008a, p. 22). The provision of subsidised access to schools seems to have been discontinued in 2010, when all such connectivity was handed over to the Department of Education (USAASA, 2010, p. 12), and to colleges in 2013.

By then a total of some R103 million had been spent on such subsidised access, with little long-term benefit to show. Strangely, the Agency appears never to have engaged with SchoolNet SA[22] in relation to either its 'cyber-lab' or ISP subsidy programmes. Its expressed desire to investigate "possible means to create a national schools network" (USAASA, 2008a, p. 8) suggests that it was entirely unaware of the existence of SchoolNet SA. Likewise, there seems to have been no attempt to interface with the USOs imposed in respect of schools by ICASA.

Equally remiss is the absence of any research study to assess the effectiveness and impact of the Agency's multi-million-rand intervention for educational connectivity.

5.6.4 *Support for Licensees*

Two sections of the legislation provided for the Fund to be utilised in support of the provision of telecommunications infrastructure.

The first of these covered financial support to Telkom (or other licensees) for the "extension of [their] telecommunication service to [under-serviced] areas and communities" in order to meet any universal-service obligations imposed via their licences (RSA, 1996, Section 66(1)(b)). No subsidies falling under this category of funding were ever paid to any licensee, despite the Agency's own review noting that it had the capacity to do so (USA, 2005, p. 50).

The second provision was introduced via the 2001 amendment to the Act, when the Under-serviced Area Licensing (USAL) model was

[22] Launched in 1997 as a national umbrella body for schools and teachers involved in ICTs and education.

introduced (see Chapter 6). It covered subsidies from the Fund to the USALs by adding a new category for "small businesses and cooperatives" providing telecommunications services in under-serviced areas (RSA, 1996, Section 66(1)(f)).

These two categories were later to be joined under a single proviso in the 2005 ECA, which introduced a technology-neutral licensing framework, and simply spoke of subsidies for "financing the construction or extension of electronic communications networks in underserviced areas" (RSA, 2005, Section 88(1)(b)).

Subsidies for the USALs were part of the planning discussion with ICASA, the Department and the Agency from the outset (Gillwald, 2002, p. 11; AVP, 2002, p. 9). The subsidy model was somewhat inchoate, with the Agency initially envisaging individual subsidies to local bidders to "assist people from these [under-served] communities to participate fully in these licences" (USA, 2002, p. 15).

A draft approach, gazetted by the Agency the following year, and peppered with grandiloquent gobbledegook, floated a combination of two models:

- Subsidised interest, long term, significantly subordinated, ZAR5 million, quasi equity loans with a 50% fully subsidised grant component for severely economically disadvantaged potential shareholders;
- Subsidised, medium term, significantly subordinated, term limited, amount limited, ZAR10 million capital guarantees to development finance institutions and commercial banks (USA, 2003, pp. 5–6).

Essentially what was being proposed was a combination of soft loans (part grants with equity rights) and capital guarantees to underwrite bank loans.

By the time the subsidy was ready to be implemented, the model had been considerably simplified into a R15 million grant per licensee, spread over three years, and subject to rollout targets being met.[23] In 2004, the Agency reported that "R50 million [had] been allocated to subsidise successful bidders for Under-serviced Area Licences, totaling [sic] R5 million per licensee over three years" (USA, 2004, p. 7). A subsequent explanatory memo issued by the Minister makes it clear that the

[23] The final subsidy guidelines were never officially gazetted.

subsidy thus comprised R15 million per licensee from the Fund, spread over three years, and "paid annually only on satisfactory roll-out of... infrastructure" (Matsepe-Casaburri, 2005, p. 5). This provision was formally carried through to the respective USAL licences (ICASA, 2004, Section 8.4).

Agreements were subsequently signed with each of the USAL licensees, covering the R15 million, but without specifying any specific conditionality relating to years two and three (Thornton, 2006, p. 6). Each of the first 7 USALs accordingly duly received their first tranche of R5 million, which appears to have been the primary source of funding in almost all cases (Thornton, 2006, p. 10). Of the seven, only two received the full subsidy, and only a further two received anything beyond the first instalment. In total, a little over R61 million (out of a possible R105 million) was paid out to the first 7 USAL licensees (see Table 5.4). No subsidies appear ever to have been paid out any of the USALs subsequently licensed in later phases of the experiment. Table 5.4 shows expenditure from the USF under each of the categories discussed above.

5.7 Useless Service Fund?

Arising from the analysis and discussion above, it is important to assess the expenditure from the Fund over the period, as accounted for by the Agency.

The ability of the Agency to manage projects and spend the funds at its disposal in a proper manner has been beset by ongoing and repeated allegations of corruption (Sidimba, 2012), and by the uncovering of irregular expenditure of at least R43 million which precipitated a forensic audit (USAASA, 2012, pp. 73ff.). More recently, USAASA has been the subject of a currently ongoing investigation by the Special Investigations Unit via special Presidential proclamation (RSA, 2014).

The recent ramping up of expenditure from the Fund in support of South Africa's belated and stalled migration to Digital Terrestrial Television (DTT) has seen spending on the provision of subsidised set-top boxes kick in over the last three years. This now makes up a substantial slice (11%) of total expenditure from the Fund, over 80% of it (some R65 million) incurred as spending surged in the most recent financial year of 2016/2017. However, this latest project too has become bogged down in allegations of tender irregularities, maladministration and bribery (Mzekandaba, 2017; Shinn, 2017).

Table 5.4 USF Expenditure (2001–2017)

Miscellaneous (includes audit fees)		*R13,662,000*
R&D		
	Needy persons definitions	R3,159,000
	National strategy/standard operating manual	R8,069,000
	Other R&D	R5,881,000
	Total R&D	**R17,109,000**
Telecentres		
	Miscellaneous expenses	R9,627,514
	Consultants	R28,595,880
	Subsidisation of capital good & services	R21,776,064
	Telecomms licensees	R3,921,000
	Communities (telecentres)	R80,493,000
	Access centre handover programme	R38,010,000
	Broadband infrastructure subsidies	R122,454,000
	ICT rapid deployment	R99,923,000
	Total telecentres	**R404,800,458**
Schools and FET colleges		
	Schools (cyber-labs)	R94,419,000
	FET subsidies	R59,226,000
	Total schools and FET colleges	**R153,645,000**
USALs		
	Amatole Telecoms	R15,000,000
	Bokamoso	R5,464,463
	Bokone	R15,000,000
	Ilizwi Telecommunications	R5,000,000
	Karabo Telecoms	R5,000,000
	Kingdom Communications	R9,900,054
	Thinta	R5,000,000
	Promotion & launches	R302,000
	Total USALs	**R61,616,194**
DTT		
	Digital Terrestrial Television	R79,924,000
	Total DTT	**R79,924,000**
Total		**R730,126,652**

Source Annual reports of the USA and USAASA, with expenditure breakdown based on report line items

A graphical breakdown of this expenditure is shown in Fig. 5.3.

Of the total expenditure from the Fund over the period, amounting to just over R730 million, the more than half has been spent on a repeated series of failed telecentre projects of one kind or another. This includes the irregular expenditure which formed the basis of the forensic audit and the

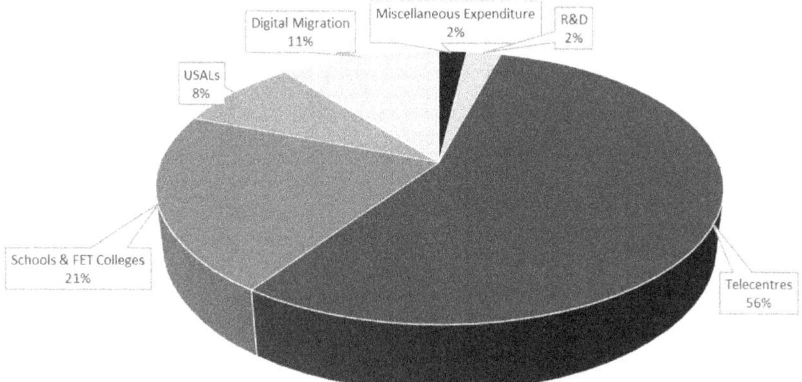

Fig. 5.3 USF expenditure breakdown (2001–2017)

SIU investigation, full details which are not available, but which appear to amount to at least R76 million,[24] possibly closer to R100 million.

A further 21% has been spent on subsidising schools and colleges, principally on cyber-labs and Internet access costs. Again, there is no cumulative information from USAASA on the status and sustainability of these interventions.

Subsidies to support the licensees in the failed USAL experiment consumed much of the remaining expenditure (8%) from the fund. Again, there is precious little to show for this expenditure. As the analysis will show, almost every single USAL seems to have collapsed, despite this subvention.

The expenditure on research and development activities over the period is *ultra vires* the Act, which only allows the payment of "subsidies" from the Fund (RSA, 2005, Section 88(1)). These monies should have been accounted for under the budget of the Agency itself, as should the 'Miscellaneous' amounts, which largely comprise Fund audit fees. That said, R&D expenditure constitutes a mere 2% of the total, a scandalously low proportion for an organisation whose mandate includes injunctions to "conduct research into and keep abreast of [ICT] developments" and

[24]The previously reported irregular expenditure of R43 million plus R33 million under the current SIU probe.

"continually [to] survey and evaluate the extent to which universal access and service have been achieved" (RSA, 2005, Section 82(4)).

Figure 5.4 compares expenditure from the Fund against licensee contributions as paid to Treasury via ICASA. What stands out starkly is the yawning gap between the levy and its associated expenditure. It must, of course, be borne in mind that licensee contributions are determined by ICASA's regulations specifying the USF levy, while the Agency's expenditure is constrained by Treasury approval and consequent Parliamentary appropriation. Nevertheless, the vast discrepancy does illustrate the tragedy of a missed opportunity. It demonstrates what could have been accomplished towards UAS with the funding potentially available, had it all been deployed effectively and efficiently. On the other hand, given the degree of wastage, mismanagement and corruption, the failure of the Fund has in some ways been a blessing in disguise.

A final point in relation to efficiency perhaps needs to be made. Even assuming the Agency had spent the funds at its disposal with proper diligence, the ratio between USAASA's institutional running costs and Fund expenditure is alarmingly high. The cumulative operational budget of the Agency over its lifespan weighs in at 95% of the total expenditure from the Fund over the same period. By way of contrast, the MDDA, an institution with an analogous mandate in the broadcasting sector, specifically stipulates that the running costs for the institution may never exceed 25% of total expenditure (RSA, 2003, p. 10). Calculated the same way, the running costs of USAASA as an institution make up a bloated, astonishingly inefficient 49% of overall total expenditure.

5.8 Conclusion

South Africa's USF appears, in the light of the preceding discussion, to have fared dismally indeed. The critical chorus sings largely from a single songbook.

For example, former IDRC staffer Tina James, who oversaw the early telecentre pilot funded by the IDRC, characterises the experience as a "shameful waste of money" (interview, 27 November 2014), noting that, despite starting off with the best of ideas and the greatest of intentions, things went wrong very quickly at the Agency.

Similarly, former academic and researcher Aki Stavrou recalls arguing very early on that the USF "needed to be readjusted" because "something had gone wrong". Somewhat diplomatically, he suggests the Fund could

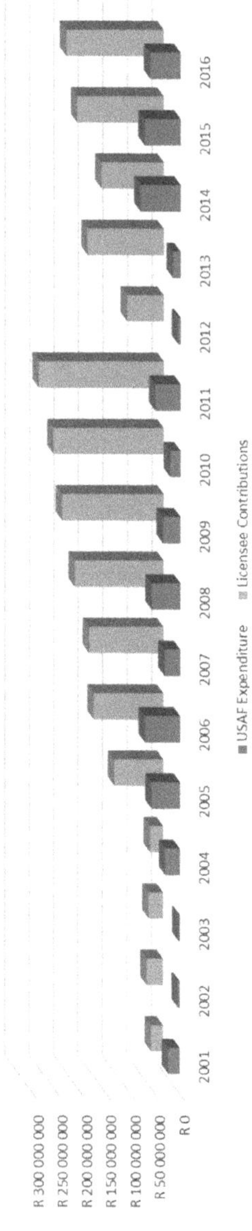

Fig. 5.4 USF expenditure vs licensee contributions

have been "better allocated at the time" (interview, 17 October 2014). Consultant and former head of policy and research at ICASA Mandla Msimang also has a gloomy assessment of the Fund, pointing to a lack of successes (interview, 7 November 2014).

A number of key factors, in addition to project-specific problems discussed above, emerge as underpinning the failures of the USF.

One of these is structural: the intersecting and overlapping mandates between the regulator and the Agency and the Minister. The Agency has found itself in the classic double-bind of being responsible for something it does not have the necessary authority to oversee.

The ability of Agency to disburse monies was significantly undermined by the extent to which the Agency has been reliant on third parties. For instance, the definition of 'under-serviced areas' (something which is fundamental to the application of UAS funding), depends upon ICASA, which took until 2012 to gazette the necessary regulations. The definition of 'needy persons' too, as noted above, lay outside the control of the Agency. Even more fundamental was the fact that the role of the Agency was seen to be that of a mere administrator of the Fund. It was designated merely to act "subject to the control and in accordance with... instructions" emanating from external structures, initially the regulator, later the Minister (RSA, 1996, Section 65(4)).

Multiple lines of accountability were further complicated by multiple lines of implementation. Instead of a single, integrated telecentre project, run from one point, a number of contending initiatives were undertaken, seemingly without any co-ordination—the Agency's telecentres, the Thusong Service Centres of the GCIS, the Post Office PITs. Even the cyber-labs operated in the face of other ICT in schools projects, such as Gauteng Online and the Western Cape's Khanya Project. Equally tellingly the cyber-labs seem to have existed in blissful ignorance of the schools USOs imposed on the operators.

There were also problems in the management of the Fund. There does not seem to have been a single formally appointed line of accountability specific to the Fund. The Agency's own consultants, for example, were to bewail the fact that there is "no dedicated USF manager" (USA, 2005, p. 74). This is a situation that persists today: a single Board exercising oversight in respect of both the Agency and the Fund, and a management structure that includes managers responsible for Finance, 'Operations' and 'Performance', but with no single point of accountability for the effectiveness of the Fund.

Further, until recently the Fund lacked a clear set of guidelines and formal procedures. The Agency's own research more than ten years ago noted that there was "neither a written charter nor a Standard Operating Procedure" (USA, 2005, p. 74), pointing out that "best international practice... [requires] a document that lays down the rules, procedures, principles and guidelines of the how the fund is administered and operated" (USA, 2005, p. 69).

In fairness, it must be noted that the Agency has recently produced a 'Universal Service and Access Fund Manual' (USAASA, 2014a)—albeit of indeterminate status. Mooted and budgeted for as far back as 2008 (USAASA, 2009b, p. 29), possibly as a result of the 2005 report, it only went out to tender in 2012, followed by a half-hearted consultative exercise late the following year (USAASA, 2013b). The actual Manual (USAASA, 2014a) dates to mid-2014, but has never been formally published. It may have been overtaken by a series of corruption scandals plaguing the Agency around the same time (ITWeb, 2013; Maake, Hofstatter, & wa Afrika, 2013), and now appears redundant given the proposed replacement of the Universal Service and Access Fund by a Digital Development Fund (DTPS, 2015, 2016).

The financial reporting and accountability in respect of the Fund is dealt with in Chapter 7 where the structure and performance of Agency as an entity is reviewed. Suffice it to note at this point that from 2013 USAASA began to issue separate annual reports and audits for the Fund (USAASA, 2014b, 2014c), possibly in response to the 2014 SIU investigation. In a similar vein, the draft Fund Manual proposes separating procurement under the Fund from USAASA's existing supply chain management structures (USAASA, 2014a).

Taken together, this suggests a track record of poor financial management of the Fund, without sufficient checks and balances, thereby opening the door to corruption and misappropriation, and thus vitiating its effectiveness in redressing South Africa's UAS gaps.

These inadequacies were compounded by the fact that the Fund seems to have been operated largely on an ad hoc basis, without a proper access gap analysis of the kind that is now considered international good practice (USA, 2005, p. 68). Indeed, in the absence of a properly integrated and comprehensive analysis of the nature, scope and extent of the various access deficits the Fund was intended to address, it is hard to see how the Agency's interventions can have been guided by anything other than glib optimism and political expediency.

It is true that there was a degree of such analysis underpinning some of the areas of proposed intervention (DNTA, 1999a; USA, 1999a, 2006a), but—with the exception of the recent but still to be ratified UAS strategy report (USAASA, 2014a)—there has been no unified analysis and consequent comprehensive set of recommendations covering the full scope of the Fund's mandate. As a result, the application of the monies available lacked focus and structure. Worse, this lack allowed telecentre millenarianism to hold sway and exposed the Fund to corruption and misappropriation.

Finally, there was clearly an issue with the management and planning of the funding generated by the Fund levy. Some have pointed to a lack of cash as under-pinning the failure of the Fund to achieve its objectives. This argument goes a little deeper than the common complaint that the Agency has consistently failed to spend the monies available to it (Perry, 2010) to argue that the appropriations approved by Treasury have been insufficient. The Agency's own consultants argued that the "USF has been under-funded from its very beginning" (USA, 2005, p. 68). This was not because the Fund levy had been set too low, as the recent Ministerial White Paper seems to imply (DTPS, 2016, p. 40). Rather, as noted above, the Agency seems to have had only the vaguest notion of how much money had been paid in by licensees to the National Revenue Fund. Neither ICASA nor the Department seem to have been very helpful in providing them with the necessary information.[25] As a result, the annual appropriations into the Fund fell, as noted above, consistently well short of the available contributions. Perhaps this is just as well, since access to greater funding is likely to have compounded the magnitude of the problem, rather than solved it.

The expenditure of some R600 million over 15 years has left little by way of long-term legacy. It seems clear, therefore, that South Africa's implementation of a USF in alignment with international good practice can largely be considered to have failed.

[25] As previously noted, one of the 2014 amendments to the ECA was designed to address this information lacuna.

References

Allchurch, N. (1998, May 8). Phone lines for Africa. *Mail & Guardian*. Retrieved from http:// mg. co. za/ article/ 1998- 05- 08- phone- lines-for- africa.

Attwood, H., & Braathen, E. (2010, September 8–10). *Telecentres and poor communities in South Africa: What have we learnt?* Paper presented at The Chronic Poverty Research Centre (CPRC) Conference, "Ten years of 'war against poverty'. What we have learned since 2000. What we should do 2010-2020", Manchester, UK. Retrieved from http:// www. chronicpoverty. org/ uploads/ publication_ files/ attwood_ braathen% 20_ telecentres. pdf.

Attwood, H., Diga, K., Braathen, E., & May, J. (2013). Telecentre FUNCTIONALITY in South Africa: Re-enabling the community ICT access environment. *Journal of Community Informatics, 9*(4). Retrieved from http:// ci- journal. net/ index. php/ ciej/ article/ view/ 970/ 1060.

AVP. (2002). *The financial viability of the under serviced area licenses [sic] in South Africa: Final report*. Midrand and Ottawa: Development Bank of Southern Africa and International Development Research Centre.

Bapela, O. (2011, May 14). Mr Obed Bapela, MP during the launch of Ulwazi Information Centre New Cross Road-14 May 2014. Pretoria: Department of Communications. Retrieved from https:// www. dtps. gov. za/ index. php? option= com_ content& view= article& id=153.

Benjamin, P. (2001). *Telecentres and universal capability: A study of the telecentre programme of the Universal Service Agency in South Africa, 1996–2000*. PhD thesis.

Benjamin, P. (2003, August 5). *Universality & telecentres.*

Benjamin, P., Stavrou, A., McCarthy, C., & Burton, P. (2000). *Telecentre 2000: Synthesis report*. Johannesburg: DRA-Development & LINK Centre.

Cell C. (2011, August). *Cell C grows revenue, subscriber base*. Johannesburg. Retrieved from http:// www. cellc. co. za/ explore/ newsroom/ cell- c- grows- revenue- subscriber- base.

Chalmers, R. (1998, February 12). Satra investing R20m in the poor. *Business Day.*

DNTA. (1999a). *Telecentre implementation plan*. Report to the Universal Service Agency and the Department of Communications, Republic of South Africa, David N. Townsend & Associates, Swampscott, MA.

DNTA. (1999b). *Universal Service Agency institutional strengthening plan*. David N: Townsend & Associates.

DoC. (1999a, May 22). Regulations relating to the Contributions to the Universal Service Fund and the apportionment thereof. *Government Gazette, 407*(20111).

DoC. (1999b, May 22). Commencement of annual contributions to the Universal Service Fund. *Government Gazette, 407*(20111).

DoC. (2001a, March 23). Public invitation to lodge written representations in relation to intended telecommunications policy directions to be issued by the Minister of Communications. *Government Gazette, 429*(22169).

DoC. (2001b, July 23). Policy Directions issued by Minister of Communications. *Government Gazette* (22503).

DoC. (2001c, August 21). Policy Directions issued by Minister of Communications. *Government Gazette, 434*(22603).

DoC. (2010, February 8). Determination issued under the Electronic Communications Act, 2005 (Act No. 36 of 2005) with regard to universal access to and the universal provision of electronic communications services and electronic communications network services. *Government Gazette* (32939).

DPTB. (1996, May 3). *Telecommunications Bill.* Pretoria: Department of Posts, Telecommunications and Broadcasting.

DSE. (1996, May 20). *Draft Telecommunications Bill, 1996.* Pretoria: Department of State Expenditure.

DTPS. (2015, March). *National integrated ICT policy review report.* Department of Telecommunications and Postal Services. Pretoria. Retrieved from http:// www. dtps. gov. za/ documents- publications/ category/ 102- ict- policy- re view- reports- 2015. html.

DTPS. (2016, October 3). National integrated ICT policy white paper. *Government Gazette, 616*(40325).

Eveleth, A. (1999, December 3). Rural link-up gets disconnected. *Mail & Guardian.*

Fuchs, R. (1998). *Little engines that did: Case histories from the global telecentre movement.* Ottawa: International Development Research Centre. Retrieved from http:// www. idrc. ca/ acacia/ engine/ index. html.

GFIA. (2012). *Summary status report: USAASA value for money audit.* Johannesburg: Gobodo Forensic and Investigative Accounting.

Gillwald, A. (2002). *Under-serviced area licences in South Africa: Steps to achieving viable operators.* Johannesburg: LINK Centre, University of the Witwatersrand. Retrieved from http:// link. wits. ac. za/ papers/ usal. pdf.

Gomez, R., Pather, S., & Dosono, B. (2012). Public access computing in South Africa: Old lessons and new challenges. *The Electronic Journal of Information Systems in Developing Countries, 52,* 1–16.

Holomisa, B. (2013, June 7). *Corruption and maladministration at USAASA.*

Hulbert, D., & Snyman, M. (2007). Determining the reasons why ICT centres fail: Six South African Case Studies. *Mousaion, 25*(2), 1–20.

ICASA. (2000, October 11). Notice of Intention to make regulations in terms of S 96 read with S 67(2) of the Telecommunications Act 103 of 1996 ("The Act") relating to Universal Service Fund Contributions by Value Added Network Service & Private Telecommunication Network Licensees. *Government Gazette* (21642).

ICASA. (2001). *Annual report 2000–2001*. Johannesburg: Independent Communications Authority of South Africa.

ICASA. (2002, March 15). Notice of intention to make regulations on annual contributions to the Universal Service Fund by telecommunication service licensees. *Government Gazette* (23237).

ICASA. (2003, August 28). Regulations in respect of the annual Contributions to the Universal Service Fund by holders of telecommunication service licences. *Government Gazette* (24508).

ICASA. (2004, November 17). Under-Serviced Area Licence in terms of section 40A of the Telecommunications Act 103 of 1996, as amended—Issued to ThintaThinta Telecomms (Proprietary) Limited (Registration No 2003/000190/07). *Government Gazette, 473*(26996).

ICASA. (2008, October 10). Universal Service and Access Fund regulations, 2008. *Government Gazette*(31499).

ICASA. (2010, September 16). Regulations in respect of the Prescribed Annual Contributions of Licensees to the Universal Service and Access Fund. *Government Gazette*.

ICASA. (2011a, February 10). USAF regulations, 2011. *Government Gazette* (34010).

ICASA. (2011b). *Supplementary analysis 2009/2010 ECNS/ECS compliance reports*. Johannesburg: Independent Communications Authority of South Africa. Retrieved from https:// www. icasa. org. za/ LegislationRegulation s/ LicensingCompliance/ CompliancePublications/ ComplianceReports/ tab id/ 474/ ctl/ ItemDetails/ mid/ 1481/ ItemID/ 851/ Default. aspx.

ISPA. (2007). *ISPA's submission on ICASA's Intention to make regulations in respect of the prescribed annual contributions of the licensee's licensed activity to the Universal Service and Access Fund*. Johannesburg: Internet Service Providers' Association.

ITU. (1994). *World telecommunication development conference, Buenos Aires 21–29 March 1994: Final report*. Geneva: International Telecommunication Union. Retrieved from http:// www. itu. int/ en/ ITU- D/ Documents/ WTDC_ 1994_ FINAL_ REPORT.PDF.

ITU. (1998). *World telecommunication development report 1998: Universal access*. Geneva: International Telecommunication Union. Retrieved from http:// w ww. itu. int/ ITU- D/ ict/ publications/ wtdr_98/.

ITU. (2003). *Trends in telecommunications reform 2003: Promoting universal access to ICTs—Practical tools for regulators*. Geneva: International Telecommunication Union.

ITWeb. (2013, October 27). Probe mooted over R500m Cell C subsidy—paper. *ITWeb*. Retrieved from http:// www. itweb. co. za/ index. php? option= co m_ content& view= article& id= 68472.

James, T. (Ed.). (2001). *An information policy handbook for Southern Africa*. Ottawa: International Development Research Centre.

Khumalo, F. (1998, August 17). *Pilot telecentre evaluation-South Africa*. Bangalore: Centre for Ecological Sciences. Retrieved from http:// ces. iisc. ernet. i n/ hpg/ envis/ doc98html/ infotel111. html.

Lewis, C. (2013). Universal access and service interventions in South Africa: Best practice, poor impact. *African Journal of Information and Communication(13)*. LINK Centre, University of the Witwatersrand.

Maake, M., Hofstatter, S., & wa Afrika, M. (2013, October 27). Dina Pule is under fire again. *Business Times*. Retrieved from http:// www. bdlive. co. z a/ businesstimes/ 2013/ 10/ 27/ dina- pule- is- under- fire- again.

Malefane, M., & Ncana, N. (2011, September 25). Digital TV officials suspended over R29m. *Sunday Times*. Retrieved from http:// www. timeslive. co. za/ s citech/ 2011/ 09/ 25/ Digital- TV- officials- suspended- over- R29m1.

Malunga, M. (1997, February 11). New players in telecom industry. *Sowetan*.

Matsepe-Casaburri, I. (2005, April 15). Questions and answers to the Minister for Under Serviced Area Licence (USAL'S) [sic] Invitation to Apply (ITA). *Government Gazette, 478*(27484).

MDDA. (2010). *Annual report 2009–10*. Johannesburg: Media Development and Diversity Agency. Retrieved from http:// www. mdda. org. za/ MDD A% 20Annual% 20Report2009_ 2010% 20. pdf.

MDDA. (2015). *MDDA annual report 2014/2015*. Johannesburg: Media Development and Diversity Agency. Retrieved from http:// media. wix. com/ ug d/ f97c7f_ e00b5bb7d6d44f2a9b0ae0c5565c20f5. pdf.

MTN. (2011). *Pioneering the way: Integrated Business Report for the year ended 31 December 2010*. Johannesburg: MTN Group Limited. Retrieved from https:// www. mtn. com/ Investors/ FinancialReporting/ Documents/ I NTEGRATEDREPORTS/ 2010/ ar_ integrated_ report2010. pdf.

My Broadband. (2009, October 11). Interconnect rates: The numbers. *MyBroadband*. Retrieved from http:// mybroadband. co. za/ news/ Cellular/ 9960. html.

Mzekandaba, S. (2017, August 7). Cloud of corruption hangs over STB tender. *ITWeb*. Retrieved from http:// www. itweb. co. za/ index. php? option= co m_ content& view= article& id= 163914: Cloud- of- corruption- hangs- ov er- STB- tender& catid=260.

Naidoo, J. (1997, May 7). Ministerial Policy Direction on Contributions to Universal Service Fund. *Government Gazette* (17984).

Ngubane, P. (1999, September 7). Phones for all—First phase before December. *Cape Times*.

Ofir, Z. (2003). *Information & communication technologies for development (Acacia): The case of South Africa*. Johannesburg: Evalnet.

Padayachie, R. (2011, May 12). Speech by the Honourable Minister of Communications, Mr Radhakrishna L Padayachie (Roy), MP at the opening of the Impendle Community Communications Centre. Pretoria: Department of Communications. Retrieved from http:// www. gov. za/ speech- honourabl e- minister- communications- mr- radhakrishna- l- padayachie- roy- mp- ope ning- impendle.

Parkinson, S. (2005). Access centres and South Africa's universal access policy. In S. Parkinson (Ed.), *Telecentres, access and development: Experience and lessons from Uganda and South Africa*. Ottawa: International Development Research Centre.

Perry, S. (2010, May). The operators' missing millions. *Brainstorm*. Retrieved from http:// www. brainstormmag. co. za/ index. php? option= com_ cont ent& view= article& id= 3855& catid= 70: cover& Itemid=108.

PMG. (2019, November 21). *USAASA – SIU—Question NW914 to the Minister of Communications*. Cape Town: Parliamentary Monitoring Group. Retrieved from https:// pmg. org. za/ committee- question/ 12878/.

Randall, E. (1996, October 4). Telkom plans to get everyone talking. *Cape Argus*.

RSA. (1996). Telecommunications Act, 1996. *No. 103 of 1996*. Pretoria: Republic of South Africa.

RSA. (2000). *The establishment of government multi-purpose community centres*. Chief Directorate: Provincial and Local Liaison. Pretoria: Republic of South Africa. Retrieved from http:// www. thusong. gov. za/ documents/ researc h/ plan. htm.

RSA. (2001, November 30). Telecommunications Amendment Act, No. 64 of 2001. *Government Gazette, 437*(22889).

RSA. (2003, October 10). Regulations in terms of section 22 of the Media Development and Diversity Agency Act (Act 14 of 2002). *Government Gazette, 460*(25570).

RSA. (2005). *Electronic Communications Act, No. 36 of 2005*. Pretoria: Republic of South Africa.

RSA. (2014, March 28). Special Investigating Units and Special Tribunals Acts, 1996 (Act No. 74 of 1996): Referral of matters to existing special investigating unit and special tribunal. *Government Gazette, 585*(37496).

SACF. (2013). *Universal access and service in South Africa: A review of USAASA and the USAF*. Johannesburg: South African Communications Forum.

SATRA. (1997, December 19). Notice in respect of contributions to the Universal Service Fund by Licensees in the Telecommunications Sector. *Government Gazette, 390*(18579).

Shinn, M. (2017, November 26). Public protector must act on set-top boxes. *TechCentral*. Retrieved from https:// techcentral. co. za/ da- wants- parliam entary- probe- ann7- deal/ 78356/.

Sidimba, L. (2012, December 28). State to subsidise poor for digital TV. *City Press*. Retrieved from http:// www. citypress. co. za/ news/ state- to- subsid ise- poor- for- digital-tv/.
SIU. (2017, March 6). *Investigations*. Special Investigating Unit. Retrieved from https:// www. siu. org. za/ investigations. html.
Stavrou, S., & Mkhize, K. (1998). *A telecommunications universal service policy framework for defining categories of needy people in South Africa*. Johannesburg: South African Telecommunications Regulatory Authority.
Stavrou, A., Whitehead, A., Wilson, M., Seloane, M., & Benjamin, P. (2001). *Presentation notes: Of recommendations on the future of the Universal Service Agency*. Pretoria: Universal Service Agency—Conference Convening Committee.
Sumbwanyambe, M., Nel, A., & Clarke, W. (2011). Challenges and proposed solutions towards telecentre sustainability: A Southern Africa case study. In P. cunningham, & M. Cunningham (Eds.), *IST-Africa 2011 conference proceedings*. IIMC International Information Management Corporation.
Telkom. (2011). *Integrated annual report 2011*. Pretoria: Telkom Group. Retrieved from http:// www. telkom. co. za/ apps_ static/ ir/ pdf/ finan cial/ pdf/ TelkomAR_ 2011. pdf.
Thornton, L. (2006). *Recommendations on how the USA and other stakeholders might Assist USALs to ensure sustainability*. Johannesburg: Universal Service and Access Agency of South Africa.
Townsend, D. (2002, December 7–8). *Telecentre options and strategies*. Global Symposium for Regulators, Hong Kong, China. Geneva: International Telecommunication Union. Retrieved from https:// www. itu. int/ ITU- D/ treg/ Events/ Seminars/ GSR/ GSR02/ Documents/ 09- USModel_ part 3_ doc. pdf.
USA. (1998, October 22). Discussion paper on definition of universal service and universal access in telecommunications in South Africa. *Government Gazette, 400*(19397). Retrieved from http:// www. polity. org. za/ polity/ govdocs/ discuss/ usa. html.
USA. (1999a, May 28). Universal access and universal service: Discussion paper. *Government Gazette, 40*(20129).
USA. (1999b). *Universal access and service definitions for South Africa: A policy recommendation to the Minister of Communications*. Johannesburg: Universal Service Agency.
USA. (2002). *Universal Service Agency: Annual report 2001–2002*. Johannesburg: Universal Service Agency.
USA. (2003, May 27). Notice of draft policy in respect of Subsidisation of the Under-Serviced Area Licencees [sic] by the Universal Service Fund in terms of section 66 (f) of the Telecommunications Act (No. 103 of 1996), as amended. *Government Gazette* (24917).

USA. (2004). *Universal Service Agency: Annual report 2003–2004*. Johannesburg: Universal Service Agency.

USA. (2005). *Universal Service Agency impact document*. Johannesburg: Universal Service Agency.

USA. (2006a). *Affordability of telecommunications services and categories of needy people in South Africa*. Johannesburg: Universal Service Agency.

USA. (2006b). *Universal Service Agency: 2005–2006 annual report*. Johannesburg: Universal Service Agency.

USAASA. (2007). *Universal Service and Access Agency of South Africa: Annual report 2006/2007*. Johannesburg: Universal Access and Service Agency of South Africa.

USAASA. (2008a). *Annual report 2007/8: Creating connections*. Johannesburg: Universal Service and Access Agency of South Africa.

USAASA. (2008b, August 15). Notice in terms of section 82(3) and sections 88(2), (3) & (4) of the Electronic Communications Act, 2005 (Act No. 36 of 2005), inviting written representations in respect of the definitions of universal service, universal access, and underserviced areas. *Government Gazette, 518*(3133).

USAASA. (2009a). *Corporate plan 2009–2014*. Johannesburg: Universal Service and Access Agency of South Africa. Retrieved from http:// www. usaasa. or g. za/ export/ sites/ usaasa/ resource- centre/ download- centre/ downloa ds/ USAASA_ Corporate_ Plan_ 2009- 2014. pdf.

USAASA. (2009b). *Annual report 2008/2009*. Johannesburg: Universal Service and Access Agency of South Africa.

USAASA. (2009c, August). *Recommendations on the definitions of universal access and service, and determination of needy persons by the Minister, and determination of underserviced areas by the Independent Communications Authority of South Africa*. Johannesburg: Universal Service and Access Agency of South Africa. Retrieved from http:// www. usaasa. org. za/ export/ sites/ usaasa/ resource- centre/ download- centre/ downloads/ USAASA_ Executive_ Sum mary_ for_ Presentation_ to_ Minister_ Aug_ 2009. pdf.

USAASA. (2010). *2009/10 annual report: Accelerating universal service and access in South Africa*. Johannesburg: Universal Service and Access Agency of South Africa.

USAASA. (2012). *Annual report 2011/2012*. Johannesburg: Universal Service and Access Agency of South Africa. Retrieved from http:// www. usaasa. or g. za/ export/ sites/ usaasa/ resource- centre/ download- centre/ downloa ds/ USAASA_ Annual_ Report_ 2011- 12. pdf.

USAASA. (2013a). *Annual report 2012/13*. Johannesburg: Universal Service and Access Agency of South Africa.

USAASA. (2013b). *National strategy on universal service & access—Consultative document*. Midrand: Universal Service and Access Agency of South Africa.

Retrieved from http:// www. usaasa. org. za/ export/ sites/ usaasa/ resource- centre/ download- centre/ downloads/ Consultative- Document- on- National- Strategy- signed. pdf.

USAASA. (2014a). *The national strategy on universal service & access report*. Johannesburg: Universal Service and Access Agency of South Africa.

USAASA. (2014b). *Annual report 2013/14*. Midrand: Universal Service and Access Agency of South Africa.

USAASA. (2014c). *USAF: The Universal Service and Access Fund annual report 2013/2014*. Johannesburg: Universal Service and Access Agency of South Africa.

USAASA. (2017). *Annual report 2016/2017: USAF, The Universal Service and Access Fund*. Johannesburg: Universal Service and Access Agency of South Africa. Retrieved from http:// www. usaasa. org. za/ export/ sites/ usaasa/ resource- centre/ download- centre/ downloads/ USAF- Annual- Report- 2016- 2017. pdf.

Vecchiatto, P. (2008a, March 27). R850m in Universal Service Access Fund. *ITWeb*. Retrieved from http:// www. itweb. co. za/ sections/ quickprint/ print. asp? StoryID= 183416.

Vecchiatto, P. (2008b, August 15). Ivy's unbelievably silly access formula. *ITWeb*. Retrieved from http:// www. itweb. co. za/ index. php? option= com_ content& view= article& id= 10278.

Vecchiatto, P. (2010, September 28). School e-rate 'is dead'. *ITWeb*. Retrieved from http:// www. itweb. co. za/ index. php? option= com_ content& view= article& id= 37230.

Vecchiatto, P., & du Toit, C. (2008, August 14). Telcos unhappy over digital billions. *ITWeb*. Retrieved from http:// www. itweb. co. za/ index. php? option= com_ content& view= article& id= 9856.

Vodacom. (2011). *Integrated report for the year ended 31 March 2011*. Johannesburg: Vodacom. Retrieved from http:// www. vodacom. com/ pdf/ annual_ reports/ ar_ 2011. pdf.

CHAPTER 6

Under-Serviced Area Licences

The award of a number of licences to operators in under-serviced areas was a bold innovation in the slow stream of South Africa's sector reform, one that first surfaced when the 1996 Telecommunications Act was being amended (RSA, 2001b).

With Telkom's legislated fixed-line monopoly ending in 2002, and the introduction of one or more fixed-line operators on the cards, the Ministry initiated a process to amend the act. This was kicked off by a stakeholder colloquium, in early 2001, attended by some 350 participants. The agenda was rather more wide-ranging, however, and included "competition and market structure, wireless spectrum usage, convergence, empowerment, universal access and new telecommunications technologies", with stakeholders invited to make "written recommendations on future policy" (ITWeb, 2001). The issues and policy questions were also germane to the planned listing of Telkom on the stock exchange.[1] In the event, some 55 stakeholder submissions were made, ranging from existing licensees and potential investors, through private individuals to the African Telecommunications Forum and the National Telephone Cooperative Association of the USA (Bridges.org, 2001).

[1] Legislative certainty was necessary to secure investor confidence for the listing which eventually took place in March 2003.

C. Lewis, *Regulating Telecommunications in South Africa*,
Information Technology and Global Governance,
https://doi.org/10.1007/978-3-030-43527-1_6

The colloquium was cast in rhetorical mode, with the opening speech by Director General Andile Ngcaba—possibly in anticipation of its contested outcomes—harking back to the consultative process leading up to the 1996 Telecommunications Act and invoking for the first time the catchphrase of 'managed liberalisation' (Ngcaba, 2001). Much of the attention at the colloquium focused on market structure, with Telkom seeking to protect its incumbency while most stakeholders favoured greater liberalisation (de Wet, 2001a).

The final outcome was the subject of see-sawing public policy vicissitudes (de Wet, 2001b), largely related to whether one or two fixed-line entrants would be introduced, and suggestive of intense behind-the-scenes contestation (DoC, 2001a, 2001b, 2001c)[2] before the Bill finally settled in favour of just a single competitor (RSA, 2001a).

However, the introduction of a new category of licences for under-serviced areas—subsequently to become known as the Under-serviced Area Licensees (USALs)—was a consistent refrain in the discussions:

> Small, medium and micro enterprises (SMMEs) and co-operatives shall be permitted to provide telecommunication services including Voice over Internet Protocol (VoIP) for the specific purpose of advancing universal access in geographic areas with a teledensity of less than 1% from 7 May 2002... using their own or leased infrastructure... [and subject to] a standard interconnection regime. (DoC, 2001a, pp. 7, 8)

6.1 Seeds and Speculations

There has been considerable speculation on the origins of the USAL model. More than likely, however, the intervention came as a result of extensive and direct lobbying from the US-based National Telephone Cooperative Association (NTCA). In a submission leading up to the February 2001 stakeholder colloquium, the NTCA had tabled a fully formulated proposal remarkably similar to what was finally enacted.

[2] The Department of Communications, under the influence of Telkom and concerned to maximise rent extraction via the IPO, was believed to support a single entrant, while the Department of Trade and Industry, subject to broader economic pressures, wanted a second competitor.

The NTCA was a surprising player in the process, given its lack of international profile either before or since.[3] However, the association had a long history and extensive experience in promoting and supporting the development of rural telecommunications co-operatives. Founded in 1954 as an offshoot of the post-war rural electrification drive in the US, the NTCA brought together a number of the beneficiaries of "long-term, low-interest loans available [from 1949] to rural telephone systems" under the Rural Electrification Act (NTCA, n.d.). As an industry association, the NTCA undertook lobbying and advocacy on behalf of its members and provided a range of support services. From 1990, the NTCA had formally established an international programme, spearheaded by the energetic and charismatic Marlee Norton. It was Marlee who was the "really important" driving force behind the USAL model in South Africa (former IDRC staffer Tina James, interview, 27 November 2014)—inspired by the NTCA's earlier successes in countries as far afield as Bolivia and Poland.

The NTCA submission arose from a late 2000 workshop on "telecommunications cooperatives" (NTCA, 2001, p. ii) in preparation for the introduction of greater liberalisation into the sector. But the NTCA had already undertaken a preparatory analysis much earlier in 2000, examining the legislative changes required if telecommunications "cooperatives are to be a considered option" (NTCA, 2001, p. 6). Even earlier, the NTCA had established a relationship with the Universal Service Agency, where it appears that they were lobbying for the setting up of telephone co-operatives (DNTA, 1999, pp. 34–35). Marlee Norton had also shared a conference platform, with acting USA head Fikile Khumalo, on the role of telecommunications co-operatives in extending services to rural communities (IIR, 1999).

However, the episteme of the USAL concept involves a rather more complex set of interactions than the consistent pattern of lobbying on the part of the NTCA. ICT sector researcher Alison Gillwald suggests that Chair and Deputy Chair of the regulator (Naepe Maepa and Eddie Funde) were active proponents of the concept (interview, 13 November 2014). Others too point to Eddie Funde as a key supporter, largely in his later role as Chair of the South African Communications Forum

[3] The driving force behind this international proselytising, other than in the personality of Marlee Norton, is unclear.

(SACF) (interviews: Mandla Msimang, 7 November 2014; Katharina Pillay, 13 January 2015). Certainly, Funde was later to claim an instrumental role for the SACF in the adoption of the USAL model (USA, 2003b, pp. 22ff.), likely perceiving a sizeable 'black economic empowerment' opportunity for its members.[4]

The 2001 NTCA submission to the Department provides a useful summary of the approach. It argues for the establishment of "locally owned telecommunications [co-operatives] that interconnect with the broader national and international network" as alternatives to the failure of the telecentre model[5] (NTCA, 2001, pp. ii and 1). Its principal recommendation was that "the exclusive licence of Telkom should be modified to provide for grant of licenses [sic] to telecommunications cooperatives in Universal Service Areas designated by the Minister" (NTCA, 2001, p. ii). The report draws on the NTCA experience in Bolivia and the US, noting their "favourable legal and regulatory climate and which combined with economic, demographic and technological developments to produce generally successful results" (NTCA, 2001, p. 7).

The report thus lobbies for appropriate conditions to ensure success, and goes on to identify a number of issues needing consideration for telecommunications co-operatives to succeed, including: limited liability protection for investors; appropriate tax structures; supportive regulatory policies and interventions; proper co-ordination between the various agencies responsible for UAS; financial support from the USF for network rollout (NTCA, 2001, pp. 7–11). The report floats a number of regulatory proposals, including: exemption from rate rebalancing; provision of local area exclusivity; special interconnection and revenue sharing arrangements with Telkom—and specifies a series of recommended legislative amendments needed (NTCA, 2001, pp. 11–14).

The core features of the USAL model are already there: the designation of under-serviced-areas; the awarding of geographically-circumscribed licences; financial support from the USF; the need for supportive policy and regulatory interventions. The report's key failure—with the wisdom

[4] The SACF was the successor to the African Telecommunications Forum (ATF), which had brought together a number of entities that had failed to secure stakes in the lucrative mobile licences awarded in 1993.

[5] The submission's co-author, Tina James, had been closely involved with previous IDRC-funded telecentre projects.

of hindsight—was its failure to recognise the potential implications of the explosive uptake of mobile telephony[6] on its proposed model.[7]

It seems probable, therefore, that the USAL concept was already under active consideration by the Department. The NTCA model is possibly what Director General Andile Ngcaba had in mind when he stated, prior to the colloquium, that "multi-level competition will be considered at the end of Telkom's exclusivity period, with a number of operators licensed to provide services at different tiers and in different geographical areas" (ITWeb, 2001).

The notion of rural licensing was already part of the broader international telecommunications epistemic community at the ITU and the World Bank, circles to which Ngcaba remained connected. For example, as early as 1994, academics Martin Cave, Mark Scanlan, and UAS expert Claire Milne had floated the idea of offering "non-overlapping franchises to operators prepared to connect and serve areas which would not prove profitable for the incumbent" (EC, p. 4). Something similar had been mooted in South Africa's even earlier Coopers & Lybrand report, which repeatedly floated the notion of "'local network operators' [which] might include cooperatives formed by local residents, or private companies" (1992, p. 25). A few years later the World Bank's Björn Wellenius had begun to author a series of policy briefs, reports and academic journal articles drawing attention to a similar model, the least-subsidy rural payphone licensing interventions being undertaken by the USF in Chile (1997, 2002a, 2002b). Some years later, Stern and his co-authors were to urge the use of the USF and the provision of asymmetric interconnection rates to support the operations of 'rural operators' (Stern, Townsend, & Monedero, 2006).

At around the same time, the telecommunications co-operatives in places as far afield as Bolivia (Calzada & Davalos, 2005; Flores, 1989) and Poland (Kontkiewicz-Chachulska, 1997) were receiving attention from researchers and policy-makers, as was the Grameen phone model of Bangladesh (Lawson & Meyenn, 2000; Richardson, Ramirez, & Haq, 2000). The epistemic tenor seems therefore to have been receptive to new UAS models.

[6] By the end of 2000, the combined subscriber base of Vodacom and MTN was already 5.4 million, growing rapidly, and poised to overtake Telkom's fixed-line tally of 5.5 million.

[7] Possibly because prepaid mobile was almost non-existent in the US at the time.

6.2 From Conceptualisation to Implementation

Shortly after the Colloquium, the Minister issued a lengthy Policy Direction, which, *inter alia*, laid the groundwork for the introduction of under-serviced area licensing (DoC, 2001a). The Minister directed that "small, medium and micro enterprises (SMMEs) and co-operatives shall be permitted to provide telecommunication services including Voice over Internet Protocol (VoiP) [sic] for the specific purpose of advancing universal access in geographic areas with a teledensity of less than 1% from 7 May 2002" and that such licensees might use "their own or leased infrastructure" (DoC, 2001a, pp. 7–8). Several regulatory provisions supporting the business case for such licensees were also set out, including that a "standard interconnection regime applicable to all SMMEs and co-operatives shall be developed by the network operators and approved by ICASA", and reiteration in respect of VANS licensees of the "prohibition to carry voice over the Internet and VANS" [sic][8] (DoC, 2001a, p. 8). The under-serviced area threshold was later raised to 5% (DoC, 2001b, p. 8), once it was realised there were almost no areas with teledensity under 1%.[9] It also excised co-operatives from the list of possible licence beneficiaries.

When the Amendment was tabled in Parliament later that year, it duly contained the necessary provisions for the award of licences to small businesses to provide "telecommunication services or facilities" in "geographic areas where less than 5% of the population has access" (RSA, 2001a, Section 40A). Further clauses allowed the USALs to utilise VoIP and provided for interconnection with the networks of existing fixed and mobile licensees. Despite the model being substantially the same as that proposed by the NTCA, it is noteworthy that the Bill too no longer contained any notion of the 'co-operatives' so central to the NTCA approach.

Only limited records survive of the consultation process. Much of the attention seems to have focused elsewhere than the USALs, on issues such as the country's WTO commitments, the independence of the regulator, the market structure of the sector and the question of what was meant by

[8] The formulation in respect of VANS licensees was corrected in the second iteration to specify a "prohibition to carry VoIP and voice" (DoC, 2001b, p. 8).

[9] The wording of the interconnection provision was also slightly amended to make ICASA solely responsible for its development (DoC, 2001b, p. 8).

'fixed-mobile'.[10] The VANS association, however, strenuously objected to the USALs being granted the VoIP privileges from which their members were still blocked (SAVA, 2001).

The final Amendment Act added a proviso privileging applications for USAL licences by "persons from historically disadvantaged groups; and [sic]… women" (RSA, 1996, Section 40A(2)(b)).[11] It became law in November 2001.

Keen to forge ahead with the issuing of USAL licences as a matter of urgency, a month later the Minister issued a list of 27 district municipalities she classified as 'under-serviced', of which 8 were earmarked for first phase licences (DoC, 2001d) (see Fig. 6.1).

According to the Minister, the determination was based on data from the 1996 census, since data from the 2001 census was not yet available (DoC, 2003c, p. 5). But this made the determination problematic. Firstly, the 1996 census did not distinguish between fixed and mobile telephony, lumping both together when counting household access to telephony. This would somewhat have skewed the figures, with mobile still relatively new to the market[12] and likely still mostly in the hands of affluent users who already had fixed-line access. Secondly, as a household survey, the census did not count business lines which are included in the definition of 'teledensity'.

However, between 1996 and 2001 the market had experienced two dramatic shifts which substantially altered the picture. Firstly, Telkom had begun to roll out its 2.69 million USO lines the following year, with its fixed-line network peaking at 5.6 million lines in 2000. Secondly, the introduction of prepaid mobile services at the end of 1996 had seen a sky-rocketing uptake of cellular telephony, often in historically under-serviced areas. By the time the under-serviced areas were designated, the number of mobile subscribers was already nearly double the number of Telkom

[10] A new concept introduced in the Bill as a category of service provision extended to PSTS licensees, it provided for wireless handsets with no or very limited base-station handover.

[11] 'Historically disadvantaged' groups, in the South African context, refer to those subject to historical discrimination, mainly on the grounds of race, gender or disability.

[12] Mobile subscriber numbers for 1996 (at which point Telkom had 3.9 million subscribers) are not available, but are likely to have been well under a million.

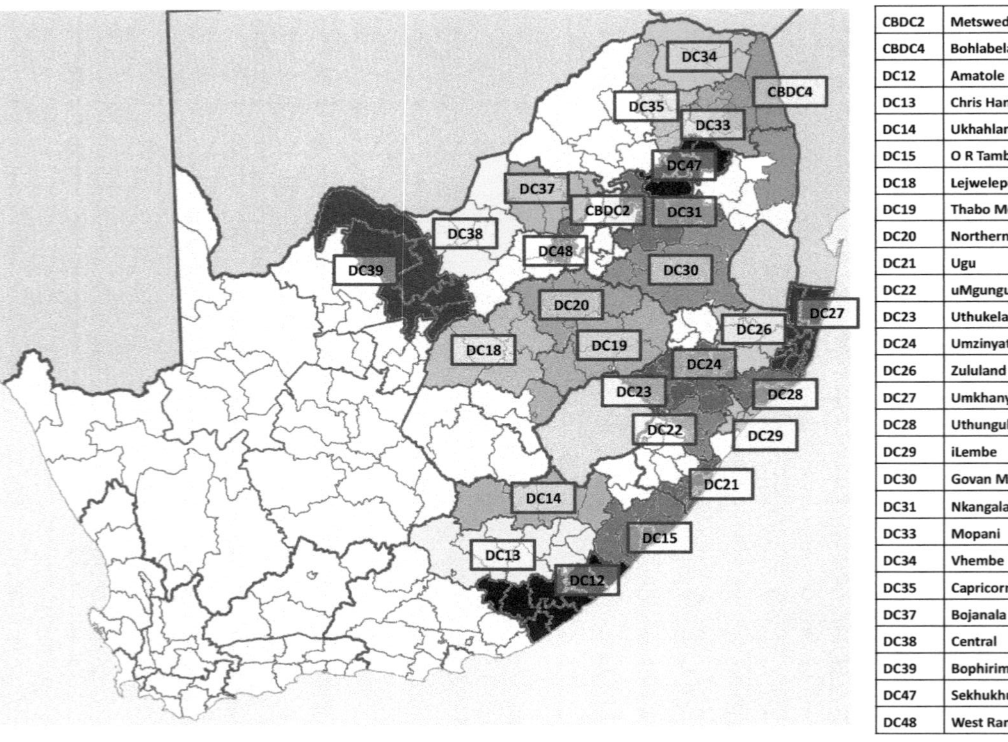

CBDC2	Metsweding
CBDC4	Bohlabela
DC12	Amatole
DC13	Chris Hani
DC14	Ukhahlamba
DC15	O R Tambo
DC18	Lejweleputswa
DC19	Thabo Mofutsanyane
DC20	Northern Free State
DC21	Ugu
DC22	uMgungundlovu
DC23	Uthukela
DC24	Umzinyathi
DC26	Zululand
DC27	Umkhanyakude
DC28	Uthungulu
DC29	iLembe
DC30	Govan Mbeki
DC31	Nkangala
DC33	Mopani
DC34	Vhembe
DC35	Capricorn
DC37	Bojanala
DC38	Central
DC39	Bophirima
DC47	Sekhukhune
DC48	West Rand

Fig. 6.1 Original 27 under-serviced licence areas

mainlines in operation.[13] This meant that the picture was substantially different than it had been at the time of the 1996 census, despite the assurance of the Minister to the contrary (DoC, 2003c, p. 5).

Gillwald suggests there was an "outcry by the incumbent fixed and mobile operators in response to the identified districts" (2002, p. 2): Telkom claimed it had exceeded 5% teledensity in some of the areas, and the mobile licensees claimed that others were "well serviced" by them.

The table below shows that at least 5 of the 27 districts were over 5% residential teledensity.[14] Further, the fact that district municipalities were used to make the demarcation meant that each under-serviced area was guaranteed to include at least one town of some size and substance. However, the inclusion of urbanised centres of economic and social activity is arguably essential for the commercial viability of the licensees (Kayani & Dymond, 1997, p. 81) (see Table 6.1).

There are, however, some surprising omissions from the list. In particular, Alfred Nzo District Municipality, centred on Mount Ayliff (population just under 5000 at the time) in the former Transkei, stands out as having the lowest teledensity in the entire country at the time: 0.54%, or a mere 2972 fixed-lines for over half a million inhabitants. Other omissions with low teledensities include Sisonke District Municipality (1.95%) and Ehlanzeni (2.73%). The last 7 entries in the table also had 2001 teledensities above the 5% threshold. In addition, it is puzzling that no Northern Cape district municipality was included.[15] Political considerations may possibly have played a role in the final selection.

8 of the 27 (2 in each of 4 provinces) were earmarked for the first round of licensing (DoC, 2001d), strangely overlooking poorly connected districts in both Mpumalanga and North-West. A few months later, presumably as a result of lobbying, a further two areas were added to the list (DoC, 2002a),[16] giving a slightly better geographic spread, but still overlooking Mpumalanga.

[13] By early 2001, MTN and Vodacom had 8.6 million subscribers, while Telkom's network had shrunk to 5 million.

[14] Bearing in mind these figures were not available to the Minister at the time.

[15] Kgalagadi District Municipality, centred on Kuruman, and with a 2001 teledensity of 3.12%, seems an obvious candidate. There were no district municipalities in Western Cape with a teledensity as low as 5%.

[16] Thabo Mafutsanyana (Free State) and Central (North West).

Table 6.1 Under-serviced areas by fixed-line teledensity[a]

District		Province	Main town	Population	Teledensity %
DC15	O. R. Tambo	Eastern Cape	Mthatha	1,676,484	0.69
DC27	Umkhanyakude District Municipality	KwaZulu-Natal	Mkuze	573,337	1.03
DC47	Sekhukhune District Municipality	Limpopo	Groblersdal	967,182	1.19
CBDC4	Bohlabela District Municipality	Limpopo	Phalaborwa	597,737	1.30
DC33	Mopani District Municipality	Limpopo	Giyani	964,237	1.42
DC34	Vhembe District Municipality	Limpopo	Thohoyandou	1,199,884	1.42
DC26	Zululand District Municipality	KwaZulu-Natal	Ulundi	804,454	1.61
DC24	Umzinyathi District Municipality	KwaZulu-Natal	Dundee	456,451	1.64
DC14	Ukhahlamba District Municipality	Eastern Cape	Barkly East	341,339	1.76
DC35	Capricorn District Municipality	Limpopo	Polokwane	1,154,693	2.36
DC13	Chris Hani District Municipality	Eastern Cape	Queenstown	810,303	2.41
DC28	Uthungulu District Municipality	KwaZulu-Natal	Richards Bay	885,967	2.43
DC39	Bophirima District Municipality[b]	North West	Vryburg	439,672	2.43
DC23	Uthukela District Municipality	KwaZulu-Natal	Ladysmith	656,987	2.70
DC37	Bojanala District Municipality	North West	Rustenburg	1,185,329	2.85
DC38	Central District Municipality[c]	North West	Mahikeng	763,000	2.85

(continued)

Table 6.1 (continued)

District		Province	Main town	Population	Teledensity %
DC29	iLembe District Municipality	KwaZulu-Natal	kwaDukuza	560,389	3.39
DC12	Amatole	Eastern Cape	East London	1,664,251	3.51
DC21	Ugu District Municipality	KwaZulu-Natal	Port Shepstone	704,030	3.51
DC30	Govan Mbeki Municipality	Mpumalanga	Ermelo	900,008	3.78
DC19	Thabo Mofutsanyane District Municipality[d]	Free State	Phuthaditjhaba	725,936	4.19
DC31	Nkangala	Mpumalanga	Middelburg	1,020,584	4.52
DC18	Lejweleputswa District Municipality	Free State	Welkom	657,012	5.01
DC20	Northern Free State District Municipality	Free State	Sasolburg	460,319	6.11
CBDC2	Metsweding District Municipality	Gauteng	Bronkhorstspruit	159,896	6.13
DC22	uMgungundlovu District Municipality	KwaZulu-Natal	Pietermaritzburg	927,847	6.38
DC48	West Rand District Municipality	Gauteng	Randfontein	744,154	6.88

[a]Data as per a spreadsheet of Census 2001 data, supplied to the author by Statistics South Africa. Some districts (e.g. DC29) changed their names subsequent to the Ministerial designation. Others (e.g. CBDC4) were later dismembered. Those districts highlighted are those selected for the first round of licensing

[b]Added in the final ITA

[c]Added to the original 8 in early 2002

[d]Added to the original 8 in early 2002, but dropped in the final ITA

6.3 Pay your Money and Get Your Licence

Licensing of the USALs then stalled for nearly a year, while ICASA was preoccupied with the ongoing brouhaha around the third mobile licence and the process to license the second network operator. Regulatory processes for the USALs—to deal with interconnection (ICASA, 2002a, 2002d) as well as ownership and control (ICASA, 2002b, 2002c) were only launched towards the end of 2002, and were then shoddily executed.[17]

The USAL licensing process itself proceeded erratically over the next few years. In December 2002, the Minister finally issued the formal Invitation to Apply (ITA)[18] and draft licence (DoC, 2002b),[19] with the latter document being revised no less than twice by ICASA (2003a, 2003b).[20] The ITA made further changes to the under-serviced areas designated for the first round of licences, leading to a slightly better geographic spread (2 each for 5 provinces, but still excluding Mpumalanga).

The process continued to be mired in delays. The Minister extended the original deadline twice (DoC, 2003a, 2003b), as ICASA struggled to manage its complexity. Not only was ICASA wrestling with the necessary enabling regulations, but the bidders were struggling to "communicate with the relevant communities" and to put in place the necessary "structures" (Weidemann, 2003a). Support and capacity building for the bids was clearly necessary, and entities like Forge Ahead BMI-T[21] (Denis Smit, interview, 20 November 2014) and the South African Communications Forum (SACF[22]) (USA, 2003b) stepped into the breach, developing business plans and providing training.

But worse, delays emanating from USAASA held up the development of the key USF funding model blueprint necessary to launch the successful USAL bidders, and make them viable. It was only in late May 2003 that the Agency tabled for comment a "draft policy" to provide subsidies to the USALs (USA, 2003a), followed a short two weeks later by a stakeholder workshop (USA, 2004, p. 15). Framed in byzantine language, it envisaged a complex two-pronged model. The final model was

[17] Both needed to have corrections issued shortly after publication. The interconnection regulations were never finalised.

[18] Under the 1996 Telecommunications Act, it was the Minister who issued the ITA and granted the licence, with the regulator doing all the remaining spadework.

[19] The draft licence provided for 'fixed mobility' which is defined as limited mobility within an undefined "Short Distance Charging Area". The annual licence fee was set at a low 0.1% of sales revenue.

[20] The revisions were largely minor and technical, although the final licence no longer defined 'fixed mobility'.

[21] Joint MD, Simon White was later part of an unsuccessful USAL bid.

[22] The SACF also embarked on a roadshow with the Universal Service Agency to create consortia and mobilise bids (USA, 2003b).

never publicly gazetted, although a "final report… was provided to the Minister after the consultation process ran its course" (Thornton, 2006, p. 6). Separate subsidy agreements were eventually signed with the individual licensees (USA, 2004, p. 14), but these were never made public. Thus, the parameters of the subsidy agreements remain unknown, save for the provision in the licences that the funds be utilised "exclusively for the acquisition and construction of infrastructure" (ICASA, 2006b, p. 12).

These delays, resulting both from a lack of institutional focus and from the complexities of the web of overlapping responsibilities, began to take their toll on the bidders. Bidder Simon White was quoted as complaining that "every month the viability of the project is limited further while the costs continue to increase", while another bewailed that few bidders had the "financial resources to sustain themselves through all these delays" (Weidemann, 2003b).

Strangely, the question of ownership and control limitations with respect to the licences was only finalised in late August (ICASA, 2003c). This was mere days ahead of the final 29 August deadline for applications. Although both draft and final regulations banned incumbent licensees (such as Telkom, MTN, Vodacom) from holding shares in any USAL applicant, and barred any entity from controlling more than one USAL, there were significant changes in the final regulations. Firstly, cross-ownership restrictions were relaxed, allowing any entity a non-controlling investment in up to 9 USALs (the draft regulations had pegged the limit at 3). Secondly, a new clause prohibited foreign investors from holding a controlling share in any USAL. It is not clear whether these changes affected any of the bids that had been submitted, a list of which was released a month later (ICASA, 2003d). Of the 10 under-serviced areas on offer, only one (DC 35, Capricorn District) attracted three bids, with two bids in four of the districts, one each in a further four, and none in one case (CBDC4 Bushbuckridge/Lowveld Municipality).

The licensing process was further delayed to allow for public comment (Weidemann, 2003c) and to run a public hearings roadshow, with sessions in each of the respective licence areas (Weidemann, 2004). As a result, it was only on 3 June 2004—two and a half years after the process had begun—that the first 7 licences were finally granted by the Minister (DoC, 2004a), in accordance with ICASA's recommendation (Fig. 6.2). A further six months were to elapse before the licences were finalised and

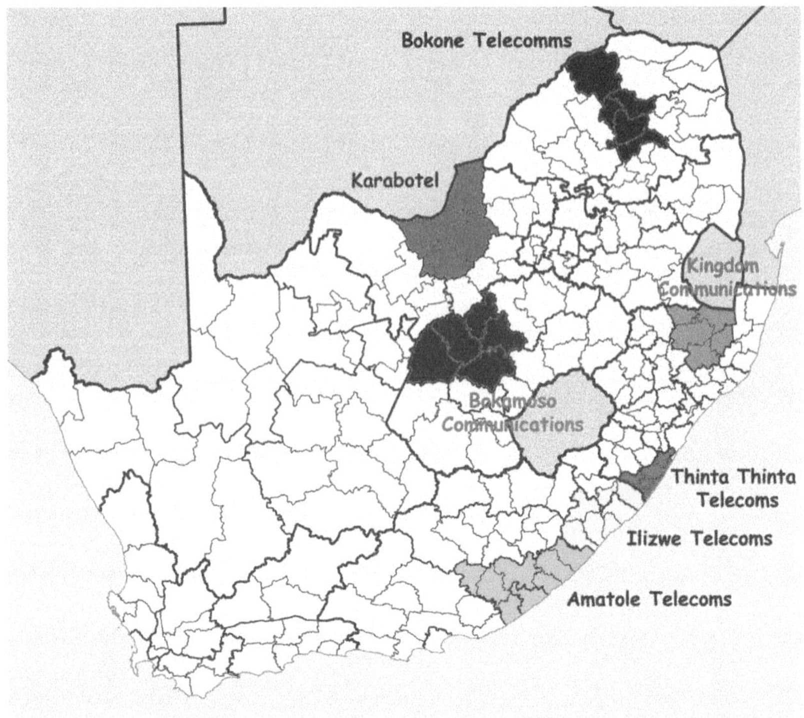

Fig. 6.2 First 7 under-serviced area licensees (*Source* Author, based on DoC [2001d])

formally issued by ICASA. Four of the licences were granted outright,[23] with three more granted conditionally[24] (DoC, 2004a). Four bids had been disqualified, and three rejected.

The provisions of the first seven USALs' licences were almost identical to the draft licence, save for the addition of a clause on roaming, and for the removal of clauses providing for exemption from number portability and carrier pre-select for a limited period. They read like any standard

[23] Bokone Telecomms, Kingdom Communications, Thinta Thinta Telecoms, Ilizwi Telecoms.

[24] Amatole Telecoms, Bokamoso Communications, KaraboTel.

telecommunications licence of the time, but it is worth noting some of their features. Each licensee:

- Held their licence for 25 years;
- Could provide "any telecommunication services including voice over Internet protocol services (VoIP), fixed-mobile services and Public Telephone Services";
- Could provide infrastructure to VANS and mobile licensees;
- Could enter into roaming agreements;
- Had 36 months to "maintain and use its network";
- Was "entitled to use any type of technology";
- Had "Roll-Out Targets and Penalties for Non-Compliance"—specified in annexures;
- Was required to pay an annual licence fee of 0.1% of "audited net operational income" (ICASA, 2006b, pp. 10–13).

With the ink barely dry on most of the licences, USAASA immediately rushed ahead to hand over the cheques for the first tranche of subsidy funding to the new licensees. Indeed, it was so proud of its achievement that it ran the handover ceremony twice (Jovanovic, 2004; Weidemann, 2005a).[25]

With unseemly haste, and with cavalier disregard for the commercial viability of the hapless recipients, the Minister moved right ahead to issue an ITA for the next 14 licences (DoC, 2005). Deadlines in this second round of applications were again slipped, with the closing date pushed out several times, and ICASA having to revise its list of applicants (ICASA, 2005a, 2005b) to cater for mergers between bidders. It took a further year to finalise the award of the second round of USALs, with the Minister granting three licences outright,[26] six conditionally,[27] and six, subject to mergers.[28] ICASA described the process as a "three-phase

[25] Only four of the licences had been signed at the time of the first ceremony. Amatole's licence was issued some months after the second event.

[26] Nkangala Telecoms, Northcom, Ukhahlamba Communications.

[27] Dinaka Telecommunications, Ilembe Communications, Metsweding Telex, Nyakatho Telecommunications, PlatiTel, ZeroPlus Trading.

[28] CH Communications & Ntwasahlobo; Thabo Mafutsanyana Telecom & Maluti Communications; Thanda Telecom, Khula Air Conditioning, Elangeni Communication & Arengo; Vhembe Telecommunications & Kwetedza Telecommunications.

licensing approach… which attaches conditions to issuing of the licences" (Senne, 2006b). Rather, it reflects on the poor quality of many of the bids, together with a growing sense of urgency to complete the USAL licensing project in the face of mounting evidence that it was in deep trouble and doomed to failure (Gillwald, 2005; Guest, 2006; Vecchiatto, 2006a). One of the six conditional licensees in this round (ZeroPlus Trading) found itself in the strange position of receiving a licence for a district that had been administratively dismembered several months earlier.[29]

Undeterred, however, the Minister issued an ITA for the remaining 6 under-serviced areas in February 2006 (DoC, 2006). These were conditionally granted by ICASA somewhat more than a year later (ICASA, 2008, p. 19)[30]—bizarrely after the new Minister had already decreed that all 27 USALs be amalgamated as 7 Provincial Under-serviced Area Network Operators (PUSANOs) (DoC, 2007).

By 2008 then, licences had formally been granted in 24 of the 27 gazetted under-serviced areas.[31] Table 6.2 lists the unfortunate recipients.

6.4 Licensed to Lose

Conceived as an innovative rural licensing model, stranded in the no-man's land between the lure of money-making opportunities and the ineptitude of bureaucratic delays, the under-serviced area licensing initiative was rapidly overtaken by events. In the three long years from the declaration of the 27 target licensing areas until the first consortium received its licence in 2005, the mobile subscriber base had ballooned to 23 million, dwarfing the country's less than 5 million fixed lines. The 27 under-serviced areas may have had less than 5% fixed-line residential teledensity, but they were likely to have had substantial and burgeoning numbers of mobile subscribers, making market entry for any USAL operator virtually impossible.

Further, partly in response to pressures from the sector, from 2003 the Ministry had begun to move towards a belated further liberalisation. On

[29] Bohlabela District was split between Ehlanzeni (Mpumalanga) and Mopani (Limpopo) District Municipalities on 1 March 2006.

[30] The announcement seems to have passed well under the radar of the trade press and only appears in the ICASA Annual Report, with no precise date attached.

[31] None of the licences was ever amended to take account of the redrawing of district boundaries or name changes.

Table 6.2 List of under-serviced licensees

USALs round 1[a] *(n=7)* *19 December 2002 ITA issued* *3 June 2004 licences granted* *November 2004 licences issued*	*USALs round 2 (n=11)* *11 January 2005 ITA issued* *14 August 2006 licences granted* *April 2007 and November 2007 licences issued*[b]	*USALs round 3 (n=6)* *7 February 2006 ITA issued* *2007/2008 licences granted*
Amatole Telecomms	Dinaka Telecommunications	Asixhumane Communications
Bokamoso Communications	Ilembe Communications	Bulani Telecommunications
Bokone Telecomms	Kwetedza Telecommunications[c]	Duzi-Cell Networking KZN
Ilizwi Telecomms	Metjodi Telecommunications[d]	Sekhukhune Telecommunications
KaraboTel	Metsweding Telex	Thetha Khuluma Telecommunications
Kingdom Communications	Nkangala Telecoms	Umzinyathi Telecommunications[e]
Thinta Thinta Telecomms	Northcom	
	Nyakatho Telecommunications	
	PlatiTel	
	Ukhahlamba Communications	
	ZeroPlus Trading	

[a]No licences were granted in: Bushbuck Ridge/Lowveld Municipality; Bophirima District (North West); Northern Free State District (Free State)
[b]Nkangala, Northcom and Ukhahlamba were the last three USALs to receive licences under the 1996 Telecomms Act. All subsequent USAL licensees were processed under the 2005 ECA
[c]A merger between Vhembe Telecommunications Company and Kwetedza Telecommunications
[d]A merger between Thabo Mafutsanyana Telecom and Maluti Communications
[e]Later known as Umzitel, possibly involved in later tender irregularities at USAASA (see Chapters 5 and 7)

the one hand, the tortuous process that was to culminate in new legislation—the 2005 Electronic Communications Act—had commenced with a stakeholder policy colloquium in July 2003, but had run into delays and controversy (Wolmarans, 2004).[32] In the meantime, in late 2004, under

[32]A draft bill had been released six months after the colloquium to howls of condemnation and ridicule.

continuing pressure from the sector, the Minister abruptly issued a set of pronouncements (DoC, 2004b) setting out important steps towards further liberalisation within the confines of the existing Act. Many of the provisions of this policy *deus ex machina*—issued a mere two months before the first USALs were to receive their licences—directly undermined the business models and potential market strategies of the USALs. Such provisions included: the full liberalisation of public payphone services, permitting 'voice over any protocol', the introduction of self-provisioning and of resale, the introduction of an e-rate discount on phone calls and Internet access charges.

Given the pressures on the new USALs due to the licensing delays, and in the light of dramatically altered market conditions, it is hardly surprising that they rushed to sign roaming agreements[33] with the mobile incumbents as they scrambled to secure a foothold in the market. Thinta Thinta was the first to do so, with an agreement allowing it to roam on the MTN network, which already covered 100% of its licence area (Mogaki, 2005). Bokamoso was quick to follow, announcing a roaming agreement with Vodacom, ahead of the fanfare launch of its services at a government *imbizo* in April 2005 (Weidemann, 2005b).[34] Shortly thereafter Vodacom[35] announced the signing of five roaming agreements with USALs, adding Amatole Telecomms, Bokone Telecomms, KaraboTel and Kingdom Communications to its growing stable (Lowman, 2005). Ilizwi Telecoms too seems to have signed up to the Vodacom network a little later (Mngcungusa, 2005). Five of the first seven licensed USALs then went on to file tariff plans with the regulator during 2005/2006 (Amatole Telecomms, Ilizwi Telecomms, KaraboTel, Kingdom Communications, Thinta Thinta Telecomms) (ICASA, 2006a, p. 11).

Although the promises to roll out their own networks within the 3 years required by their agreements with the USA were trotted out with each announcement, none had even started to do so by year's end. This was because their applications for the necessary spectrum remained stalled

[33] Most of these were really resale agreements, with rebranding.

[34] Bokamoso (B-Tel) subsequently switched to Telkom (Telkom, 2005), reportedly because the reseller agreement with Vodacom was "unfavourable" (Thornton, 2006, p. 18).

[35] Vodacom's Tjaart le Roux was the driving force behind this. It is unclear whether this was simply a commercial drive, animated by financial or altruistic motives, or whether it was part of a more cynical business strategy to emasculate the USALs.

at ICASA (Mngcungusa, 2005). Nearly a year later the USALs were still waiting for spectrum (Guest, 2006)!

As a result, the USALs were essentially reduced to MVNOs,[36] with no networks of their own, reselling the services of the mobile incumbents. Their contracts with the mobile operators included voicemail, emergency services calls, with the necessary MVNO branding support: "assistance with respect to the manufacturing of SIM cards and prepaid re-charge vouchers (with USAL branding and programmed on the USALs number plan)" (Vodacom, 2005). But they faced a crucial, crippling difference: their customers were unable to roam outside their designated under-serviced area. Selling a service that offered only limited mobility within a market dominated by fully mobile providers was a recipe for failure.

It soon became clear that the USALs were in serious trouble (Gillwald, 2005; Guest, 2006; Vecchiatto, 2006a). Alerted, in part by its own workshops with the USALs (Vecchiatto, 2006b), and by an impact study, which pointed out that the "viability" of the USALs had been "severely impacted" (USA, 2005, p. 33) by delays and other market factors,[37] the Agency commissioned external specialists to conduct a USAL review[38] and to "propose recommendations to strengthen their business cases and ensure their sustainability" (USA, 2006).

The results of this were more startling and starker than any had anticipated and began to filter out ahead of the formal tabling of the report (Vecchiatto, 2006a, 2006b). The report makes grim reading. It concludes bleakly that "without significant intervention... most if not all of the USALs will not survive" (Thornton, 2006, pp. 1, 2). The report shows the USALs to be in dire straits, undermined by poor organisational functioning, "weak" corporate governance practices, largely unable to manage basic "regulatory compliance", and severely financially constrained (Thornton, 2006, pp. 9ff.). The USALs are described as primarily reliant on funding from the USF to survive, with the overwhelming bulk of its disbursements (R35,000 at the time) having been spent on "start-up and operating costs" (Thornton, 2006, p. 12). By that stage, the six operational USALs had a mere 17,000 estimated subscribers between them,

[36] A mobile virtual network operator (MVNO) sells mobile phone services to customers using infrastructure and facilities leased from a mobile operator.

[37] Including the threat of several million SIM cards anticipated from the mobile licensees under the 1800 MHz spectrum *quid pro quo*.

[38] Covering the first 7 USAL licensees.

with estimated ARPUs barely a quarter of the national average, well below the threshold for survival (Thornton, 2006, pp. 14ff.).

The report goes on to hone in on three major bottlenecks confronting the USALs:

- Lack of access to capital, for both operational and capital expenditure, which it describes as "one of the most acute limitations" facing the USALs—due both to difficulties in raising loans and securing equity, and to the small size of the subsidies from the USF, which it describe as "not adequate";
- Failure on the part of ICASA to assign the necessary spectrum in the WiMax (in one case) and CDMA (for the remainder) bands, on which the USALs' "current business plans" were reliant[39];
- Failure to on the part of ICASA to extend "cost based interconnection" beyond the PSTS to the mobile licensees (Thornton, 2006, pp. 27ff.).

Accordingly, the report's main recommendations mirror the three key issues:

- Increase in and changes in respect of allocation of the USF Subsidy;
- Access to CDMA (and other necessary) or alternative spectrum;
- Promulgation and enforcement of interconnection regulations to ensure cost-based interconnection with all other telecommunications service providers (Thornton, 2006, p. 27).

It is clear that the dire situation of the USALs was due to policy and regulatory failure, with ineptitude and delays creating a crisis for the luckless licensees. The report remains circumspect when it comes to pointing fingers, but does recommend a range of supplementary, "supporting interventions" to be undertaken by the Department, the regulator and the Agency (Thornton, 2006, pp. 27ff.).

The findings, described by one of the research team on the report as "absolutely damning" (Justine Limpitlaw, personal communication, 20 January 2015), were duly presented to the Minister, supported by the

[39] One USAL did manage to secure a test licence in the 850 MHz band.

unfortunate USALs. In response, the Minister's "face became grimly set in stone" (Justine Limpitlaw, personal communication, 20 January 2015).

The final report was presented at a conference some months later (Senne, 2006c) and generated some column inches in the trade press (Guest, 2006; Senne, 2006c). Perhaps many, like USAASA Board member Bibi Khan, were "tired of being in workshops where we discuss the problems that USALs are facing" and blamed the hapless USALs for not taking "responsibility for their sustainability" (Senne, 2006c). Khan had clearly not read the report closely, since it laid most of the blame squarely at door of the policy-makers and regulatory bodies, her own included.

The impact of this damning report on policy and regulation was precisely zero. The new legislation contained no licensing category appropriate to USALs, and ICASA was soon consumed with the mammoth task of converting all its legacy licences, thus leaving little room to focus on the USALs. Subsequent pleas by several of the USALs to the Parliamentary Portfolio Committee on Communications, describing their dire predicament and calling for the recommendations of the report to be implemented, were met with scant sympathy: one ANC MP brusquely told the USALs present[40] to be "self-critical and assess internal problems" (PMG, 2007).

It was over a year later that the Minister suddenly again picked up the issue of the USALs in the course of another round of policy directions. These included the following bizarre injunction to ICASA: "where there is more than one licence in a province, merge the licences and issue one Provincial Under-Serviced Area Network Operator (PUSANO) licence" (DoC, 2007, p. 9). Few at the time seem to have appreciated the enormity or the folly of this solution to the predicament of the USALs. Essentially, it amounted to enforcing mergers between the holders of USAL licences (and holders-to-be, since six licences were already in process under the Minister's own ITA), some functional and some having already collapsed. It would have reduced 27 USAL licensees to 7 PUSANO licensees.[41] And it sounded the death knell for the ill-fated USAL model.

Despite breezy assurances from USAASA that all was well (Glazier, 2007; Motloung, 2008), none of the mergers ever went through. The USALs themselves were kept in the dark while the regulator tried to

[40] The record suggests several were present, but only Bokamoso is named.

[41] Two of the country's nine provinces had no gazetted under-serviced areas.

work out how to proceed, before they issued an open letter to ICASA demanding clarity and action (Senne & Jones, 2007). ICASA was later to explain that it had refused to implement the Minister's policy direction on the grounds that it was *ultra vires* the ECA (ICASA, 2009). In many places, there was also no longer much left to merge: two journalists were only able to trace one (Ilembe Communications) of the eight-round two USALs they attempted to contact (du Toit & Senne, 2007). In the meantime, ICASA went ahead and issued class infrastructure and individual service licences to 25 of the 27 USALs.

With the various regulatory delays and policy vacillations, all hope of securing the desperately needed investment in the USALs evaporated. Despite the fact that their licences prohibited the USALs from seeking additional external investment (ICASA, 2006b, p. 15), a number had approached South Africa's Industrial Development Corporation (IDC, a state-owned development finance institution), as well as Lucent Technologies, a WiMax vendor. While the IDC had been keen to invest some R215 million in the first set of USALs (Thornton, 2006, p. 11), their loan pre-conditions (chiefly: equity participation,[42] but also possession of a spectrum licence) appear never to have been met, and no loans were ever finalised.

By the beginning of 2008 then, none of the original seven USALs had rolled out a network, and only three remained "viable", according to USAASA CEO James Theledi (Senne, 2008). Unfortunately, his bleak summary of the situation, while accurate, again shifts the blame to the USALs, and fails to recognise any policy, regulatory or contextual contribution to the collapse of the project:

> We gave USALs money; spent many years since they were licensed in December 2004 waiting for them to begin offering services; and now it's 2008 and they have not finalised interconnection agreements, they don't have networks, have challenges of liquidation [sic] and can't bring together a roll-out plan. (Senne, 2008)

It fell to the incoming Minister to administer the last rites. He finally conceded that the USAL model as a "concept and the possible remedy had not worked" (Vecchiatto, 2009).

[42] Equity participation would have required prior written approval from ICASA, but also compliance with the ownership and control regulations.

A policy direction abolishing the PUSANO folly followed a few months later (DoC, 2009). This left some 25 ill-fated USALs without a formal concessionary licence category, albeit able to build their own provincial network infrastructure and able to offer fixed or mobile services countrywide.[43] However, they now faced a market effectively fully liberalised[44] with over 400 VANS operators able to roll out their own networks and offer telephony services in direct competition to the USALs. It was an environment in which few if any of the USALs would be able to survive.

The fate of most of the jinxed USAL licensees remains unclear, even today. Of the original 7 pioneers, only Amatole Telecomms appears still to survive, albeit offering wireless ISP services very different from what was originally envisaged. The difficulty of establishing their status is compounded by the failure of ICASA to maintain an up-to-date and accurate database of licensees. By the time ICASA embarked on an exercise to clean up their database in 2014, three of the original seven had either deregistered or were untraceable, or both (ICASA, 2014a). Of the remaining 20, a further 9 had either deregistered or were untraceable, or both.

Of the subsequent 17, not one appears to have survived. The most optimistic numbers from the above amount to a mere 17,000 GSM MVNO customers, with no figures for customers on the USALs' own networks. Some R61 million from the USF by way of subsidies, along with unknown amounts from small-scale investors and entrepreneurs, seems to have been almost entirely wasted.

6.5 From Business Case to Basket Case

Behind to failure of the model, and the collapse of the individual licensees, lie many untold stories of personal loss and financial disaster. BMI-Tech's Denis Smit recalls that people lost their houses and communities lost their

[43] Thanks to holding individual service licences, although they would need to secure roaming rights for customers travelling beyond the reach of their provincially delimited infrastructure licences.

[44] The landmark 'Altech judgement' had seen VANS licensees gain national infrastructure licences.

savings[45] (interview, 20 November 2014). There are persistent rumours that one investor, facing financial ruin, committed suicide[46] (Alison Gillwald, interview, 9 May 2017).

What then are the likely causes of this debacle?

The USAL licensing intervention found ready resonance with the groundswell of popular opposition to Telkom's fixed-line monopoly. Accordingly, from the outset there was considerable focus on the part of researchers and stakeholders on how to ensure the economic viability and commercial success of the USALs, and to protect them from falling victim to the market power and dominance of the fixed and mobile incumbents.

The NTCA proposal (2001) had already touched on what it viewed as critical success factors and key enabling regulatory interventions. A subsequent report commissioned by the DBSA and the IDRC looked directly at financial viability for the USALs, covering both capital and operational expenditure, as well as sources of revenue. Its financial modelling projected the USALs breaking even after three years—with only limited support by way of "start-up subsidies" from the USF in "marginal" cases (AVP, 2002, p. 29). But it was predicated on two key measures being put in place, namely:

- regulations providing asymmetric interconnection (which it viewed as a "make or break" issue [AVP, 2002, p. 24]) and facilities sharing; and
- the creation of a "Shared Platform Company" which would provide "Operating Support System / Business Support Systems" (largely network management and customer service activities) (AVP, 2002, p. 29).

The LINK Centre's Alison Gillwald also wrote extensively—and with an increasing degree of frustration—on the USALs and their waning possibilities for commercial survival (Gillwald, 2002, 2003, p. 9, 2005; Gillwald & Esselaar, 2004, p. 16). Similar concerns were shared by other commentators (Chetty, Blake, & McPhie, 2006; van der Merwe, 2002).

[45] Several of the shareholdings appear to have been through community savings groups known as 'stokvels'.

[46] 'Urban legend' or not, it is a meme for how the USALs spelt financial ruin for many of the communities, individuals and small businesses that had invested in them.

It is important, therefore, to assess the factors upon which the survival of this brave licensing experiment hinged.

6.5.1 Asymmetric Termination

A viable USAL business case rests principally on cost structures and revenue streams. Interconnect payments to upstream operators for outgoing calls and termination revenues for incoming calls from other networks are two key streams of expenditure and revenue for any small-scale operator. The balance between the two becomes all the more critical in a high-cost, low-revenue environment, with small volumes of call origination.

These market and cost dynamics have long been recognised, and underpinned earlier World Bank research which recommended "skewed interconnection agreements [as] an effective means of encouraging the start–up and early growth of rural network operators" (Kayani & Dymond, 1997, p. 85). A similar counter-intuitive recommendation called for "regulators to allow [rural] operators, at least for an initial period, to price their services above those in urban areas" and to implement cost-based "geographic de-averaging... [to] reflect more closely the costs of terminating a call in a... more costly rural area" (Dymond & Oestmann, 2003, pp. 60 and 63). The case is reinforced by greater willingness to pay on the part of consumers denied access because of their remote rural location. A subsequent World Bank report elaborated the same set of ideas (Dymond, 2004).

A number of commentators recognised that the imposition of an asymmetric termination rate regime for the USALs was critical to a successful business model. Gillwald early mounted an extended plea for the imposition of "cost based asymmetrical interconnection prices" in order to ensure a "sustainable business case" (2002, pp. 12–13). Regulatory law expert Dominic Cull agreed: "the policy of using an asymmetric interconnection regime as a mechanism for subsidising service provision in under-serviced areas was one of the underpinnings of the 2002 policy relating to Under-Serviced Area Licensees (USALs)" (2008, p. 2). An asymmetric interconnection regime is also implicit in the "revenue sharing procedures" of the initial NTCA submission (NTCA, 2001, p. 14). Certainly, it was the critical *sine qua non* of the business model proposed by the DBSA and the IDRC (AVP, 2002).

ICASA's draft interconnection regulations to cater for the USALs (ICASA, 2002a, 2002d) did not go nearly far enough. They proposed a

30% 'differential' in interconnection charges, but only applicable to long-distance call interconnection with Telkom. Unsurprisingly, the DBSA report viewed the draft regulations with dismay, pointing out that the existing fixed-to-mobile differential in the market exceeded 70% (AVP, 2002, p. 8), stating that the proposal was far too low and would make the "USAL business unviable". They called for a "minimum differential of 55-60%" (AVP, 2002, pp. 19 and 29).

The incumbent operators were hostile to even a limited degree of interconnection asymmetry. According to former DBSA staffer Heloise Emdon,[47] the incumbents resolutely opposed an asymmetric interconnection market, suggesting instead that any USAL revenue shortfall be paid for out of the USF (interview, 28 October 2014).

> It became evident that the mobile operators would not enter into viable commercial asymmetric termination agreements with the USALs, which undermined the [USAL] licences… sabotaging potential business models. (Heloise Emdon, personal communication, 23 June 2017)

The draft regulations, likely as a result of this kind of pressure, never came into force. By mid-2003, the Minister was taking the application of the existing interconnection guidelines to the USALs as a *fait accompli* (DoC, 2003c, p. 5).

But the notion of asymmetric termination continued to bubble along in the background. ICASA Councillor Mamodupi Mohlala was to claim some years later that the "cellphone operators were still studying the proposed [asymmetrical interconnection] model" (Otter, 2007). In a similar vein, as late as 2008 Minister Ivy Matsepe-Casaburri called upon ICASA to "consider favourable interconnection rates in the traffic that originates on the networks operated by such [USAL] operators" (Parliament, 2008, pp. 14, 15).

The failure to impose active asymmetry in respect of interconnection with the USALs dealt a fatal blow to their prospects of success. Gillwald and Esselaar give this as a key reason for describing the USALs as "doomed" (2004, p. 16), while Cull views it as "pivotal", declaring that "There is little doubt in [my] mind that this is one of the principal reasons for the failure of the USAL project" (2008, p. 2).

[47] Emdon had been pivotal in developing and lobbying for the DBSA / IDRC business model for the USALs.

Not only was an asymmetric termination rate regime denied the USALs, but interconnection was actively blocked by new entrant Cell C. The USAASA report summarises the situation:

> The interconnection arrangements do not extend to Cell C. It apparently wants to negotiate its own interconnection agreement with each of the USALs. None of the USALs has signed such an agreement with Cell C because Cell C desires a geographically bound arrangement, which is unacceptable to the USALs. The USALs are thus currently unable to interconnect with Cell C. (Thornton, 2006, p. 18)

It is unclear what Cell C intended by the 'regional' interconnect agreement repeatedly referred to in that report. Its technical feasibility is unclear—but its intent is plain. It was an anti-competitive refusal that undermined the ability of the USALs to compete for customers.[48] Amatole did mount a formal anti-competitive conduct challenge to Cell C's refusal, but this was never ruled on by the Competition Tribunal.

Asymmetric interconnection, with marginal or smaller operators able to charge higher termination fees than those with significant market power, has since become a mainstream regulatory intervention (ERG, 2008). Indeed, in the face of significant opposition from fixed and mobile incumbents (Tubbs, 2014), it is what underpins South Africa's 2014 mobile termination rate regulations (ICASA, 2014b), albeit at a differential far lower than that deemed necessary to ensure the viability of the USALs.

6.5.2 *Shared Platform Company*

The second major business case pillar for the USALs was the creation of a 'Shared Platform Company' to minimise costs, reduce overheads and achieve economies of scale for them by pooling network management and customer service activities under a single, shared entity (AVP, 2002, p. 29).

The idea, however, found limited traction, with no institutional support from either the Agency or the DBSA (from whom the idea emanated). It was left to four of the USALs—Bokamoso Communications, Bokone Telecomms, Kingdom Communications and Thinta Thinta Telecomms (Thornton, 2006, p. 125)—to attempt to institutionalise this

[48] At the time Cell C itself was seeking to get a foothold in the market.

as a 'Shared Services Group'. The Agency's report spells out its functions in some detail:

> The intention behind this SSG is to allow the USALs to increase choice of services and packages via ownership and control of certain network and support components. Shared components will include a billing platform, OSS / BSS[49] functions, certain network operations functions, OTS (On-site Technical Support services) a NOC (Network Operations Centre) and customer call centre – all in support of services on the CDMA network. The SSG will make these services available to [each USAL] for a monthly fee and gives the USAL access to certain scale economies normally only available to larger organisations. (Thornton, 2006, p. 101)

The 'Shared Services Group' (SSG) never got off the ground, unfunded by the Agency, and with its partners collapsing. It would certainly have presented management, co-ordination and accountability challenges, but it was a case of too little too late. Amatole, which eschewed its services, is still a going concern. Two others that did likewise are not. The concept of establishing an SSG does, nevertheless, present an intriguing and potentially viable cost-saving model in a marginal market environment.

6.5.3 *Funding and the Subsidy Scheme*

Financial support for the licensees from the Universal Service Fund was the third key pillar of support for the USALs. The small size of the subsidy—R15 million in three annual tranches—has been criticised as insufficient to ensure viability for the USALs (Gillwald, 2005, p. 11; MyBroadband, 2005). Worse, the insistence by the tax authorities that the subsidy was subject to corporate tax (Thornton, 2006, p. 13), meant that each USAL would effectively receive only a little over R10 million in total.

Part of the problem is that the size of the USF subsidy had no empirical basis. The figures in the draft policy are mere thumb-sucks, presented (USA, 2003a) without analysis or justification, limited by the level of allocations to the fund at the time.[50] R15 million was far below the cost

[49] Respectively, operational and business support systems.

[50] The appropriation to the USF in 2003/2004 was a mere R25 million, insufficient to pay a full first tranche to all 7 USALs.

of constructing a network. Ilizwi Telecomms and Kingdom Communications had budgeted respectively R60 million and R63 million, while Bokone Telecomms was seeking funding to the value of some R70 million (Thornton, 2006, pp. 69, 87 and 112). KaraboTel elsewhere corroborates the figure of R60 million (MyBroadband, 2005). R15 million over three years was clearly never going to be enough to launch a USAL in the absence of a further substantial capital injection.

With many of the USALs unable to finance network construction, the Agency's report recommended that the subsidy be "increased substantially" and that "operating expenditure and capital expenditure be availed and administered separately" (Thornton, 2006, p. 2). This latter recommendation was because many of the USALs had been forced to utilise the USF grant, earmarked for network rollout, simply to keep themselves afloat.

There were also problems with the implementation and monitoring of the funding agreements signed by the Agency with the first seven USALs. Indeed, there is almost no assessment of USAL progress in the annual reports of USAASA,[51] and no further monitoring and evaluation studies were ever commissioned or conducted. Only R61 million of the planned R105 million was disbursed, with only two of USALs receiving their full R15 million, and only another two ever receiving a second tranche. Several USALs reported difficulties and delays in receiving their funds from USAASA. In addition, none of the subsequent USAL licensees ever received any funding from the USF, for reasons that were never given.

Together with the failure of any of the USALs to secure additional external funding, this meant that they were doomed for the most part to slide slowly into financial collapse.

The USF subsidies for the USALs were, in summary, poorly conceptualised, under-funded, ill-executed and badly monitored, another contributing factor in their demise.

6.5.4 *The Spectre of Spectrum*

Most of the USALs had planned to deploy CDMA networks, with two opting for WiMax. This would have been apparent in the bids submitted

[51] Aside from: (USAASA, 2007, pp. 12–14, 2008b, p. 16).

to ICASA during 2003. It is therefore inexplicable why the USAL licences were issued without spectrum having been assigned.

Given the delays in the licensing process, ICASA had ample time to complete the necessary spectrum groundwork. Although the regulator had initiated a consultation in 2002 into the feasibility of CDMA licensees (such as the USALs and the SNO) sharing certain frequency bands with broadcasters in order to deliver wireless access (ICASA, 2004), the process dragged badly. It took the regulator a full 18 months to initiate "full-scale research into these sharing possibilities" (ICASA, 2004, p. 8). And it was only in 2006—nearly two years later and more than a year after the USALs had received their licences—that ICASA gazetted its intention to open Channel 65 (822–830 MHz) for "non-broadcasting services", and a further 10 months before it formally determined to open up Channels 65 and 66 (822–838 MHz) (ICASA, 2006c). The delay—more than four years in total—is both inexplicable and inexcusable, and had a vitiating impact on the ability of the USALs to roll out their own networks and services timeously.

The failure timeously to assign spectrum to the USALs was inimical to their ability to achieve rollout targets and secure commercial viability. It is an impact often overlooked by commentators (Gillwald, 2005; Lewis, 2013), but one which surfaces repeatedly in trade press accounts (Guest, 2006; Mngcungusa, 2005; Senne, 2006a). Indeed, one of the main recommendations of the Agency's report was that "Icasa make spectrum available to USALs, immediately" (Thornton, 2006, p. 2).

By that time, however, it was already too late for most of the USALs, with lack of access to spectrum yet another key contributor to their demise.

6.5.5 *Market Morass*

Between the gestation of the concept of under-serviced area licensing around 2000, and the issuing of the first seven licences from late 2004, there had been dramatic swings in the market.

By the time the USALs were ready to enter the market, fixed-line teledensity, upon which their licensed areas had been predicated, was already in terminal decline. By 2005, Telkom's rollout had shrunk to 4.7 million mainlines, down 14% from its 2000 peak, largely due to the mass disconnection of subscribers unable to pay their bills. By contrast, mobile subscriptions had increased dramatically, surpassing 23 million in 2005.

Fixed-mobile substitution was substantially reshaping the market (Esselaar & Stork, 2005; Hodge, 2005).

Research commissioned by USAASA shows that in rural communities and small villages—the very areas that had been determined as 'under-serviced' on the basis of having residential fixed-line teledensity below 5%—mobile penetration was already very substantial, an order of magnitude greater, with more than half of all adults connected (USAASA, 2008a).[52]

This dramatically altered competitive landscape was what faced the USALs as they attempted to secure market share in an environment where average mobile teledensity had already reached 50%. Worse, entering the market as MVNOs meant that they were signing up customers, albeit under their own branding, to use the very networks that were to be their competition. And with GSM having eclipsed CDMA as the standard for mobile connectivity, they were unable to compete.

The problem was compounded by discriminatory pricing practices from the mobile incumbents. For example, "Bokone discovered that the wholesale rate offered by Vodacom was in fact higher than the retail rate offered to subscribers" (Thornton, 2006, p. 61). Telecomms lawyer Justine Limpitlaw concurs: "the mobile operators (principally Vodacom, but also MTN) were charging the USALs more for calls roaming on their networks than they were charging their own customers" (personal communication, 20 January 2015). The report commissioned by the Agency goes on to set out a detailed litany of dubious contractual and pricing practices inflicted on the USALs (Thornton, 2006, pp. 19, 33, 77, 123 and 124).

The broader market and regulatory environment were also adversely impacted by the unexpected set of Ministerial determinations, which came into effect just as the USALs were being licensed, and cut the ground out from under their market and business case (Gillwald & Esselaar, 2004, p. 16). These included: lifting the prohibition on VoIP; liberalising the payphone market; and permitting all operators to provide their own infrastructure. Removing the competitive advantage of being able to offer VoIP services (prohibited to other licensees before then) was probably the most telling, but many USALs' business plans also called for

[52]The data is drawn from the 2006 South African Audience Research Foundation's All Media Products Survey, which uses a nationally representative sample of personal in-home interviews.

entry into Telkom's payphone market. In the event the proliferation of informal, street-side vendors offering payphone services on their mobile handsets, followed by the proliferation of mobile access, cut the ground out from under that market.

6.5.6 *Institutional Failures*

The USALs were also let down by the policy and regulatory institutions in the environment.

The foot-dragging of ICASA in the licensing process and in assigning desperately needed spectrum is inexcusable, as was the failure to impose a suitable asymmetric interconnection framework. The licences issued by the regulator were also too rigid, with stringent BEE-inspired ownership and control limitations that prevented access to equity investors.

USAASA too failed the USALs. There is little evidence of real practical support or proper business training having been supplied to the USALs. The Shared Services Group, which might have offered essential support services, remained a pipe dream. The very limited financial assistance from the USF left the USALs under-capitalised, unable even to meet operational expenses. The Agency, aside from a single belated evaluation report, made little effort to monitor and evaluate the progress of the USALs, and failed to intervene once problems were manifest.

The various Ministers, who oversaw the policy and its implementation, also need to shoulder a share of the blame. Pushing ahead with licensing a further 17 consortia, when it was already clear that the first 7 were in serious difficulty, smacks of reckless disregard for the evidence. Further, little regard was given to the likely impact of the 2004 Ministerial determinations—or indeed of the subsequent Electronic Communications Act—upon the viability and future of the USALs. Finally, the policy zigzags around the promulgation and subsequent rescinding of the PUSANO model show a disregard for the practical consequences on existing licensees of changing policies mid-stream.

6.5.7 *Co-operatives*

Some commentators feel that the commercial USAL model that was implemented was a betrayal of the original co-operative vision (NTCA,

2001, pp. 2–3). Former IDRC staffer Tina James, co-author of that pivotal submission, describes herself as "very disappointed" with the way the concept of "telecomms co-operatives" was lost in the final legislation:

> The USALs were supposed to be owned by the people in the areas. The model was based on sweat equity and the sharing of resources like engineering skills and financial expertise - but instead you got a whole lot of private sector investors coming in. (interview, 27 November 2014)

Instead the USAL legislation is imbued with the economic empowerment approach so characteristic of South Africa's democratic transition. It refers only to "small businesses" as potential licensees, privileging ownership by "historically disadvantaged groups", including women (RSA, 1996, Section 40A (2)). It plays into the hands of a rent-seeking, managerial enrichment approach to empowerment rather than a broader-based, economic upliftment one (Ponte, Roberts, & van Sittert, 2007; Tangri & Southall, 2008). And the scramble to create USAL consortia and submit bids was reminiscent of the mêlée surrounding the much earlier mobile licence awards. If black economic empowerment was the goal, what eventuated was little short of tragic denouement.

6.5.8 Into the Sunset

A number of other issues bedevilled the USAL experiment. The USAASA report repeatedly refers to lack of management and administrative skills, lack of regulatory compliance, and lapses of corporate governance (Thornton, 2006). This was largely caused by the emphasis on "ownership and control" and "empowerment" as key criteria in awarding the licence at the expense of business planning and technical competencies (Gillwald, 2002, p. 4).

Several commentators have laid the blame for the USAL fiasco at the feet of competing and conflicting policy objectives. The USAASA report refers to an IDRC description of the USAL policy intervention as representing:

> a flawed convergence of two distinct goals - an empowerment model to broaden ownership and control of telecommunications to previously disadvantaged individuals residing locally in historically under-serviced and marginalised Districts; and a regulatory model to introduce competition in

> such Districts as the best way to grow the market. Both of these are laudable goals, and each would work well if part of another model. The flaw lies in trying to achieve them through the same mechanism. (Thornton, 2006, pp. 21–22)

It is a criticism that may over-simplify: it is not unusual for a single intervention to be driven by more than one policy objective. The goals listed by the various commentators above are not *ipso facto* contradictory. They did, however, require careful co-ordination between the various policy and regulatory entities within the sector, and for careful regulatory impact assessment, and integration with other interventions that held definite consequences for the USAL venture (such as the Ministerial determinations).

The USAL adventure, then, was inadequately conceived and poorly executed. The ensuing challenges and bottlenecks together resulted in the collapse of the intervention. Today, only one of the original licensees survives, applying a very different business model from that originally envisaged. Years of effort, the expenditure of taxpayers' money, the loss of substantial sums of entrepreneurial capital, have together made almost no impact on universal access and service for the poor and marginalised rural communities that were the intended beneficiaries of the intervention. The USALs became a mere footnote to UAS in the sector.

References

AVP. (2002). *The financial viability of the under serviced area licenses [sic] in South Africa: Final report.* Midrand and Ottawa: Development Bank of Southern Africa & International Development Research Centre.

Bridges.org. (2001, May 2). *South Africa telecommunications overview, commentary, and statistics (policy brief)*. Cape Town: Bridges.org. Retrieved from http://www.bridges.org/publications/123.

Calzada, J., & Davalos, A. (2005). Cooperatives in Bolivia: Customer ownership of the local loop. *Telecommunications Policy, 29*(5), 387–407.

Chetty, M., Blake, E., & McPhie, E. (2006). VoIP deregulation in South Africa: Implications for underserviced areas. *Telecommunications Policy, 30*(5–6), 332–344.

Coopers & Lybrand. (1992). *Telecommunications sector strategy study for the Department of Posts and Telecommunications.* Pretoria: Department of Posts and Telecommunications.

Cull, D. (2008, June). *Note on the 2008 Department of Communications budget speech*. Cape Town: Ellipsis Regulatory Solutions. Retrieved from http://www.ellipsis.co.za/wp-content/uploads/2008/07/note_doc_budget_speech_2008.pdf.

de Wet, P. (2001a, February 5). Stakeholders veto telecomms duopoly. *ITWeb*. Retrieved from http://www.itweb.co.za/index.php?option=com_content&view=article&id=98653:stakeholders-veto-telecomms-duopoly&catid=260.

de Wet, P. (2001b, August 16). Government's amazing contortion act. *ITWeb*. Retrieved from http://www.itweb.co.za/index.php?option=com_content&view=article&id=93821:governments-amazing-contortion-act&catid=79&Itemid=2354.

DNTA. (1999). *Universal Service Agency Institutional Strengthening Plan*. David N. Townsend & Associates.

DoC. (2001a, March 23). Public invitation to lodge written representations in relation to intended telecommunications policy directions to be issued by the Minister of Communications. *Government Gazette, 429*(22169).

DoC. (2001b, July 23). Policy directions issued by Minister of Communications. *Government Gazette*(22503).

DoC. (2001c, August 21). Policy directions issued by Minister of Communications. *Government Gazette, 434*(22603).

DoC. (2001d, December 18). Determination of under serviced areas. *Government Gazette(22954)*. Pretoria: Department of Communications.

DoC. (2002a, February 21). General notice. *Government Gazette*(23164).

DoC. (2002b, December 19). Invitation to Apply for the provision of telecommunications services in the under serviced areas in terms of section 34 (2) of the Telecommunications Act, 1996 (Act 103 of 1996). *Government Gazette*(24204).

DoC. (2003a, April 16). Minister of Communications: Extention [sic] of closing date for under service [sic] area licenses [sic]. *Government Gazette*(24755).

DoC. (2003b, June 18). Minister of Communications: Extention [sic] of closing date for under service [sic] area licenses [sic]. *Government Gazette*(25113).

DoC. (2003c, August 22). Queries and answers to the Minister for under serviced area license [sic] (USAL's) [sic] Invitation to Apply (ITA). *Government Gazette*(25385).

DoC. (2004a, June 3). *Matsepe-Casaburri: Announcement on under serviced area licences*. Pretoria: Ministry of Communications. Retrieved from http://www.polity.org.za/article/matsepecasaburri-announcement-on-under-serviced-area-licences-03062004-2004-06-03.

DoC. (2004b, September 3). Determinations of dates in terms of the Telecommunications Act (Act No 103 of 1996). *Government Gazette, 471*(26763).

DoC. (2005, January 11). Invitation to apply for the provision of telecommunications services in the under serviced areas in terms of section 34 (2) of the Telecommunications Act, 1996 (Act 103 of 1996). *Government*(27166).

DoC. (2006, February 7). Invitation to apply for the provision of telecommunications services in the under serviced areas in terms of section 34 (2) of the Telecommunications Act, 1996 (Act 103 of 1996). *Government Gazette*(28478).

DoC. (2007, September 17). Policies and policy directions drafted in terms of section 3(1) and (2) of the Electronic Communications Act, 2005 (Act No. 36 of 2005). *Government Gazette, 507*(30308).

DoC. (2009, August 19). Amendment of Policies and Policy Directions issued under the Electronic Communications Act, 2005 (Act No. 36 of 2005) with regard to Provincial Under-Serviced Area Network Operator (PUSANO) Licences. *Government Gazette*(32509).

du Toit, C., & Senne, D. (2007, October 1). ICASA denies USAL shambles. *ITWeb*. Retrieved from http://www.itweb.co.za/index.php?option=com_content&view=article&id=6551&catid=182.

Dymond, A. (2004). *Telecommunications challenges in developing countries: Asymmetric interconnection charges for rural areas*. Washington, DC: World Bank. Retrieved from http://documents.worldbank.org/curated/en/881171468780577005/pdf/284020PAPER0WBWP027.pdf.

Dymond, A., & Oestmann, S. (2003). The role of sector reform in achieving universal access. In ITU (Ed.), *Trends in telecommunications reform*. Geneva: International Telecommunication Union. Retrieved from http://www.inteleconresearch.com/pdf/TTR03_Chapter_3.pdf.

EC. (1994). *Meeting universal service obligations in a competitive telecommunications sector*. Brussels: European Commission. Retrieved from http://bookshop.europa.eu/en/meeting-universal-service-obligations-in-a-competitive-telecommunications-sector-pbCV8394757/.

ERG. (2008). *ERG's Common Position on symmetry of fixed call termination rates and symmetry of mobile call termination rates*. Brussels: European Regulators Group. Retrieved from http://www.irg.eu/streaming/erg_07_83_mtr_ftr_cp_12_03_08.pdf?contentId=543020&field=ATTACHED_FILE.

Esselaar, S., & Stork, C. (2005). Mobile cellular telephone: Fixed-line substitution in sub-Saharan Africa. *The African Journal of Information and Communication, 6*, 64–73.

Flores, W. (1989). The telephone cooperatives in Bolivia. In A. Castilla & M. Cruz (Eds.), *Telecommunications and development in Spain and Ibero-America*. Madrid: Hispanic-American Association of Research Centres and Telecommunication Enterprises.

Gillwald, A. (2002). *Under-serviced area licences in South Africa: Steps to achieving viable operators*. Johannesburg: LINK Centre, University of the Witwatersrand. Retrieved from http://link.wits.ac.za/papers/usal.pdf.

Gillwald, A. (2003). *Stimulating investment in network extension: The case of South Africa*. Johannesburg: LINK Centre. Retrieved from https://idl-bnc-idrc.dspacedirect.org/handle/10625/42382.

Gillwald, A. (2005, Summer). A closing window of opportunity: Under-serviced area licensing in South Africa. *Information Technologies and International Development, 2*(4), 1–19.

Gillwald, A., & Esselaar, S. (2004). *South African 2004 ICT sector performance review*. Johannesburg: LINK Centre.

Glazier, D. (2007, December 6). Provincial USALs to merge soon. *iWeek*. Retrieved from http://www.iweek.co.za/in-the-know/provincial-usals-to-merge-soon.

Guest, K. (2006, October 2). A licence to fail. *Brainstorm*. Retrieved from http://www.brainstormmag.co.za/technology/10308-a-licence-to-fail.

Hodge, J. (2005). Tariff structures and access substitution of mobile cellular for fixed line in South Africa. *Telecommunications Policy, 29*, 493–505. https://doi.org/10.1016/j.telpol.2005.05.001.

ICASA. (2002a, August 20). Notice of intention to prescribe supplementary guidelines for interconnection of underserviced areas in terms of section 40A (6) and section 43 of the Telecommunications Act No. 103 of 1996 as amended ("the act"). *Government Gazette*(23771).

ICASA. (2002b, August 20). Notice of intention to prescribe regulations in terms of section 52 of the Telecommunications Act of 1996 as amended, which limits the ownership and control of licences granted in terms of section 40A. *Government Gazette*.

ICASA. (2002c, August 27). Notice of correction on draft regulations published in terms of section 52 of the Telecommunications Act of 1996 as amended which limit ownership and control in licenses [sic] granted in terms of section 40A published on the 20 of August 2002. *Government Gazette*(23789).

ICASA. (2002d, October 4). Notice of correction on draft supplementary guidelines for interconnection of underserviced areas in terms of section 40A(6) and section 43 of the Telecommunications Act No. 103 of 1996 as amended ("the act"). *Government Gazette*(23914).

ICASA. (2003a, January 27). Draft licence for underserviced area licences to be issued pursuant to section 40A. *Government Gazette*(24320).

ICASA. (2003b, August 8). Draft licence for underserviced area licences to be issued pursuant to section 40A. *Government Gazette*(25343).

ICASA. (2003c, August 22). Limitation of ownership and control of section 40A licenses [sic]. *Government Gazette*(25386).

ICASA. (2003d, September 23). Notice of applications received for under-serviced area licences pursuant to an Invitation to Apply (ITA) issued by the Minister of Communications on the 19th of December 2002 in general notice number 3458 in Government Gazette number 24204. *Government Gazette*(25498).

ICASA. (2004, February 3). Notice in terms of section 27 of the Telecommunications Act (Act 103 of 1996 as amended) read in conjuction [sic] with section 29 of the IBA Act (Act 153 of 1993) regarding amendment of Notice 3.9.2 of the radio frequency band plan for frequencies… *Government Gazette*(25990).

ICASA. (2005a, July 1). Telecommunications Act (103/1996): Notice regarding applications received by the authority for under-serviced area licences. *Government Gazette, 481*(27756).

ICASA. (2005b, September 6). Notice regarding applications received by the authority for the underserviced area licences, in terms of section 34(3)(A) of the Telecommunications Act No. 103 of 1996, as amended ("the Act"). *Government Gazette*(28008).

ICASA. (2006a). *Annual report 2005/6.* Johannesburg: Independent Communications Authority of South Africa.

ICASA. (2006b, February 9). Under-serviced area licence in terms of section 40A of the Telecommunications Act 103 of 1996, as amended, issued to Amatole Telecommunications Services (Proprietary) Limited (registration no. 2004/013673/07). *Government Gazette*(28484).

ICASA. (2006c, October 31). Outcome of the process initiated by notice in the Government Gazette No. 28547 of 22 February 2006. *Government Gazette*(29345).

ICASA. (2008). *Annual report 2007/8.* Johannesburg: Independent Communications Authority of South Africa.

ICASA. (2009). *Annual report 2008/9.* Johannesburg: Independent Communications Authority of South Africa.

ICASA. (2014a, April 11). General notice to licensees who have failed to respond to requests for compliance information. *Government Gazette*(37549).

ICASA. (2014b, September 30). Call Termination Regulations, 2014. *Government Gazette, 591*(38042).

IR. (1999). *Rural telecoms: 13th–16th September 1999, The Lord Charles Hotel, Cape Town, South Africa.* London: Institute for International Research.

ITWeb. (2001, January 10). Colloquium to push telecommunications amendment. *ITWeb.* Retrieved from http://www.itweb.co.za/index.php?option=com_content&view=article&id=99249.

Jovanovic, D. (2004, November 24). SMEs drive telecoms for the poor. *ITWeb.* Retrieved from http://www.itweb.co.za/index.php?option=com_content&view=article&id=18832:smes-drive-telecoms-for-the-poor&catid=69.

Kayani, R., & Dymond, A. (1997). *Options for rural telecommunications development*. Washington, DC: World Bank. Retrieved from http://elibrary.worldbank.org/doi/pdf/10.1596/0-8213-3948-6.

Kontkiewicz-Chachulska, H. (1997). Recent evolution of telecommunications in the region of Central Europe. *Telecommunications and Energy in Systemic Transformation* (pp. 153–196). Basel: Springer.

Lawson, C., & Meyenn, N. (2000, March). Bringing cellular phone service to rural areas. *Public Policy for the Private Sector*(205). Retrieved from http://rru.worldbank.org/Documents/PublicPolicyJournal/256Musta-031103.pdf.

Lewis, C. (2013). Universal access and service interventions in South Africa: Best practice, poor impact. *African Journal of Information and Communication, 13*, 95–107.

Lowman, S. (2005, April 21). USALs piggyback on Vodacom. *ITWeb*. Retrieved from http://www.itweb.co.za/sections/quickprint/print.asp?StoryID=151447.

Mngcungusa, N. (2005, December 13). USAL companies still not independent. *ITWeb*. Retrieved from http://www.itweb.co.za/index.php?option=com_content&view=article&id=127321:usal-companies-still-not-independent&catid=260.

Mogaki, I. (2005, February 23). Telecoms boost for rural KZN. *ITWeb*. Retrieved from http://www.itweb.co.za/sections/quickprint/print.asp?StoryID=149967.

Motloung, M. (2008, March 28). Please try again later. *Financial Mail*. Retrieved from http://secure.financialmail.co.za/08/0328/technology/hfeat.htm.

MyBroadband. (2005, May 12). Off to a cautious start. *MyBroadband*. Retrieved from https://mybroadband.co.za/nephp/296.html.

Ngcaba, A. (2001, February 2). *Speech by the Director General of Communications, Andile Ngcaba, at the Telecommunications Colloquium*. Retrieved from http://www.polity.org.za/polity/govdocs/speeches/2001/sp0204.html.

NTCA. (2001, January 19). *Telecommunications and integrated rural development in South Africa: Telecommunications cooperatives as a mechanism for supporting sustainable economic development*. Arlington, VA: National Telephone Cooperative Association.

NTCA. (n.d). *History of rural telecommunications*. Arlington, VA: National Telecommunications Cooperative Association. Retrieved from http://www.ntca.org/about-ntca/history-of-rural-telecommunications.html.

Otter, A. (2007, May 22). Rural telecoms discussion focuses on connecting poor. *MyBroadband*. Retrieved from https://mybroadband.co.za/news/telecoms/61-rural-telecoms-discussion-focuses-on-connecting-poor.html.

Parliament. (2008). *Proceedings of Extended Public Committee—Old Assembly Chamber, Tuesday, 3 June 2008.* Cape Town: Parliament of the Republic of South Africa. Retrieved from http://www.parliament.gov.za/live/commonrepository/Processed/20130507/145781_1.doc.

PMG. (2007, February 13). *Communications Portfolio Committee: Interaction with underserviced area licensees.* Cape Town: Parliamentary Monitoring Group. Retrieved from https://pmg.org.za/committee-meeting/7706/.

Ponte, S., Roberts, S., & van Sittert, L. (2007). 'Black economic empowerment' (BEE), business and the state in South Africa. *Development and Change, 38*(5), 933. https://doi.org/10.1111/j.1467-7660.2007.00440.x.

Richardson, D., Ramirez, R., & Haq, M. (2000). *Grameen Telecom's village phone programme in rural Bangladesh: A multi-media case study–Final report.* Ottawa: Government of Canada. Retrieved from http://gianlucasalvatori.nova100.ilsole24ore.com/wp-content/uploads/sites/31/files/finalreport.pdf.

RSA. (1996). *Telecommunications Act, 1996. No. 103 of 1996.* Pretoria: Republic of South Africa.

RSA. (2001a). *Telecommunications Amendment Bill.* Pretoria: Republic of South Africa.

RSA. (2001b, November 30). Telecommunications Amendment Act, No. 64 of 2001. *Government Gazette, 437*(22889).

SAVA. (2001). *Representations in respect of the Telecommunications Amendment Bill (B 65-2001).* Johannesburg: South African Value Added Network Services Association. Retrieved from http://pmg-assets.s3-website-eu-west-1.amazonaws.com/docs/2001/appendices/sava.htm.

Senne, D. (2006a, March 13). Hope for USALs on spectrum issue. *ITWeb.* Retrieved from http://www.itweb.co.za/index.php?option=com_content&view=article&id=113444:hope-for-usals-on-spectrum-issue&catid=260.

Senne, D. (2006b, August 15). USALs granted. *ITWeb.* Retrieved from http://www.itweb.co.za/index.php?option=com_content&view=article&id=116786:usals-granted&catid=260.

Senne, D. (2006c, August 31). USALs told to stop complaining. *ITWeb.* Retrieved from http://www.itweb.co.za/index.php?option=com_content&view=article&id=117165:usals-told-to-stop-complaining&catid=260.

Senne, D. (2008, January 22). Bleak future for USALs. *ITWeb.* Retrieved from http://www.itweb.co.za/sections/quickprint/print.asp?StoryID=181132.

Senne, D., & Jones, C. (2007, December 12). Phase two USALs left hanging. *ITWeb.* Retrieved from http://www.itweb.co.za/sections/quickprint/print.asp?StoryID=180603.

Stern, P., Townsend, D., & Monedero, J. (2006). *New models for universal access in Latin America*. Montreal/Boston/Madrid: Regulatel/World Bank/ECLAC. Retrieved from http://www.ictregulationtoolkit.org/Documents/Document/Document/3511.

Tangri, R., & Southall, R. (2008). The politics of black economic empowerment in South Africa. *Journal of Southern African Studies, 34*(3), 699–716.

Telkom. (2005, October 10). Telkom helps USALs to break communication barriers. *ITWeb*. Retrieved from http://www.itweb.co.za/index.php?option=com_content&view=article&id=125887:telkom-helps-usals-to-break-communication-barriers&catid=260.

Thornton, L. (2006). *Recommendations on how the USA and other stakeholders might assist USALs to ensure sustainability*. Johannesburg: Universal Service and Access Agency of South Africa.

Tubbs, B. (2014, February 12). ICASA knuckles down on Vodacom, MTN. *ITWeb*. Retrieved from http://www.itweb.co.za/index.php?option=com_content&view=article&id=70801:ICASA-knuckles-down-on-Vodacom-MTN&catid=260.

USA. (2003a, May 27). Notice of draft policy in respect of subsidisation of the under-serviced area licensees [sic] by the Universal Service Fund in terms of section 66 (f) of the Telecommunications Act (No. 103 of 1996), as amended. *Government Gazette*(24917).

USA. (2003b). *Report on the cooperatives workshop held on the 18th July 2003 at the Volkswagen marketing conference centre*. Johannesburg: Universal Service Agency.

USA. (2004). *Universal Service Agency: Annual report 2003–2004*. Johannesburg: Universal Service Agency.

USA. (2005). *Universal Service Agency impact document*. Johannesburg: Universal Service Agency.

USA. (2006). *Universal Service Agency: 2005–2006 annual report*. Johannesburg: Universal Service Agency.

USAASA. (2007). *Universal Service and Access Agency of South Africa: Annual report 2006/2007*. Johannesburg: Universal Access and Service Agency of South Africa.

USAASA. (2008a, March 18). *USAASA: Budget, strategy plan and priorities for 2008/09*. Johannesburg: Universal Service and Access Agency of South Africa.

USAASA. (2008b). *Annual report 2007/8: Creating connections*. Johannesburg: Universal Service and Access Agency of South Africa.

van der Merwe, C. (2002, September 2). Big bucks for minor licences. *Brainstorm*. Retrieved from http://www.brainstormmag.co.za/index.php?option=com_content&view=article&id=1724.

Vecchiatto, P. (2006a, March 8). USALs in deep trouble. *ITWeb*. Retrieved from http://www.itweb.co.za/index.php?option=com_content&view=article&id=113363:usals-in-deep-trouble&catid=260.

Vecchiatto, P. (2006b, March 14). Naiveté compounds USALs' problems. *ITWeb*. Retrieved from http://www.itweb.co.za/index.php?option=com_content&view=article&id=113486:naivet-compounds-usals-problems&catid=260.

Vecchiatto, P. (2009, June 25). Nyanda waves regulatory big stick. *ITWeb*. Retrieved from http://www.itweb.co.za/index.php?option=com_content&view=article&id=23936:nyanda-waves-regulatory-big-stick&catid=260&Itemid=59.

Vodacom. (2005, April 20). *Vodacom and USAL's [sic] bring cellular to rural areas*. Johannesburg: Vodacom. Retrieved from http://news.itweb.co.za/office/vodacom/0504201234.htm.

Weidemann, R. (2003a, April 16). Extension for rural telecoms. *ITWeb*. Retrieved from http://www.itweb.co.za/index.php?option=com_content&view=article&id=81013:extension-for-rural-telecoms&catid=260.

Weidemann, R. (2003b, July 10). Bidders disillusioned by rural licence delays. *ITWeb*. Retrieved from http://www.itweb.co.za/index.php?option=com_content&view=article&id=79148:bidders-disillusioned-by-rural-licence-delays&catid=260.

Weidemann, R. (2003c, October 20). Public gets chance to comment on USALs. *ITWeb*. Retrieved from http://www.itweb.co.za/index.php?option=com_content&view=article&id=76796:public-gets-chance-to-comment-on-usals&catid=260.

Weidemann, R. (2004, March 2). ICASA set to deliberate USAL bids. *ITWeb*. Retrieved from http://www.itweb.co.za/index.php?option=com_content&view=article&id=73955:icasa-set-to-deliberate-usal-bids&catid=260.

Weidemann, R. (2005a, January 27). Agency hands R5m to USALs. *ITWeb*. Retrieved from http://www.itweb.co.za/index.php?option=com_content&view=article&id=120449:agency-hands-r5m-to-usals&catid=260.

Weidemann, R. (2005b, April 8). B-Tel inks deal with Vodacom. *ITWeb*. Retrieved from http://www.itweb.co.za/index.php?option=com_content&view=article&id=121992:b-tel-inks-deal-with-vodacom&catid=260.

Wellenius, B. (1997, February). *Extending telecommunications service to rural areas—The Chilean experience*. Retrieved from http://siteresources.worldbank.org/EXTFINANCIALSECTOR/Resources/282884-1303327122200/105welle.pdf.

Wellenius, B. (2002a). *Closing the gap in access to rural communications: Chile 1995–2002*. Washington, DC: World Bank. Retrieved from http://www-wds.worldbank.org/external/default/WDSContentServer/WDSP/IB/2002/03/22/000094946_0203070403326/Rendered/PDF/multi0page.pdf.

Wellenius, B. (2002b). Closing the gap in access to rural Communication: Chile 1995–2002. *info*, *4*(3).

Wolmarans, R. (2004, February 5). It is just a bad law. *Mail & Guardian*. Retrieved from https://mg.co.za/article/2004-02-05-it-is-just-a-bad-law.

CHAPTER 7

Universal Service (and Access) Agency (of SA)

Establishing a specific, dedicated body like the Universal Service Agency, not merely to oversee and manage the Universal Service Fund, but also to engage in activities of a quasi-policy and quasi-regulatory nature, was unique for the time.

One commentator described the Agency as "a unique institution.... an institutional experiment, keenly watched by some institutional observers in South Africa and around the world" (DNTA, 1999, p. 3). These functions in other jurisdictions are overwhelmingly (65%) housed either within the regulator or directly under the control of the regulator (ITU, 2013). A few others, including Canada, Jamaica, Pakistan and the US, house their USFs under independent administrative and financial structures. But only Mauritania's Agence de promotion de l'Accès universel aux services (APAUS) and the Ghana Investment Fund for Electronic Communication (GIFEC), both established after the USA, have a similar structure (ITU, 2013), although neither is involved in policy or regulation to the same extent as the Agency.

The Agency has been responsible for the USF, was involved in providing funding support to the USALs, and had a role to play in relation to the USOs. This gives it a unique involvement in South Africa's UAS interventions. That set of cross-cutting responsibilities and accountabilities, and their consequent challenges of co-jurisdiction and co-ordination, may also to a degree be responsible for some of the areas of failure within the set of interventions under examination.

C. Lewis, *Regulating Telecommunications in South Africa*,
Information Technology and Global Governance,
https://doi.org/10.1007/978-3-030-43527-1_7

7.1 Establishing the Agency

The establishment of the Universal Service Agency was officially announced shortly after the promulgation of the Telecommunications Act, in February 1997, with Mlungisi Hlongwane appointed as its first head (Malunga, 1997). The Agency was initially staffed mainly by cadres drawn from the COSATU-affiliated trade union in the sector, POTWA, or from the ANC-aligned umbrella body for the civics, SANCO. Hlongwane himself was a former POTWA President, as was Lefty Monyokolo, the USA's head of projects and partnerships, who had also been on the Eminent Persons Group during the drafting of the 1996 White Paper. Heading regulatory affairs was Tshepo Rantho, former President of the National Community Media Forum (NCMF) and former member of the ComTask team. Fikile Khumalo, former Secretary-General of the National Telecommunications Forum (NTF), headed up research.

Several commentators have suggested that the appointment of so many former trade unionists was a deliberate strategy. Former USA staffer Peter Benjamin suggests it was an easy opportunity for Director General Ngcaba to give a role for labour in the new sector arrangements (interview, 13 August 2014). Former IBA Councillor Felleng Sekha has a rather more cynical view, describing the appointments as a "masterstroke" designed to head off union opposition to the privatisation of Telkom (interview, 5 December 2014). The fact that COSATU and its affiliates had been firm advocates of UAS may also have been a consideration. The consequence, however, was the appointment of a leadership that were beholden to Ngcaba.

The appointment of the head of the Agency was at the sole discretion of the Minister (RSA, 1996, Section 60(1)), reinforcing that chain of command. It was only with the adoption of the 2005 Electronic Communications Act, that a Board was introduced to provide good governance and promote fiduciary responsibility (RSA, 2005, Section 81), but that too was appointed—controversially so—at the pleasure of the Minister.

A further consequence was the staffing of the Agency with people who, whatever their track record in the mass democratic movement and their passion for UAS, had little of the technocratic background and managerial skills necessary to administer a fund and engage in policy research and lobbying. Former IDRC programme manager Tina James describes the appointments as "problematic", pointing out that the USA staff "didn't have the right background; they didn't have the right skills; they didn't understand tender processes" (interview, 27 November 2014).

In addition, as former unionists, many of the new staff carried with them the baggage of South Africa's fractious industrial relations history: a highly adversarial mindset towards business and an often confrontational approach. As Benjamin notes, this cost the Agency "much goodwill" in its dealings with the private sector (2001, p. 101).[1]

7.2 Mandate of the Agency

It is worth reflecting on the mandate that the 1996 Telecommunications Act had bestowed upon Hlongwane and his team in order to address the legacy of the *apartheid* digital divide and to ensure the provision of UAS.

Equally bedevilling to the work of the Agency was the level of vagueness with which the functions of the Agency were spelt out. They included:

a. ... promote the goal of universal service;
b. encourage, facilitate and offer guidance in respect of any scheme to provide... [UAS]...;
c. foster the adoption and use of new methods of attaining [UAS];
d. stimulate public awareness of the benefits of telecommunication services (RSA, 1996, Section 59(1)).

Further, the Agency was tasked with assisting the Minister to determine what constituted 'universal access' and 'universal service' (RSA, 1996, Section 59(2)). In addition, it had an extensive policy and advocacy function, including to undertake research, conduct investigations, issue information and table recommendations relating to UAS (RSA, 1996, Section 59(3)). Most importantly, the USA was put in charge of managing and administering the USF (RSA, 1996, Section 59(4)). These functions were to remain largely unchanged and were carried through into the 2005 ECA.

It was a daunting slew of objectives, ranging from advocacy and research, through policy support to the disbursement and management of

[1]The point is echoed by former IDRC staffer Tina James (interview, 27 November 2014).

funding. The emphasis on rolling out telecentres, however, looms large in public statements and press reports at the time (Allchurch, 1998; Koopman, 1998)—this despite the fact that it was nowhere specified as an area of activity under the USF. Minister Jay Naidoo's perspective was even more simplistic, and equally *ultra vires*, when he described the USA as an entity "whose objective is to set up 'telecentres' in rural areas which will ensure access to telephones and the Internet, funded through a universal service fund" (Naidoo, 1997).

The Agency's first mission statement reads:

> The vision of the USA is to be the world leader in promoting universal access and universal service to telecommunications and information services as an empowerment vehicle for disadvantaged communities...
>
> The USA will promote affordable Universal Access and Universal Service in Information and Communication Technologies for disadvantaged communities in South Africa, in order to facilitate development, empowerment and economic growth. (DNTA, 1999, p. 4)[2]

Benjamin quotes the first business plan of the newly formed Agency, adopted in 1997, as setting out the following objectives for its first full year in operation, in terms that are worryingly vague and apparently without targets, deliverables or timeframes:

- Establish the USA as an efficient and effective organisation;
- Raise awareness of the issue of Universal Service;
- Run and learn from pilot telecentre projects through the Universal Service Fund;

[2] Both statements have undergone a number of revisions over the years. They are now as follows:

Vision: Universal Access and Service to ICT for All.
Mission: To facilitate the rollout of adequate Information and Communication Technology (ICT) infrastructure to enable universal access to under-serviced areas in South Africa.

- To facilitate ICT service to under-serviced areas and thereby contributing [sic] to the reduction of poverty and unemployment in South Africa.
- To promote and pursue the goal of Universal Access and Services [sic] and contribute to the sharing and preservation of information in order to build South Africa's sustainable knowledge society.

- Co-ordinate stakeholders in this field to work together for Universal Service;
- Research and make recommendations on how regulation and other public policy instruments can be used to promote universal service;
- Establish procedures for collection of statistics on Universal Access and Universal Service (2001, pp. 100–101).

7.3 'Organisational Strengthening'

Recognising the challenges of establishing a new institution, with an untested mandate, headed by staff with limited managerial skill and little experience in administering, disbursing and accounting for project funding, or in undertaking or commissioning research, it was early decided to provide capacity-building support to the fledgling Agency. Once again it fell to Canada's IDRC, supported by the UNDP, to commission and fund the necessary organisational development intervention (DNTA, 1999). A team of consultants spent six months working with the USA to provide what was termed "institutional strengthening" (DNTA, 1999, p. 3).

The most surprising aspect of this intervention was its headline recommendation that the USA break sharply away from the "traditional focus" of UAS on "voice telephone service alone", and move to a "predominant emphasis on access to the Internet", in line with the telecentre implementation plan the consultants were drafting in parallel (DNTA, 1999, pp. 4, 5). This lies well outside the 'institutional strengthening' scope of the consultancy. It also borders on altering the legislated mandate of the Agency. While the Act, although it was drafted before the explosion of the Internet, does cover a fairly broadly defined set of 'telecommunications services' (within which the Internet might fall), it seems clear that the primary focus of the Agency was intended to be the telephony access gap.

At the time, South Africa had some 8.4 million telephony subscribers, 60% of them fixed-line subscribers, in a population of 43 million (i.e. 20% total teledensity). The country was still therefore far off universal access or service in respect of voice telephony. And, while it is true that UAS interventions need to pay attention to the full continuum of services (Msimang, 2003, p. 35), such a specifically targeted shift in focus towards the Internet surely requires substantive and in-depth research into access patterns and market dynamics. Possibly the consultants were under pressure to legitimate the Agency's telecentre implementation plan they were developing in parallel.

The report's organisational development recommendations are more mainstream and contain several useful assessments and interesting proposals, although these should be seen against the consultants' baseline assumption that telecentres were to be the core of the work of the USA.

Foremost amongst the report's findings is that the Agency had, under pressure from both the Minister and public expectation, "deviated" from its core policy mandate to become a "project management organisation", too directly "involved in the process of telecentre implementation" (DNTA, 1999, p. 8). As a consequence, its staff had become overwhelmed by "day-to-day logistics and crisis management", for which they lacked the necessary skills and training (DNTA, 1999, p. 8).

Elsewhere the report is forthright in cautioning against hands-on project implementation:

> it is not the job of the USA to implement telecentres nor to do any other type of specific project implementation, unless it is on a pilot project basis. Long terms [sic] project implementation by the USA is contrary to the spirit of the Telecommunications Act and inconsistent with the use of the USF resources. (DNTA, 1999, p. 22)

The consultants go on the recommend that "expertise for tasks such as project implementation and specialised evaluation and monitoring should be outsourced" (DNTA, 1999, pp. 15–16).[3]

The report's analysis is concerned over the organisation's union-derived organisational culture, which coloured its internal functioning and affected its ability to interface effectively with the private sector. It notes, rather diplomatically, that the "USA's institutional orientation and staff experience is not equipped to fully understand the dynamics of private sector participation in the provision of public services" (DNTA, 1999, p. 8).

The report elsewhere suggests the Agency's work is too closely aligned to the "skills and main interests" of its staff of former unionists, and calls for the USA to "return to a strong policy emphasis" (DNTA, 1999, pp. 8

[3] Worryingly, the report sees nothing amiss in assigning both implementation and evaluation to the same external entity.

and 10–11). As a result, topping the list of recommendations is the need to "restructure the USA, creating an agency focused on what it does best: policy making and policy implementation" (DNTA, 1999, p. 19).

The report does seem to be aware of the structural complexities created by having a "triad" of entities dealing with UAS, calling for "close co-operation with SATRA, in order to create a new strategic foundation and focus between the agencies" (DNTA, 1999, pp. 11 and 14). Its final recommendations further call for an "external advisory group that includes one delegate from the DoC and one from SATRA" to be established (DNTA, 1999, p. 19). This was in addition to establishing an internal "advisory committee", which would include "other experts upon need and invitation" (DNTA, 1999, p. 19).

The report also proposes a "flat [organisational] structure" with four programmes intended to:

- provide "training... for telecentres" and SMMEs, "focusing on business management and operations skills";
- "promote... telecentre value-added services";
- undertake "research and develop ICT cooperatives"; and
- focus on "universal service policy and research" (DNTA, 1999, p. 19).

Unfortunately, it is a structure inadequately grounded in the functions of the Agency as set out in its empowering legislation, hence the degree to which the telecentres project is over-represented in the recommended organogram. There is, for example, no mention of subsidies from the USF for 'needy persons'[4] or for the 'extension' of Telkom's PSTS, both of which had funding allocations by Ministerial Policy Direction. There is also no mention of the kind of careful access gap analysis that is now a mainstay of international good practice in order to determine USF priorities and expenditures (Blackman & Srivastava, 2011; ITU, 2011).

The flattened structure was never implemented. By 2016, the initial staff of 14 had swelled to 62, of whom 19 were spread across four different grades of either "top" or "senior" management (USAASA, 2016, p. 62).

[4]Which term the consultants do not like and suggest be changed (DNTA, 1999, p. 22), despite the Act.

7.4 Organisational Function and Dysfunction

With almost all primary documentation from the period having disappeared,[5] the extent to which the consultants' recommendations were implemented remains unclear. None of the subsequent assessments of the Agency (Stavrou, Whitehead, Wilson, Seloane, & Benjamin, 2001; USA, 2005; USAASA, 2014b) was to focus on evaluating the organisational functioning, performance and effectiveness of the USA.[6]

Organisational structure and function can, however, be interpolated to a degree from the Agency's surviving annual reports, which reflect an organisational structure that seems to have been reconfigured on an annual basis. In 2002, following the "restructuring of the organization to enable it to carry out its new responsibilities as outlined in the Ministerial Policy Directions and Telecommunications Act as amended", the Agency comprised three divisions: 'Finance & Administration', 'Implementation & Delivery', and 'Research, Marketing & Public Education' (USA, 2002, pp. 1 and 16). By the following year, the first two had been renamed 'Finance and Human Resources' and 'Programmes', respectively (USA, 2003, p. Slide 8). A year later these had become 'Corporate Services', 'Projects Services' and 'Information & Knowledge Management' (USA, 2004), which, in turn, were rearranged a mere two years later into 'Regulatory & Corporate Affairs', 'Human Resources', 'Projects Services' and 'Financial Management & Information Technology' (USA, 2006d). It is hard to see how the organisation could function effectively and deliver on its core programmes[7] and overall mandate if the deck chairs were in a constant state of rearrangement.

It is also hard to see how an organisation can function effectively and to deliver on its mandate if the top management too is continually changing (see Table 7.1). From its inception, throughout its lifetime, the leadership of the Agency responsible for UAS has been in continual crisis, having gone through no fewer than seventeen CEOs and acting CEOs in its 20-year life span, seven of whom were in an acting capacity. The longest

[5] The USA's own later case study was also forced to "focus on secondary and tertiary sources" (USA, 2005, p. 1).

[6] The recent National Strategy does make a recommendation on the structure of the Agency going forward (USAASA, 2014b, pp. 5–1ff.).

[7] Themselves in a state of constant flux.

Table 7.1 Heads of USA/USAASA

From	*To*	*Name*	*Tenure (months)*
December 1996	August 1998	Mlungisi Hlongwane	20
August 1998	May 2000	Fikile Khumalo (acting)	21
May 2000	2002	Maite Letsoalo	?
2002	2003	Dipuo Mvelase	?
April 2003	May 2006	Dr Sam Gulube	37
June 2006	November 2006	Ms Motlatso Ramadiba (acting)	5
December 2006	February 2007	Dr Raymond Ngcobo	2
February 2007	May 2007	Cassandra Gabriel (acting, Board Chairperson)	3
June 2007	November 2008	James Theledi	17
November 2008	March 2009	Phineas Moleele (acting)	4
March 2009	July 2010	Winile Lamani (acting)	16
July 2010	October 2011/March 2012	Phineas Moleele	15
October 2011	1 October 2012	Themba Phiri and Sam Vilakazi (DoC caretakers)	12
1 October 2012	31 March 2013	Ms Pumla Radebe (acting, Board Chairperson)	6
1 April 2013	31 March 2016	Zam Nkosi	35
1 April 2016	23 May 2016	Makhotso Moiloa (acting)	2
24 May 2016		Lumko Mtimde	

Source USA/USAASA annual reports

tenure to date (Dr Sam Gulube) lasted a little over three years. Considerably shorter was the tenure of Dr Raymond Ngcobo, who lasted a mere two months before resigning (USAASA, 2007, p. 43).

Such turnover in leadership speaks to a troubled organisation, both as cause and consequence. It likely underpins the almost constant state of structural reorganisation and undermines the ability to create and follow through on sustainable actions and initiatives.

Many of the appointments were based on the 'struggle credentials' of the appointees. Beyond Mlungisi Hlongwane (then President of SANCO, and a former President of POTWA) and Fikile Khumalo (former head of the National Telecommunications Forum, site of much of the negotiation for a new sectoral dispensation), other heads included: former MK and Operation Vula veteran and then SACP Deputy Chair Dipuo Mvelase; MK veteran and former SANDF officer, Dr Sam Gulube; and former ANC Department of Information and Publicity media officer, Cassandra Gabriel.

What is also striking is the number of internal appointees serving in an acting capacity. In several instances, the Chair of the Board acted as CEO, and over one period of particular crisis the role was filled by two senior officials from the Department.

The circumstances under which the appointments were made are not always clear, since the Head of the Agency was initially appointed directly by the Minister (RSA, 1996, Section 60(1)). Under the 2005 ECA, this responsibility was transferred to the Board, which in turn was appointed by the Minister (RSA, 2005, Sections 81 and 83). In both cases, the process is thus effectively removed from stakeholder input and from public scrutiny. With little by way of press coverage in the early years, little is known of the circumstances surrounding the arrival and departure of the early CEOs. It does, however, seem clear that Mlungisi Hlongwane resigned because of mounting tensions with the Minister (Aki Stavrou, interview, 17 October 2014).

The resignation of the Agency's longest-serving head, Dr Sam Gulube, coincided with the release of the damning indictment of the USALs project, but was claimed to be unrelated, with "personal reasons" being cited (Gedye, 2006). Gulube himself claimed to be returning to his "first passion, clinical health services" (Gedye, 2006).

Other departures were far more explicitly linked to scandal. In 2008, a new regime, under former Deputy Director General at the Department of Public Enterprises James Theledi, ran rapidly off the rails despite an initially positive reception (Muller, 2008). In September of that year, Chief Financial Officer, Keith Keys, was suspended and subsequently resigned, having been found guilty of financial mismanagement (IOL, 2008). Shortly thereafter, Theledi himself was suspended, following a sexual harassment scandal involving another USAASA senior executive (Czernowalow, 2008) and finally axed in March 2009 (Mawson, 2009).

His eventual successor, Phineas Moleele, was soon implicated in serious "financial mismanagement" and was amongst a group of six senior managers placed on "precautionary suspension" in October 2011 while a "forensic investigation" was undertaken (Rasool, 2011c). Aside from the CEO, the group comprised CFO Andrew Hlubi, Head of Business Development Services Molefi Mollo, Supply Chain Manager Archie Mbatha, Head of Performance Thandeka Mngadi and IT Manager Thato Matsepe (GFIA, 2012; Rasool, 2012c), and included the four most senior executives of the organisation. An attempt by three of the group to challenge their suspension was thrown out of the Labour Court (Rasool, 2012a). Matsepe and Mollo subsequently resigned (Rasool, 2012a, 2012c), and Moleele was able to negotiate an exit settlement, which allegedly included a substantial cash pay-out (Rasool, 2012d) "once disciplinary proceedings against him [had] commenced" (Rasool, 2012b). The fate of the other three is not known.

The second-longest serving CEO, Zam Nkosi, also presided over his share of controversy and allegations of corruption. This time the furore concerned his own qualifications and selection for the position, as well as allegations of corruption. Nkosi's appointment was called into question in an open letter from opposition MP Bantu Holomisa to President Zuma, alleging several irregularities in the process (Holomisa, 2013). *Inter alia*, Holomisa alleged that Nkosi did not possess the required qualifications, that Board Chair Pumla Radebe was improperly involved in his appointment process, and drew attention to allegations of tender fraud at waste management utility, Pikitup, that had accompanied Nkosi's abrupt departure thence (2013, p. 2). Holomisa's letter went on to make a series of possibly more serious allegations of corruption at the Agency (some of which were covered in the earlier discussion on telecentres, others of which will be examined below), and led to the establishment of a formal investigation under the Special Investigation Unit (SIU) (RSA, 2014).

In addition, the irregular circumstances of Nkosi's appointment appeared to have included improper interference by the then Minister for Communications, Dina Pula, in the appointment process. As a result of its investigation, as well as based on a "forensic investigation done by auditors SizweNtsalubaGobodo", the SIU filed papers in the North Gauteng High Court asking for the appointment to be declared unlawful and to be set aside (Bailey, 2014b). The SIU held that the Minister had unlawfully interfered in the process, which was the responsibility of the Board alone, by rejecting their shortlist, and by advising "the chair to recommend to the board to restart the process of finding a CEO again and to do so by following a headhunting process" (2014b). The SIU investigation also encompassed charges of mismanagement against Nkosi, including "making irregular and or unlawful appointments and promotions of certain officials" (Bailey, 2014b). It is not clear what happened to the court application of the SIU. Its investigation into the more serious allegations of corruption relating to Cell C and broadband tenders—both of which are discussed below—remains ongoing and incomplete (SIU, 2017).

In February 2016, in answer to a Parliamentary question, the new Minister stated that the case (No 43250/14) was "defended and ongoing" (Parliament, 2016). However, at the end of the following month, Nkosi's contract was quietly allowed to lapse (Mzekandaba, 2016), his erstwhile mentor having herself resigned two months earlier (Moyo, 2015), and the case was eventually withdrawn (PMG, 2016).

In the light of the events outlined above, it is clear that the leadership of the Agency has been unstable and lacking much semblance of continuity. Sadly, the two major episodes of collusion and corruption at the very top of the organisation were never prosecuted in court. Those involved were simply allowed to slip away and take up new positions, and the reports implicating them have yet to see the public light of day.

7.5 Fingers in the USF Pie

Oversight and financial management of the USF was one of the core responsibilities of the Agency. While the available annual reports of the Agency provide separate financial statements for the Fund, the formal audit reports on these have been relatively unremarkable. The audit opinion from the state Auditor-General's office[8] has largely been formally 'unqualified' over the years, albeit with 'emphasis of matter' statements[9] in many instances. The three main substantive episodes of corruption involving the USF, however, found more space in the public gallery than in the dry pages of annual reports. It is, therefore, important to examine each of these scandals in some detail.

[8] Statutory body with audit oversight of a wide range of state entities.

[9] Used to draw attention to areas of significant uncertainty that need to be taken into account when reading the financial statements.

7.5.1 Forensics and Fiddles

The first of the major corruption scandals to have hit the Agency focused on the rollout of telecentres and featured corruption in the appointment and payment of telecentre suppliers. Without repeating the discussion from Chapter 5, it is important to examine here the institutional circumstances under which this episode occurred.

The scandal first broke in the press in late 2011, but had clearly been brewing for some time (Ncana & Mokone, 2011). A majority of the USAASA Board began to take action on the basis of the various delivery failures that had been uncovered in mid-2011 during site visits by then Board member Shaun Pather, and which pointed to corruption and non-delivery. The rest of the Board clearly believed that more than just a few senior managers were involved, holding, as a result, a number of meetings without informing their Chair Louis Moahlodi. The latter was to describe these meetings as "secret" and "unprocedural" (Ncana & Mokone, 2011). An internal audit report, conducted on their instruction, uncovered widespread misappropriation of funds amounting to at least R29 million (USD4 million). Issues uncovered by the report included:

- Tender fraud, including "irregularities in appointing service providers" without the required "competitive bidding" processes;
- Financial fraud, with some service providers "paid for doing nothing", as well as "payments worth millions going to companies that had not completed projects";
- "Duplication of services";
- Problems with contracts, including some that "could not be found" and others that "did not specify the start and end dates" (Malefane & Ncana, 2011).[10]

It is a damning list of practices, pointing to organised corruption. The size of the cabal of staffers involved—six were eventually suspended—suggests systematic and active collusion, whether by commission or omission. Former Board member Shaun Pather describes it as an "entwined web" of patronage and corruption (interview, 27 March 2015).

[10]Again, this 'internal audit report' was never made public, although a copy was leaked to the *Sunday Times*.

Noteworthy is that the group seems to have enjoyed protection from Board Chair Louis Moahlodi, who is described as having a "close relationship with the suspended officials" (Malefane & Ncana, 2011). Indeed, all (excluding the CEO) had been appointed under Moahlodi's tenure within the short space of a few months: CFO Andrew Hlubi—3 June 2010; Head of Performance Thandeka Mngadi—16 July 2010; Head of Business Development Services Molefi Mollo—1 September 2010; Supply Chain Manager Archie Mbatha and ICT Manager Thato Matsepe—13 December 2010 (USAASA, 2011, Slides 25 and 26).

On the basis of damning evidence from the internal investigation, the Board took a decision to suspend three of the staff closely implicated—CFO Andrew Hlubi, Business Development Manager Molefi Mollo and Supply Chain Manager Archie Mbatha—and approached the Minister to order an urgent forensic audit. At the same time, the Board also informed the Minister of the "impasse between its four members and the chairman", stating that they anticipated "resistance and difficulty" from him in the investigation (Malefane & Ncana, 2011).

To its credit, the Department promptly ordered a "forensic investigation" (Rasool, 2011b). Unfortunately, the resultant forensic audit report, by Durban-based firm 'Forensic Investigation Risk & Recovery Management', which underpinned the suspension, charging and dismissal of a number of senior Agency staff being charged, was never made public. The author does, however, have a copy of the subsequent 'Summary Status Report' (GFIA, 2012).

A corresponding audit of external suppliers, titled the 'USAASA Value for Money Audit' (GFIA, 2012), was undertaken by Gobodo Forensic and Investigative Accounting, and duly completed in May 2013 (PMG, 2016). Its terms of reference were:

a. Investigate and express an opinion on the value for money derived from the listed tenders and/or contracts awarded to service providers
b. Investigate and conduct background inquiries of firms or individuals
c. Investigate and can conduct [sic] the verification of equipment supplied to access centres around the country and determine the value of money thereof
d. Gather documentary evidence
e. Review project related documentation, including contract documents of the list of service provider which render the services and/or

goods to USAASA with a view of expressing an opinion on the value for money

f. Conduct interviews of involved parties, including the service providers and project managers is [sic] required (PMG, 2016).

Key amongst the Gobodo recommendations were that criminal charges be laid against two companies, whose transgressions were covered in considerable detail, viz:

- MI Holdings, for price gouging "assisted by misrepresentation from USAASA officials" on the supply of IT equipment to telecentres to the value of R12 million [USD1.7 million];
- Dan Young, for invoice fraud related to the relocation and refurbishment of the USAASA Head Office, amounting to R773,000 [USD100,000] (GFIA, 2012).

Although, as an audit, the report does not go into specific detail, it raised questions in respect of another four projects, highlighting value for money problems relating to payments and the delivery of services, viz:

- Annix Telecommunications, for the rapid deployment project, worth R19.2 million (USD2.7 million);
- Umzitel, for the Msinga connectivity project, worth of R13.5 million (USD2 million);
- Rockwett Systems, for broadcasting digital migration, worth R12.9 million (USD2 million);
- Mzumbe Ekhaya, for the ICT Hubs project, worth R5.5 million (USD800,000) (GFIA, 2012).

The audit was unable to make findings on a further 5 projects due to "lack of information", clearing 9 others, mostly far smaller in scope (GFIA, 2012).

Details, however, surfaced in the press, showing that substantial sums of money had been paid for services that were never delivered. The key contract, with Annix Telecommunications, specified 44 telecentres in the first year, with a payment R19 million (USD2.7 million) tied to the delivery of 20 such "access centres" in the first quarter. However, "only one centre was completed before the end of the first quarter.... the Ulwazi[11] centre in the Western Cape" (Rasool, 2011a). In return for this spectacular shortfall in delivery, the "service provider" was paid R15,000,000 (USD2 million) (Rasool, 2011a). Further, even after being exposed, the "service provider was reappointed, and again, funds were already being disbursed" (Rasool, 2011c).

In another case, the "signature of a board member, Vusi Ngcobo, was forged to approve a tender of R12-million" (USD1.7 million) (Mokone & Malefane, 2011).

Finally, the tender for the 'Rapid Deployment' project at uMsinga[12] had been awarded to Umzitel, one of the failed round three USALs[13]—surprisingly, given that national providers Vodacom and Telkom had been amongst the unsuccessful bidders (Shaun Pather, interview, 1 April 2015). Pather queried the award, and the Board asked for an independent engineering firm to assess the technical solution. USAASA staff, however, ignored the Board decision and went ahead and signed the contract—to the value of some R30 million (USD4 million).

In the face of the evidence, those implicated sought to prevaricate. CEO Moleele claimed that "USAASA preferred to take remedial rather than punitive action" (Rasool, 2011a), while suspended managers Mollo and Hlubi claimed that Board Chair Moahlodi was "on their side and was against their suspension" and demanded they be given an "opportunity to respond" (Mokone & Malefane, 2011).

The key USAASA annual report, which should have covered the events outlined above, is unfortunately only available as a presentation to the Portfolio Committee. This document merely contains a tantalising and elliptical summary: to the effect that "internal systems were tested and found to be ineffective, including deficiencies in the supply chain management process, information technology and human resources, risk

[11] Opened with much pre-election fanfare by Deputy Minister Obed Bapela in May 2011 (Bapela, 2011).

[12] Msinga Local Municipality is in rural KwaZulu-Natal, some 60 km to the east of the infamous Nkandla homestead of President Jacob Zuma.

[13] According to the Department, "UMZITEL, a former USAL, was appointed by USAASA, to implement the broadband network in uMsinga" (DoC, 2011). Then known as Umzinyathi Telecomms, they had been a successful USAL applicant for Umzinyathi District Municipality.

and prevention plan and compliance with approved delegation of authority", going on to state that unspecified "corrective action is being taken" (USAASA, 2011, p. Slide 33).

The following year's annual report contains numerous references to the "forensic investigation", and its deleterious impact on ongoing project implementation, but makes no mention of any actual findings (USAASA, 2012d). That year's financial statements list "irregular expenditure" amounting to R22.7 million (USD3 million) in 2010/2011 and R19.5 million (USD3 million) in 2011/2012 "as a result of non-compliance with [supply chain management] policies" and "bidding processes", along with payment of R2.7 million (USD400,000) to a "supplier without a valid contract" (USAASA, 2012d, pp. 53, 74 and 90). It outlines the sanctions being imposed: "dismissal of the CFO, a final written warning for the Executive manager: Performance and a demotion for the Senior manager: SCM. Criminal and civil charges are in the process of being instituted" (USAASA, 2013b, p. 84).

There was, however, some discussion of the forensic audit when USAASA presented its annual report to the Parliamentary Portfolio Committee, showing the network of corruption to have been centred on the "Project [Management] Office" and a "database of experts", both of which had been established in late 2010 (PMG, 2011a), after the appointments mentioned above. This office appears to have been designed as a specific vehicle for nefarious purposes, a "tenderpreneurship tool to create and give out work to targeted individuals and businesses" (Shaun Pather, interview, 27 March 2015). The members of the Board had become "extremely concerned by the substantial amounts that were paid to the experts and the [Project Management Office]... [and that] "delegated authority was being exceeded" (PMG, 2011a). It may have been these latter amounts that swelled the amount squandered by USAASA to "approximately R92 million" (USD13 million) (PMG, 2012). Later reports were to place the figure as high as R110 million (USD16 million) (Sidimba, 2012).

It is not easy to correlate these figures against the Auditor-General's comments available in the available annual reports. These list "irregular expenditure" amounting to R19.5 million (USD3 million), along with "fruitless and wasteful" expenditure amounting to R47.3 million (USD7 million) between 2010 and 2012 (USAASA, 2012d, pp. 53 and 79). The following year the Auditor-General issued a "qualified" audit opinion because of being "unable to confirm the project... [and] accrued expenses" to the value of some R57 million (USD8 million) and because of the "lack of a [sic] sound and reliable processes in place to identify and measure on the number of completed centres" (USAASA, 2013b, pp. 44 and 48).

The Portfolio Committee unexpectedly turned on the entire Board, accusing it of having "failed in the execution of its fiduciary duties" and asking "why the Board as it currently stood should not be dissolved" (PMG, 2011b). Board Chair Moahlodi resigned a few days later (USAASA, 2012d, p. 5). The incoming Minister[14] then dissolved the remainder of the Board and appointed senior departmental officials Sam Vilakazi and Themba Phiri as "executive caretakers" (Labour Court, 2011).

As noted previously, the CFO was dismissed, and three others resigned. It appears that the remaining two got off very lightly given the seriousness and the extent of the financial irregularities, with a "final written warning" and a "demotion" respectively (USAASA, 2013b, p. 83). Despite the talk of taking "civil action to recover the money USAASA had lost" and instituting "criminal action… against those involved" (PMG, 2012), and the fact that some 26 charges were reportedly laid against three of the managers involved (Sidimba, 2012), along with criminal sanctions recommended by the value for money audit, nothing appears ever to have come to court, and nothing further seems to have happened to any of the perpetrators.

In the event, by then the Agency was already embroiled in yet another scandal and forensic investigation, this time conducted by the country's statutory anti-corruption Special Investigation Unit.

7.5.2 *Shenanigans and the SIU*

The SIU investigation into the appointment and actions of the CEO, then Zam Nkosi, along with improper expenditure from the USAF (RSA, 2014) had been triggered by an open letter from opposition MP Bantu Holomisa (IOL, 2014), directly to President Jacob Zuma,[15] setting out

[14] A sudden cabinet reshuffle in the midst of the crisis had seen well-regarded Minister Roy Padayachie replaced by Dina Pule, later to be disgraced in a corruption scandal of her own. The reasons for dissolving the Board may well have been in retribution for their role in exposing the corruption at USAASA: Minister Padayachie had just re-appointed three of them following the stand-off with the Portfolio Committee (McConnachie & Mawson, 2011).

[15] MP Holomisa bypassed the then responsible Minister, Dina Pule, since she was implicated.

a number of allegations of "corruption and maladministration" in respect of USAASA, and pointing to the "looting of State resources" (Holomisa, 2013). The level of detail in Holomisa's open letter suggests it had been based on documents leaked by one or more concerned USAASA staffers.

The Board of USAASA was quick to respond to the letter, saying it had decided to "institute an independent investigation into ALL [sic] allegations" and to "place on suspension" two unnamed staff members, as well as to investigate how "confidential third party information" had been leaked (USAASA, 2013a). The Ministry was much slower to respond, largely because Minister Dina Pule was axed in early July, as part of another cabinet reshuffle,[16] but eventually announced that it had appointed "independent investigators to look into the allegations of possible corruption and maladministration" (BusinessTech, 2013a).

The investigation by forensic investigating firm SizweNtsalubaGobodo appears to been taken back to the Board and the well-regarded new Minister, Yunus Carrim, some months later (Jacobs, 2013a), with the result that a formal SIU investigation (which required an official proclamation to be issued by President Zuma) was instituted early the following year. The Board's primary action, however, seems instead to have been in pursuit of the "whistleblowers" (Jacobs, 2013a).

The mandate of the SIU proclamation is terse, covering the three main areas set out in the Holomisa letter, instructing investigation into:

- maladministration in relation to the recruitment process [leading to the 2013 appointment of the CEO]...
- The Agency's funding, by way of a subsidy in the amount of R500 million (USD71 million), to a service provider for the construction and expansion of an electronic communications network for Emalahleni Local Municipality... and any related unauthorised, irregular or fruitless and wasteful expenditure...
- The procurement by the Agency of services in relation to the Rapid Deployment of Public Access Facilities Programme... and any related unauthorised, irregular or fruitless and wasteful expenditure... (RSA, 2014).

[16]The primary cause of her dismissal appears to have been the 'ICT Indaba' scandal, which saw substantial amounts of conference funding siphoned off to a company owned by her romantic partner.

Once again, analysis of what transpired is hampered by the non-availability of the final report from the SIU—the investigation remains ongoing and incomplete (SIU, 2017), forcing us once again to rely on what third-party documentation is available.

The issues relating to the appointment of CEO Zam Nkosi have already been analysed above.

The second area of investigation relates to an allegation involving mobile operator Cell C. An amount of R500 million (USD71 million) of irregular funding was apparently almost granted for a Cell C project to construct an electronic communications network in eMalahleni Local Municipality in the Eastern Cape. The detailed slew of leaked documentation cited by Holomisa lends credence to his version of the events. It was an unsolicited request for funding, which reached USAASA via Minister Pule, leading in turn to a Cell C presentation to "USAASA management", and an instruction from CEO Nkosi to Business Development Manager Mmatlou Morudu to proceed with the necessary funding. Morudu, however, to his enormous credit, refused to authorise the payment, citing his "duty of professional care and competence", and pointing out that the instruction was *ultra vires*—"the Act clearly articulates that such application must be adjudicated via a competitive tender" (Holomisa, 2013). While Morudu's principled and procedural stance had the effect of blocking the payment of the R500 million from the USAF to Cell C, it appears that it led, in turn, to the dismissal of Morudu, and a subsequent court case on his part against USAASA (Bailey, 2014a; BusinessTech, 2013b).

Cell C, for its part, insisted that the proposal, which had "stemmed from [Head of Regulatory Affairs] Mothibi Ramusi" was fully above board, describing it as a "'transparent application' in terms of section 88 of the ECA".[17] Cell C went on to wash its hands of culpability, stating "we will cooperate with authorities if requested to do so as we have acted completely within the law at all times" (ITWeb, 2013).

Strangely, no-one seems to have commented on the price tag for the proposal, accepting the inflated R500 million figure without question. While it is true that the USF account held about R750 million (USD100 million) in it at the time, almost all of this was earmarked for set-top box subsidies, and it is doubtful that the diversion of much of these funds to Cell C would have passed audit muster.

[17] Which allows for licensees to be paid subsidies "for the purpose of financing the construction or extension of electronic communications networks in under-serviced areas".

The third strand of corruption allegations dealt with tender manipulation on a multi-million rand contract awarded in 2012, in part to Mthinte Communications (the other successful bidder being Hawkstone Marketing) (USAASA, 2012c). Hawkstone and Mthinthe had been selected from an initial field of 22 companies (USAASA, 2012b) that had submitted reverse subsidy[18] bids for a 'Rapid Deployment Project' to roll out what are described as "public access centres", but which look suspiciously like the failed USA telecentres of old (USAASA, 2012a).

Accusations of non-delivery and overpayment were also reported in the press in respect of both companies, with one report apparently having had sight of leaked documents additional to those referenced by Holomisa: it cites an internal USAASA document as stating that Hawkstone had been overpaid by R3.8 million (USD550,000) despite delivering only 8 out of its contracted 32 telecentres, while Mthinte has been overpaid by R7.5 million despite delivering only 19 of its contracted 33 telecentres (de Klerk, 2013). Holomisa gives little detail on Hawkstone, or the issue of non-delivery, but alleges that Mthinte was overpaid to the tune of over R10 million (USD1.4 million) on what should have been a R24 million (USD3.4 million) tender. The allegations of tender fraud include paying Mthinte 100% of the cost of the rollout, despite their winning bid being pegged at an 80% subsidy, and irregularly adding "branding" to the original contract (Holomisa, 2013).

USAASA's own reaction to Holomisa's allegations bordered on the incoherent. A spokesperson described the allegations as "just hallucination", labelling the whistle-blowers as "habitual liars", and claimed that "to prosecute [USAASA] in the public gallery without following procedures is tantamount to character assassination" (Jacobs, 2013b). Following the SIU proclamation, USAASA issued a further statement, stating on the one hand that the "Boards have instructed management to cooperate fully and truthfully with the SIU", but on the other labelling the allegations as "unfounded" and a "desperate ploy". It went on to allege a bizarre conspiracy concocted by nameless parties seeking to take control of the USF, and "peddled in the media [as] a deliberate and unfortunate creation in the quest for control over the organization's existing as well as future funds" (USAASA, 2014a).

[18]With the exception of ISP iBurst and failed USAL Umzinyathi Telecomms, the list of bidders mostly comprises hitherto unknown entities.

In the absence of the final report from the SIU investigation, it is impossible to be certain of the full extent and nature of the corruption around the USF. The Hawkstone and Mthinthe allegations certainly seem to point to a repeat of the 2011 fiasco around the Project Management Office. If not outright tender fraud, there seem certainly to have been major lapses in financial management and corporate governance. Other recent instances of corruption, such as the late 2014 suspension of another (unnamed) USAASA staffer on charges of "corruption and maladministration" (USAASA, 2014c) simply underline the point. Likewise, the uncovering by opposition parliamentarian, Marian Shinn, of an illegal transfer of R4.7 million (USD600,000) from the USAF to cover USAASA's tax bill does suggest chaotic financial controls (MyBroadband, 2012). Shinn notes with some disappointment that once "the tax payment from the USAF was paid back to Treasury from USAASA's funds and accounted for in their books, Treasury saw no need to take further action taken against the officials concerned" (personal communication, 10 February 2015).[19]

7.5.3 *Set-Top Stealing*

A fresh round of corruption allegations has latterly surfaced at USAASA, this time involving tenders for the set-top boxes needed in the country's migration to digital terrestrial television. The tender to manufacture these devices runs to over R4 billion (USD300 million) and was unaccountably awarded to a "panel" comprising all 27 bidders (van Zyl, 2015). An investigation into the tender was instigated by Treasury and has led in turn to yet another forensic investigation. This appears to have uncovered substantial contraventions of supply chain management policies, and went so far as to recommend that the "production process of STBs be stopped with immediate effect and a process that will lead to the integrity and value for money be initiated" (DoC, 2016)—a clear indication of substantial corruption afoot. The investigation continues to simmer, with the Competition Commission allegedly investigating price collusion between bidders, and recent press reports alleging bidder Altech agreed to pay a

[19] A late 2019 answer by the Minister to a Parliamentary question, as this book was in press, gives some glimpse into the findings of the still-unpublished SIU report. It refers to numerous irregularities surrounding the contract with Mthinthe Communications, amounting to "financial misconduct", for which prosecution was recommended.

bribe of R54 million (USD7.5 million) to one of the sons of then President Jacob Zuma in order to secure the contract (wa Afrika, 2017). With the Minister keeping the report under wraps, the shadow Minister of Communications has called for the Public Protector[20] to investigate (Shinn, 2017).

Under the management of USAASA, the impacts and achievements of the USF have been, as the analysis has shown, extremely limited. The rollout of telecentres was ill-conceived, well short of targets, plagued with problems and unsustainable. Further, no subsidies were ever paid to needy persons. No subsidies were paid for the extension of communications networks, aside from the near-miss involving Cell C. Payments to the USALs were insufficient and ineffective. Despite being considered as part of the canon of international good practice, the implementation of the USF in South Africa thus appears to have been a barely mitigated failure of policy implementation.

There were clearly a number of factors contributing to the failures of the Agency in respect of the USF. In the absence of stringent financial procedures and controls, those overseeing the USF seem to have been concerned less with the impact of their interventions upon the communications poor, and more focused on exploiting the Fund as an avenue for personal enrichment. The constantly changing and unstable leadership of the Agency, coupled with poorly qualified staff, and a lack of skilled financial and management expertise, seem to have contributed to an environment where staff placed private, corrupt agendas above the public interest. It is true that the Agency has belatedly developed a formal Manual setting out funding guidelines and operating procedures for the Fund (USAASA, 2014b), but its existence has not been widely publicised, and it is not available via the Agency's website.

There seem to be inherent structural challenges facing institutions such as the Agency, charged with allocating, disbursing and accounting for public funds. Opportunities for corruption seem to be engendered in any environment where this trusteeship is not subject either to adequate public scrutiny or to the necessary organisational checks, balances and controls. Surprisingly, international good practice does not appear to have taken account of or examined the potential for corruption and misappropriation of funds in respect of USFs worldwide. Both recent global studies on USFs (GSMA, 2013; ITU, 2013) remain strangely silent on the issue.

[20] A statutory investigative office focusing on government maladministration, improper conduct by government functionaries, and corruption with respect to public monies.

Yet, it is difficult to believe that the expenditure of substantial sums of public money through USFs, has not been seen as an opportunity for illegal personal gain in countries other than South Africa.

7.6 Research, Advocacy and Policy Support

Although the primary responsibility of the Agency has been the oversight, expenditure and accountability of finds via the USF, its mandate extends more widely than a financial and fiduciary one, to include advocacy, research and policy support. It is therefore important to look at the performance of the Agency in respect of each of these functional areas.

7.6.1 Research

The enabling legislation of the Agency sets out a number of areas of research focus, including requirements that it:

a. undertake such investigations into matters relating to its functions as it may consider necessary…
b. conduct research into and keep abreast of developments…
c. continually survey and evaluate the extent to which [UAS has] been achieved…
d. issue information from time to time… (RSA, 2005, Section 82(4)).

Former USA researcher Katharina Pillay has suggested that research should have been the primary mandate of the Agency (interview, 13 January 2015). That may be overstating the case, but research is clearly an important pillar for its work. The Agency requires data, reports and information for it to function effectively in other areas, and as an input for the policy-maker and the regulator. However, the Agency's publications output—a primary indicator of research activity—belies this. In fact, research output has consumed less than 3% of USF expenditure to date.[21] Moreover, the list of formally issued research reports and documents[22] is, by any standard, a paltry output over its 20 years of existence. It comprises:

- 'Affordability of Telecommunications Services and Categories of the Needy People in South Africa' (USA, 2006a);
- 'Analysis of the Extent to which the Objectives of the Telecommunications Act (103 of 1996), As Amended, were Achieved (in the Period 1997 to 2004)' (Schofield & Sithole, 2006);
- 'ICT Penetration in South Africa Project Report' (USA, 2006b);
- 'Recommendations on How the USA and other Stakeholders Might Assist USALs to Ensure Sustainability' (Thornton, 2006);
- 'Community Telephone Services Market Study' (USA, 2006c);
- 'The National Strategy on Universal Service & Access Report' (USAASA, 2014b);
- 'Universal Service and Access Fund Manual' (USAASA, 2014b).

Formal research activity seems to have taken place only in two brief spurts, around 2006 and again in 2014. None of the reports appears to have been formally published and issued. Only one report (Thornton, 2006) appears to have enjoyed any level of coverage in the trade press. Others made only a brief appearance on the website of the Agency. None is currently available for download. Further, some of the research (Schofield & Sithole, 2006; USA, 2006c) seems to have focused on issues unrelated to the mandate of the Agency. Only one report (USA, 2006b) can be said to evaluate the extent of UAS in South Africa. None examine the roll-out and effectiveness of the Agency's flagship telecentre programme, on which over 62% of USF funding to date has been expended.

This is not to say that there was no ongoing internal research activity and capacity at USAASA over the years. However, the Agency has never had a section or division with research as its primary mandate. Further, lack of access to the necessary data and information to enable the Agency to assess, monitor and track progress in respect of UAS has been widely

[21] Arguably, this too is *ultra vires* the Act (which provides that the Fund must be "utilised exclusively for the payment of subsidies"), and should have been funded from the core USAASA budget rather than via the USF.

[22] Research related to formal regulatory notice and comment procedures (USA, 1998; USAASA, 2008b) has been omitted from the list, but is equally sparse.

reported as an ongoing problem (Ngubane, 1999). A particular bottleneck has been the persistent refusal of the operators to release rollout data on the grounds that it was "commercially sensitive", and the failure to audit their USO compliance (Stavrou et al., 2001, p. 2). As a result, the USA was unable to establish a "national Geographical Information System (GIS), crucial to the monitoring of such a roll-out". In fact, despite later claims that "a Geographical Information System is currently being developed" (USA, 2002, p. 2), and that "maps can be accessed through the link on the Agency website called GIS Mapping" (USAASA, 2008a, p. 24), it languishes on the wish-list.

7.6.2 Advocacy

The Agency's mandate also includes several advocacy objectives. These include injunctions to:

> a. strive to promote the goal of universal access and universal service…
> b. encourage, facilitate and offer guidance in respect of any scheme to provide [UAS]…
> c. foster the adoption and use of new methods of attaining universal access and universal service (RSA, 2005, Section 82(1)).

The original 1996 Act contained and additional advocacy injunction to "stimulate public awareness of the benefits of telecommunication services" (RSA, 1996, Section 59(1)(d)), which was not carried through to the 2005 ECA.

An early evaluation of the work of the Agency was scathing in its assessment of performance in this area, stating that "creating public awareness…. has simply not occurred" (Stavrou et al., 2001, p. 3), and going on to find that

> Advocacy, through representation to the Ministers office, DoC and ICASA, was yet another function that the USA should have undertaken. The record shows that these rarely happened, and when they did they tended to be of an adversarial nature. (Stavrou et al., 2001, p. 3)

The stance of the Agency may have mellowed somewhat in subsequent years, but its advocacy track record has remained scant and relatively low-key. While it has made formal submissions on an ongoing basis to the various notice and comment processes in the sector and has conducted a number of workshops over the years, its profile as an advocate of UAS has largely flown beneath the radar.

7.6.3 Policy Support

Finally, the Agency is enjoined to provide support for policy-making and regulation. Specifically, it is required to:

> e. make recommendations [on request] to the Minister in relation to policy on any matter relating to universal access and universal service...
> f. advise the [ICASA on request] on any matter relating to universal access and universal service...
> g. continually evaluate the effectiveness of this Act and things done in terms thereof towards the achievement of the goal of universal access and universal service... (RSA, 2005, Section 82(4)).

Here the Agency's track record has been rather better, despite a number of hiccups, and albeit only in respect of a single area. The two sets of processes through which the Agency sought to secure definitions for 'universal access', 'universal service', 'under-serviced areas', and 'needy persons' have already been charted. The first, covering all four definitions (USA, 1998, 1999a, 1999b), was conducted in terms of the 1996 Telecommunications Act, but ultimately foundered on the desk of the Minister whose responsibility it was to issue the necessary regulations. A second attempt (USAASA, 2008b, 2009a, 2009b) was rather more successful, leading to a corresponding Ministerial determination this time (DoC, 2010), and, ultimately, a set of regulations from ICASA, defining under-serviced areas (ICASA, 2012b).

The Agency has done little, if anything, when it comes to evaluating the impact of legislation, and its consequent sets of regulations, on achieving UAS. Arguably, this ongoing watchdog role is amongst the central functions of the Agency, one which would have allowed it to influence and shape policy pronouncements, legislative amendments and regulatory interventions. However, there is simply no evidence that the Agency ever conducted a regulatory impact assessment of this nature and scope.

7.7 Assessing the Work of the Agency

In late 2000, with the Agency approaching the end of its initial lifespan, a task team was appointed by Director General Andile Ngcaba to review the work of the USA and to make a recommendation on its future (Stavrou et al., 2001). Somewhat surprisingly, given its assessment of the performance of the Agency, the team was unequivocal in its insistence that the Agency should continue to exist until "it is deemed that universal access and service in telecommunications and related information services has been achieved". Their report was strident in its condemnation of any attempt to close the USA down, branding this as "immoral and a crime of negligence towards the constituents [sic] of South Africa" (Stavrou et al., 2001, pp. 4 and 6).

This was despite an assessment which is damning. The report itemises a litany of failures in respect of the core objectives of the Agency. Three of these were cases where the specific "performance was within the control of the USA", and which "failed because of incompetence". In a further eight instances, objectives were judged as ones that "could not have be met because their performance was linked to both support and performance of other institutions and organisations" (Stavrou et al., 2001, pp. 1–3).

Surprisingly, the USA escapes very lightly on its lead project, the telecentres, which is listed amongst the areas where failure is attributed to external factors. This is despite the project being described as "ad hoc" and having a "number of inherent problems", resulting in "one-sided dependency relationships between the telecentres and the USA that have largely resulted in their breakdown" (Stavrou et al., 2001, p. 2).

The assessment also deals with the failure at the time to achieve definitions for 'universal access', 'universal service' and 'needy persons'. However, this area of failure does highlight the extent to which the Agency was dependent upon the regulator and the Minister in carrying out its work. ICASA, in particular, is singled out for lack of the "socio-political will" to establish and convene the necessary co-ordinating structures (Stavrou et al., 2001, p. 2).

The report also highlights some of the staffing and leadership problems that have already been discussed above. It describes problems of "staff turnover, particularly that of the Head" as being "far from acceptable". And it goes on to point to internal organisational development problems—the "reshuffling of portfolios… [with the result that] skilled personnel have found themselves in positions that they neither desired nor are equipped to handle" (Stavrou et al., 2001, p. 3).

The report does make some interesting recommendations, amongst them that:

- The Agency take over monitoring of the USOs of the operators;
- The governance of the Agency be assumed by a Board of Directors to be appointed by the Minister;
- The universal service levy be hiked to "2% of gross revenue", but that a "'play or pay' principle" be adopted, with a "financial incentive [for operators] to play";
- The name of the Agency be changed from the rather unfortunate USA to "Universal Service Development Agency (USDA)" (Stavrou et al., 2001, pp. 7, 11, 14 and 15).

There are a number of other recommendations, mainly reconfirming the status quo in respect of the Agency. Of those above, only the establishment of an oversight Board was implemented directly in the 2001 amendment to the Act. The USA did change its name, however—to the even more unfortunate and cumbersome Universal Service and Access Agency of South Africa (USAASA).

However, the value of the assessment was limited by its primary mandate to pronounce on the future of the USA as an institution. As a result, the authors seem far more concerned with arguing for the USA's continuation, than with exposing its failings and proposing corrective actions.

The establishment of a governing Board for the Agency was adopted as policy shortly afterwards, in a Ministerial directive, which dealt, *inter alia*, with the "restructuring" of the Agency, emphasising its role to "evaluate and monitor implementation of universal access projects" and setting out a Board to "provide oversight" (DoC, 2001). The Board was duly established when the Act was amended (RSA, 2001), although, as noted, the functions of the Agency were left almost entirely unchanged.

The work of the Agency was again evaluated some years later through a 2005 'impact' study, commissioned by USAASA itself. This rather rambling assessment describes itself as a "written, in-depth case study of South

Africa's Universal Service Agency" (USA, 2005, p. 1). The report's assessment of the USA's track record in relation to the various areas of its mandate is unremittingly negative. In a detailed, often repetitive catalogue evaluating each of the USA's functional areas, the report finds a number of these "too vague to permit a meaningful assessment", and judges the Agency as having neither "capacity or budget" in respect of others (USA, 2005, pp. 42–54).

The overall conclusion of the report is, however, both strident and damning. Contextualising its final assessment somewhat tendentiously against the "consensus in professional, academic as well as telecom sector literature... that South Africa's telecommunications policy is a failure", it characterises the USA as a "creature of [that] policy" and views its legislated "mandate [as having] set the Agency up to fail" (USA, 2005, p. 93). Key identified areas of failure on the part of the USA include:

- Having "made [telecentre] implementation its core function";
- Neglecting to "monitor and analyze the RSA telecom sector" (USA, 2005, pp. 93–94).

The report goes on to call for:

> The mandate for the Universal Service Agency [to be] improved...
> The Agency's budget and the funds allocated to the Universal Service Fund [to be] increased dramatically...
> The USA's human resource capacity [to be] increased, particularly with respect to research and analytical skill sets (USA, 2005, p. 95).

7.8 Conclusion

On the basis of the preceding discussion, it is hard to see the Agency as anything short of a failed institution caught up in failed policy implementation.

To be fair, the Agency was placed in a difficult structural position from the outset, caught between the Ministry and the regulator and the operators, with much of its mandate outside of its own control, and with neither enforcement nor regulatory powers. It shared overlapping co-jurisdiction with the regulator on many aspects of UAS implementation, monitoring and enforcement, without any sort of formal co-ordinating structure. This is the sort of situation Limpitlaw is referring to when she describes USAASA as being in a “bizarre regulatory space” (2014, p. 5265). Similarly, the USA assessment report describes the Agency as “weakly embedded in South Africa’s regulatory space” (USA, 2005, p. 20). BMI-Tech CEO Denis Smit likewise bewails the “conflicting mandate” between the Agency and the regulator (interview, 20 November 2014). In addition, the work of the Agency has also been undermined by a debilitating combination of lack of support from the Department on the one hand, and continual Ministerial interference on the other. Such structural limitations have made it very difficult for the agency to be effective and to make an impact.

Nonetheless, there was much the Agency could have achieved, had it not tripped up on its own internal limitations. Lack of capacity and inappropriate skills sets have been enumerated above. Combined with a weak, unstable and constantly changing leadership, with several CEOs embroiled in one form of misconduct or another, this left the entity unable to intervene systematically or effectively. It also opened the door to financial mismanagement and corruption. From the earliest irregularities involving the IDRC funding, through the forensic audit and subsequent SIU investigation, both involving misappropriation of telecentre funding, there has been hardly a period when the Agency has been free from the taint of scandal.

Arguably, external pressures exacerbated the personal enrichment opportunities that were presented by having control over large sums of money in the absence of competent management and the necessary strict financial controls. As noted, there was considerable pressure on the Agency from Ministers looking for the glamour of flagship projects and an opportunity to make political capital out of cutting telecentre ribbons. Sustainability of access and lived benefits for disadvantaged communities took a back seat to showcase politics.

As a result, over R600 million (USD86 million) of funding available in the USF has been spent, but with almost nothing by way of tangible, sustainable results to show for it. Contrast this with over R2 billion (USD285 million) in operator contributions over the same period. Funding on this scale, properly and judiciously spent, would have made a real difference in providing access to communications services and content to the digitally disadvantaged in South Africa.

In consequence, the Agency has failed to deliver on almost all of the core areas of its mandate. Its research related to UAS in South Africa has been almost non-existent, and what there was, lacked both profile and impact. In advocacy, the Agency has been weak and ineffectual. It is only when it comes to support for and input into regulation that the Agency can claim any level of success: several sets of definitions that were developed and promulgated. However, the Agency's influence on the broader policy agenda has been non-existent.

It remains unclear as to why the creation of a separate institutional entity to drive UAS was so strongly driven. It does seem likely, though, that the primary motivation was to ensure that UAS remained at the forefront of policy implementation. Providing an institutional counterweight to the sector regulator in order to offset the possibility of regulatory capture, given the ANC's mistrust of much of the bureaucratic baggage likely to be carried over into the new state environment, seems also to have played a role. Using the Agency as a vehicle to reward an important labour and community constituency through the initial staffing appointments may also have been a consideration. The very motivations behind the creation of the USA then likely consigned it to the margins of policy implementation.

It seems highly unlikely that the establishment of the USA was in any way related to a premediated agenda of corruption. The opportunities for personal plunder were comparatively small and piecemeal (particularly in early years when the Fund was capped), and pale into insignificance against those presented by the arms deal, and via high-spending state institutions such as Eskom, the government pension fund, PRASA and SAA. In any event, the beneficiaries of corruption via the USF appear to have been a very different set of individuals, unconnected to those who established the USA in the first place. What does seem clear is that access to, and the ability to manipulate, the expenditure of large sums of a money allows the lure of lucre to shine brightly. This is especially so in an environment that is sliding slowly towards becoming a kleptocratic state.

It is further unclear why corrective action has been so slow and so limited in scope. It is true that some legislative amendments seem to have been triggered by specific events or particular reports. But, for example, the introduction of a governing Board seems a fairly limited response to the 2000 review of the USA (Stavrou et al., 2001), even if that in turn was more concerned with ensuring the continuation of the USA as an entity than with identifying weaknesses and proposing corrective action. Similarly, the SIU investigation seems to have been the trigger for the insertion into the Act of a number of clauses stressing the fiduciary duties of the Board and the appointment, conditions of employment and removal of the CEO (RSA, 2005, Sections 81A, 82A–82E). The fundamental structural issues and institutional shortcomings of the Agency seem never to have been properly analysed or adequately addressed. It is only with the recent White Paper that a decision has been taken to dissolve USAASA, and to assign its policy-making functions to the Department and its regulatory functions to ICASA (DTPS, 2016, p. 171).[23] As a consequence, regulatory interventions to achieve UAS may be strengthened and streamlined, but at the expense of UAS becoming far less of a policy priority.

USAASA appears therefore to have come to the end of its lifespan. It has become an institution that seems to have failed on almost every level. It is hard to point to a single, sustained instance where its programmes can be said to have succeeded. As an entity, its processes and procedures have become tainted with corruption, and it has become politically discredited.

Indeed, the creation and work of the Agency are viewed by many as having been "fatally flawed" (Denis Smit, interview, 20 November 2014). It is hardly surprising, then, that former IDRC staffer Tina James can conclude thus:

> I think the USA is one of the most shameful things this country has done. I can't believe how we wasted so much money for so long where the need was so great. (interview, 27 November 2014)

References

Allchurch, N. (1998, May 8). Phone lines for Africa. *Mail & Guardian*. Retrieved from http://mg.co.za/article/1998-05-08-phone-lines-for-africa.

Bailey, C. (2014a, May 18). Luthuli House dragged into labour case. *Independent Online*. Retrieved from http://www.iol.co.za/news/politics/luthuli-house-dragged-into-labour-case-1689938.

Bailey, C. (2014b, June 22). SIU nails Dina Pule's man. *Independent Online*. Retrieved from http://www.iol.co.za/news/crime-courts/siu-nails-dina-pule-s-man-1.1707113.

Bapela, O. (2011, May 14). Mr Obed Bapela, MP during the launch of Ulwazi Information Centre New Cross Road-14 May 2014. Pretoria: Department

[23] At the same time, the USF is to be replaced by a "Digital Development Fund", far broader in scope and resourced by a significantly higher levy.

of Communications. Retrieved from /https://www.dtps.gov.za/index.php?option=com_content&view=article&id=153.

Benjamin, P. (2001). *Telecentres and universal capability: A study of the Telecentre Programme of the Universal Service Agency in South Africa, 1996–2000* (PhD thesis).

Blackman, C., & Srivastava, L. (2011). From availability to use: Universal access and service. In C. Blackman & L. Srivastava (Eds.), *Telecommunications regulation handbook* (pp. 151–177). Washington, DC and Geneva: World Bank, infoDev, & International Telecommunication Union. Retrieved from http://www.infoDev.org/en/Document.1069.pdf.

BusinessTech. (2013a, July 15). Usaasa to be investigated for corruption. *BusinessTech*. Retrieved from http://businesstech.co.za/news/telecommunications/42017/usaasa-to-be-investigated-forcorruption/.

BusinessTech. (2013b, October 27). Cell C's R500 million Usaasa broadband rollout proposal investigated. *BusinessTech*. Retrieved from http://businesstech.co.za/news/mobile/48433/cell-cs-r500-million-usaasa-broadband-rollout-proposal-investigated/.

Czernowalow, M. (2008, September 16). USAASA suspends CEO. *ITWeb*. Retrieved from http://www.itweb.co.za/index.php?option=com_content&view=article&id=11066:usaasa-suspends-ceo&catid=69.

de Klerk, A. (2013, June 24). ICT contract in tatters on non-delivery. *Daily Dispatch*. Retrieved from http://www.dispatchlive.co.za/news/ict-contract-in-tatters-on-non-delivery/.

DNTA. (1999). *Universal Service Agency Institutional Strengthening Plan*. David N. Townsend & Associates.

DoC. (2001, July 23). Policy directions issued by Minister of Communications. *Government Gazette*(22503).

DoC. (2010, February 8). Determination issued under the Electronic Communications Act, 2005 (Act No 36 of 2005) with regard to Universal access to and the universal provision of electronic communications services and electronic communications network services. *Government Gazette*(32939).

DoC. (2011). *Annual report 2010/2011*. Pretoria: Department of Communications.

DoC. (2016, September 14). *Minister Faith Muthambi addresses a joint-committees' digital migration state of readiness meeting*. Pretoria: Department of Communications. Retrieved from http://www.doc.gov.za/minister-faith-muthambi-addresses-joint-committees%E2%80%99-digital-migration-state-readiness-meeting.

DTPS. (2016, October 3). National integrated ICT policy white paper. *Government Gazette, 616*(40325).

Gedye, L. (2006, May 12). USA loses its head. *Mail & Guardian*. Retrieved from http://m.mg.co.za/article/2006-05-12-usa-loses-its-head.

GFIA. (2012). *Summary status report: USAASA value for money audit*. Johannesburg: Gobodo Forensic and Investigative Accounting.

GSMA. (2013). *Survey of universal service funds: Key findings*. London: GSM Association. Retrieved from http://www.gsma.com/publicpolicy/wp-content/uploads/2013/04/GSMA-USF-Key-findings-final.pdf.

Holomisa, B. (2013, June 7). *Corruption and maladministration at USAASA*.

ICASA. (2012b, September 10). Under-serviced areas definition regulations. *Government Gazette, 567*(35675).

IOL. (2008, September 4). USAASA CFO steps down. *Independent Online*. Retrieved from http://www.iol.co.za/news/south-africa/usaasa-cfo-steps-down-415115.

IOL. (2014, March 25). *Zuma orders Usaasa graft probe*. Johannesburg: Independent Online. Retrieved from http://www.iol.co.za/news/crime-courts/zuma-orders-usaasa-graft-probe-1.1666242#.VNnRkC7qWXc.

ITU. (2011). *SADC toolkit on universal access funding and universal service fund implementation*. Geneva: International Telecommunication Union. Retrieved from http://www.itu.int/ITU-D/projects/ITU_EC_ACP/hipssa/Activities/SA/CRASA/Toolkit%20Final%20Report.pdf.

ITU. (2013). *Universal service funds and digital inclusion for all*. Geneva: International Telecommunication Union. Retrieved from http://www.itu.int/en/ITU-D/Regulatory-Market/Documents/USF_final-en.pdf.

ITWeb. (2013, October 27). Probe mooted over R500m Cell C subsidy—Paper. *ITWeb*. Retrieved from http://www.itweb.co.za/index.php?option=com_content&view=article&id=68472.

Jacobs, M. (2013a, November 20). No answers yet on USAASA allegations. *ITWeb*. Retrieved from http://www.itweb.co.za/?id=69170:No-answers-yet-on-USAASA-allegations.

Jacobs, M. (2013b, November 22). USAASA slams corruption allegations. *ITWeb*. Retrieved from http://www.itweb.co.za/index.php?option=com_content&view=article&id=69228.

Koopman, A. (1998, February 17). 2000 rural schools will 'leap-frog' onto the Web. *Cape Times*.

Labour Court. (2011, February 24). *Judgment Case no: J 2951/2011*. Johannesburg: The Labour Court of South Africa. Retrieved from http://www.saflii.org/za/cases/ZALCJHB/2012/21.pdf.

Limpitlaw, J. (2014). South Africa. In C. Long & P. Brisby (Eds.), *Global telecommunications law and practice*. London: Sweet & Maxwell.

Malefane, M., & Ncana, N. (2011, September 25). Digital TV officials suspended over R29m. *Sunday Times*. Retrieved from http://www.timeslive.co.za/scitech/2011/09/25/Digital-TV-officials-suspended-over-R29m1.

Malunga, M. (1997, February 11). New players in telecom industry. *Sowetan*.

Mawson, N. (2009, October 2). Theledi blocks USAASA CEO appointment. *ITWeb*. Retrieved from http://www.itweb.co.za/index.php?option=com_content&view=article&id=26810:theledi-blocks-usaasa-ceo-appointment.

McConnachie, K., & Mawson, N. (2011, October 24). Dina Pule: New comms minister. *ITWeb*. Retrieved from http://www.itweb.co.za/index.php?option=com_content&view=article&id=48546.

Mokone, T., & Malefane, M. (2011, October 16). Parliament censures troubled state TV agency [sic] for 'playing politics'. *Sunday Times*. Retrieved from http://www.timeslive.co.za/local/2011/10/16/parliament-censures-troubled-state-tv-agency-for-playing-politics.

Moyo, A. (2015, December 3). USAASA boss calls it quits. *ITWeb*. Retrieved from http://www.itweb.co.za/index.php?option=com_content&view=article&id=148298:USAASA-boss-calls-it-quits.

Msimang, M. (2003). Universal access and service: An overview. In *ITU, Trends in Telecommunication Reform 2003—Promoting Universal Access to ICTs: Practical tools for regulators* (pp. 29–50). Geneva: International Telecommunication Union.

Muller, R. (2008, March 27). Please try again later. *MyBroadband*. Retrieved from http://mybroadband.co.za/news/telecoms/3307-please-try-again-later.html.

MyBroadband. (2012, October 19). DA: USAASA "plundered" R4.7 million from fund. *MyBroadband*. Retrieved from http://mybroadband.co.za/news/general/62660-da-usaasa-plundered-r4-7-million-from-fund.html.

Mzekandaba, S. (2016, April 18). USAASA CEO makes quiet exit. *ITWeb*. Retrieved from http://www.itweb.co.za/index.php?option=com_content&view=article&id=151642:USAASA-CEO-makes-quiet-exit.

Naidoo, J. (1997, July 10). Deregulation must await mass roll-out. *Business Day*.

Ncana, N., & Mokone, T. (2011, September 18). Fur flies at state TV [sic] access agency. *Sunday Times*.

Ngubane, P. (1999, September 7). Phones for all—First phase before December. *Cape Times*.

Parliament. (2016, February 11). *Written reply—Question No: 125*. Parliament of the Republic of South Africa: National Assembly.

PMG. (2011a, October 13). *2010/11 annual reports of the Universal Service Access Agency of South Africa and the National Electronic Media Institute of South Africa*. Cape Town: Parliamentary Monitoring Group. Retrieved from https://pmg.org.za/committee-meeting/13524/.

PMG. (2011b, October 19). *Universal Service & Access Agency of SA on its annual report 2010/11; Communications Budget Review and Recommendation Report*. Cape Town: Parliamentary Monitoring Group. Retrieved from https://pmg.org.za/committee-meeting/13586/.

PMG. (2012, October 10). *Universal Service and Access Agency of South Africa & National Electronic Media Institute of South Africa annual report 2011/12*. Cape Town: Parliamentary Monitoring Group. Retrieved from https://pmg.org.za/committee-meeting/14993/.

PMG. (2016, October 21). *National Assembly: Written reply—Question No: 2314*. Cape Town: Parliament of the Republic of South Africa. Retrieved from https://pmg.org.za/files/RNW2314-161114.docx.

PMG. (2019, November 21). *USAASA – SIU—Question NW914 to the Minister of Communications*. Cape Town: Parliamentary Monitoring Group. Retrieved from https://pmg.org.za/committee-question/12878/.

Rasool, F. (2011a, September 22). USAASA overpays, under-serves. *ITWeb*. Retrieved from http://www.itweb.co.za/index.php?option=com_content&view=article&id=47462:usaasa-overpays-underserves.

Rasool, F. (2011b, October 5). USAASA under investigation. *ITWeb*. Retrieved from http://www.itweb.co.za/index.php?option=com_content&view=article&id=47870:usaasa-under-investigation.

Rasool, F. (2011c, October 20). USAASA CEO suspended. *ITWeb*. Retrieved from http://www.itweb.co.za/index.php?option=com_content&view=article&id=48434.

Rasool, F. (2012a, March 14). USAASA labour case dismissed. *ITWeb*. Retrieved from http://www.itweb.co.za/index.php?option=com_content&view=article&id=52600.

Rasool, F. (2012b, March 29). Golden handshake for USAASA CEO. *ITWeb*. Retrieved from http://www.itweb.co.za/index.php?option=com_content&view=article&id=53068.

Rasool, F. (2012c, August 22). Suspended USAASA exec resigns. *iWeek*. Retrieved from http://www.iweek.co.za/in-the-know/suspended-usaasa-exec-resigns.

Rasool, F. (2012d, October 17). R220m of USAF untouched. *ITWeb*. Retrieved from http://www.itweb.co.za/index.php?option=com_content&view=article&id=59357:R220m-of-USAF-untouched&catid=118.

RSA. (1996). *Telecommunications Act, 1996. No 103 of 1996*. Pretoria: Republic of South Africa.

RSA. (2001, November 30). Telecommunications Amendment Act, No 64 of 2001. *Government Gazette, 437*(22889).

RSA. (2005). *Electronic Communications Act, No 36 of 2005*. Pretoria: Republic of South Africa.

RSA. (2014, March 28). Special Investigating Units and Special Tribunals Acts, 1996 (Act No 74 of 1996): Referral of matters to existing special investigating unit and special tribunal. *Government Gazette, 585*(37496).

Schofield, A., & Sithole, H. (2006). *Achievement of the Telecommunications Act objectives: Analysis of the extent to which the objectives of the Telecommunications*

Act (103 of 1996), as amended were achieved (in the period 1997 to 2004). Johannesburg: Universal Service Agency. Retrieved from http://www.usa.org.za/docs/gen/Achievements%20of%20the%20Objectives%20of%20the%20Telecom%20Act%20of%201996%2020.pdf.

Shinn, M. (2017, November 26). Public protector must act on set-top boxes. *TechCentral.* Retrieved from https://techcentral.co.za/da-wants-parliamentary-probe-ann7-deal/78356/.

Sidimba, L. (2012, December 28). State to subsidise poor for digital TV. *City Press.* Retrieved from http://www.citypress.co.za/news/state-to-subsidise-poor-for-digital-tv/.

SIU. (2017, March 6). *Investigations.* Retrieved from Special Investigating Unit: https://www.siu.org.za/investigations.html.

Stavrou, A., Whitehead, A., Wilson, M., Seloane, M., & Benjamin, P. (2001). *Presentation notes: Of recommendations on the future of the Universal Service Agency.* Pretoria: Universal Service Agency—Conference Convening Committee.

Thornton, L. (2006). *Recommendations on how the USA and other stakeholders might assist USALs to ensure sustainability.* Johannesburg: Universal Service and Access Agency of South Africa.

USA. (1998, October 22). Discussion paper on definition of universal service and universal access in telecommunications in South Africa. *Government Gazette, 400*(19397). Retrieved from http://www.polity.org.za/polity/govdocs/discuss/usa.html.

USA. (1999a, May 28). Universal access and universal service: Discussion paper. *Government Gazette, 40*(20129).

USA. (1999b). *Universal access and service definitions for South Africa: A policy recommendation to the Minister of Communications.* Johannesburg: Universal Service Agency.

USA. (2002). *Universal Service Agency: Annual report 2001/2002.* Johannesburg: Universal Service Agency.

USA. (2003). *Universal Service Agency 2002/2003 annual report.* Johannesburg: Universal Service Agency.

USA. (2004). *Universal Service Agency: Annual report 2003–2004.* Johannesburg: Universal Service Agency.

USA. (2005). *Universal Service Agency impact document.* Johannesburg: Universal Service Agency.

USA. (2006a). *Affordability of telecommunications services and categories of needy people in South Africa.* Johannesburg: Universal Service Agency.

USA. (2006b). *ICT penetration in South Africa: Project report.* Johannesburg: Universal Service Agency. Retrieved from http://www.saide.org.za/resources/thutong/0000027996/0000026677/0000026672/ICT%2520Penetration%2520Study%2520Report%25202005-6.pdf.

USA. (2006c). *Community telephone services market study*. Johannesburg: Universal Service Agency.

USA. (2006d). *Universal Service Agency: 2005–2006 annual report*. Johannesburg: Universal Service Agency.

USAASA. (2007). *Universal Service and Access Agency of South Africa: Annual report 2006/2007*. Johannesburg: Universal Service and Access Agency of South Africa.

USAASA. (2008a). *Annual report 2007/8: Creating connections*. Johannesburg: Universal Service and Access Agency of South Africa.

USAASA. (2008b, August 15). Notice in terms of section 82 (3) and sections 88 (2), (3) & (4) of the Electronic Communications Act, 2005 (Act No 36 of 2005), inviting written representations in respect of the definitions of universal service, universal access, and underserviced areas. *Government Gazette, 518*(3133).

USAASA. (2009a, April 30). *Position paper and recommendations to the Minister of Communications and the Independent Communications Authority of South Africa regarding definitions of universal service, universal access, under-serviced areas and needy persons*. Johannesburg: Universal Service and Access Agency of South Africa. Retrieved from http://www.usaasa.org.za/export/sites/usaasa/resource-centre/download-centre/downloads/USAASA_Definitions_Position_Paper.pdf.

USAASA. (2009b, August). *Recommendations on the definitions of universal access and service, and determination of needy persons by the minister, and determination of underserviced areas by the Independent Communications Authority of South Africa*. Johannesburg: Universal Service and Access Agency of South Africa. Retrieved from http://www.usaasa.org.za/export/sites/usaasa/resource-centre/download-centre/downloads/USAASA_Executive_Summary_for_Presentation_to_Minister_Aug_2009.pdf.

USAASA. (2011, November 1). *USAASA annual report 2010/2011: Presentation to the Parliament [sic] Portfolio Committee*. Johannesburg: Universal Service and Access Agency of South Africa.

USAASA. (2012a). *Invitation to bid*. Johannesburg: Universal Service and Access Agency of South Africa. Retrieved from http://www.usaasa.org.za/export/sites/usaasa/tenders/2012/downloads/USAASA_Apply_for_Subsidy.PDF.

USAASA. (2012b). *Bid Number: USAF/HO/01/2012*. Johannesburg: Universal Service and Access Agency of South Africa. Retrieved from http://www.usaasa.org.za/export/sites/usaasa/tenders/2011/downloads/List_of_Bidders_Rapid_Deployment_Tender.pdf.

USAASA. (2012c). *USAASA Bid No: USAF/HO/01/2012: Notification of award of subsidies for the deployment of ICT public access facilities in under serviced [sic] areas*. Johannesburg: Universal Service and Access Agency of South Africa. Retrieved from http://www.usaasa.org.za/export/sites/usaasa/tenders/2011/downloads/Rapid_Deployment_Project_Notification_of_Award.pdf.

USAASA. (2012d). *Annual report 2011/2012*. Johannesburg: Universal Service and Access Agency of South Africa. Retrieved from http://www.usaasa.org.za/export/sites/usaasa/resource-centre/download-centre/downloads/USAASA_Annual_Report_2011-12.pdf.

USAASA. (2013a, June 20). *USAASA board resolves to investigate UDM allegations*. Johannesburg: Universal Service and Access Agency of South Africa. Retrieved from http://www.usaasa.org.za/export/sites/usaasa/resource-centre/download-centre/downloads/PRESS-RELEASE-June-20-2013.pdf.

USAASA. (2013b). *Annual report 2012/13*. Johannesburg: Universal Service and Access Agency of South Africa.

USAASA. (2014a, April 1). *USAASA welcomes SIU probe*. Johannesburg: Universal Service and Access Agency of South Africa. Retrieved from http://companies.mybroadband.co.za/usaasa/2014/04/01/usaasa-welcomes-siu-probe/.

USAASA. (2014b). *The national strategy on Universal Service & Access Report*. Johannesburg: Universal Service and Access Agency of South Africa.

USAASA. (2014c, September 3). *USAASA confirms the suspension of a staff member*. Retrieved from http://companies.mybroadband.co.za/usaasa/2014/09/03/usaasa-confirms-the-suspension-of-a-staff-member/.

USAASA. (2016). *Annual report 2015/2016*. Johannesburg: Universal Service and Access Agency of South Africa. Retrieved from http://www.usaasa.org.za/export/sites/usaasa/resource-centre/download-centre/downloads/USAASA-Annual-Report-2015-2016.pdf.

van Zyl, G. (2015, April 16). Set-top box tender winners revealed. *News24*. Retrieved from http://www.fin24.com/Tech/News/Set-top-box-tender-winners-revealed-20150416.

wa Afrika, M. (2017, August 6). Another Zuma son accused of 'seeking bribe' to clinch deal. *Sunday Times*. Retrieved from https://www.timeslive.co.za/sunday-times/news/2017-08-05-another-zuma-son-accused-of—seeking-bribe-to-clinch-deal/.

CHAPTER 8

UAS Policy: From Conception to Outcomes

The preceding chapters have documented the evolution of a canon of international good practice in relation to UAS policy, together with how those precepts and prescriptions were adopted and adapted in South Africa, and how the implementation of each of the major interventions played out over the two decades post-democracy.

During this period the deep digital donga separating 'white' and 'black' South Africa has slowly silted up, leaving merely a shallow scar across the landscape. At the same time, the ICT landscape has changed fundamentally—from basic telephony towards ubiquitous Internet access and the widespread availability of high-speed, high-bandwidth broadband. National broadband strategies have become the new *de rigueur* form of international good practice, both in South Africa (DoC, 2013) and indeed globally (Oliver, 2015), thus opening up new fissures in access, new axes of deprivation (McHenry et al., 2016). While income may today have replaced race as the primary determinant of deprivation (World Wide Worx, 2017, p. 7), an Internet digital divide (and, by extension, a broadband one) remains a central obstacle to providing ICT infrastructure, services and content to all South Africans.

The preceding chapters have presented both a structured historical exposition of events and an analysis of their consequences and outcomes. The tools of regime theory and policy transfer have been used to organise and reconstruct these events on the basis of the available evidence,

C. Lewis, *Regulating Telecommunications in South Africa*,
Information Technology and Global Governance,
https://doi.org/10.1007/978-3-030-43527-1_8

drawing on key informant interviews and analysis of the extant documentation. The further lens of policy success and policy failure provides a heuristic tool to assess the extent to which the series of UAS interventions described in the preceding chapters met the RDP's stirring telecommunications vision of "universal affordable access for all" (ANC, 1994, Section 2.8.4).

These lessons, in turn, hold important implications for future policy and regulatory interventions designed to ensure nationwide, reasonably priced access to high-speed, high-bandwidth broadband infrastructure, services and content.

8.1 Policy Success or Policy Failure?

As we have seen, South Africa adopted and implemented a series of policy and regulatory interventions drawn from international good practice and designed to achieve UAS in respect of ICT infrastructure, services and content. The imposition of USOs upon licensees (Chapter 4) and the deployment of a USF (Chapter 5) are the most direct examples. The two remaining planks of South Africa's UAS policy were, as noted, less directly derived from international good practice, but remained consistent with its principles and practices. They were: the awarding of rural licences to under-serviced area licensees (USALs) (Chapter 6) and the establishment of an institutional entity dedicated to UAS, now the Universal Service and Access Agency of South Africa (USAASA) (Chapter 7).

The implementation of each of these interventions, along with their associated developments and consequent outcomes was beset by problems of formulation, implementation and monitoring, and bedevilled by areas of outright failure. Indeed, the effectiveness of each has been the subject of widespread public criticism and academic scepticism. Equally importantly, the policy-makers themselves abandoned one of the interventions, when policy directions regarding the future of the USALs were withdrawn (DoC, 2009), and are currently proceeding to dismantle another, with the announced dismemberment of USAASA (DTPS, 2016, p. 171).

8.1.1 The Process of UAS Policy in SA

These failures notwithstanding, the overall policy goal of achieving affordable UAS for all, especially for rural areas and poor communities, remains unchallenged. It remains politically untenable to question the need for

UAS in South Africa, as it is to deny the country's *apartheid* legacy of glaring socio-economic disparities. There seems to be general acceptance of the remaining specific interventions themselves, now that the USALs have faded from the public memory, and with the closure of USAASA now planned.

The outcome of ICASA's 2010 USO review is illustrative. Although the major licensees were predictably unanimous in their critique of their existing USOs, preferring to see the Universal Service Fund (USF) as the chosen form of intervention, there was no opposition to UAS interventions per se. For example, the Internet Service Providers' Association agreed that "there is no real debate that USAOs [broadly speaking]... have a role to play in meeting UA and US objectives" (ISPA, 2010, p. 5). ICASA was therefore able to extend the existing USOs—albeit after dropping the "SIM card and handset distribution obligations" and reducing the number of schools to be connected, and promising to undertake a regulatory impact assessment (Ellipsis, 2017). More recently, although a number of aspects of Government's recent White Paper have proven highly controversial, there was little criticism of the plan to broaden the current USF into a new Digital Development Fund (DDF) (DTPS, 2016).

Having said that, there remain a number of difficult and contested issues which may taint the legitimacy of UAS policy in the long-term. The memory of how the initial enthusiasm for the USAL experiment rapidly turned into dismay, scorn and ridicule, still lingers. The poorly performing and corruption-riddled USAASA has similarly remained a consistent object of public scorn, with its recently announced demise seen as the logical outcome of years of maladministration and ineffective inactivity (Mzekandaba, 2016). And, while the USF model remains widely acceptable, both the ongoing maladministration of the existing fund and the proposal to hike the levy to 1% of licensees' turnover have been widely condemned (Gopal, 2015). Similarly, the regulator's ongoing moves to tinker with the existing USOs by way of undertaking a regulatory impact assessment, as well as proposing amendments in some cases (Ellipsis, 2017),[1] suggests less than universal satisfaction with the mechanics of the current regime.

[1] ICASA has proposed to reduce Telkom's payphone obligation from 120,000 to 25,000—the company currently claims to have a mere 20,000 in service (McLeod, 2016). The promised impact assessment did not materialise.

Despite considerable grumbling at the process of overall policy formulation over the years, the outcomes have largely been accepted. The public furore around the various drafts of the 1996 White Paper notwithstanding, the resultant 1996 Act was implemented without formal challenge. There were similar rumblings leading up to the 2005 Electronic Communications Act (Buckland, 2004), and, more recently, a degree of furore around several of the controversial positions adopted in the 2016 ICT White Paper (McLeod, 2017).[2] And, although both Parliament and the Regulator adhere to strict notice and comment procedures, some commentators continue to express fundamental reservations around the agenda and transparency of policy in the sector (Horwitz & Currie, 2007, p. 458). However, the legitimacy and process of UAS policy formulation and implementation have to date escaped fundamental challenge.

Nevertheless, the poor track-record in respect of the USALs and USAASA, in particular—where the myth of policy success continued to be peddled in the face of mounting, indeed overwhelming, evidence to the contrary—has left the Department and the regulator perceived as being out of touch with the evidence of implementation in practice, reluctant to acknowledge policy failures, and lacking any vision for viable, alternative solutions. For example, the recent ICT Policy White Paper (DTPS, 2016) remains very thin, almost silent, on concrete and specific measures to undercut maladministration and looting in respect of the proposed, and much more lucrative, DDF. In a similar vein, the recent proposals by ICASA to amend the USOs imposed on Telkom, WBS and Sentech (Ellipsis, 2017) show little by way of measures to obviate the shortcomings of their predecessors.

8.1.2 UAS Programmes in SA

Although each of the four core features of UAS policy was duly carried out in accordance with their legislative mandate, implementation in almost every case, as the previous chapters have shown, has largely failed the objectives of UAS policy.

The USOs, as noted, were duly written into the operator licences. However, when it came to carrying out the obligations, the operators were largely left to their own devices. The necessary co-ordination

[2] The proposed provisions for a so-called Wireless Open Access Network (WOAN) licensee.

structures and clear implementation guidelines never materialised, either because of weak and overlapping mandates between ICASA and USAASA, or as a result of regulatory inefficiency and lack of capacity. Monitoring and enforcement of compliance was either almost entirely ineffective from the side of the regulator—for many of the same reasons—or actively obfuscated and blocked by the licensees. As a result, the execution of the USOs has remained haphazard, and only very loosely in line with objectives.

Although the USF was established relatively expeditiously, with the necessary regulatory measures put in place to ensure a somewhat circuitous flow of funding towards UAS projects, the actual disbursement of UAS funding has been, as noted, little short of disastrous. Expenditure was heavily skewed in favour of the highly problematic telecentre programme (which was, at least initially, beyond the legal mandate of the Fund)—at the expense of support for 'needy persons'. Worse, the Fund has continued to be bedevilled by repeated episodes of alleged corruption, with some four substantial incidents stretching across its entire 20-year lifespan.

The USALs project, intended to license commercially-viable operators in under-serviced areas and communities, similarly failed its envisaged objectives. Predicated on a highly questionable assessment of the market, the project was plagued by delays, undermined by policy and regulatory moves towards greater liberalisation, weakened by lack of financial and capacity-building support, and overtaken by the burgeoning prepaid mobile market, before being finally abandoned as a policy.

Finally, the Agency, USAASA as it is now titled, failed dismally to live up to its projected flagship role of defending and advancing the cause of UAS. Its institutional positioning and legislative mandate placed it on a weak footing from the outset. Coupled with low levels of skilled capacity and repeated leadership turnover, this led the organisation to fall victim to financial maladministration and corruption. As a result, what was delivered fell far short of the envisaged objectives, so much so that it is now slated for closure.

Taken together, the picture that emerges suggests that, although there was progress in implementation across the four programmes, this fell far short of the intentions of the policy. Too many aspects of the programme were undermined by a catalogue of failures. Implementation of the policy became the subject of much controversy, as noted in the preceding chapters. Operationalisation of the policy thus became highly controversial and very difficult to defend.

Although universal affordable access to telecommunications infrastructure, services and content, has largely been achieved in South Africa, certainly for voice telephony, this has occurred largely despite, rather than because of the various components of the UAS programme. While it is true that the USOs and the USF did achieve some rollout and provide some measure of ICT access to those who would otherwise not have enjoyed this, the overwhelming bulk South African households (96%) with functional access to telephony (Stats SA, 2017, p. 49) owe this to market forces, because of the post-2000 explosion of prepaid mobile. Indeed, but for this uptake, which saw UAS outcomes achieved by unintended means, the overall UAS policy programme might have generated far more controversy than has in fact been the case. The overall progress towards UAS has nevertheless been offset by too many unintended outcomes and a substantial level of controversy around each of the programmes.

From the programmatic perspective of efficiency and effectiveness, the ability to deliver within specified timeframes, in accordance with planned budgets, and in alignment with functional specifications, has been limited at best. For example, the limited monitoring and evaluation of the licensee USOs that took place, suggests grave functionality problems. Most of the lines within Telkom's USO rollout were disconnected in short order; and high percentages of the mobile CSTs were either untraceable or out of operation. In addition, the shenanigans surrounding the USF suggest widespread misapplication and misappropriation of funds. Further, almost all the 24 USALs collapsed, at the cost of nearly R62 million in wasted USF funding, and with severe financial impact on the luckless bidders and their employees. The resultant unwanted and negative media attention visited on these three programme components, and on the Agency itself, has overshadowed the relatively limited successes across the overall UAS programme.

However, where licensee views on UAS issues have been canvassed, the responses have largely been negative. While this is certainly self-interested, it does suggest that the policy must be viewed as a reputational liability. ICASA's 2010 review of the USOs and the USF levies does not seem to have been due to stakeholder pressure, but many of the responses do suggest that the policy agenda was under some pressure. For example, the country's largest mobile operator bluntly referred to the "failure of the existing USAOs to deliver genuine benefits for South African citizens [unlike] competitive markets" (Vodacom, 2010, p. 25). Most argued for

USOs to be dropped, since they had "proven to be ineffective", in favour of contributions to the USF—subject to the development of a "clear framework identifying how the funds are to be utilised" (ICASA, 2012, pp. 7 and 10).[3]

Political fallout from the various UAS interventions seems to have been relatively limited. This is in part due to the complex and inchoate lines of accountability in South Africa's ICT sector: it is not always readily apparent where policy responsibility lies between the Minister, the Department, Parliament, the regulator, the Agency. However, the line ministers and the department (first DoC, now DTPS), have similarly been the subject of ongoing political comment and criticism (Horwitz & Currie, 2007; Tubbs, 2013; Vegter, 2009) over the years.[4]

Nevertheless, many aspects of the policy have proven controversial, with influential stakeholder SA Communications Forum describing the "current UAS model [as] ineffective" and consultancy Research ICT Africa calling instead for the "use of market forces to extend access" (DoC, 2014b, pp. 80–81). The ICT Policy Green Paper consultation elicited very limited support for the continuation of USAASA and widespread calls for its dissolution (DoC, 2014b, pp. 80–90). At the same time, most stakeholders viewed the USF as the most viable of the UAS options, with many calling for it to be made more effective and efficient.

It is true that government has had to concede that "growth in South Africa's ICT sector has not brought affordable, universal access to the full range of communications services [and that the] performance of most state interventions in the ICT sector has been disappointing" (NPC, 2012, p. 190). Nevertheless, UAS continues to enjoy prominence in most areas of ICT policy going forward. For example, the National Development Plan reaffirms the "priority goal of achieving affordable and truly universal access" (NPC, 2012, p. 191). Similarly, South Africa's national broadband plan, SA Connect, sets "universality… universal access

[3] This assessment predates, and is arguably thus not yet coloured by, the revelations of maladministration and corruption that began to surface in 2012 (see Chapter 5).

[4] Interestingly, the multi-party Parliamentary Portfolio Committee in Parliament, to whom the Minister, the Department, the regulator and the Agency, are formally politically accountable, has largely escaped the critical public eye.

to broadband services" (DoC, 2013, p. 17) as one of its ten guiding principles, and the recent ICT Policy White Paper deals extensively with what it refers to as "universal service and access" (DTPS, 2016, pp. 25–36).

Government, through the Minister and the Department, is not wont to expend a great deal of time or resources on defending specific aspects of ICT policy. However, actions in this case speak louder than words. The abandoning in 2009 of the ten-year-long failed USAL experiment (DoC, 2009; Vecchiatto, 2009) has already been noted. More recently, USAASA faces being merged with ICASA, and the USAF is to be repurposed into a DDF (DTPS, 2016).

Accordingly, the level of political benefit to government as the policy-maker, and the institutions tasked with policy implementation, ICASA and USAASA, has been mixed. Government has been able to sustain its commitment to the broad and general moral imperative of providing UAS, as evidenced by the degree to which that commitment remains prominent in ongoing policy formulation. One of the perhaps unintended benefits of the regulatory state with its arms-length entities responsible for policy execution is that criticism for process and particularly programme failures is deflected onto those institutions. Indeed, such deflections allow government to escape or delay accountability in many areas and respects. For example, the programmatic failure of Telkom's line roll-out and payphone USOs has largely been attributed to ICASA's failures of specification and enforcement (Hodge, 2004). Likewise, the wastage and corruption surrounding the USF have rebounded to the discredit of USAASA, its weak governance structures and processes, and its lack of effective financial processes and controls (Lewis, 2013, pp. 101–102). Similarly, government has been able to escape much of the direct blame for the collapse of the USALs experiment and for the institutional failures of USAASA itself. In addition, as noted previously, the issues of policy furore and contestation have tended to lie in areas of more direct financial consequence to operators and users, such as competition in the market, regulatory independence, licensing and pricing of services, and access to spectrum (Horwitz & Currie, 2007).

8.2 The UAS Trajectory in South Africa

This book has set out to chart South Africa's UAS trajectory, from the rise of international good practice in respect of UAS, through its adoption, adaptation and implementation in national policy and practice, up to its outcomes and impacts on the country's sector and its people.

8.2.1 UAS: The Rise of International Good Practice

South Africa's pursuit of UAS as a central pillar of its ICT policy did not occur in a vacuum. Although the lack of access by so many of its population to telecommunications infrastructure and services was particularly acute and was coloured by the country's unique *apartheid* past, South Africa was by no means the only country to have grappled with a stark and glaring digital divide.

At the advent of democracy in South Africa, in 1994, the challenge of 'universal service' (as it was then referred to) had already been confronted by a range of countries and international groupings. In Chapter 2, the analysis sets out to identify in the phenomenon of telecomms reform the roots of these universal service strategies that were beginning to coalesce into a canon of international good practice.

In the early 1980s, as noted, a number of powerful pressures associated with the advent of neo-liberalism—economic, technological, geopolitical and social—began to force changes in the structure of global telecommunications market, hitherto largely consisting of state-owned national monopolies. Riding on the back of these technological changes that had been enabled by digitisation and the rise of IT, the drivers were nevertheless fundamentally economic, as businesses sought to exploit the new technologies on the one hand, and to gain access to the new markets offered by technological change. What was at stake was firm ownership, market structure and governance of the sector, with demands for privatisation and the introduction of competition at the forefront.

The contestation for change played itself out at several levels. At the country level, it led to the privatisation of British Telecom in the UK, and to the AT&T divestiture settlement in the US. But the pressures soon spilled over into international fora, including the European Union (EC, 1987) and the OECD (1991), before being taken up at the International Telecommunication Union (ITU) (1991), as well as, to a lesser extent, and through the World Bank and the IMF. The same pressures were subsequently to feature prominently at the post-GATT negotiations leading up to the creation of the WTO (1995).

Together, these various institutions acted as a relatively coherent, if disparate, international regime, loosely aligned to the broad perspectives of the 'Washington consensus', sharing many "implicit or explicit principles, norms, rules, and decision-making procedures" (Krasner, 1982, p. 186). It was this cluster of transnational institutions that provided the broad arena in which international stakeholders could contend for hegemony and codification of a reformed telecommunications regime.

The key features of this new regime involved:

- Privatising the state-owned incumbent providers of services;
- Introducing competition into the market;
- Establishing an independent regulator to oversee the market (Wallsten, 2001, p. 3).

In consequence, UAS came to be raised by the defenders of the continued monopoly provision of telecommunications services by the state-owned incumbent. Such an arrangement, it was argued, was necessary in order to finance the rollout of infrastructure and services to poor customers and remote communities at affordable prices—to provide for 'universal service' no less.

To counter this, those pushing for reform of the sector began to propose a series of universal service interventions that were compatible with liberalised markets where the incumbent operator had been partially or fully privatised. Specifically, two principal forms of intervention stand out in the documentation and the literature as the two key planks of international good practice, viz:

- The imposition of universal service obligations (USOs) on licensees;
- The establishment of a USF to finance UAS interventions (ITU, 2003).

Much of the formulation of this body of knowledge derived from a series of research reports, organisational documents and academic journal articles, many of them authored by members of a loosely coherent epistemic community of experts and academics.

What, then, were the factors underpinning and enabling the emergence of these various components of telecomms reform and UAS international good practice? Clearly, the pressures towards sector reform—technological, economic, political and social—were key drivers. But the existence of important global regimes, including the ITU as a global multilateral forum dealing with the sector, provided the battlegrounds in which the old principles and norms could be assailed, vanquished and displaced. And the epistemic communities of practice, research and writing provided the weaponry that enabled victory in many of the individual clashes, providing a growing body of countervailing international good practice.

8.2.2 UAS: Adoption and Implementation in South Africa

Chapter 3 documents and discusses the advent of telecomms reform in South Africa, from its first tentative pre-1994 steps up to the 1996 passage of the landmark Telecommunications Act. In particular, the chapter examines how UAS came to be at the forefront of policy and enshrined in legislation, along with key, specific UAS provisions embodied in that legislation.

The global pressures towards telecommunication reform described above had also been felt in *apartheid* South Africa, despite its global isolation, leading the regime to undertake its first, faltering steps (de Villiers, 1989) towards reform of a sector historically characterised, like so many others, by a state-owned, integrated monopoly provider of telecommunications and postal services. International good practice began to filter through more strongly (Coopers & Lybrand, 1992) into the policy direction of the sector in the first few years after the 1990 unbanning of the ANC. Posts and telecommunications were separated, Telkom corporatised, and two GSM licences awarded. But these faltering steps towards sector reform had been highly and bitterly contested by the newly unbanned ANC, which viewed telecomms reform as a key component within its overall socio-economic vision (ANC, 1994).

It was the political, economic and social landscape facing the incoming ANC government that dictated the pre-eminence of UAS within its telecommunications policy prescriptions after 1996. In particular, a stark and glaring historical division cut the overwhelming majority of 'black' South Africans off from the economic and social benefits enabled by the kind of access to telephony enjoyed by almost all their 'white' compatriots—a 'digital donga' created and perpetuated by decades of *apartheid* oppression. As the voice of the hitherto-disenfranchised majority, recognising this context of telecommunications deprivation, the ANC government thus came to place the "universal and affordable provision of telecommunication services" (RSA, 1996, Section 2(a)) at the forefront of ICT sector policy as part of its commitment to a better life for all—although it did seek to balance this with ensuring that the benefits of telecommunications provision also accrued to business and the economy.

As a result, therefore, the ANC fought bitterly against the imposition of early telecomms reform measures by the then-governing National Party. This was partly driven by political hostility towards the regime, but also by mistrust of its underlying agendas, as well as a deep desire to impose its own stamp on the timing, pace and content of reform. For example, only the inclusion of strong UAS measures (and BEE requirements) in the mobile licences finally persuaded the ANC to back down from its hostility to them.

The ANC was, as noted, perhaps uniquely positioned in the face of telecomms reform and its associated global and institutional pressures, given the degree to which its head of ICT policy, Andile Ngcaba, had been involved within the structures and processes of the ITU. At the same time, it was acutely aware of a dire shortage of skills and experience in this key area. As a result, Ngcaba moved rapidly to set up an ICT policy think-tank, the Centre for the Development of Information and Telecommunications Policy (CDITP), and to recruit and develop a cadre of expertise, while engaging in policy research and development focused on transformation of the sector. The resultant epistemic network, which included international exposure and progressive expertise, was able further to entrench UAS within the policy debate and in opposition to a simplistic liberalisation of the sector.

In parallel, and partly as a counterweight to the influence of business interests and the power of the existing fixed licensee in particular, the ANC then moved to set up the National Telecommunications Forum as a multilateral stakeholder forum to discuss and agree future policy for the sector. The ensuing process, which ran until the passage of the 1996 Telecommunications Act, albeit beset by vicissitudes and controversy, led to the negotiated compromise between stakeholder elites so vividly characterised by Horwitz (2001).

The 1996 Act, then, was one that set South Africa firmly on the road to telecomms reform, establishing an independent sector regulator, and paving the way for the subsequent partial privatisation of Telkom and the gradual introduction of more competition over the years—in a process later to be characterised as 'managed liberalisation'.

The Act also embodied the key components of international good practice. In particular, these included: the imposition of USOs upon licensees; and the creation of a USF, under the direction of a unique, dedicated Agency, financed by a levy imposed on licensees, and intended to subsidise 'needy' users and to support network rollout. Together this was a slew of UAS interventions widely welcomed and warmly applauded (ITU, 1998).

The adoption of UAS, along with these key UAS interventions, was thus the outcome of a complex interplay of factors, rather than simple policy transfer. Driven by the realities of a peculiarly South African digital divide, along with the political imperatives of contesting for and achieving power, the ANC was uniquely positioned to place UAS at the forefront of telecommunications policy. Wary of simple-minded adoption of international practice, it sought to develop a model of ICT sector reform grounded in the country's unique economic and social context, accommodating the overall direction of ICT sector reform while imbuing it with national characteristics. The resultant policy mix was, thus, a uniquely compelling example of policy learning and adaptation in the context of a hegemonic international telecomms reform regime.

8.2.3 *UAS: Outcomes and Impacts*

South Africa's engagement with ICT sector reform, and with the new global regime preaching its tripartite gospel of privatisation, competition and regulation, via the ITU, the WTO and the World Bank, thus led to the adaptation and adoption of its key policy precepts, albeit with a specifically South African flavour. Telkom was partially privatised, firstly through a strategic equity partnership, then via an IPO. Competition, in the form of the first two mobile licensees, was accepted and gradually expanded under the doctrine of 'managed liberalisation' (Ngcaba, 2001). At first, it was ISPs and VANS that began to infiltrate the market (Lewis, 2005), but, from 2001, additional mobile, fixed and USAL licences were awarded, before government effectively lost its stranglehold over licensing, following the 2008 Altech ruling.

In order to achieve its stated policy objective of providing universal, affordable access to ICT infrastructure, services and content, government adopted a slew of UAS measures, some directly derived from prevailing international good practice, but others rather more innovative. Four main areas of intervention were undertaken. A series of USOs were imposed upon providers via their licences. Levies were imposed upon licensees, aggregated into a USF, and expended on a variety of UAS interventions. A dedicated entity was created to superintend the achievement of UAS and to administer the USF. Finally, from 2001, a series of licences were awarded to operators to provide infrastructure and services in defined areas of low teledensity.

The subsequent introduction of a series of non-overlapping rural licensees, the infamous USALs, informed by direct lobbying from the US-based NTCA (2001), with a degree of alignment with similar international good practice initiatives (Kayani & Dymond, 1997; Wellenius, 2002), faltered and died, with only one of the original licensees known to have survived.

The detailed chronicle and analysis set out in Chapters 4–7 suggests that the implementation of the interventions was substantially flawed, beset by programmatic failures, unable to achieve its intended outcomes.

For example, the impact of the USOs imposed via the operator licences has been limited at best. Initially, these comprised access line rollout and payphone installation in the case of Telkom, and network coverage and community service telephone (CST) provision in the case of the mobile licensees. This was later supplemented by the distribution of SIM cards and handsets, and the provision of Internet access to public schools and institutions for people with disabilities. But the fixed-line network is now in terminal decline, with the very existence of payphones under threat. While CSTs appear relatively thriving, they form a very small percentage of the market. The SIM card and handset distribution has been abandoned, and the Internet access USOs failed to get any real traction due to failures of co-ordination. It was only the required rollout of a mobile network with extensive geographic coverage that produced any lasting and substantial impact. It was this network that provided the infrastructure which was the basis for the explosive uptake of prepaid services from around 2000. As a result, the mobile market was able to eclipse the most optimistic projections, and to achieve universal access to telephony.

The USOs might have performed better, had they been better conceived and executed. They were often, as noted, poorly specified—which allowed licensees to dodge compliance by inflating numbers, fudging counts and gerrymandering locations to meet reporting targets. The USOs were also poorly monitored and enforced, with a lack of regulatory capacity to conduct independent audits of operator reports, and a failure of political will to enforce proper compliance.

The USF, as noted, fared little better. As in the case of so many other jurisdictions (GSMA, 2013, pp. 101–104), it has proven far easier to impose a levy on licensees and to accumulate a substantial pot of money, than to expend the funds thus garnered upon meaningful and effective

UAS interventions. Further, even the imposition and collection of the USF levy, more especially the onward transmission to the actual bank account for the Fund, was not without its difficulties. However, it was the expenditure from the Fund that proved to be most problematic, in terms of both project choice and programme management, with maladministration and corruption a particular blight. Indeed, the Fund, as noted, has failed in almost every aspect of its mandate, with little to show for some R730 million (USD100 million) spent since its inception.

Under pressure from the Department, and paying loose attention to the strictures of the Act, the focus of the Fund came to rest on telecentre implementation, an intervention that was to consume nearly two-thirds of all expenditure over the years, despite repeated and overwhelming evidence of rollout and sustainability failures of this model. Indeed, as recently as late 2017, an ICASA connectivity audit of an USAASA project to connect schools and clinics in the under-serviced Chief Albert Luthuli Local Municipality in rural Mpumalanga province produced a shocking finding: of 21 sites audited, "only one (1) clinic was found to have [both] installed equipment and Internet connectivity" (USAASA, 2017, p. 60). What makes the audit finding all the more shocking is that it measured only raw connectivity, included no examination of service access, uptake or usage, and hence gives only the most basic indication of actual project effectiveness.

Direct subsidies to 'needy persons' to fund access ICT infrastructure and services, originally intended to be the primary focus of the Fund, never eventuated—unless one counts the recent launch of the hand-out of subsidised television set-top boxes to poor households (MyBroadband, 2015) as part of South Africa's troubled rollout of digital terrestrial television. Similarly, with the exception of some wasted subsidies to the hapless USALs, nothing was ever paid to any other licensee for the extension of the PSTN.

Although establishing a USF continues to be seen as good international practice, in South Africa at least the outcome has been largely at odds with the intention. Chapter 5 shows a critical disjuncture between the Fund's legislated scope and actual expenditure: project areas outside the original purview were actively pursued, while core mandate areas were simply ignored. As a result, apart from showcasing institutional ineptitude and offering opportunities for corruption and rent-seeking, the USF has little of enduring substance to show for its 17 years of existence.

The process of awarding of a series of USALs to some 24 luckless consortia marks the third area of substantive policy and programme intervention by South Africa in support of UAS. Chapter 6 chronicles the trajectory of that ill-fated experiment—from enthusiastic inception in 2001 to ignominious demise in 2009. It provides a clear example of UAS policy that was noble in conception but hapless in execution. As noted, today a solitary USAL continues to exist, albeit operating in a market far removed from its original mandate. The USAL venture was a programme that fell foul of a number of failures in execution. Implementation was slow and haphazard, a key failing for a UAS model that was dependent on a complex mesh of interlocking critical success factors: financial backing, access to spectrum, the provision of an asymmetric termination regime, managerial capacity and administrative support. But, critically, the USALs were dumped into a market that was on the cusp of a transformation that was to undermine the entire model, as prepaid mobile overtook and then left fixed-line telephony floundering in its wake. The resultant market pressures were to force upon the policy-makers further liberalisation of the market that crippled the ability of the USALs to compete. The USAL venture today is little more than a ghost ship adrift on the sea of UAS policy, wallowing, abandoned and derelict.

The final plank of South Africa's UAS policy—the establishment of a dedicated UAS institution—has similarly proven to be riven by cracks. The Agency created in 1997 continues in 2017 to exist, marking time as it awaits the legislation that will mark its demise (TechFinancials, 2017). Its imminent closure comes in consequence of a long history of organisational weakness and implementation failure, chronicled in Chapter 7. The Agency failed dismally to discharge its principal mandate: the management of the USF. In part, this was due to weaknesses in staffing, administration and management, coupled with a continual turnover of leadership. These organisational development weaknesses, in turn, opened the door to maladministration in respect of the public funds entrusted to the Agency, and created opportunities for rent-seeking activities through corruption and venality. No fewer than four such major episodes have occurred over the Agency's 20-year history: ranging from the debacle of the early IDRC-funded telecentres, through the 2012 forensic audit and the 2014 SIU investigation, up to the latest set-top procurement scandal. The converse of these manifest and high-profile scandals has been the Agency's neglect of several key areas of its mandate: research, advocacy and policy support.

What started as a flagship institution for the digital divide and standard-bearer for UAS, became, over its lifespan, a synonym for organisational ineffectiveness, financial mismanagement and project failure.

While the programmatic outcomes set out above are overwhelmingly negative, consideration from a process and political point of view (as per the heuristic of policy success and failure [McConnell, 2010]) does suggest a rather more nuanced approach. Although the UAS programme has in many instances been a case of so little achieved with so much, the processes of policy formulation, legislation and regulation have largely been able to retain their legitimacy, as has the political status of both UAS as a policy imperative, along with the main international good practice models of USOs and a USF.

A number of commentators and analysts have documented the fractures between UAS policy and its execution (Benjamin, 2002; Gillwald, 2005a; Hodge, 2004; Lewis, 2013), but few if any have been able to account for the implementation slippages in substantial and explanatory detail. Several analyses (Horwitz, 2001) have been concerned with the political dynamics underpinning policy formulation. A number have pointed to problems underpinning policy formulation itself: political interference (Horwitz & Currie, 2007) or, commonly, failure to introduce sufficient competition (Gillwald, 2005b; Horwitz & Currie, 2007). But limited attention has been given to the possible structural causes of implementation failures, the systemic disconnects that allow policy so well-intentioned and so closely aligned to international good practice to go so badly astray.

On the one hand, policy design did work relatively well, the caveats of the commentators cited above aside. Consultation and negotiation with stakeholders was robust and did lead to modifications of policy design, as Horwitz has so clearly shown (2001), and as the current public controversy surrounding the ICT White Paper suggests (Schofield, 2017). Legislation and regulation are drafted by skilled ICT lawyers, advised by consultants of international standing, and are promulgated at the outcome of 'notice-and-comment' procedures that are usually robust and well-informed.

On the other, as has been shown, it is in the implementation of the resultant policies, laws and regulations that things have so often gone awry. Further, the roots of so many slippages between UAS policy design and UAS programme outcomes are manifold, multifaceted and complex, as the chapters above have sought to show. Nonetheless, there do appear to be some common denominators to this cluster of policy failures.

One of the problem areas lies in the lack of articulation and interaction between various policy strands. Policies have too often been adopted with limited understanding of their dependencies, or without any attempt at regulatory impact assessment. For example, the dependence of the USAL business model on an asymmetric interconnection regime was never factored into the legislative mandate or the regulatory regime. Neither does there seem to have been any attempt to appreciate and deal with impact on the viability of the USALs caused by subsequent moves towards greater liberalisation.

In addition, legislation, and sometimes regulation, has on occasion failed to anticipate how the modalities and exigencies of implementation might unfold. For example, the poor specification of USOs opened the door to creative compliance on the part of the operators, and weak monitoring and enforcement provisions weakened the ability of both the regulator and the Agency ensure adequate compliance.

Further, there seems to have been a failure to appreciate the complexities of the interplay between the various institutions, and the difficulties of managing overlapping mandates in respect of complex implementations. For instance, there are too many areas of UAS intervention where ICASA and USAASA have interlocking mandates. These include: the imposition, monitoring and impact of the licensee USOs; collections for and expenditure from the USF (where the Minister too has a directive role); and the licensing of and provision of support for the USALs.

Moreover, lack of co-ordination and consultation seems to have bedevilled implementation where more than one responsible entity was involved. For example, in the implementation of the USOs to public schools, where the involvement of the responsible Department was clearly necessary, the regulator seems to have been unable to either establish the necessary structures or to ensure they were functional. Proper co-ordination would have been all the more essential, given that so many parties were involved—the more so because schools were being provided with connectivity from two major, disparate sources: the licensee USOs, initially covering some 20,500 schools[5]; and funding from the USF,

[5] Later slashed to 5250.

covering both schools and FET colleges to the tune of over R150 million (USD20 million). A similar lack of co-ordination between ICASA, USAASA and the DoC clearly undermined the management of the USF.

The lack of capacity within both policy formulation and policy implementation structures is an oft-cited factor underpinning many of the implementation problems and failures, both in the ICT sector (DTPS, 2015, p. 157; Hawthorne, 2014, pp. xvii and 90; Lloyd, 2013) and more generally (Franks, 2014; Nengwekhulu, 2009; Walters, 2014). Indeed, it is hard not to lay much of the blame for the slippages between UAS policy formulation and UAS policy implementation on a lack of institutional capacity. Chapter 7 showed that USAASA was undermined by problems with staffing and poor organisational design and development from the outset. Similarly, ICASA's poor level of regulatory and administrative capacity at levels below that of top management is the stuff of legend. The Department too, particularly since the departure of Director General Andile Ngcaba at the end of 2003, has been afflicted by serious capacity constraints. Mistrust of the bona fides and agendas of civil servants inherited from the previous regime, coupled with the changes in demographic profile under the policy of 'black economic empowerment', aided by attractive severance packages offered to *apartheid*-era bureaucrats, have all left a cadre short on skills and thin on institutional memory. As a result, there were few in management with a deep appreciation of the environment and an in-depth grasp of the issues. This, in turn, led to slow implementation of policies, an inability to move expeditiously and decisively, poor understanding and co-ordination of linkages between programmes, compounded by extensive reliance on external experts and consultants with limited levels of embedded awareness. It has also led to poor management and administration of programmes, as well as a lack of monitoring and enforcement, which together have opened gaps for corruption and venality.

This is not to downplay the role of the major operators themselves in the overall ineptitude of UAS policy implementation. The limitations in regulatory and implementation capacity, together with the resultant lack of monitoring and enforcement, created many opportunities for creative compliance by licensees, particularly in respect of their USOs. While licensees are impelled publicly to acknowledge the need for USOs and to support their imposition, commercial bottom-line imperatives exert countervailing pressures. Since every USO means in effect an enforced internal cross-subsidy, using revenue from high-revenue customers to finance the delivery of services to uneconomic areas and customers, and to support pilot projects, they cut into profit margins. The resultant financial pressures incentivise licensees to cut the costs of USO implementation, for example, by locating CSTs in areas closer to the existing network rather than in areas of greatest need, or by skimping on costly technology or expensive post-implementation support, or through looking for opportunities for commercial arbitrage, or simply by looking for ways in which to fudge the numbers. Similar accounting pressures exist in relation to contributions to the USF, where the confusion surrounding the 2009 contribution changes was eagerly grasped upon by all except Vodacom, saving the others of millions on annual report balance sheets.

8.2.4 Interventions to Secure UAS

The resultant overall picture that emerges is one UAS policy design and intervention that was well-intentioned—largely influenced by the international good practice regime, and shaped in important ways by localised policy learnings that imparted a uniquely South African flavour—but one that was weakened and undermined by multiple instances of implementation failure. The question then arises whether the international good practice models should still be considered as such.

Significant problems have been shown to exist with the imposition of USOs on ICT sector licensees. First off, overly specific and excessively detailed specification of the USOs has created difficulties. Tight specification appears to encourage creative compliance, as noted when Telkom was able to dodge its line targets, and the mobile licensees were able to fudge their CST targets by including those in peri-urban areas. Moreover, precise definitions are easily overtaken by technology shifts and rendered redundant by changes in the market. It has really only been the relatively generalised network coverage targets of the mobile licensees that have had a lasting impact on UAS. Further, close specification requires close monitoring, something which has proven beyond the capacity and political will of ICASA to enforce.

This is a lesson the regulator seems reluctant to learn. ICASA has recently issued draft revisions to the USOs imposed on WBS, Telkom and Sentech. These will see: a substantial downwards revision in Telkom's payphone targets (from 120,000 to 25,000, to be placed at various priority locations, such as ports of entry) as well as a new requirement to provide Internet connectivity to 3631 "public health institutions" (ICASA, 2017a). Sentech will now be required to develop and "provide [an] eLearning Solution Platform" to all Technical & Vocational Education & Training Colleges (TVETs) within 4 years, as well as to implement "Internet access provisions" to TVETs allocated by ICASA (2017b). WBS will be required to provide "connectivity" to 62 TVETs allocated to it by ICASA (2017c).

USOs also impact on the market, sometimes in unexpected ways. As has already been noted, USOs are effectively an enforced internal cross-subsidy, redirecting revenue derived from existing customers to subsidise potential customers. In some cases, USOs operate at a market price: Telkom's rollout of its 2.69 million new lines was expected to earn revenue at the prevailing rates for installation, rental and calls. In other cases, USOs operate outside and below the retail market, introducing market distortions; for example, the CSTs imposed on the mobile licensees had to be funded by them and generated revenue for the recipients via asymmetrical, discounted tariffing, allowing for a substantial retail mark up.

Both approaches have the potential of raising prices, albeit marginally, to existing and potential customers. They also cut into profit margins, providing incentives for creative compliance in the absence of stringent regulatory enforcement alluded to above. The discounted CST tariffing also presented possibilities for commercial arbitrage, which Cell C recognised and was quick to exploit. Cell C was also quick to recognise that the SIM handout USO offered it an opportunity to reach millions of potential new customers and to increase its subscriber base quite dramatically.

And yet policy-makers remain wedded to the concept of obliging licensees to provide services to remote areas and poor communities. Australia, for example, although phasing out its "anachronistic and costly" funding for incumbent Telstra to provide universal service, plans to replace this with a "Universal Service Guarantee" (Reichert, 2017), which appears very much akin to what has been described as a 'universal service obligation'. Others have argued for shifting the universal service obligation away from an administrative imposition towards a market-based, 'pay-or-play', contestable model (Reynolds, Ockerby, Janssen, & Hird, 2008, pp. 31ff.).

International spectrum management good practice is now moving towards the imposition of rural coverage obligations attached to high-demand spectrum auctions, a proposal first advanced by Cave and Hatta (2008).

This has not always been successful, as Brazil's 2012 spectrum auction demonstrates. Although there were four successful bidders (the country's mobile incumbents, unsurprisingly) in the valuable 2.5 GHz band, no bids were received in the 450 MHz band, more suited to rural deployment. As a result, the regulator decided—*post facto*—to allocate some 450 MHz spectrum to each of the winning bidders, and to impose rural rollout obligations upon them (*TeleGeography*, 2012).

Cave continues to advocate spectrum USOs as a "workable and competitive means of 'buying' the attainment of equity objectives" (Cave & Nicholls, 2017, p. 377). The approach has indeed been widely adopted in the EU, with recent spectrum auctions in Denmark, Germany and Sweden having sought to impose rural service obligations on successful bidders (Ricknäs, 2010; Siong, 2012). Rural coverage obligations have also recently been attached to spectrum auctions by the French regulator, ARCEP (MobileEurope, 2016), with the UK's Ofcom also having announced plans to do so (Ofcom, 2017). As with any USO, its imposition implies an increased regulatory burden in respect of monitoring and enforcement, as the establishment by ARCEP of an 'observatory' for this purpose illustrates. A slightly different approach in the USA proposes to redirect some auction revenues towards UAS, requiring that "ten percent of the proceeds be directed toward wireless infrastructure projects in rural areas" (Szal, 2018), presumably via something similar to a USF.

The continued value and relevance of such funds remain open to question. A global assessment undertaken by the GSMA—whose members have something of a vested interest in the outcome—describes the model as "inefficient and ineffective", concluding that "USFs do not appear to be the most appropriate mechanism to achieve universal service and further social and economic development" (GSMA, 2013, pp. 4–5). Certainly, some of the GSMA's critique applies to USAASA's USAF: namely, that "levies… have been established without any substantive analysis regarding the actual service funding or subsidy levels needed"; that expenditure has been subjected to "political intervention or interference" and has "failed to take into account… sustainability concerns". The GSMA concludes that "alternative approaches… [e.g. USOs] are often more effective than USFs" (GSMA, 2013, pp. 4–5). Surprisingly, questions of corruption and maladministration receive no attention.

By contrast, and equally unsurprisingly, given its role in the global international good practice regime purveying the USF model, the ITU's own assessment, which came out in the same year, presents a far less gloomy picture and makes no such recommendation for the discontinuation of the model. Instead, recognising the "numerous challenges and pitfalls" besetting USFs, and setting out critical success factors for their implementation, it concludes with a series of recommendations intended to "'future proof' USFs to the greatest practical extent". These include the need for: "flexible" responsiveness to the changing environment; greater "transparency, visibility and accountability"; and, more emphasis on "sustainability" of their interventions (ITU, 2013, pp. 116ff.). This report does include a rather more substantive reference to "allegations… of financial mismanagement associated with a number of funds"[6] (ITU, 2013, p. 13), but falls short of specifics as to how this might be addressed for the future.

A recent analysis of USFs in several countries around the Indian subcontinent bases itself on an examination of "disbursement rates" (the ratio between USF collections and actual fund expenditures) and concludes that "universal service schemes in the case-study countries are failing" (Samarajiva & Hurulle, 2017, p. 23). USFs are thus viewed as rent-seeking initiatives in effect, with "money… being extracted from current consumers of telecom services and… being kept unspent (or used for purposes other than the intended)" (Samarajiva & Hurulle, 2017, p. 23). The authors further refer to a World Bank assessment of UAS more generally, which pointed out the "universal access programs [have been] largely superseded by the rollout of phone services by the private sector" (World Bank, 2011, p. ix)—as we saw in the case of South Africa, thanks to prepaid mobile market in particular.

While it is a truism that it is far easier to amass levies into a USF than it is to spend them effectively, it is still too early to dismiss a carefully conceived USF, efficiently managed, based on a research-based assessment of the 'true access gap' beyond the market, publicly accountable and subject to clear sustainability management. And, although disbursement ratios are clearly a key metric of USF performance, they surely cannot be the only one. Further, both qualitative research (into issues such as user perceptions, social and economic impact, successes and failures, and more) and quantitative indicators (numbers of telecentres, schools, clinics sustainably

[6] Aside from a brief mention of Pakistan, USAASA is the sole specific case cited in any detail, although the report does claim that in several instances "entire senior fund management teams have been replaced".

implemented, bandwidth consumed, and more) are essential for monitoring and evaluation, for policy analysis and policy learning.

Even though the USALs were, as noted in Chapter 6, largely an unmitigated failure, the allure of licensing small-scale rural or community providers in areas where the major operators are reluctant to venture continues to entice (Heimerl, Hasan, Ali, Parikh, & Brewer, 2015; Mathee, Mweemba, Pais, Van Stam, & Rijken, 2007; Navarro, et al., 2016; Ó Siochrú & Girard, 2005; Rey-Moreno, Sabiescu, Siya, & Tucker, 2015; Westerveld, 2012). Some approaches focus on the economic impacts and challenges of technological choice (Johnson & Roux, 2008; Zaidi & Lan, 2017), which, as noted, was one of the key challenges undermining the ability of the USALs to get off the ground in the face of the explosion of prepaid mobile access. Most argue in favour of a bottom-up approach, either co-operative or community-based (Heimerl et al., 2015; Ó Siochrú & Girard, 2005; Rey-Moreno et al., 2015), along the lines of the original approach argued for by the first proponents of the USAL model.

Even in respect of the co-operative "community ownership" approach, favoured ahead of a more entrepreneurial model by Ó Siochrú and Girard, it is clear that the success of pilot projects like these is dependent upon a conducive policy and regulatory framework. Viability requires the elaboration of a "specific national policy strand" in support of the community-based model, supported by an enabling "regulatory environment", together with concrete mechanisms for "financing and investment" and a range of training and "capacity-building" interventions (Ó Siochrú & Girard, 2005, pp. 45–53). Such an approach deserves greater policy protection and regulatory support than was afforded South Africa's luckless USALs, but it is likely to remain a small-scale model, only able to meet demand, provide access and deliver returns at the shoestring end of the market.

Finally, it seems doubtful that experimenting with institutional arrangements in the way that was attempted though the creation of the USA, is likely to produce much by way of benefit. The comment of Blackman and Srivastava in respect of the USA and similar bodies alludes to the "bizarre regulatory space" (Limpitlaw, 2014, p. 5265) occupied by such entities and provides a succinct summary of the value of the approach:

> While a completely separate agency elevates the status of UAS and creates at least the appearance of even greater independence, it may come at a

> higher cost as well as with increased complexities of coordination. (2011, p. 173)

While it seems that none of the main UAS intervention practices is entirely without merit, many are fraught with inherent challenges and pitfalls. Policy-makers and regulators embarking on this route—either de novo, or in respect of new services such as broadband—would therefore do well to approach with caution. Creative compliance is an obvious obstacle, particularly in respect of USOs. Careful anticipation of unwanted outcomes, driven by the desire of licensees to game the system, seems absolutely essential. Regulators might do well to adopt scenario planning and modelling of options and outcomes ex ante. Likewise, it seems that excessively detailed and technology-specific prescription of USO targets is a recipe for obsolescence. When it comes to expenditure from USFs, it seems that there is much room for improvement. Intervention design and implementation management need to be underpinned by far greater reliance on needs assessment and access gap research. Addressing UAS shortfalls needs to be seen far less as an infrastructure, supply-side problem, and far more as a question of dealing with ongoing sustainability and demand-side challenges through providing long-term support structures, building skills and capacity, and developing demand. The potential for corruption needs to be recognised as an inherent, structural consequence of USF design, and specific management, accountability and transparency measures put in place to counter it. In all cases, UAS interventions need to include an inbuilt, independent, publicly available research component to identify implementation shortcomings and to assess short-term impacts and longer-term outcomes, so that proper policy learning and feedback can increase effectiveness.

8.3 Concluding Thoughts

The preceding pages and chapters constitute an extended and in-depth case study of UAS policy and its implementation in South Africa. The analysis has charted the rise of an ICT policy regime, impelled by the forces driving telecomms reform, formulating and propagating a series of best practice interventions intended to ensure that the liberalisation of markets in the sector remains—despite its turn towards a private-sector, profit-driven model—able to provide widespread, affordable access to

ICT infrastructure, services and content to those either too remote or too poor to be able to acquire or sustain such access on their own resources.

The analysis has shown how South Africa's transition to democracy in the early 1990s and the legacy of a racially determined digital donga placed a commitment to UAS at the forefront of ICT policy and its reform by the incoming ANC government. It has further shown how this, in turn, led the country to draw from international good practice, as well as to innovate, with the intention of ensuring that the ICT sector was able to provide economic benefits, social development and cultural enrichment to all its citizens.

Each of the major planks of UAS intervention that were adopted, adapted and implemented in South Africa came to be marred with greater or lesser degrees of failure, principally at the programmatic, implementation level. USOs came largely to be a series of empty milestones, creatively complied with by licensees, poorly monitored and enforced by regulators, and ultimately overtaken by technological and market innovation, swept aside in the avalanche of prepaid mobile subscriptions. The USF, so easily collected from licensees, became mired in expenditure on ill-executed, unsustainable telecentres and other poorly conceived projects, swallowed in a quagmire of corruption and maladministration. A well-intentioned attempt to liberalise the market and empower small-scale entrepreneurs through the awarding of rural telecommunications licences foundered in implementation delays and policy vacillation. The establishment of a flagship body to champion the cause of UAS collapsed into ineffectiveness, poor management and corruption.

It is a sad and salutary tale of noble policy intention, animated by international best practice, but substantially undermined by programmatic implementation failure.

The digital donga in respect of telecommunications access has substantially silted up over the years. But it has not been planned policy interventions that have filled it in. Rather it has been technological development and market innovation.

However, those self-same technologies and markets are now throwing up new digital divides in relation to broadband access and fibre rollout. As policy-makers and regulators ponder new interventions to stem these new and widening divides, they would do well to heed the perspective on the now-ubiquitous mobile telephone offered some thirty-five years ago:

An executive gets into his car and travels across London. As he goes, he talks to his secretary on the telephone. Until now, that scenario has been limited to a privileged 3 000 or 4 000. In the PWV area, only 140 mobile phones are in use - though the number is to be increased to 512 by mid-year, says SAPO. The restricting factor has been a shortage of applicable radio channels. Now an ingenious development called cellular radio promises to turn this into a mass market. (FM, 1983, p. 32)

References

ANC. (1994). *The reconstruction and development programme: A policy framework*. Johannesburg: African National Congress.

Bate, D. (2014). *Connecting people: Accelerating universal service and access to communications services in South Africa*. DPA thesis, University of South Africa.

Benjamin, P. (2002). Reviewing universal access in South Africa. *Southern African Journal of Information and Communication, 2*(1). Retrieved from http://hdl.handle.net/10520/AJA20777213_5.

Blackman, C., & Srivastava, L. (2011). From availability to use: Universal access and service. In C. Blackman & L. Srivastava (Eds.), *Telecommunications regulation handbook* (pp. 151–177). Washington, DC and Geneva: World Bank, infoDev, & International Telecommunication Union. Retrieved from http://www.infoDev.org/en/Document.1069.pdf.

Bovens, M. (2010). A comment on Marsh and McConnell: Towards a framework for establishing policy success. *Public Administration, 88*(2), 584–585. https://doi.org/10.1111/j.1467-9299.2009.01804.x.

Bovens, M., & 't Hart, P. (2016). Revisiting the study of policy failure. *Journal of European Public Policy, 23*(5), 653–666. https://doi.org/10.1080/13501763.2015.1127273.

Buckland, M. (2004, March 1). The great convergence sideshow. *Brainstorm*. Retrieved from http://www.brainstormmag.co.za/white-noise/9864-the-great-convergence-sideshow.

Cave, M., & Hatta, K. (2008). Universal service obligations and spectrum policy. *Info, 10*(5/6). https://doi.org/10.1108/14636690810904715.

Cave, M., & Nicholls, R. (2017). The use of spectrum auctions to attain multiple objectives: Policy implications. *Telecommunications Policy* (41), 367–378. http://dx.doi.org/10.1016/j.telpol.2016.12.010.

Cogburn, D. (2004). Elite decision-making and epistemic communities: Implications for global information policy. In S. Braman (Ed.), *The emergent global information policy regime* (pp. 154–178). Houndsmills, UK: Palgrave Macmillan.

Coopers & Lybrand. (1992). *Telecommunications sector strategy study for the department of posts and telecommunications*. Pretoria: Department of Posts and Telecommunications.

de Villiers, W. (1989). *Summarised report on the study by Dr W J De Villiers concerning the strategy, policy, control structure and organisation of posts and telecommunications*. Pretoria: Department of Posts and Telecommunications.

DoC. (2009, August 19). Amendment of policies and policy directions issued under the Electronic Communications Act, 2005 (Act No. 36 of 2005) with regard to Provincial Under-Serviced Area Network Operator (PUSANO) Licences. *Government Gazette* (32509).

DoC. (2013, December 6). South Africa connect: Creating opportunities, ensuring inclusion—South Africa's broadband policy. *Government Gazette* (37119).

DoC. (2014a, January 24). Department of communications: National integrated ICT Policy Green Paper. *Government Gazette, 583*(37261).

DoC. (2014b). *ICT Green Paper submissions: Phase II report*. Pretoria: Department of Communications.

Dolowitz, D., & Marsh, D. (2000). Learning from abroad: The role of policy transfer in contemporary policy-making. *Governance: An International Journal of Policy and Administration, 13*(1), 5–24.

DTPS. (2015, March). *National integrated ICT policy review report*. Department of Telecommunications and Postal Services. Pretoria. Retrieved from http://www.dtps.gov.za/documents-publications/category/102-ict-policy-review-reports-2015.html.

DTPS. (2016, October 3). National integrated ICT Policy White Paper. *Government Gazette, 616*(40325).

Dyzenhaus, D. (2007). The pasts and future of the rule of law in South Africa. *South African Law Journal, 124*(4), 734–761.

EC. (1987). *Towards a dynamic European economy: Green Paper on the development of the common market for telecommunications services and equipment*. Brussels: Commission of the European Communities. Retrieved from http://ec.europa.eu/green-papers/pdf/green_paper_telecom_services__common_market_com_87_290.pdf.

Ellipsis. (2017, February 20). *Review of Universal Service and Access Obligation (USAO) framework*. Retrieved from http://www.ellipsis.co.za/review-of-universal-service-and-access-obligation-usao-framework/.

Financial Mail. (1983, April 29). It's for you. *Financial Mail*.

Flyvbjerg, B. (2011). Case study. In N. Denzin & Y. Lincoln (Eds.), *The Sage handbook of qualitative research* (4th ed.). Thousand Oaks, CA: Sage.

Franks, P. (2014, November). The crisis of the South African public service. *The Journal of the Helen Suzman Foundation, 74*, 48–56.

Frederickson, H. (2004). *Whatever happened to public administration? Governance, governance, everywhere*. Ontario: Queens University Institute of Governance. Retrieved from http://citeseerx.ist.psu.edu/viewdoc/download?doi=10.1.1.537.8624&rep=rep1&type=pdf.

Gillwald, A. (2005a, Summer). A closing window of opportunity: Under-serviced area licensing in South Africa. *Information Technologies and International Development, 2*(4), 1–19.

Gillwald, A. (2005b). Good intentions, poor outcomes: Telecommunications reform in South Africa. *Telecommunications Policy* (29), 469–491. https://doi.org/10.1016/j.telpol.2005.05.005.

Gillwald, A., Moyo, M., & Stork, C. (2013). *Understanding what is happening in ICT in South Africa: A supply- and demand-side analysis of the ICT sector*. Cape Town: Research ICT Africa. Retrieved from http://www.researchictafrica.net/docs/South_Africa_Country_Report_2013_Final.pdf.

Gopal, S. (2015, May 25). Fears as Usaasa 'tax' set to rise. *TechCentral*. Retrieved from https://techcentral.co.za/fears-as-usaasa-tax-set-to-rise/56903/.

GSMA. (2013). *Survey of Universal Service Funds: Key findings*. London: GSM Association. Retrieved from http://www.gsma.com/publicpolicy/wp-content/uploads/2013/04/GSMA-USF-Key-findings-final.pdf.

Haas, P. (1992, Winter). Introduction: Epistemic communities and international policy coordination. *International Organization, 46*(1), 1–35.

Hawthorne, R. (2014). *Review of economic regulation of the telecommunications sector*. Johannesburg: Centre for Competition, Regulation and Economic Development, University of Johannesburg. Retrieved from https://static1.squarespace.com/static/52246331e4b0a46e5f1b8ce5/t/537f2e60e4b0b4236d47a5bb/1400843872601/1400407_EDD-UJ_RECBP_Project+Report_App10_Telecommunications+Sector+Review_Final.pdf.

Heimerl, K., Hasan, S., Ali, K., Parikh, T., & Brewer, E. (2015). A longitudinal study of local, sustainable, small-scale cellular networks. *Information Technologies & International Development, 11*(1), 1–19.

Hills, J. (2007). *Telecommunications and empire*. Champaign: University of Illinois Press.

Hodge, J. (2004, March). Universal service through roll-out targets and licence conditions: Lessons from telecommunications in South Africa. *Development Southern Africa, 21*(1), 205–225.

Horwitz, R. (2001). *Communication and democratic reform in South Africa*. Cambridge: Cambridge University Press.

Horwitz, R., & Currie, W. (2007). Another instance where privatization trumped liberalization: The politics of telecommunications reform in South Africa—A ten-year retrospective. *Telecommunications Policy, 31*, 445–462.

Howlett, M. (2012). The lessons of failure: Learning and blame avoidance in public policy-making. *International Political Science Review, 33*(5), 539–555. https://doi.org/10.1177/0192512112453603.

ICASA. (2012, September 10). General Notice - Findings on Review of Universal Service Access [sic] Obligations ("USAO"). *Government Gazette, 567*(35674).

ICASA. (2017a, January 26). Request for amendment of public payphone universal service obligations by Telkom SA SOC Limited. *Government Gazette, 619* (40575), 12–21.

ICASA. (2017b, January 26). Request for amendment of Sentech SOC Ltd Universal Service and Access Licence Obligations. *Government Gazette* (40575).

ICASA. (2017c, January 26). Request for Amendment of WBS Universal Service and Access Licence Obligations. *Government gazette* (40575).

ISPA. (2010). *ISPA submission in response to the discussion document on the review of Universal Service and Access Obligations.* Johannesburg: Internet Service Providers' Association. Retrieved from http://www.ellipsis.co.za/wp-content/uploads/2010/12/ISPA_Submission_USAO_Discussion_Document_20101112.pdf.

ITU. (1991). *Tomorrow's ITU: The challenges of change—Report of the high level committee to review the structure and functioning of the International Telecommunication Union (ITU).* Geneva: International Telecommunication Union.

ITU. (1998). *World telecommunication development report 1998: Universal access.* Geneva: International Telecommunication Union. Retrieved from http://www.itu.int/ITU-D/ict/publications/wtdr_98/.

ITU. (2003). *Trends in telecommunications reform 2003: Promoting universal access to ICTs—Practical tools for regulators.* Geneva: International Telecommunication Union.

ITU. (2013). *Universal service funds and digital inclusion for all.* Geneva: International Telecommunication Union. Retrieved from http://www.itu.int/en/ITU-D/Regulatory-Market/Documents/USF_final-en.pdf.

Johnson, D., & Roux, K. (2008). Building rural wireless networks: Lessons learnt and future directions. *Proceedings of the 2008 ACM workshop on Wireless Networks and Systems for Developing Regions* (pp. 17–22). ACM.

Kayani, R., & Dymond, A. (1997). *Options for rural telecommunications development.* Washington, DC: World Bank. Retrieved from http://elibrary.worldbank.org/doi/pdf/10.1596/0-8213-3948-6.

Klemperer, P. (2004). *Auctions: Theory and practice.* Princeton, NJ: Princeton University Press.

Krasner, S. (1982). Structural causes and regime consequences: Regimes as intervening variables. *International Organization, 36*(2), 185–205.

Lewis, C. (2005, Spring). Negotiating the net: The Internet in South Africa (1990–2003). *Information Technologies and International Development, 2*(3), 1–28. Retrieved from http://mitpress.mit.edu/journals/pdf/ITID_2_3_1_0.pdf.

Lewis, C. (2013). Universal access and service interventions in South Africa: Best practice, poor impact. *African Journal of Information and Communication* (13), 95–107.

Limpitlaw, J. (2014). South Africa. In C. Long & P. Brisby (Eds.), *Global telecommunications law and practice*. London: Sweet & Maxwell.

Lloyd, L. (2013). *Evaluation of ICASA*. Johannesburg: Open Society Institute.

Mathee, K., Mweemba, G., Pais, A., Van Stam, G., & Rijken, M. (2007). *Bringing internet connectivity to rural Zambia using a collaborative approach*. IEEE.

McConnell, A. (2010). Policy success, policy failure and grey areas in-between. *Journal of Public Policy, 30*(3), 345–362. https://doi.org/10.1017/S0143814X10000152.

McHenry, G., Carlson, E., Lewis, M., Goldberg, R., Goss, J., & Chen, C. (2016, September 27). The digital divide is closing, even as new fissures surface. *TPRC 44: The 44th research conference on communication, information and internet policy 2016*. https://dx.doi.org/10.2139/ssrn.2757328.

McLeod, D. (2006, August 11). Electronic Communications Act. All eyes on Icasa. *Financial Mail*.

McLeod, D. (2016, November 16). Telkom wants to get rid of payphones. *TechCentral*. Retrieved from https://www.techcentral.co.za/telkom-wants-to-get-rid-of-payphones/70095/.

McLeod, D. (2017, January 25). ICT White Paper 'not constitutional'. *TechCentral*. Retrieved from https://www.techcentral.co.za/ict-white-paper-unconstitutional/71367/.

Melody, W. (Ed.). (1997). *Telecom reform: Principles, policies and regulatory practices*. Lyngby: Den Private Ingeniørfond, Technical University of Denmark. Retrieved from http://lirne.net/resources/tr/telecomreform.pdf.

MobileEurope. (2016, February 19). France's Arcep to track rural coverage with new observatory. *MobileEurope*. Retrieved from https://www.mobileeurope.co.uk/press-wire/france-s-arcep-to-track-rural-coverage-withnew-observatory.

Moyo, A. (2015, October 22). ICASA paints 'bleak picture' of itself. *ITWeb*. Retrieved from http://www.itweb.co.za/index.php?option=com_content&view=article&id=147204&A=FIN&S=Financial&O=E&E=3-17558.

MyBroadband. (2015, December 17). First digital TV set top boxes roll out. *MyBroadband*. Retrieved from https://mybroadband.co.za/news/broadcasting/150213-first-digital-tv-set-top-boxes-roll-out.html.

Mzekandaba, S. (2016, October 3). End of the road for USAASA. *ITWeb*. Retrieved from http://www.itweb.co.za/index.php?option=com_content&view=article&id=156344:End-of-the-road-for-USAASA&catid=260.

Navarro, L., Viñas, R., Barz, C., Bonicioli, J., Braem, B., Freitag, F., & Vilata-i-Balaguer, I. (2016, July). Advances in wireless community networks with the community-lab testbed. *IEEE Communications Magazine*, 20–27.

Nengwekhulu, R. (2009). Public service delivery challenges facing the South African public service. *Journal of Public Administration, 44*(2), 341–363. Retrieved from http://hdl.handle.net/10520/EJC51708.

Ngcaba, A. (2001, February 2). *Speech by the director general of communications, Andile Ngcaba, at the telecommunications colloquium.* Retrieved from http://www.polity.org.za/polity/govdocs/speeches/2001/sp0204.html.

NPC. (2012). *Our future—Make it work: National Development Plan 2030.* Pretoria: National Planning Commission. Retrieved from http://www.npconline.co.za/MediaLib/Downloads/Downloads/NDP%202030%20-%20Our%20future%20-%20make%20it%20work.pdf.

NTCA. (2001, January 19). *Telecommunications and integrated rural development in South Africa: Telecommunications cooperatives as a mechanism for supporting sustainable economic development.* Arlington, VA: National Telephone Cooperative Association.

Ó Siochrú, S., & Girard, B. (2005). *Community-based networks and innovative technologies: New models to serve and empower the poor.* New York, NY: United Nations Development Program. Retrieved from http://p-ced.com/reference/community-based_nets.pdf.

OECD. (1991). Universal service and rate restructuring in telecommunications, No. 23. *OECD Digital Economy* (4). http://dx.doi.org/10.1787/237454868255.

Ofcom. (2017, July 11). *Ofcom sets rules for mobile spectrum auction.* London: Office for Communications. Retrieved from https://www.ofcom.org.uk/about-ofcom/latest/media/media-releases/2017/ofcom-sets-rules-formobile-spectrum-auction.

Oliver, C. (2015). Monitoring the implementation of broadband plans and strategies. In *Trends in telecommunication reform 2015: Getting ready for the digital economy.* Geneva: International Telecommunication Union.

Reichert, C. (2017, December 12). USO to be axed in 2020 for universal service guarantee. *ZDNet.* Retrieved from http://www.zdnet.com/article/uso-to-be-axed-in-2020-for-universal-service-guarantee/.

Rey-Moreno, C., Sabiescu, A., Siya, M., & Tucker, W. (2015). Local ownership, exercise of ownership and moving from passive to active entitlement: A practice-led inquiry on a rural community network. *The Journal of Community Informatics, 11*(2).

Reynolds, P., Ockerby, J., Janssen, M., & Hird, T. (2008). *Reforming universal service policy: A report for GSM Europe.* London: GSM Association. Retrieved from http://www.gsma.com/gsmaeurope/wp-content/uploads/2012/03/usofinalreport0208.pdf.

Ricknäs, M. (2010, May 21). Germany ends frequency auction, Preps rural broadband. *PC World.* Retrieved from https://www.pcworld.com/article/196874/article.html.

Riege, A. (2003). Validity and reliability tests in case study research: A literature review withe "hands-on" applications for each research phase. *Qualitative Market Research, 6*(2).

RSA. (1996). *Telecommunications Act, 1996. No. 103 of 1996*. Pretoria: Republic of South Africa.

Samarajiva, R., & Hurulle, G. (2017). Measuring disbursement efficacy of universal service funds: Case studies from India, Malaysia, Pakistan & Sri Lanka. *SSRN*. https://doi.org/10.2139/ssrn.304425.

Schofield, A. (2017, March 22). ICT policy could prove disastrous for SA. *TechCentral*. Retrieved from https://www.techcentral.co.za/ict-policy-could-prove-disastrous-for-sa/72676/.

Schramm, W. (1971, December). *Notes on case studies of instructional media projects*. Stanford: California Institute for Communication Research, Stanford University. Retrieved from http://files.eric.ed.gov/fulltext/ED092145.pdf.

Sidler, V. (2016, March 29). Fibre to everywhere is in South Africa's near-term future. *Business Tech*. Retrieved from http://businesstech.co.za/news/industry-news/118194/fibre-to-everywhere-is-in-south-africas-near-term-future/.

Singh, J. (2002). Introduction: Information technologies and the changing scope of global power and governance. In J. Rosenau & J. Singh (Eds.), *Information technologies and global politics: The changing scope of power and governance* (pp. 1–38). New York, NY: SUNY Press.

Siong, A. (2012). *Digital dividend, the Danish way*. London: DotEcon. Retrieved from https://www.dotecon.com/publications/digital-dividend-the-danish-way/.

Stats SA. (2017). *General household survey 2016*. Pretoria: Statistics South Africa. Retrieved from http://www.statssa.gov.za/publications/P0318/P03182016.pdf.

Stavrou, A., Whitehead, A., Wilson, M., Seloane, M., & Benjamin, P. (2001). *Presentation notes: Of recommendations on the future of the universal service agency*. Pretoria: Universal Service Agency—Conference Convening Committee.

Szal, A. (2018, February 8). Spectrum auction legislation introduced in congress. *Wireless Week*. Retrieved from https://www.wirelessweek.com/news/2018/02/spectrum-auction-legislation-introducedcongress.

TechFinancials. (2017, October 10). South Africa plans to dissolve USAASA. *TechFinancials*. Retrieved from https://techfinancials.co.za/2017/10/10/south-africa-plans-to-dissolve-usaasa/.

TeleGeography. (2012, June 13). Big four secure frequencies in Brazil's 4G auction, but 450MHz band fails to excite. *TeleGeography*. Retrieved from https://www.telegeography.com/products/commsupdate/articles/2012/06/13/big-four-securefrequencies-in-brazils-4g-auction-but-450mhz-band-fails-to-excite/.

Tubbs, B. (2013, August 8). Fourth time lucky? *ITWeb*. Retrieved from http://www.itweb.co.za/index.php?option=com_content&view=article&id=66430:Fourth-time-lucky-&catid=260.

USAASA. (2017). *Comprehensive report on Mpumalanga connectivity*. Johannesburg: Universal Service and Access Agency of South Africa.

van der Heijden, J. (2012). Different but equally plausible narratives of policy transformation: A plea for theoretical pluralism. *International Political Science Review, 34*(1), 57–73. https://doi.org/10.1177/0192512112453604.

Vecchiatto, P. (2009, June 25). Nyanda waves regulatory big stick. *ITWeb*. Retrieved from http://www.itweb.co.za/index.php?option=com_content&view=article&id=23936:nyanda-waves-regulatory-big-stick&catid=260&Itemid=59.

Vegter, I. (2009, January 8). After poison ivy. *ITWeb*. Retrieved from http://www.itweb.co.za/index.php?option=com_content&view=article&id=13677:afterpoison-ivy&catid=79&Itemid=2354.

Vodacom. (2010). *Vodacom (Pty) Ltd's written submission in response to the discussion document on the review of universal service and access obligations framework (Notice 807, Government Gazette 33467 of 17 August 2010)*. Johannesburg: Vodacom. Retrieved from http://www.ellipsis.co.za/wp-content/uploads/2010/12/Vodacom-Submission-USAO-Review-12Nov2010.pdf.

Walford, G. (2007). Classification and framing of interviews in ethnographic interviewing. *Ethnography and Education, 2*(2), 145–157. https://doi.org/10.1080/17457820701350491.

Wallsten, S. (2001). An econometric analysis of telecom competition, privatization, and regulation in Africa and Latin America. *The Journal of Industrial Economics, 49*(1), 1–19.

Walters, J. (2014). Public transport policy implementation in South Africa: Quo vadis? *Journal of Transport and Supply Chain Management, 8*(1). http://dx.doi.org/10.4102/jtscm.v8i1.134.

Wellenius, B. (2002). *Closing the gap in access to rural communications: Chile 1995–2002*. Washington, DC: World Bank. Retrieved from http://www-wds.worldbank.org/external/default/WDSContentServer/WDSP/IB/2002/03/22/000094946_0203070403326/Rendered/PDF/multi0page.pdf.

Westerveld, R. (2012). Inverse telecommunications: The future for rural areas in developing countries? In T. Egyedi & D. Mehos (Eds.), *Inverse infrastructures: Disrupting networks from below* (pp. 187–207). Cheltenham, UK: Edward Elgar.

Williamson, J. (1990). What Washington means by policy reform. In *Latin American adjustment: How much has happened?* Washington, DC: Peterson Institute for International Economics.

World Bank. (2011). *An evaluation of world bank group activities in information and communication technologies: Capturing technology for development*.

Washington, DC: Independent Evaluation Group, World Bank. Retrieved from http://ieg.worldbankgroup.org/sites/default/files/Data/reports/ict_evaluation.pdf.

World Wide Worx. (2017). *Internet access in South Africa 2017: A comprehensive study of the Internet access market in South Africa, and its key drivers.* Johannesburg: World Wide Worx.

WTO. (1995). *Annex on telecommunications.* Geneva: World Trade Organisation. Retrieved from http://www.wto.org/english/tratop_e/serv_e/12-tel_e.htm.

Yin, R. (1994). *Case study research: Design and methods* (2nd ed.). Beverly Hills, CA: Sage.

Zaidi, Z., & Lan, K. (2017). Wireless multihop backhauls for rural areas: A preliminary study. *PloS One, 14*(4).

Glossary

3G Third-generation mobile telecommunications technology network or service. A basic broadband standard, providing a minimum data transfer rate of 200 k/bits/sec.

Access network The part of the telecommunications network that provides the direct connection to the end user often referred to as the 'last mile' or the 'local loop'

ADSL Asymmetric Digital Subscriber Line, a data communications technology that enables high-speed data transmission over copper telephone lines

ANC African National Congress, founded in 1912, former national liberation movement, governing party in South Africa since 1994

Apartheid System of racial segregation in South Africa, enforced through legislation by the ruling National Party (1948–1994), severely curtailing the freedoms, rights and movements of the majority 'blacks', 'coloureds' and 'Indians' in order to maintain 'white' minority rule

ARPU Average revenue per user, revenue benchmark commonly used in mobile communication services

Asymmetric regulation Application of differential regulatory requirements to different regulated entities, usually based on their levels of market power or market share or differing USOs (qv)

C. Lewis, *Regulating Telecommunications in South Africa*, Information Technology and Global Governance, https://doi.org/10.1007/978-3-030-43527-1

AT&T American multinational telecommunications company, headquartered in Dallas, Texas, with roots in American Telephone & Telegraph Corporation (founded 1885)

ATF African Telecommunications Forum, established in 1993 as a 'black' economic empowerment consortium in the sector, succeeded by SACF (qv)

ATU African Telecommunications Union, successor since 1999 to Pan-Africa Telecommunications Union, specialised agency of the African Union focused on ICTs

AU African Union. Established in 2002, as a continental union, successor to the OAU (qv)

Backbone The core part of a telecommunications network that handles the major voice and data traffic of a country

Backhaul High-capacity fixed or wireless connectivity dedicated to the transport of communication signals from base stations to the core network

Bandwidth The range of frequencies available for the transmission of signals or data, usually measured in bits per second (bit/s)

Bantustan Territory set aside under the policy of *apartheid* (qv) for 'black' South Africans on the basis of ethnic homogeneity

Base station A radio transmitter/receiver and antenna used in the mobile cellular network, which maintains communications with handsets, etc. within a given cell and which transmits traffic to other components of the network

Basic service The provision and carriage of voice telephony service

BBBEE/BEE (Broad-based) Black Economic Empowerment. SA government policy aimed at increasing wealth and participation in the economy by groups historically disadvantaged under *apartheid* (qv)

BEREC Body of European Regulators for Electronic Communications, established by the European Parliament in 2009

Best effort Traffic delivery standard in which the network endeavours to ensure that the traffic is delivered, but provides no guarantee that all traffic will be delivered

Broadband High-capacity Internet access, usually 1 M/bit/s in one or both directions, or as defined by the regulatory authorities from time to time

BS Broadcasting Service, a category of electronic communications service and licence as defined in the ECA (qv)

BSS Business Support Systems. IT systems used by operators to manage customer-facing activities, including product and customer management, orders and billing

BT British Telecom (UK), incumbent fixed-line operator, privatised in 1984

Carrier Pre-select Process whereby a telephony subscriber whose line is maintained by one company can choose to have some of their calls automatically routed across a different company's network

CDMA Code division multiple access, a technology for digital transmission of radio signals

CDITP Centre for the Development of Information Technology Policy, ANC think tank established in 1991, focusing on ICT sector reform

Cell-C Mobile telecommunications operator (South Africa), controversially awarded SA's third mobile licence in June 2001

Cellular Mobile telephony service provided by a network of base stations, each of which covers the area of one geographic cell within the total service area

Cherry-picking Pejorative conceptual metaphor referring to the practice of selectively providing telecommunications services to high-revenue customers in preference to less profitable users.

CODESA Convention for a Democratic South Africa, pre-1996 negotiating forum involving the National Party, the ANC (qv) and a number of other political organisations

Connectivity The capability to provide end users with connections to communication networks such as the Internet

Convergence Phenomenon marked by the increasing integration of previously discrete ICT infrastructure and devices, services and content, such as broadcasting, telecommunications and the Internet

COSATU Congress of South African Trade Unions, historically ANC-aligned trade union federation, founded in 1985

Coverage The extent of a mobile or wireless network, usually measured in terms of geographic (territorial area) or population coverage

CPE Customer premises equipment, end user devices connected to the telecommunications network, such as telephones, handsets and computers

Cream-skimming See 'Cherry-picking' (qv)

CST Community service telephone, a universal access model, providing subsidised telephony services to under-serviced areas

CUASA Communications Users Association of South Africa, umbrella body representing business users of telecommunications services, established in 2001

CWU Communication Workers' Union, an affiliate of COSATU, organising workers in the ICT sector, established in 1996

Cybercafé Place where one can use a computer with Internet access for a fee. Also known as an Internet café

DBSA The Development Bank of Southern Africa, established in 1983 to support *apartheid*-created 'bantustans', now supporting developmental infrastructure provision across Africa

DECT Digital enhanced cordless telecommunications, a radio technology standard for cordless telephony

Digital divide Economic and social inequality between categories of persons in respect of access to, use of, or knowledge of ICTs (qv), usually highlighting disparities according to demographic categories such as wealth, geographic location, race, gender, education

DoC Department of Communications, formerly the Department of Posts and Telecommunications, later split into Department of Telecommunications and Postal Services (DTPS) and Department of Communications (DoC) in May 2014

Dominance Regulatory classification of an operator with the largest share in a given market segment, or that is otherwise able to exercise significant market power

dti Department of Trade and Industry (South Africa), government department responsible for commercial and industrial policy

DTPS See DoC (qv)

e-rate The provision of discounted rates to eligible educational institutions to fund access to telecommunications, the Internet and related services

EC European Commission, executive body of the EU (qv)

ECA Electronic Communications Act, No. 36 of 2005, as amended in 2007 & 2014

ECS Electronic Communications Service, a category of communications service licence, as defined in the ECA (qv)

ECNS Electronic Communications Network Service, a category of communications infrastructure licence, as defined in the ECA (qv)

End user The individual or organisation that originates or is the final recipient of information carried over a communications network (i.e. the consumer)

EPG Eminent Persons Group, five-person task team appointed to advise and oversee the drafting of the 1996 White Paper and Telecommunications Act

Essential facilities Critical network facilities that may act as bottlenecks to national or international connectivity

EU European Union, politico-economic union established in 1993, currently with 28-member states located primarily in Europe

***Ex-ante* regulation** Regulation which involves setting specific rules or restrictions to prevent anti-competitive or otherwise undesirable market activity by operators before it occurs

***Ex-post* regulation** Regulation which deals with anti-competitive or undesirable market conduct after transgressions occur, by applying sanctions or corrective measures

Exclusivity Temporary period of monopoly granted, usually to the incumbent licensee, either to entice investors or in return for achieving rollout targets

FABCOS Foundation for African Business and Consumer Services, a national association of rural and township small businesses, founded in 1988

FCC Federal Communications Commission, US regulatory agency for interstate communications, created in 1934

FTTH Fibre-to-the-home, provision of a high-speed, fibre-optic, Internet connection to provide a broadband (qv) service at household level

Functional separation Requiring an operator (usually a vertically integrated dominant operator) to establish independently operated business divisions

G-7 Grouping of seven major advanced economies (Canada, France, Germany, Italy, Japan, the UK, and the US)

Gateway A network node or switch for providing access to another network

GATS General Agreement on Trade in Services, founding treaty of the WTO

GATT General Agreement on Tariffs and Trade, a multilateral agreement regulating international trade with effect from January 1948

GCIS Government Communication and Information System, government propaganda agency established in 1998

GDP Gross domestic product

GEAR Growth, Employment, and Redistribution, ANC macroeconomic policy framework, adopted in 1996

Green Paper Official consultation document issued by government for public debate in preparation for major policy or legislative changes

GSM Global System for Mobile Communications, dominant global technology for mobile telephony networks

GSMA GSM Association, global association of mobile operators and related companies

Household penetration A measure of access to telecommunications, showing the proportion of total households within a defined geographical area reached by the specified service

IBA Independent Broadcasting Authority, established in 1993 to regulate broadcasting, later merged with SATRA (qv) to form ICASA (qv)

ICASA Independent Communications Authority of South Africa, converged ICT sector regulator in South Africa, established in 2000

ICC International Chamber of Commerce, founded in 1919 as an international business association

ICT Information and communications technologies

ICT4D The uses of Information and Communications Technologies for socio-economic development

IDC Industrial Development Corporation, government-owned national development finance institution set up in 1940

IDRC International Development Research Centre (Canada), established in 1970 as a semi-independent body supporting research in developing countries

IMF International Monetary Fund, established in 1944

Incumbent Existing operator in a market when it is opened to competition

infoDev A global multi-donor programme in the World Bank (qv) Group, set up in 1995, with a focus on ICT for development

Information society Social order in which the creation, distribution, use, integration and manipulation of information is a significant economic, political and cultural activity

Infrastructure sharing Sharing between operators of agreed components of the network

Interconnection Physical and logical connection, linking two operator networks

Internet Interconnected global communications networks that use the Internet protocol

INTUG International Telecommunications Users' Group, international association of business users of telecommunications, founded in 1974

IP Internet protocol, used to encode data packets for transmission over the Internet or other network

IPO Initial public offering of company shares on the stock market

ISAD Information Society and Development, conference held in Midrand, South Africa, 13–15 May 1996

ISPA Internet Service Providers' Association, established in 1996

ISP Internet Service Provider, company offering access to the Internet and online services

ITRs International Telecommunications Regulations, binding international treaty, adopted through the ITU (qv) in 1988

ITU International Telecommunication Union, formed in 1865, now a specialised agency of the United Nations responsible for issues concerning information and communications technologies

Knowledge economy System of production and consumption based on intellectual capital and information production

Leased line A point-to-point permanently connected communication channel or circuit rented out by a network operator to an individual subscriber

Least subsidy auction Competitive tender process whereby bidders compete for a licence or project award based on the lowest level of subsidy requested

Liberalisation (1) generally, the relaxation of previous government restrictions affecting the ICT sector, through privatisation of the incumbent operator, the introduction of competition, and the establishment of a national regulatory authority; (2) more specifically, the introduction of competition in the ICT sector

Lifeline Tariff A pricing structure that involves the provision of a free or subsidised block of services

LTE Long-Term Evolution, a telephone and mobile broadband communication standard, offering high-speed data access

M2M Machine-to-machine communication

Market efficiency gap Component of universal access and service model that exhorts policy-makers and regulators to achieve UAS goals by stimulating market forces and removing regulatory blockages

MDDA Media Development and Diversity Agency, established in 2002 to support and fund community and small commercial media

MERG Macro-Economic Research Group (South Africa), formed by the ANC in November 1991 as an econometric think-tank

MFN Most Favoured Nation status, a method of ensuring non-discriminatory treatment amongst WTO members

MPCC Multi-Purpose Community Centre, a telecentre offering a broad range of ICT services

MTN Mobile Telephone Networks, second largest mobile telecommunications operator in South Africa, licensed in 1993

MVNO Mobile virtual network operator, selling mobile phone services without owning its own wireless network infrastructure

NABVU National Association of Business Voice Users (South Africa)

NAFCOC National African Federated Chamber of Commerce, established in 1964 as an umbrella body for 'black' traders

NAIL New African Investments Limited, founded in the early 1990s by prominent Soweto activist Dr Nthatho Motlana as a vehicle for black economic empowerment

Neo-liberalism Pejorative term for the twentieth-century resurgence of nineteenth-century ideas associated with laissez-faire economic liberalism

NeoTel Second fixed-line telecommunications operator in South Africa, licensed in 2005

NGN Next-generation Network, generic term for packet-switched, high-bandwidth, quality-of-service enabled, converged services

Non-discrimination Condition requiring an operator not to apply less favourable technical and commercial conditions to a competitor

NRF National Revenue Fund, Treasury account specified in the Constitution, into which all money received by the national government must be paid

NTCA National Telephone Cooperative Association, US-based association of independent, community-based rural and small-town telecommunications companies, established in 1954

NTF National Telecommunications Forum, stakeholder body established as a negotiating platform in the lead-up to the 1996 Telecommunications Act

NTPP National Telecommunications Policy Project, established in 1995 as a stakeholder negotiating vehicle to prepare Green and White papers on telecommunications

NTUG National Telematics User Group (South Africa), founded in 1978 as an association of business users of telecommunications services

OAU Organisation of African Unity (1963–2002), forerunner of the African Union (AU, qv)

OECD Organisation for Economic Co-operation and Development, international economic organisation of 34 developed countries

Ofcom Office of Communications (UK), converged super-regulator for telecomms, broadcasting and postal services, established in 2003

Oftel Office for Telecommunications (UK), telecomms regulator from its establishment in 1984 until its absorption into Ofcom (qv) in 2003

OSS Operational Support Systems. Computer systems used by operators to control and manage their networks, and to support network management functions

Packet Block or grouping of data that is treated as a single unit for transmission within a communications network

PABX Private automatic branch exchange, automatic telephone switching system within a private enterprise

Pay or Play Mechanism whereby licensees may opt to fulfil their USOs (qv) either through implementation of approved universal access and service projects or via contributions to agreed financial mechanisms such as the USF (qv)

PAYE Pay as you earn income tax

PIT Public Information Terminal, a self-service, Internet-connected kiosk, developed jointly by the DoC (qv) and SAPO (qv) in 1998

PNC-ISAD Presidential National Commission on the Information Society and Development, established in 2001 by President Thabo Mbeki

POTWA Posts and Telecommunications Workers' Association, COSATU-aligned trade union, organising mainly 'Black' workers at SAPT (qv), founded in 1986, later merged into CWU (qv)

Privatisation Process of transferring ownership or control of a telecommunications or other enterprise, partially or fully, from state ownership to the private sector

PSTN Public switched telephone network

PSTS Public switched telephone service, provided over the PSTN (qv)

PTN Private telecommunications network

PTT Postal, telegraph, and telephone entity, typically a state-owned incumbent monopoly service provider

Public Protector Statutory institution in South Africa, empowered to investigate maladministration and improper conduct by government functionaries, including corruption and mismanagement of public monies

QoS Quality of service, a measure (mostly quantitative) of the performance of a telecommunications network

Regulator Regulatory Authority, a public entity established in law by government, with responsibility to exercise authority and supervision over a designated area of economic or social activity

Regulatory capture Politically corrupt institutional failure, in which a regulatory authority advances the narrow sectoral interests of one or more of the specific groups that it is charged with regulating

Regulatory state Model of governance where the state pursues an economic policy through arm's-length regulation rather than direct intervention

Resale Offering to users or customers, for profit, ICT services obtained from another ICT service provider

RIA Regulatory Impact Assessment, a report providing a detailed and systematic appraisal of the potential impacts of a new regulation

Roaming Arrangement allowing customers of one mobile operator to access mobile services via the network of another when outside to coverage area of their own service provider

SABC South African Broadcasting Corporation, state-owned, public service broadcaster, established in 1936

SACF South African Communications Forum, successor to the African Telecommunications Forum, formed in 2001 as a non-profit, membership-based industry association

SADC Southern African Development Community, inter-governmental organisation, currently comprising 15 southern African countries

SANCO South African National Civics Organisation, launched in 1992

SAPO South African Post Office, established in 1991 through the separation of SAPT (qv) into postal and telecommunications companies

SAPT South African Posts and Telecommunications, state-owned integrated entity providing telecommunications and postal services until 1991

SARS South African Revenue Service, administratively autonomous tax-collection agency of the South African government

SATRA South African Telecommunications Regulatory Authority, established in 1997, and later merged with the IBA (qv) to form ICASA (qv)

Sentech Established in 1992 as the signal distribution (qv) division of the SABC (qv)

Signal distribution Process of conveying radio or television signals from a broadcasting service provider and transmitting them to the end user

SIM Subscriber identity module, an integrated circuit, used to identify and authenticate subscribers on the mobile network

SIU Special Investigating Unit, South African statutory anti-corruption investigative body, established in 1996

Smart subsidy zone Component of universal access and service model that identifies people and communities too poor or too remote to be reached by market-based regulatory measures alone, but who are able to sustain access to communications services after initial support (e.g. free handset, subsidised base station, etc.)

Smartphone A mobile phone, typically having a touchscreen interface, providing advanced, Internet-enabled functionality

SME Small or medium enterprise

SMP Significant market power, the ability of a firm in a defined market, either individually or jointly with others, to exercise dominance

SMS Short Message Service, a widely used mobile telephony service providing text messages

Soweto South Western Townships, *apartheid*-created dormitory township for 'black' South Africans outside Johannesburg

Stats SA Statistics South Africa, national statistical agency

TBVC states Transkei, Bophuthatswana, Venda, and Ciskei, four nominally independent homeland states created under grand *apartheid's* (qv) Bantustan (qv) programme

Telecentre A public place where people can access computers, the Internet, and other digital technologies

Teledensity A measurement of access to telecommunications within a defined geographic area, calculated by dividing the number of subscribers to a specific service (e.g. mobile) by the corresponding total population

Telecommunications Domestic or international transmission of information by wire, radio waves, optical media or other electromagnetic systems

Telephony Voice telecommunications, point-to-point voice communication in real-time

Telkom Incumbent telecommunications operator in South Africa, successor to SAPT (qv)

True access gap Component of universal access and service model that identifies people and communities too poor or too remote to be reached by market-based regulatory measures, and therefore requiring permanently ongoing support to enjoy access to communications services

UAS Universal Access and Service, currently preferred ITU (qv) terminology, an umbrella term, loosely covering both universal access (qv) and universal service (qv)

UK United Kingdom

UN United Nations

Universal Access Policy to make ICT infrastructure and services available, at affordable prices, to as many people as possible through common points or shared end-user facilities

Universal Service Policy to make ICT infrastructure and services available, throughout the country at affordable prices so that they are accessible to anyone, regardless of geographical location

US United States of America

USA Universal Service Agency, state entity set up in 1997 under the 1996 Telecommunications Act to promote and facilitate universal access and service, and to manage the Universal Service Fund

USAASA Universal Service and Access Agency of South Africa, successor to the USA (qv) under the 2005 Electronic Communications Act

USAF Universal Service and Access Fund (South Africa), successor to South Africa's USF (qv) under the 2005 Electronic Communications Act

USAL Under-serviced area licensee (South Africa), category of licence, covering areas with low fixed-line teledensity, created under the 2001 amendment to the 1996 Telecommunications Act

USAO Universal Service and Access Obligation (South Africa), term adopted by ICASA (qv) to refer to USOs

USF Universal Service Fund: (i) a fund into which contributions imposed on operators or derived from other sources are paid for the purpose of providing basic and advanced ICT infrastructure and services to under-serviced areas, communities or individuals who cannot afford such services on their own; (ii) the fund (South Africa) set up for this purpose under the control of the USA (qv) in terms under the 1996 Telecommunications Act

USO Universal Service Obligation, mandatory stipulation imposed on operators, requiring, *inter alia*, network rollout or service provision to under-serviced areas and communities

VANS Value-added network services, ICT services provided over public or private networks which, in some way, add value to the basic carriage

Vodacom Largest mobile telecommunications operator in South Africa, licensed in 1993

VoIP Voice over IP, generic term used to describe the techniques used to carry voice traffic by means of Internet Protocol

VSAT Very small aperture terminal, a two-way satellite ground station with a small dish antenna

White Paper Official public document issued by government setting out policy positions, usually in preparation for major legislative changes

WiFi Short-range wireless local area computer networking technology that allows electronic devices to interconnect

WiMax Worldwide Interoperability for Microwave Access, a fixed wireless communications standard providing long-range, high-bandwidth wireless connectivity

World Bank United Nations international financial institution, created at the 1944 Bretton Woods Conference

WSIS World Summit on the Information Society, series of ICT conferences (2003, Geneva & 2005, Tunis) sponsored by the United Nations

WTO World Trade Organisation, intergovernmental organisation to regulate international trade under GATS (qv), established in 1995

CPSIA information can be obtained
at www.ICGtesting.com
Printed in the USA
BVHW021113260720
584695BV00010B/44